EUROPEAN COMMISSION

Pharmaceutical Sector

Coordinated instruments

Position on 31.12.1994

EN

Calatoguing data can be found at the end of the publication.

Luxembourg: Office for Official Publications of the European Communities, 1995

ISBN 92-827-0020-8

Printed in Luxembourg

NOTICE

This document is a compilation without official status and is intended solely as a guide to Community legislation on the subject concerned; it has been drawn up on the basis of texts made available originally in the Info 92 database.

Neither the European Commission nor any person acting on its behalf can be held liable for the use made of the information contained herein.

*
* *

Your attention is also drawn to another Commission publication of a more practical nature entitled "the rules governing medicinal products in the European Community"(*), which, in addition to Community acts, includes explanatory notes on trials, opinions and advice for those applying for authorizations and a guide to good production practices, making it easier to understand, interpret and implement Community rules.

While we strongly recommend that publication to those wanting a full understanding of the pharmaceuticals sector and an overview of the related issues, it should in no way be confused with the present document, which merely attempts to provide, in a coordinated form, the relevant Community legislation for information purposes.

(*) The rules governing medicinal products

Volume I   -   The rules governing medicinal products for human use in the European Union
                Catalogue No - CO-86-94-319-EN-C / ISBN-92-826-9207-8

Volume II   -   Notice to applicants for marketing authorizations for medicinal products for human use in
                the Member States of the European Community
                Catalogue No - CB-55-89-293-EN-C / ISBN-92-825-9503-X

Volume III -   Guidelines on the quality, safety and efficacy of medicinal products for human use
                Catalogue No - CB-55-89-843-EN-C / ISBN-92-825-9619-2

Volume III -   Addendum
                Catalogue No - CB-59-90-936-EN-C / ISBN-92-826-0421-7

Volume III -   Addendum No 2
                Catalogue No - CO-75-92-558-EN-C / ISBN-92-826-4550-9

Volume IV   -   Good manufacturing practice for medicinal products Directorate-General Internal Market and
                Industrial Affairs
                Catalogue No - CO-71-91-760-EN-C / ISBN-92-826-3180-X

Volume VA   -   The rules governing veterinary medicinal products in the European Community
                Catalogue No - CO-77-92-384-EN-C / ISBN-92-826-5174-6

Volume VB   -   Notice to applicants for marketing authorization for veterinary medicinal products in the
                European Community
                Catalogue No - CO-78-93-443-EN-C / ISBN-92-826-5780-9

Volume VI   -   Establishment by the European Community of maximum residue limits (MRLs) for residues
                of veterinary medicinal products in foodstuffs of animal origin
                Catalogue No - CO-71-91-768-EN-C / ISBN-92-826-3173-7

Volume VII -   Guidelines for the testing of veterinary medicinal products
                Catalogue No - CO-86-94-383-EN-C / ISBN-92-826-9269-8

EXPLANATORY NOTE

This publication contains all the Community legislation relating to the sector in question. Texts which have been amended are set out in coordinated form incorporating all the changes made to the original instruments. Texts which have not been amended are reproduced from the Official Journal.

Instruments which could not be included for technical reasons will be available in a later version.

Cover page (the boxes preceding the coordinated text)

The coordinated text is preceded by the following information (see examples):

1) *A Notice*

This points out that the text is intended for information only and cannot therefore be regarded as legally binding.

> The consolidated version below is supplied by the Commission for information only; it confers no rights and imposes no obligations separate from those conferred or imposed by the acts formally adopted and published, which continue to be only authentic ones.

2) *The basic instrument*

Information relating to the basic instrument is set out as follows:

--   the identification number in the CELEX database:
     378L0664;

--   the full title of the instrument

     78/664/EEC: COUNCIL DIRECTIVE OF 25 JULY 1978 LAYING DOWN SPECIFIC CRITERIA OF PURITY FOR ANTIOXIDANTS WHICH MAY BE USED IN FOODSTUFFS INTENDED FOR HUMAN CONSUMPTION

--   the reference to the Official Journal in which the instrument was published:
     OFFICIAL JOURNAL No L 223, 14/08/1978, P. 30;

--   the date on which the Member States were notified of the instrument
     DATE OF NOTIFICATION: 31/07/1978;

--   in the case of Directives, the date of transposition (the date by which Member States must have amended their own legislation to bring it into line with Community rules):
     DATE OF TRANSPOSITION: 01/02/1980; SEE ART. 3.

3) *Amending instruments*

These are set out in chronological order, as follows:

-- the identification number in the CELEX database;

-- the abridged title of the instrument, followed by a number in square brackets indicating the source of the amendment incorporated in the text: **[No]**;

-- the reference to the Official Journal in which the instrument was published;

-- the date on which the Member States were notified of the instrument;

-- in the case of Directives, the date of transposition.

AMENDED BY

382L0712
82/712/EEC: COUNCIL DIRECTIVE OF 18 OCTOBER 1982 [1]
OFFICIAL JOURNAL No L 297, 23/10/1982, P. 31
DATE OF NOTIFICATION: 29/10/1982
DATE OF TRANSPOSITION: 30/06/1984; SEE ART. 2

The coordinated text

The coordinated text includes only the articles and annexes of the instrument and not the citations or recitals.

Amendments are incorporated in the instrument as follows (see examples):

1) *Incorporation of amendment*

-- An amendment replacing or supplementing the original text is shown as follows:

" amending text " [No];

Article 5

" 1. Notwithstanding Article 2 (1), Member States may authorize the use of hexamethylenetetramine:

a) in semi-preserved fish and fishery products whose pH is more than 4.5, provided that, when the product is marketed, the level of this substance does not exceed 500 mg/kg;
b) in caviar (sturgeon eggs) and other fish eggs, not smoked, provided that, when the product is marketed, the level of this substance does not exceed 1g/kg " [10]

N.B. To show that an amendment has been made the new text is put in inverted commas followed by a number in square brackets. Where the inverted commas denote an amendment, a space is inserted between them and the text.

--   An amendment made for the <u>sole</u> purpose of deleting part of the original text is indicated as follows:

"..." [No]:

3. "..." [17];

--   On the cover page of some coordinated instruments reference is made to amending instruments that have no effect on the basic text. These usually involve amendments which have been subsequently repealed, and accordingly no longer figure in the coordinated text.

2)   Source of amendment

--   The source of an amendment can be found by means of the number in square brackets immediately following the new text; this number refers back to the details of the amending instrument on the cover page:

" b) in caviar (sturgeon eggs) and other fish eggs, not smoked, provided that, when the product is marketed, the level of this substance does not exceed 1g/kg " [10]

3)   Comments in square brackets [ ]

--   These are used to provide information which may be helpful in understanding the amendments; they do not form part of the text:

" 2. " [17] " by way of derogation from article 1, member States may maintain the provisions of their national laws relating to the use of formaldehyde in grano padano cheese provided that when the final product is marketed, the level of formaldehyde, free and/or combined, shall not exceed 0.5 milligram per kilogram. " [14]

3. "..." [17]

[the paragraph was inserted by [14]; [17] deletes 5(2) and 5(3)(b), 5(3)(a) becomes 5(2)]

4)   Annexes

The annexes are coordinated in the same way as the substantive provisions.
It should be noted that:

--   the presentation of tables differs from that in the Official Journal;

--   drawings and symbols cannot be reproduced and the Official Journal should therefore be consulted.

Abbreviations

For instruments

R :   Regulation

L :   Directive

D :   Decision

AA :   Act of Accession

For the institutions

CS :   Council

COM :   Commission

A reference is to be read as follows:

L	CS	69/414	OJ
Type of instrument: Directive	Author: Council	Year/number of the Directive or Decision	*Official Journal of the European Communities*
OJ L	OJ C	291/69	SE
Official Journal L series	Official Journal C series	Number of the Official Journal/year	Special Edition
JO			
Journal officiel des Communautés européennes			

CONTENTS

Coordinated instruments

Pharmaceutical Sector

DETAILED LIST OF INSTRUMENTS

	Type of instrument	OJ/SE	Page
Texts relating to marketing authorizations for medicinal products for human use			
Free movement of medicinal products - European Agency for medicinal products	R CS 2309/93	OJ L 214/93	19
Approximation of legislation relating to medicinal products - A	L CS 65/65	SE 1965-1966, p. 20	41
	amended by:		
	L CS 66/454	SE 1965-1966, p. 168	
	L CS 75/319	OJ L 147/75	
	L CS 83/570	OJ L 332/83	
	L CS 87/21	OJ L 15/87	
	L CS 89/341	OJ L 142/89	
	L CS 89/342	OJ L 142/89	
	L CS 89/343	OJ L 142/89	
	L CS 92/27	OJ L 113/92	
	L CS 92/73	OJ L 297/92	
	L CS 93/39	OJ L 214/93	
Approximation of legislation relating to medicinal products - B	L CS 75/319	OJ L 147/75	53
	amended by:		
	L CS 78/420	OJ L 123/78	
	L CS 83/570	OJ L 332/83	
	L CS 89/341	OJ L 142/89	
	L CS 89/342	OJ L 142/89	
	L CS 89/343	OJ L 142/89	
	L CS 89/381	OJ L 181/89	
	L CS 92/27	OJ L 113/92	
	L CS 92/73	OJ L 297/92	
	L CS 93/39	OJ L 214/93	
Placing on the market of high-technology medicinal products, particularly those derived from biotechnology	L CS 87/22	OJ L 15/87	75
	repealed by:		
	L CS 93/41	OJ L 214/93	79
Immunological medicinal products	L CS 89/342	OJ L 142/89	81
Radiopharmaceuticals	L CS 89/343	OJ L 142/89	83
Medicinal products derived from human blood or human plasma	L CS 89/381	OJ L 181/89	87

---

[1]   p. 111
[2]   p. 217

---

[3] p. 111
[4] p. 217

	Type of instrument	OJ/SE	Page
Conditions governing the preparation, placing on the market and use of medicated feedingstuffs in the Community	L CS 90/167	OJ L 92/90	275
Economic environment of veterinary medicinal products			
Creation of a supplementary protection certificate for medicinal products	R CS 1768/92	OJ L 182/92	285
Other relevant texts applicable to medicinal products for human and/or veterinary use			
Liability for defective products	L CS 85/374	OJ L 210/85	293
Contained use of genetically modified micro-organisms	L CS 90/219	OJ L 117/90	299
	amended by: L CS 94/51	OJ L 297/94	
Guidelines for classification referred to in Article 4 of Directive 90/219 (genetically modified micro-organisms)	D COM 91/448	OJ L 239/91	313
Deliberate release into the environment of genetically modified organisms	L CS 90/220	OJ L 117/90	317
	amended by: L CS 94/15	OJ L 103/94	
Principles of good laboratory practice and the verification of their application for tests on chemical substances	L CS 87/18	OJ L 15/87	333
Protection of animals used for experimental and other scientific purposes	L CS 86/609	OJ L 358/86	335
Setting-up a pharmaceutical committee	D CS 75/320	OJ L 147/75	363

Texts relating to marketing authorizations for medicinal products for human use

I

(Acts whose publication is obligatory)

COUNCIL REGULATION (EEC) No 2309/93

of 22 July 1993

laying down Community procedures for the authorization and supervision of medicinal products for human and veterinary use and establishing a European Agency for the Evaluation of Medicinal Products

THE COUNCIL OF THE EUROPEAN COMMUNITIES,

Having regard to the Treaty establishing the European Economic Community, and in particular Article 235 thereof,

Having regard to the proposal from the Commission [1],

Having regard to the opinion of the European Parliament [2],

Having regard to the opinion of the Economic and Social Committee [3],

Whereas Council Directive 87/22/EEC of 22 December 1986 on the approximation of national measures relating to the placing on the market of high-technology medicinal products particularly those derived from biotechnology [4] has established a Community mechanism for concertation, prior to any national decision relating to a high-technology medicinal product, with a view to arriving at uniform decisions throughout the Community; whereas this route should be followed, particularly in order to ensure the smooth functioning of the internal market in the pharmaceutical sector;

Whereas the experience acquired as a result of Directive 87/22/EEC has shown that it is necessary to establish a centralized Community authorization procedure for technologically advanced medicinal products, in particular those derived from biotechnology; whereas this procedure should also be available to persons responsible for placing on the market medicinal products containing new active substances which are intended for use in human beings or in food-producing animals;

Whereas in the interest of public health it is necessary that decisions on the authorization of such medicinal products should be based on the objective scientific criteria of the quality, the safety and the efficacy of the medicinal product concerned to the exclusion of economic or other considerations; whereas, however, Member States should exceptionally be able to prohibit the use on their territory of medicinal products for human use which infringe objectively defined concepts of public order or public morality; whereas, moreover, a veterinary medicinal product may not be authorized by the Community if its use would contravene the legal measures laid down by the Community within the framework of the common agricultural policy;

Whereas, in the case of medicinal products for human use, the criteria of quality, safety and efficacy have been extensively harmonized by Council Directive 65/65/EEC of 26 January 1965 on the approximation of provisions laid down by law, regulation or administrative action relating to medicinal products [5], and the Second Council Directive 75/319/EEC of 20 May 1975 on the approximation of provisions laid down by law, regulation and administrative action relating to proprietary medicinal products [6], and by Council Directive 75/318/EEC of 20 May 1975 on the approximation of the laws of the Member States relating to analytical pharmaco-toxicological and clinical standards and protocols in respect of the testing of medicinal products [7];

Whereas in the case of veterinary medicinal products, the same results have been achieved by Council Directive 81/851/EEC of 28 September 1981 on the approximation

---

[1] OJ No C 330, 31. 12. 1990, p. 1, and
OJ No C 310, 30. 11. 1991, p. 7.
[2] OJ No C 183, 15. 7. 1991, p. 145.
[3] OJ No C 269, 14. 10. 1991, p. 84.
[4] OJ No L 15, 17. 1. 1987, p. 38.

---

[5] OJ No 22, 9. 2. 1965, p. 369/65. Directive last amended by Directive 92/27/EEC (OJ No L 113, 30. 4. 1992, p. 8).
[6] OJ No L 147, 9. 6. 1976, p. 13. Directive last amended by Directive 92/27/EEC (OJ No L 113, 30. 4. 1992, p. 8).
[7] OJ No L 147, 9. 6. 1975, p. 1. Directive last amended by Commission Directive 91/507/EEC (OJ No L 270, 26. 9. 1991, p. 32).

of the laws of the Member States relating to veterinary medicinal products (¹) and by Council Directive 81/852/EEC of 28 September 1981 on the approximation of the laws of the Member States relating to analytical, pharmaco-toxicological and clinical standards and protocols in respect of the testing of veterinary medicinal products (²);

Whereas the same criteria must be applied to medicinal products which are to be authorized by the Community;

Whereas only after a single scientific evaluation of the highest possible standard of the quality, safety or efficacy of technologically advanced medicinal products, to be undertaken within the European Agency for the Evaluation of Medicinal Products, should a marketing authorization be granted by the Community by a rapid procedure ensuring close cooperation between the Commission and Member States.

Whereas Council Directive 93/39/EEC of 14 June 1993 amending Directive 65/65/EEC, 75/318/EEC and 75/319/EEC in respect of medicinal products (³) has provided that in the event of a disagreement between Member States about the quality, safety or efficacy of a medicinal product which is the subject of the decentralized Community authorization procedure, the matter should be resolved by a binding Community decision following a scientific evaluation of the issues involved within a European medicinal product evaluation agency; whereas similar provisions have been laid down in respect of veterinary medicinal products by Council Directive 93/40/EEC of 14 June 1993 amending Directives 81/851/EEC and 81/852/EEC on the approximation of the laws of the Member States relating to veterinary medicinal products (⁴);

Whereas the Community must be provided with the means to undertake a scientific evaluation of medicinal products which are presented for authorization in accordance with the centralized Community procedures; whereas, furthermore, in order to achieve the effective harmonization of the administrative decisions taken by Member States in relation to individual medicinal products which are presented for authorization in accordance with decentralized procedures, it is necessary to provide the Community with the means of resolving disagreements between Member States about the quality, safety and efficacy of medicinal products;

Whereas it is therefore necessary to establish a European Agency for the Evaluation of Medicinal Products ('the Agency');

Whereas the primary task of the Agency should be to provide scientific advice of the highest possible quality to the Community institutions and the Member States for the exercise of the powers conferred upon them by Community legislation in the field of medicinal products in relation to the authorization and supervision of medicinal products;

Whereas it is necessary to ensure close cooperation between the Agency and scientists working within the Member States;

Whereas, therefore, the exclusive responsibility for preparing the opinions of the Agency on all matters relating to medicinal products for human use should be entrusted to the Committee for Proprietary Medicinal Products created by the Second Council Directive 75/319/CEE; whereas in respect of veterinary medicinal products this responsibility should be entrusted to the Committee for Veterinary Medicinal Products created by Directive 81/851/EEC;

Whereas the establishment of the Agency will make it possible to reinforce the scientific role and independence of these two Committees, in particular through the establishment of a permanent technical and administrative secretariat;

Whereas it is also necessary to make provisions for the supervision of medicinal products which have been authorized by the Community, and in particular for the intensive monitoring of adverse reactions to those medicinal products through Community pharmacovigilance activities in order to ensure the rapid withdrawal from the market of any medicinal product which presents an unacceptable level of risk under normal conditions of use;

Whereas the Commission, working in close cooperation with the Agency, and after consultation with Member States, should also be entrusted with the task of coordinating the discharge of the various supervisory responsibilities of Member States and in particular the provisions of information about medicinal products, monitoring the respect of good manufacturing practices, good laboratory practices and good clinical practices;

Whereas the Agency should also be responsible for coordinating the activities of the Member States in the field of the monitoring of adverse reactions to medicinal products (pharmacovigilance);

Whereas it is necessary to provide for the orderly introduction of Community procedures for the authorization of medicinal products alongside the national procedures of the Member States which have already been extensively harmonized by Directives 65/65/EEC, 75/319/EEC and 81/851/EEC; whereas it is therefore appropriate in the first instance to limit the obligation to use the new Community procedure to certain medicinal products; whereas the scope of the Community procedures should be reviewed in the light of experience at the latest six years after the entry into force of this Regulation;

(¹) OJ No L 317, 6. 11. 1981, p. 1. Directive last amended by Directive 93/40/EEC (OJ No 214, 24. 8. 1993).
(²) OJ No L 317, 6. 11. 1981, p. 16. Directive last amended by Directive 93/40/EEC (OJ No 214, 24. 8. 1993).
(³) See page 22 of this Official Journal.
(⁴) See page 31 of this Official Journal.

Whereas risks to the environment may be associated with medicinal products containing or consisting of genetically modified organisms; whereas therefore it is necessary to provide for an environmental risk assessment of such products similar to that provided for by Council Directive 90/220/EEC of 23 April 1990 on the deliberate release into the environment of genetically modified organisms (¹), together with the assessment of the quality, safety and efficacy of the product concerned within a single Community procedure;

Whereas the Treaty does not provide, for the adoption of a uniform system at Community level, as provided for by this Regulation, powers other than those of Article 235,

HAS ADOPTED THIS REGULATION:

TITLE I

DEFINITIONS AND SCOPE

Article 1

The purpose of this Regulation is to lay down Community procedures for the authorization and supervision of medicinal products for human and veterinary use and to establish a European Agency for the Evaluation of Medicinal Products.

The provisions of this Regulation shall not affect the powers of the Member States' authorities as regards the price setting of medicinal products or their inclusion in the scope of the national health system of the Member States' authorities or their inclusion in the scope of the social security schemes on the basis of health, economic and social conditions. For example, the Member States may choose from the marketing authorization those therapeutic indications and pack sizes which will be covered by their social security organizations.

Article 2

The definitions laid down in Article 1 of Directive 65/65/EEC and those laid down in Article 1 (2) of Directive 81/851/EEC shall apply for the purposes of this Regulation.

The person responsible for placing the medicinal products covered by this Regulation on the market must be established in the Community.

Article 3

1. No medicinal product referred to in Part A of the Annex may be placed on the market within the Community unless a marketing authorization has been granted by the Community in accordance with the provisions of this Regulation.

2. The person responsible for placing on the market a medicinal product referred to in Part B of the Annex may request that authorization to place the medicinal product on the market be granted by the Community in accordance with the provisions of this Regulation.

3. Before entry into force of this Regulation and after consultation of the Committee for Proprietary Medicinal Products, Parts A and B of the Annex as regards medicinal products for human use shall be re-examined in the light of scientific and technical progress with a view to making any amendments necessary which will be adopted under the procedure laid down in Article 72.

4. Before entry into force of this Regulation and after consultation of the Committee for Veterinary Medicinal Products, Parts A and B of the Annex as regards veterinary medicinal products shall be re-examined in the light of scientific and technical progress with a view to making any amendments necessary which will be adopted under the procedure laid down in Article 72.

5. The procedures referred to in paragraphs 3 and 4 shall continue to apply after entry into force of this Regulation.

Article 4

1. In order to obtain the authorization referred to in Article 3, the person responsible for placing a medicinal product on the market shall submit an application to the European Agency for the Evaluation of Medicinal Products, hereinafter referred to as 'the Agency', set up under Title IV.

2. The Community shall issue and supervise marketing authorizations for medicinal products for human use in accordance with Title II.

3. The Community shall issue and supervise marketing authorizations for veterinary medicinal products in accordance with Title III.

(¹) OJ No L 117, 8. 5. 1990, p. 15.

TITLE II

AUTHORIZATION AND SUPERVISION OF MEDICINAL PRODUCTS FOR HUMAN USE

CHAPTER 1

Submission and examination of applications — authorizations — renewal of authorization

Article 5

The Committee for Proprietary Medicinal Products established by Article 8 of Directive 75/319/EEC, in this Title referred to as 'the Committee', shall be responsible for formulating the opinion of the Agency on any question concerning the admissibility of the files submitted in accordance with the centralized procedure, the granting, variation, suspension or withdrawal of an authorization to place a medicinal product for human use on the market arising in accordance with the provisions of this Title and pharmacovigilance.

Article 6

1.　An application for authorization for a medicinal product for human use must be accompanied by the particulars and documents referred to in Articles 4 and 4a of Directive 65/65/EEC, in the Annex to Directive 75/318/EEC and in Article 2 of Directive 75/319/EEC.

2.　In the case of a medicinal product containing or consisting of genetically modified organisms within the meaning of Article 2 (1) and (2) of Directive 90/220/EEC, the application must also be accompanied by:

— a copy of any written consent or consents of the competent authorities to the deliberate release into the environment of the genetically modified organisms for research and development purposes where provided for by Part B of Directive 90/220/EEC,

— the complete technical dossier supplying the information requested in Annexes II and III to Directive 90/220/EEC and the environmental risk assessment resulting from this information; the results of any investigations performed for the purposes of research or development.

Articles 11 to 18 of Directive 90/220/EEC shall not apply to medicinal products for human use containing or consisting of genetically modified organisms.

3.　The application must also be accompanied by the fee payable to the Agency for the examination of the application.

4.　The Agency shall ensure that the opinion of the Committee is given within 210 days of the receipt of a valid application.

In the case of a medicinal product containing or consisting of genetically modified organisms, the opinion of the Committee shall respect the environmental safety requirements laid down by Directive 90/220/EEC to ensure that all appropriate measures are taken to avoid adverse effects on human health and the environment which might arise from the deliberate release or placing on the market of genetically modified organisms. During the process of evaluating applications for marketing authorizations for products containing or consisting of genetically modified organisms, necessary consultations will be held by the rapporteur with the bodies set up the Community or the Member States in accordance with Directive 90/220/EEC.

5.　The Commission shall, in consultation with the Agency, the Member States and interested parties, draw up detailed guidance on the form in which applications for authorization are to be presented.

Article 7

In order to prepare its opinion, the Committee:

(a) shall verify that the particulars and documents submitted in accordance with Article 6 comply with the requirements of Directives 65/65/EEC, 75/318/EEC and 75/319/EEC, and examine whether the conditions specified in this Regulation for issuing a marketing authorization for the medicinal product are satisfied;

(b) may ask for a State laboratory or a laboratory designated for this purpose to test the medicinal product, its starting materials and, if need be, its intermediate products or other constituent materials in order to ensure that the control methods employed by the manufacturer and described in the application documents are satisfactory;

(c) may, where appropriate, request the applicant to supplement the particulars accompanying the application within a specific time limit. Where the Committee avails itself of this opinion, the time limit laid down in Article 6 shall be suspended until such time as the supplementary information requested has been provided. Likewise, this time limit shall be suspended for the time allowed to the applicant to prepare oral or written explanations.

Article 8

1.　Upon receipt of a written request from the Committee, a Member State shall forward the information establishing that the manufacturer of a medicinal product or the importer from a third country is able to manufacture the medicinal product concerned and/or carry out the necessary control tests in accordance with the particulars and documents supplied pursuant to Article 6.

2. Where it considers it necessary in order to complete its examination of an application, the Committee may require the applicant to submit to a specific inspection of the manufacturing site of the medicinal product concerned. The inspection, which shall be completed within the time limit referred to in Article 6, shall be undertaken by inspectors from the Member State who possess the appropriate qualifications and who may, if need be, be accompanied by a rapporteur or expert appointed by the Committee.

Article 9

1. Where the opinion of the Committee is that:

— the application does not satisfy the criteria for authorization set out in this Regulation, or

— the summary of the product characteristics proposed by the applicant in accordance with Article 6 should be amended, or

— the labelling or package leaflet of the product is not in compliance with Council Directive 92/27/EEC of 31 March 1992 on the labelling of medicinal products for human use and on package leaflets (¹), or

— the authorization should be granted subject to the conditions provided for in Article 13 (2),

the Agency shall forthwith inform the applicant. Within 15 days of receipt of the opinion, the applicant may provide written notice to the Agency that he wishes to appeal. In that case he shall forward the detailed grounds for his appeal to the Agency within 60 days of receipt of the opinion. Within 60 days of the receipt of the grounds for appeal, the Committee shall consider whether its opinion should be revised, and the conclusions reached on the appeal shall be annexed to the assessment report referred to in paragraph 2.

2. Within 30 days of its adoption, the Agency shall forward the final opinion of the Committee to the Commission, the Member States and the applicant together with a report describing the assessment of the medicinal product by the Committee and stating the reasons for its conclusions.

3. In the event of an opinion in favour of granting the relevant authorization to place the medicinal product concerned on the market, the following documents shall be annexed to the opinion:

(a) a draft summary of the product characteristics, as referred to in Article 4a of Directive 65/65/EEC;

(b) details of any conditions or restrictions which should be imposed on the supply or use of the medicinal product concerned, including the conditions under which the medicinal product may be made available to patients, having regard to the criteria laid down in Council Directive 92/26/EEC of 31 March 1992 concerning the classification for the supply of medicinal products for human use (²), without prejudice to the provisions in Article 3 (4) of that Directive;

(c) the draft text of the labelling and package leaflet proposed by the applicant, presented in accordance with Directive 92/27/EEC, without prejudice to the provisions of Article 7 (2) of that Directive;

(d) the assessment report.

Article 10

1. Within 30 days of receipt of the opinion, the Commission shall prepare a draft of the decision to be taken in respect of the application, taking account of Community law.

In the event of a draft decision which envisages the granting of marketing authorization, the documents referred to in Article 9 (3) (a), (b) and (c) shall be annexed.

Where, exceptionally, the draft decision is not in accordance with the opinion of the Agency, the Commission shall also annex a detailed explanation of the reasons for the differences.

The draft decision shall be forwarded to the Member States and the applicant.

2. A final decision on the application shall be adopted in accordance with the procedure laid down in Article 73.

3. The rules of procedure of the Committee referred to in Article 73 shall be adjusted to take account of the tasks incumbent upon it in accordance with this Regulation.

These adjustments shall involve the following:

— except in cases referred to in the third subparagraph of paragraph 1, the opinion of the Standing Committee shall be obtained in writing,

— each Member State is allowed at least 28 days to forward written observations on the draft decision to the Commission,

— each Member State is able to require in writing that the draft decision be discussed by the Standing Committee, giving its reasons in detail.

Where, in the opinion of the Commission, the written observations of a Member State raise important new questions of a scientific or technical nature which have

---

(¹) OJ No L 113, 30. 4. 1992, p. 8.

(²) OJ No L 113, 30. 4. 1992, p. 5.

not been addressed in the opinion of the Agency, the Chairman shall suspend the procedure and refer the application back to the Agency for further consideration.

The provisions necessary for the implementation of this paragraph shall be adopted by the Commission in accordance with the procedure laid down in Article 72.

4. The Agency shall, upon request, inform any person concerned of the final decision.

Article 11

Without prejudice to other provisions of Community law, the authorization provided for in Article 3 shall be refused if, after verification of the information and particulars submitted in accordance with Article 6, it appears that the quality, the safety or the efficacy of the medicinal product have not been adequately or sufficiently demonstrated by the applicant.

Authorization shall likewise be refused if the particulars and documents provided by the applicant in accordance with Article 6 are incorrect or if the labelling and package leaflets proposed by the applicant are not in accordance with Directive 92/27/EEC.

Article 12

1. Without prejudice to Article 6 of Directive 65/65/EEC, a marketing authorization which has been granted in accordance with the procedure laid down in this Regulation shall be valid throughout the Community. It shall confer the same rights and obligations in each of the Member States as a marketing authorization granted by that Member State in accordance with Article 3 of Directive 65/65/EEC.

The authorized medicinal products shall be entered in the *Community Register of Medicinal Products* and shall be given a number which must appear on the packaging.

2. The refusal of a Community marketing authorization shall constitute a prohibition on the placing on the market of the medicinal product concerned throughout the Community.

3. Notification of marketing authorization shall be published in the *Official Journal of the European Communities,* quoting in particular the date of authorization and the number in the Community Register.

4. Upon request from any interested person, the Agency shall make available the assessment report of the medicinal product by the Committee for Proprietary Medicinal Products and the reasons for its opinion in favour of granting authorization, after deletion of any information of a commercially confidential nature.

Article 13

1. Authorization shall be valid for five years and shall be renewable for five-year-periods, on application by the holder at least three months before the expiry date and after consideration by the Agency of a dossier containing up-to-date information on pharmacovigilance.

2. In exceptional circumstances and following consultation with the applicant, an authorization may be granted subject to certain specific obligations, to be reviewed annually by the Agency.

Such exceptional decisions may be adopted only for objective and verifiable reasons and must be based on one of the causes mentioned in Part 4 G of the Annex to Directive 75/318/EEC.

3. Some products may be authorized only for use in hospitals or for prescription by some specialists.

4. Medicinal products which have been authorized by the Community in accordance with the provisions of this Regulation shall benefit from the 10-year period of protection referred to in point 8 of the second paragraph of Article 4 of Directive 65/65/EEC.

Article 14

The granting of authorization shall not diminish the general civil and criminal liability in the Member States of the manufacturer or, where applicable, of the person responsible for placing the medicinal product on the market.

CHAPTER 2

Supervision and sanctions

Article 15

1. After an authorization has been issued in accordance with this Regulation, the person responsible for placing the medicinal product on the market shall, in respect of the methods of production and control provided for in points 4 and 7 of the second paragraph of Article 4 of Directive 65/65/EEC, take account of technical and scientific progress and make any amendments that may be required to enable the medicinal products to be manufactured and checked by means of generally accepted scientific methods. The aforementioned person must apply for approval for these amendments in accordance with this Regulation.

2. The person responsible for placing the medicinal product on the market shall forthwith inform the Agency, the Commission and the Member States of any new information which might entail the amendment of the particulars and documents referred to in Articles 6 or 9 or in the approved summary of the product characteristics. In particular the aforementioned person

shall forthwith inform the Agency, the Commission and the Member States of any prohibition or restriction imposed by the competent authorities of any country in which the medicinal product is placed on the market and of any other new infomation which might influence the evaluation of the benefits and risks of the medicinal product concerned.

3. If the person responsible for placing the medicinal product on the market proposes to make any alteration to the information and particulars referred to in Articles 6 and 9, he shall submit an application to the Agency.

4. The Commission shall, in consultation with the Agency, adopt appropriate arrangements for the examination of variations to the terms of a marketing authorization.

These arrangements shall include a notification system or administrative procedures concerning minor variations and define precisely the concept of 'a minor variation'.

These arrangements shall be adopted by the Commission in the form of an implementing Regulation in accordance with the procedure laid down in Article 72.

Article 16

In the case of medicinal products manufactured within the Community, the supervisory authorities shall be the competent authorities of the Member State or Member States which have granted the manufacturing authorization provided for in Article 16 of Directive 75/319/EEC in respect of the manufacture of the medicinal product concerned.

In the case of medicinal products imported from third countries, the supervisory authorities shall be the competent authorities of the Member States in which the controls referred to in Article 22 (1) (b) of Directive 75/319/EEC are carried out unless appropriate arrangements have been made between the Community and the exporting country to ensure that those controls are carried out in the exporting country and that the manufacturer applies standards of good manufacturing practice at least equivalent to those laid down by the Community.

A Member State may request assistance from another Member State or the Agency.

Article 17

1. The supervisory authorities shall have responsibility for verifying on behalf of the Community that the person responsible for placing the medicinal product on the market or the manufacturer or importer from third countries satisfies the requirements laid down in Chapter IV of Directive 75/319/EEC and for exercising supervision over such persons in accordance with Chapter V of Directive 75/319/EEC.

2. Where, in accordance with the second paragraph of Article 30 of Directive 75/319/EEC, the Commission is informed of serious differences of opinions between Member States as to whether the person responsible for placing the medicinal product on the market or a manufacturer or importer established within the Community is satisfying the requirements referred to in paragraph 1, the Commission may, after consultation with the Member States concerned, request an inspector from the supervisory authority to undertake a new inspection of the aforementioned person, the manufacturer or the importer; the inspector in question may be accompanied by an inspector from a Member State which is not party to the dispute and/or by a rapporteur or expert nominated by the Committee.

3. Subject to any arrangements which may have been concluded between the Community and third countries in accordance with the second subparagraph of Article 16, the Commission may, upon receipt of a reasoned request from a Member State, the Committee for Proprietary Medicinal Products, or on its own initiative, require a manufacturer established in a third country to submit to an inspection. The inspection shall be undertaken by appropriately qualified inspectors from the Member States, who may, if appropriate, be accompanied by a rapporteur or expert nominated by the Committee. The report of the inspectors shall be made available to the Commission, the Member States and the Committee for Proprietary Medicinal Products.

Article 18

1. Where the supervisory authorities or the competent authorities of any other Member State are of the opinion that the manufacturer or importer from third countries is no longer fulfilling the obligations laid down in Chapter IV of Directive 75/319/EEC, they shall forthwith inform the Committee and the Commission, stating their reasons in detail and indicating the course of action proposed.

The same shall apply where a Member State or the Commission considers that one of the measures envisaged in Chapter V or Va of Directive 75/319/EEC should be applied in respect of the medicinal product concerned or where the Committee for Proprietary Medicinal Products has delivered an opinion to that effect in accordance with Article 20.

2. The Commission shall in consultation with the Agency forthwith examine the reasons advanced by the Member State concerned. It shall request the opinion of the Committee within a time limit which it shall determine having regard to the urgency of the matter. Whenever practicable, the person responsible for placing the medicinal product on the market shall be invited to provide oral or written explanations.

3. The Commission shall prepare a draft of the Decision to be taken which shall be adopted in accordance with Article 10.

However, where a Member State has invoked the provisions of paragraph 4, the time limit provided for in Article 73 shall be reduced to 15 calendar days.

4. Where urgent action is essential to protect human or animal health or the environment, a Member State may suspend the use on its territory of a medicinal product which has been authorized in accordance with this Regulation. It shall inform the Commission and the other Member States no later than the following working day of the reasons for its action. The Commission shall immediately consider the reasons given by the Member State in accordance with paragraph 2 and shall initiate the procedure provided for in paragraph 3.

5. A Member State which has adopted the suspensive measures referred to in paragraph 4 may maintain them in force until such time as a definitive decision has been reached in accordance with the procedure laid down in paragraph 3.

6. The Agency shall, upon request, inform any person concerned of the final decision.

CHAPTER 3

Pharmacovigilance

Article 19

For the purpose of this Chapter, the definitions given in Article 29b of Directive 75/319/EEC shall apply.

Article 20

The Agency, acting in close cooperation with the national pharmacovigilance systems established in accordance with Article 29a of Directive 75/319/EEC, shall receive all relevant information about suspected adverse reactions to medicinal products which have been authorized by the Community in accordance with this Regulation. If necessary the Committee may, in accordance with Article 5, formulate opinions on the measures necessary to ensure the safe and effective use of such medicinal products. These measures shall be adopted in accordance with the procedure laid down in Article 18.

The person responsible for placing the medicinal product on the market and the competent authorities of the Member States shall ensure that all relevant information about suspected adverse reactions to medicinal products authorized in accordance with this Regulation are brought to the attention of the Agency in accordance with the provisions of this Regulation.

Article 21

The person responsible for the placing on the market of a medicinal product authorized by the Community in accordance with the provisions of this Regulation shall have permanently and continuously at his disposal an appropriately qualified person responsible for pharmacovigilance.

That qualified person shall be responsible for the following:

(a) the establishment and maintenance of a system which ensures that information about all suspected adverse reactions which are reported to the personnel of the company and to medical representatives, is collected, evaluated and collated so that it may be accessed at a single point within the Community;

(b) the preparation of the reports referred to in Article 22 for the competent authorities of the Member States and the Agency in accordance with the requirements of this Regulation;

(c) ensuring that any request from the competent authorities for the provision of additional information necessary for the evaluation of the benefits and risks of a medicinal product is answered fully and promptly, including the provision of information about the volume of sales or prescriptions for the medicinal product concerned.

Article 22

1. The person responsible for placing the medicinal product on the market shall ensure that all suspected serious adverse reactions occurring within the Community to a medicinal product authorized in accordance with the provisions of this Regulation which are brought to his attention by a health care professional, are recorded and reported immediately to the Member States in whose territory the incident occurred, and in no case later than 15 days following the receipt of the information.

The person responsible for placing the medicinal product on the market shall ensure that all suspected serious unexpected adverse reactions occurring in the territory of a third country, are reported immediately to Member States and the Agency and in no case later than 15 days following the receipt of the information.

The arrangements for the reporting of suspected unexpected adverse reactions which are not serious, whether arising in the Community or in a third country, shall be adopted in accordance with Article 26.

2. In addition, the person responsible for placing the medicinal product on the market shall be required to maintain detailed records of all suspected adverse reactions occurring within or outside the Community which are reported to him by a health care professional. Unless other requirements have been laid down as a condition of the granting of the marketing authorization by the Community, these records shall be submitted to the Agency and Member States immediately upon request or at least every six months during the first two years following authorization and once a year for the following three years. Thereafter, the records shall be submitted at five-yearly intervals together with the application of renewal of the authorization, or immediately upon request. These records shall be accompanied by a scientific evaluation.

Article 23

Each Member State shall ensure that all suspected serious adverse reactions occurring within their territory to a medicinal product authorized in accordance with the provisions of this Regulation which are brought to their attention are recorded and reported immediately to the Agency and the person responsible for placing the medicinal product on the market, and in no case later than 15 days following the receipt of the information.

The Agency shall inform the national pharmacovigilance systems.

Article 24

The Commission in consultation with the Agency, Member States, and interested parties, shall draw up guidance on the collection, verification and presentation of adverse reaction reports.

The Agency, in consultation with the Member States and the Commission, shall set up a data-processing network for the rapid transmission of data between the competent Community authorities in the event of an alert relating to faulty manufacture, serious adverse reactions and other pharmacovigilance data regarding medicinal products marketed in the Community.

Article 25

The Agency shall collaborate with the World Health Organization on international pharmacovigilance and shall take the necessary steps to submit promptly to the World Health Organization appropriate and adequate information regarding the measures taken in the Community which may have a bearing on public health protection in third countries and shall send a copy thereof to the Commission and the Member States.

Article 26

Any amendment which may be necessary to update the provisions of this chapter to take account of scientific and technical progress shall be adopted in accordance with the provisions of Article 72.

TITLE III

AUTHORIZATION AND SUPERVISION OF VETERINARY MEDICINAL PRODUCTS

CHAPTER 1

Submission and examination of applications — authorization — renewal of authorization

Article 27

The Committee for Veterinary Medicinal Products established by Article 16 of Directive 81/851/EEC, in this Title referred to as 'the Committee', shall be responsible for formulating the opinion of the Agency on any question concerning the admissibility of the files submitted in accordance with the centralized procedure, the granting, variation, suspension or withdrawal of an authorization to place a veterinary medicinal product on the market arising in accordance with the provisions of this Title and pharmacovigilance.

Article 28

1. An application for authorization for a veterinary medicinal product must be accompanied by the particulars and documents referred to in Articles 5, 5a and 7 of Directive 81/851/EEC.

2. In the case of a veterinary medicinal product containing or consisting of genetically modified organisms within the meaning of Article 2 (1) and (2) of Directive 90/220/EEC, the application must also be accompanied by:

— a copy of any written consent or consents of the competent authorities to the deliberate release into the environment of the genetically modified organisms for research and development purposes where provided for in Part B of Directive 90/220/EEC,

— the complete technical dossier supplying the information requested in Annexes II and III to Directive 90/220/EEC and the environmental risk assessment resulting from this information; the results of any investigations performed for the purposes of research or development.

Articles 11 to 18 of Directive 90/220/EEC shall not apply to veterinary medicinal products containing or consisting of genetically modified organisms.

3. The application shall also be accompanied by the fee payable to the Agency for the examination of the application.

4. The Agency shall ensure that the opinion of the Committee is given within 210 days of the receipt of a valid application.

In the case of a veterinary medicinal product containing or consisting of genetically modified organisms, the opinion of the Committee shall respect the environmental safety requirements laid down by Directive 90/220/EEC to ensure that all appropriate measures are taken to avoid adverse effects on human health and the environment which might arise from the deliberate release into the environment or placing on the market of genetically modified organisms. During the process of evaluating applications for marketing authorizations for veterinary medicinal products containing or consisting of genetically modified organisms, necessary consultations shall be held by the rapporteur with the bodies set up by the Community or the Member States in accordance with Directive 90/220/EEC.

5.   The Commission shall, in consultation with the Agency, the Member States and interested parties, draw up detailed guidance on the form in which applications for authorization are to be presented.

Article 29

In order to prepare its opinion, the Committee:

(a) shall verify that the particulars and documents submitted in accordance with Article 28 comply with the requirements of Directives 81/851/EEC and 81/852/EEC and examine whether the conditions specified in this Regulation for issuing a marketing authorization are satisfied;

(b) may ask for a State laboratory or a laboratory designated for this purpose to test the veterinary medicinal product, its starting materials and, if need be, its intermediate products or other constituent materials in order to ensure that the control methods employed by the manufacturer and described in the application documents are satisfactory;

(c) may request a State laboratory or laboratory designated for this purpose to verify, using samples provided by the applicant, that the analytical detection method proposed by the applicant in accordance with point 8 of the second paragraph of Article 5 of Directive 81/851/EEC is suitable for use in routine checks to reveal the presence of residue levels above the maximum residue level accepted by the Community in accordance with the provisions of Council Regulation (EEC) No 2377/90 of 26 June 1990 laying down a Community procedure for the establishment of maximum residue limits of veterinary medicinal products in foodstuffs of animal origin (¹);

(d) may, where appropriate, request the applicant to supplement the particulars accompanying the application within a specific time limit. Where the Committee avails itself of this option, the time limit laid down in Article 28 shall be suspended until such time as the supplementary information requested has been provided. Likewise, this time limit shall be

suspended for the time allowed to the applicant to prepare oral or written explanations.

Article 30

1.   Upon receipt of a written request from the Committee, a Member State shall forward the information establishing that the manufacturer of a veterinary medicinal product or the importer from a third country is able to manufacture the veterinary medicinal product concerned and/or carry out the necessary control tests in accordance with the particulars and documents supplied pursuant to Article 28.

2.   Where it considers it necessary in order to complete its examinination of an application, the Committee may require the applicant to submit to a specific inspection of the manufacturing site of the veterinary medicinal product concerned. The inspection, which shall be completed within the time limit referred to in Article 28, shall be undertaken by inspectors from the Member State who possess the appropriate qualifications and who may, if need be, be accompanied by a rapporteur or expert appointed by the Committee.

Article 31

1.   Where the opinion of the Committee is that:

— the application does not satisfy the criteria for authorization set out in this Regulation,

    or

— the summary of the product characteristics proposed by the applicant in accordance with Article 28 should be amended,

    or

— the labelling or package insert of the product is not in compliance with Directive 81/851/EEC,

    or

— the authorization should be granted subject to the conditions provided for in Article 35 (2),

the Agency shall forthwith inform the applicant. Within 15 days of receipt of the opinion, the applicant may provide written notice to the Agency that he wishes to appeal. In that case he shall forward the detailed grounds for his appeal to the Agency within 60 days of receipt of the opinion. Within 60 days of the receipt of the grounds for appeal, the Committee shall consider whether its opinion should be revised, and the reasons for the conclusion reached on the appeal shall be annexed to the assessment report referred to in paragraph 2.

2.   Within 30 days of its adoption, the Agency shall forward the final opinion of the Committee to the Commission, the Member States and the applicant together with a report describing the assessment of the veterinary medicinal product by the Committee and stating the reasons for its conclusions.

(¹) OJ No L 224, 18. 8. 1990, p. 1. Regulation last amended by Regulation No 762/92 (OJ No L 83, 28. 3. 1992, p. 14).

3. In the event of an opinion in favour of granting the relevant authorization to market the veterinary medicinal product, the following documents shall be annexed to the opinion:

(a) the draft summary of the product characteristics, as referred to in Article 5a of Directive 81/851/EEC; where necessary this will reflect differences in the veterinary conditions pertaining in the Member States;

(b) in the case of a veterinary medicinal product intended for administration to food-producing animals, a statement of the maximum residue level which may be accepted by the Community in accordance with Regulation (EEC) No 2377/90;

(c) details of any conditions or restrictions which should be imposed on the supply or use of the veterinary medicinal product concerned, including the conditions under which the veterinary medicinal product may be made available to users, in accordance with the criteria laid down in Directive 81/851/EEC;

(d) the draft text of the labelling and package insert proposed by the applicant, presented in accordance with Directive 81/851/EEC;

(e) the assessment report.

Article 32

1. Within 30 days of receipt of the opinion, the Commission shall prepare a draft of the decision to be taken in respect of the application, taking account of Community law.

In the event of a draft decision which envisages the granting of marketing authorization, the documents referred to in Article 31 (3) (a), (b), (c) and (d) shall be annexed.

Where, exceptionally, the draft decision is not in accordance with the opinion of the Agency, the Commission shall also annex a detailed explanation of the reasons for the differences.

The draft decision shall be forwarded to the Member States and the applicant.

2. A final decision on the application shall be adopted in accordance with the procedure laid down in Article 73.

3. The rules of procedure of the Committee referred to in Article 73 shall be adjusted to take account of the tasks incumbent upon it in accordance with this Regulation.

These adjustments shall involve the following:

— except in the cases referred to in the third subparagraph of paragraph 1, the opinion of the Standing Committee shall be obtained in writing,

— each Member State is allowed at least 28 days to forward written observations on the draft decision to the Commission,

— each Member State is able to require in writing that the draft decision be discussed by the Standing Committee giving its reasons in detail.

Where, in the opinion of the Commission, the written observations of a Member State raise important new questions of a scientific or technical nature which have not been addressed in the opinion of the Agency, the Chairman shall suspend the procedure and refer the application back to the Agency for further consideration.

The provisions necessary for the implementation of this paragraph shall be adopted by the Commission in accordance with the procedure laid down in Article 72.

4. The Agency shall, upon request, inform any person concerned of the final decision.

Article 33

Without prejudice to other provisions of Community law, the authorization provided for in Article 3 shall be refused if, after verification of the information and particulars submitted in accordance with Article 28, it appears that:

1. the veterinary medicinal product is harmful under the conditions of use stated at the time of the application for authorization, has no therapeutic effect or the applicant has not provided sufficient proof of such effect as regards the species of animal which is to be treated, or its qualitative and quantitative composition is not as stated;

2. the withdrawal period recommended by the applicant is not long enough to ensure that foodstuffs obtained from treated animals do not contain residues which might constitute a health hazard for the consumer or is insufficiently substantiated;

3. the veterinary medicinal product is offered for sale for a use prohibited under other Community provisions.

Authorization shall likewise be refused if the particulars and documents provided by the applicant in accordance with Article 28 are incorrect or if the labelling and package inserts proposed by the applicant are not in accordance with Chapter VII of Directive 81/851/EEC.

Article 34

1. Without prejudice to Article 4 of Council Directive 90/677/EEC of 13 December 1990 extending the scope of Directive 81/851/EEC on the approximation of the laws of the Member States relating to veterinary medicinal

products ([1]), and laying down additional provisions for immunological veterinary medicinal products, a marketing authorization which has been granted in accordance with the procedure laid down in this Regulation shall apply throughout the Community. It shall confer the same rights and obligations in each of the Member States as a marketing authorization granted by that Member State in accordance with Article 4 of Directive 81/851/EEC.

The authorized veterinary medicinal products shall be entered in the Community Register of Medicinal Products and shall be given a number which must appear on the packaging.

2. The refusal of a Community marketing authorization shall constitute a prohibition on the placing on the market of the veterinary medicinal product concerned throughout the Community.

3. Notification of marketing authorization shall be published in the *Official Journal of the European Communities*, quoting in particular the date of authorization and the number in the Community Register.

4. Upon request from any interested person, the Agency shall make available the assessment report of the veterinary medicinal product by the Committee for Veterinary Medicinal Products and the reasons for its opinion in favour of granting authorization, after deletion of any information of a commercially confidential nature.

Article 35

1. Authorization shall be valid for five years and shall be renewable for five-year periods, on application by the holder at least three months before the expiry date and after consideration by the Agency of a dossier containing up-to-date information on pharmacovigilance.

2. In exceptional circumstances and following consultations with the applicant, authorization may be granted subject to certain specific obligations, to be reviewed annually by the Agency.

Such exceptional decisions may be adopted for objective and verifiable reasons.

3. Veterinary medicinal products which have been authorized by the Community in accordance with the provisions of this Regulation shall benefit from the 10-year period of protection referred to in point 10 of the second paragraph of Article 5 of Directive 81/851/EEC.

Article 36

The granting of authorization shall not diminish the general civil and criminal liability in the Member States of the manufacturer or, where applicable, of the person responsible for placing the veterinary medicinal product on the market.

([1]) OJ No L 373, 31. 12. 1990, p. 26.

CHAPTER 2

Supervision and sanctions

Article 37

1. After an authorization has been issued in accordance with this Regulation, the person responsible for placing the veterinary medicinal product on the market shall, in respect of the methods of production and control provided for in points 4 and 9 of the second paragraph of Article 5 of Directive 81/851/EEC, take account of technical and scientific progress and make changes that may be required to enable the veterinary medicinal product to be manufactured and checked by means of generally accepted scientific methods. The aforementioned person must apply for approval for these changes in accordance with this Regulation.

Upon a request from the Commission, the person responsible for placing the veterinary medicinal product on the market shall also review the analytical detection methods provided for in point 8 of the second paragraph of Article 5 of Directive 81/851/EEC and propose any changes which may be necessary to take account of technical and scientific progress.

2. The person responsible for placing the veterinary medicinal product on the market shall forthwith inform the Agency, the Commission and the Member States of any new information which might entail the amendment of the particulars and documents referred to in Articles 28 and 31 or in the approved summary of the product characteristics. In particular the aforementioned person shall forthwith inform the Agency, the Commission and the Member States of any prohibition or restriction imposed by the competent authorities of any country in which the veterinary medicinal product is marketed and of any other new information which might influence the evaluation of the benefits and risks of the veterinary medicinal product concerned.

3. If the person responsible for placing the veterinary medicinal product on the market proposes to make any alteration to the information and particulars referred to in Articles 28 and 31, he shall submit an application to the Agency.

4. The Commission shall, in consultation with the Agency, adopt appropriate arrangements for the examination of variations to the terms of a marketing authorization.

These arrangements shall include a notification system or administrative procedures concerning minor variations and define precisely the concept of 'a minor variation'.

These arrangements shall be adopted by the Commission in the form of an implementing Regulation in accordance with the procedure laid down in Article 72.

Article 38

In the case of veterinary medicinal products manufactured within the Community, the supervisory authorities shall be the competent authorities of the Member State or Member States which have granted the manufacturing authorization provided for in Article 24 of Directive 85/851/EEC in respect of the manufacture of the veterinary medicinal product concerned.

In the case of veterinary medicinal products imported from third countries, the supervisory authorities shall be the competent authorities of the Member States in which the controls referred to in Article 30 (1) (b) of Directive 81/851/EEC are carried out unless appropriate arrangements have been made between the Community and the exporting country to ensure that those controls are carried out in the exporting country and that the manufacturer applies standards of good manufacturing practice at least equivalent to those laid down by the Community.

A Member State may request assistance from another Member State or the Agency.

Article 39

1. The supervisory authorities shall have responsibility for verifying on behalf of the Community that the person responsible for placing the veterinary medicinal product on the market, or manufacturer or importer from third countries satisfies the requirements laid down in Chapter V of Directive 81/851/EEC and for exercising supervision over such persons in accordance with Chapter VI of Directive 81/851/EEC.

2. Where, in accordance with the second paragraph of Article 39 of Directive 81/851/EEC, the Commission is informed of serious differences of opinion between Member States as to whether the person responsible for placing the veterinary medicinal product on the market or a manufacturer or importer established within the Community is satisfying the requirements referred to in paragraph 1, the Commission may, after consultation with the Member States concerned, request an inspector from the supervisory authority to undertake a new inspection of the aforementioned person, the manufacturer or the importer; the inspector in question may be accompanied by an inspector from a Member State which is not party to the dispute and/or by a rapporteur or expert nominated by the Committee.

3. Subject to any arrangements which may have been concluded between the Community and third countries in accordance with the second paragraph of Article 38, the Commission may, upon receipt of a reasoned request from a Member State, the Committee for Veterinary Medicinal Products, or on its own initiative, require a manufacturer established in a third country to submit to an inspection. The inspection shall be undertaken by appropriately qualified inspectors from the Member States, who may, if appropriate, be accompanied by a rapporteur or expert nominated by the Committee. The report of the inspectors shall be made available to the Commission, the Member States and the Committee for Veterinary Medicinal Products.

Article 40

1. Where the supervisory authorities or the competent authorities of any other Member State are of the opinion that the manufacturer or importer from third countries is no longer fulfilling the obligations laid down in Chapter V of Directive 81/851/EEC, they shall forthwith inform the Committee and the Commission, stating their reasons in detail and indicating the course of action proposed.

The same shall apply where a Member State or the Commission considers that one of the measures envisaged in Chapter VI of Directive 81/851/EEC should be applied in respect of the veterinary medicinal product concerned or where the Committee for Veterinary Medicinal Products has delivered an opinion to that effect in accordance with Article 42.

2. The Commission shall in consultation with the Agency forthwith examine the reasons advanced by the Member State concerned. It shall request the opinion of the Committee within a time limit to be determined by the Commission having regard to the urgency of the matter. Whenever practicable, the person responsible for placing the veterinary medicinal product on the market shall be invited to provide oral or written explanations.

3. The Commission shall prepare a draft of the Decision to be taken which shall be adopted in accordance with the procedure laid down in Article 32.

However, where a Member State has invoked the provisions of paragraph 4, the time limit provided for in Article 73 shall be reduced to 15 calendar days.

4. Where urgent action is essential to protect human or animal health or the environment, a Member State may suspend the use on its territory of a veterinary medicinal product which has been authorized in accordance with this Regulation. It shall inform the Commission and the other Member States no later than the following working day of the reasons for its action. The Commission shall immediately consider the reasons given by the Member State in accordance with paragraph 2 and shall initiate the procedure provided for in paragraph 3.

5. A Member State which has adopted the suspensive measures referred to in paragraph 4 may maintain them in force until such time as a definitive decision has been reached in accordance with the procedure laid down in paragraph 3.

6. The Agency shall, upon request, inform any person concerned of the final decision.

CHAPTER 3

Pharmacovigilance

Article 41

For the purpose of this Chapter, the definitions given in Article 42 of Directive 81/851/EEC shall apply.

Article 42

The Agency, acting in close cooperation with the national pharmacovigilance systems established in accordance with Article 42a of Directive 81/851/EEC, shall receive all relevant information about suspected adverse reactions to veterinary medicinal products which have been authorized by the Community in accordance with this Regulation. If necessary the Committee may, in accordance with Article 27, formulate opinions on the measures necessary to ensure the safe and effective use of such veterinary medicinal products. These measures shall be adopted in accordance with the procedure laid down in Article 40.

The person responsible for placing the veterinary medicinal product on the market and the competent authorities of the Member States shall ensure that all relevant information about suspected adverse reactions to veterinary medicinal products authorized in accordance with this Regulation are brought to the attention of the Agency in accordance with the provisions of this Regulation.

Article 43

The person responsible for the placing on the market of a veterinary medicinal product authorized by the Community in accordance with the provisions of this Regulation shall have permanently and continuously at his disposal an appropriately qualified person responsible for pharmacovigilance.

That qualified person shall be responsible for the following:

(a) the establishment and maintenance of a system which ensures that information about all suspected adverse reactions which are reported to the personnel of the company and to its representatives is collected, evaluated and collated so that it may be accessed at a single point within the Community;

(b) the preparation of the reports referred to in Article 44 for the competent authorities of the Member States and the Agency in accordance with the requirements of this Regulation;

(c) ensuring that any request from the competent authorities for the provision of additional information necessary for the evaluation of the benefits and risks of a veterinary medicinal product

is answered fully and promptly, including the provision of information about the volume of sales or prescriptions for the veterinary medicinal product concerned.

Article 44

1. The person responsible for placing a veterinary medicinal product on the market shall ensure that all suspected serious adverse reactions occurring within the Community to a veterinary medicinal product authorized in accordance with the provisions of this Regulation which are brought to his attention are recorded and reported immediately to the Member States in whose territory the incident occurred, and in no case later than 15 days following the receipt of the information.

The aforementioned person shall ensure that all suspected serious unexpected adverse reactions occurring in the territory of a third country, are reported immediately to the Member States and the Agency and in no case later than 15 days following the receipt of the information.

The arrangements for the reporting of suspected unexpected adverse reactions which are not serious, whether arising in the Community or in a third country, shall be adopted in accordance with Article 48.

2. In addition, the person responsible for placing a veterinary medicinal product on the market shall be required to maintain detailed records of all suspected adverse reactions occurring within or outside the Community which are reported to him. Unless other requirements have been laid down as a condition of the granting of the marketing authorization by the Community, these records shall be submitted to the Agency and Member States immediately upon request or at least every six months during the first two years following authorization and once a year for the following three years. Thereafter, the records shall be submitted at five-yearly intervals together with the application of renewal of the authorization, or immediately upon request. These records shall be accompanied by a scientific evaluation.

Article 45

Each Member State shall ensure that all suspected serious adverse reactions occurring within their territory to a veterinary medicinal product authorized in accordance with the provisions of this Regulation which are brought to their attention are recorded and reported immediately to the Agency and the person responsible for placing the veterinary medicinal product on the market, and in no case later than 15 days following the receipt of the information.

The Agency shall inform the national pharmacovigilance systems.

Article 46

The Commission in consultation with the Agency, Member States, and interested parties, shall draw up guidance on the collection, verification and presentation of adverse reaction reports.

The Agency, in consultation with the Member States and the Commission, shall set up a data-processing network for the rapid transmission of data between the competent Community authorities in the event of an alert relating to faulty manufacture, serious adverse reactions and other pharmacovigilance data regarding veterinary medicinal products marketed in the Community.

Article 47

The Agency shall cooperate with international organizations concerned with veterinary pharmacovigilance.

Article 48

Any amendment which may be necessary to update the provisions of this Chapter to take account of scientific and technical progress shall be adopted in accordance with the provisions of Article 72.

TITLE IV

THE EUROPEAN AGENCY FOR THE EVALUATION OF MEDICINAL PRODUCTS

CHAPTER 1

Tasks of the Agency

Article 49

A European Agency for the Evaluation of Medicinal Products is hereby established.

The Agency shall be responsible for coordinating the existing scientific resources put at its disposal by the competent authorities of the Member States for the evaluation and supervision of medicinal products.

Article 50

1. The Agency shall comprise:

(a) the Committee for Proprietary Medicinal Products, which shall be responsible for preparing the opinion of the Agency on any question relating to the evaluation of medicinal products for human use;

(b) the Committee for Veterinary Medicinal Products, which shall be responsible for preparing the opinion of the Agency on any question relating to the evaluation of veterinary medicinal products;

(c) a Secretariat, which shall provide technical and administrative support for the two Committees and ensure appropriate coordination between them;

(d) an Executive Director, who shall exercise the responsibilities set out in Article 55;

(e) a Management Board, which shall exercise the responsibilities set out in Articles 56 and 57.

2. The Committee for Proprietary Medicinal Products and the Committee for Veterinary Medicinal Products may each establish working parties and expert groups.

3. The Committee for Proprietary Medicinal Products and the Committee for Veterinary Medicinal Products

may, if they consider it appropriate, seek guidance on important questions of a general scientific or ethical nature.

Article 51

In order to promote the protection of human and animal health and of consumers of medicinal products throughout the Community, and in order to promote the completion of the internal market through the adoption of uniform regulatory decisions based on scientific criteria concerning the placing on the market and use of medicinal products, the objectives of the Agency shall be to provide the Member States and the institutions of the Community with the best possible scientific advice on any question relating to the evaluation of the quality, the safety, and the efficacy of medicinal products for human or veterinary use, which is referred to it in accordance with the provisions of Community legislation relating to medicinal products.

To this end, the Agency shall undertake the following tasks within its Committees:

(a) the coordination of the scientific evaluation of the quality, safety and efficacy of medicinal products which are subject to Community marketing authorization procedures;

(b) the transmission of assessment reports, summaries of product characteristics, labels and package leaflets or inserts for these medicinal products;

(c) the coordination of the supervision, under practical conditions of use, of medicinal products which have been authorized within the Community and the provision of advice on the measures necessary to ensure the safe and effective use of these products, in particular by evaluating and making available through a database information on adverse reactions to the medicinal products in question (pharmacovigilance);

(d) advising on the maximum limits for residues of veterinary medicinal products which may be accepted in foodstuffs of animal origin in accordance with Regulation (EEC) No 2377/90.

(e) coordinating the verification of compliance with the principles of good manufacturing practice, good laboratory practice and good clinical practice;

(f) upon request, providing technical and scientific support for steps to improve cooperation between the Community, its Member States, international organizations and third countries on scientific and technical issues relating to the evaluation of medicinal products;

(g) recording the status of marketing authorizations for medicinal products granted in accordance with Community procedures;

(h) providing technical assistance for the maintenance of a database on medicinal products which is available for public use;

(i) assisting the Community and Member States in the provision of information to health care professionals and the general public about medicinal products which have been evaluated within the Agency;

(j) where necessary, advising companies on the conduct of the various tests and trials necessary to demonstrate the quality, safety and efficacy of medicinal products.

Article 52

1. The Committee for Proprietary Medicinal Products and the Committee for Veterinary Medicinal Products shall each consist of two members nominated by each Member State for a term of three years which shall be renewable. They shall be chosen by reason of their role and experience in the evaluation of medicinal products for human and veterinary use as appropriate and shall represent their competent authorities.

The Executive Director of the Agency or his representative and representatives of the Commission shall be entitled to attend all meetings of the Committees, their working parties and expert groups.

Members of each Committee may arrange to be accompanied by experts.

2. In addition to their task of providing objective scientific opinions to the Community and Member States on the questions which are referred to them, the members of each Committee shall ensure that there is appropriate coordination between the tasks of the Agency and the work of competent national authorities, including the consultative bodies concerned with the marketing authorization.

3. The members of the Committees and the experts responsible for evaluating medicinal products shall rely on the scientific assessment and resources available to the national marketing authorization bodies. Each Member State shall monitor the scientific level of the evaluation

carried out and supervise the activities of members of the Committees and the experts it nominates, but shall refrain from giving them any instruction which is incompatible with the tasks incumbent upon them.

4. When preparing the opinion, each Committee shall use its best endeavours to reach a scientific consensus. If such a consensus cannot be reached, the opinion shall consist of the position of the majority of members and may, at the request of those concerned, include the divergent positions with their grounds.

Article 53

1. Where, in accordance with the provisions of this Regulation, the Committee for Proprietary Medicinal Products or the Committee for Veterinary Medicinal Products is required to evaluate a medicinal product, the Committee shall appoint one of its members to act as rapporteur for the coordination of the evaluation, taking into consideration any proposal from the applicant for the choice of a rapporteur. The Committee may appoint a second member to act as co-rapporteur.

The Committee shall ensure that all its members undertake the role of rapporteur or co-rapporteur.

2. Member States shall transmit to the Agency a list of experts with proven experience in the assessment of medicinal products who would be available to serve on working parties or expert groups of the Committee for Proprietary Medicinal Products or the Committee for Veterinary Medicinal Products, together with an indication of their qualifications and specific areas of expertise.

This list shall be updated as necessary.

3. The provision of services by rapporteurs or experts shall be governed by a written contract between the Agency and the person concerned, or where appropriate between the Agency and his employer. The person concerned, or his employer, shall be remunerated in accordance with a fixed scale of fees to be included in the financial arrangements established by the Management Board.

4. On a proposal from the Committee for Proprietary Medicinal Products or the Committee for Veterinary Medicinal Products, the Agency may also avail itself of the services of rapporteurs or experts for the discharge of other specific responsibilities of the Agency.

Article 54

1. The membership of the Committee for Proprietary Medicinal Products and the Committee for Veterinary Medicinal Products shall be made public. When each appointment is published, the professional qualifications of each member shall be specified.

2. Members of the Management Board, Committee members, rapporteurs and experts shall not have financial or other interests in the pharmaceutical industry which could affect their impartiality. All indirect interests which could relate to this industry shall be entered in a register held by the Agency which the public may consult.

Article 55

1. The Executive Director shall be appointed by the Management Board, on a proposal from the Commission, for a period of five years, which shall be renewable.

2. The Executive Director shall be the legal representative of the Agency. He shall be responsible:

— for the day-to-day administration of the Agency,

— for the provision of appropriate technical support for the Committee for Proprietary Medicinal Products and the Committee for Veterinary Medicinal Products, and their working parties and expert groups,

— for ensuring that the time limits laid down in Community legislation for the adoption of opinions by the Agency are respected,

— for ensuring appropriate coordination between the Committee for Proprietary Medicinal Products and the Committee for Veterinary Medicinal Products,

— for the preparation of the statement of revenue and expenditure and the execution of the budget of the Agency,

— for all staff matters.

3. Each year, the Executive Director shall submit to the Management Board for approval, while making a distinction between the Agency's activities concerning medicinal products for human use and those concerning veterinary medicinal products:

— a draft report covering the activities of the Agency in the previous year, including information about the number of applications evaluated within the Agency, the time taken for the completion of the evaluation and the medicinal products authorized, rejected or withdrawn,

— a draft programme of work for the coming year,

— the draft annual accounts for the previous year,

— the draft budget for the coming year.

4. The Executive Director shall approve all financial expenditure of the Agency.

Article 56

1. The Management Board shall consist of two representatives from each Member State, two representatives of the Commission and two representatives appointed by the European Parliament. One representative shall have specific responsibilities relating to medicinal products for human use and one relating to veterinary medicinal products.

Each representative may arrange to be replaced by an alternate.

2. The term of office of the representatives shall be three years. It shall be renewable.

3. The Management Board shall elect its Chairman for a term of three years and shall adopt its rules of procedure.

Decisions of the Management Board shall be adopted by a majority of two-thirds of its members.

4. The Executive Director shall provide the Secretariat of the Management Board.

5. Before 31 January each year, the Management Board shall adopt the general report on the activities of the Agency for the previous year and its programme of work for the coming year and forward them to the Member States, the Commission, the Council and the European Parliament.

CHAPTER 2

Financial provisions

Article 57

1. The revenues of the Agency shall consist of a contribution from the Community, and the fees paid by undertakings for obtaining and maintaining a Community marketing authorization and for other services provided by the Agency.

2. The expenditure of the Agency shall include the staff, administrative, infrastructure and operational expenses and expenses resulting from contracts entered into with third parties.

3. By 15 February each year at the latest, the Director shall draw up a preliminary draft budget covering the operational expenditure and the programme of work anticipated for the following financial year, and shall forward this preliminary draft to the Management Board together with an establishment plan.

4. Revenue and expenditure shall be in balance.

5. The Management Board shall adopt the draft budget and forward it to the Commission which on that basis shall establish the relevant estimates in the preliminary draft general budget of the European Communities, which it shall put before the Council pursuant to Article 203 of the Treaty.

6. The Management Board shall adopt the Agency's final budget before the beginning of the financial year,

adjusting it where necessary to the Community subsidy and the Agency's other resources.

7.   The Director shall implement the Agency's budget.

8.   Monitoring of the commitment and payment of all the Agency's expenditure and of the establishment and recovery of all the Agency's revenue shall be carried out by the financial controller appointed by the Management Board.

9.   By 31 March each year at the latest, the Director shall forward to the Commission, the Management Board and the Court of Auditors the accounts for all the Agency's revenue and expenditure in respect of the preceding financial year.

The Court of Auditors shall examine them in accordance with Article 206a of the Treaty.

10.   The Management Board shall give a discharge to the Director in respect of the implementation of the budget.

11.   After the Court of Auditors has delivered its opinion, the Management Board shall adopt the internal financial provisions specifying, in particular, the detailed rules for establishing and implementing the Agency's budget.

Article 58

The structure and the amount of the fees referred to in Article 57 (1) shall be established by the Council acting under the conditions provided for by the Treaty on a proposal from the Commission, following consultation of organizations representing the interests of the pharmaceutical industry at Community level.

CHAPTER 3

General provisions governing the Agency

Article 59

The Agency shall have legal personality. In all Member States it shall benefit from the widest powers granted by law to legal persons. In particular it may acquire and dispose of real property and chattels and institute legal proceedings.

Article 60

1.   The contractual liability of the Agency shall be governed by the law applicable to the contract in question. The Court of Justice of the European Communities shall have jurisdiction to give judgment pursuant to any arbitration clause contained in a contract concluded by the Agency.

2.   In the case of non-contractual liability, the Agency shall, in accordance with the general principles common to the laws of the Member States, make good any damage caused by it or its servants in the performance of their duties.

The Court of Justice shall have jurisdiction in any dispute relating to compensation for such damages.

3.   The personal liability of its servants towards the Agency shall be governed by the relevant conditions applying to the staff of the Agency.

Article 61

The Protocol on the Privileges and Immunities of the European Communities shall apply to the Agency.

Article 62

The staff of the Agency shall be subject to the rules and regulations applicable to officials and other staff of the European Communities.

In respect of its staff, the Agency shall exercise the powers which have been devolved to the appointing authority.

The Management Board, in agreement with the Commission, shall adopt the necessary implementing provisions.

Article 63

Members of the Management Board, members of Committees, and officials and other servants of the Agency shall be required, even after their duties have ceased, not to disclose information of the kind covered by the obligation of professional secrecy.

Article 64

The Commission may, in agreement with the Management Board and the relevant Committee, invite representatives of international organizations with interests in the harmonization of regulations applicable to medicinal products to participate as observers in the work of the Agency.

Article 65

The Management Board shall, in agreement with the Commission, develop appropriate contacts between the Agency and the representatives of the industry, consumers and patients and the health professions.

Article 66

The Agency shall take up its responsibilities on 1 January 1995.

TITLE V

GENERAL AND FINAL PROVISIONS

Article 67

All decisions to grant, refuse, vary, suspend, withdraw or revoke a marketing authorization which are taken in accordance with this Regulation shall state in detail the reasons on which they are based. Such decisions shall be notified to the party concerned.

Article 68

1. An authorization to place on the market a medicinal product coming within the scope of this Regulation shall not be refused, varied, suspended, withdrawn or revoked except on the grounds set out in this Regulation.

2. An authorization to place on the market a medicinal product coming within the scope of this Regulation shall not be granted, refused, varied, suspended, withdrawn or revoked except in accordance with the procedures set out in this Regulation.

Article 69

Without prejudice to Article 68, and without prejudice to the Protocol on the Privileges and Immunities of the European Communities, each Member State shall determine the penalties to be applied for the infringement of the provisions of this Regulation. The penalties must be sufficient to promote compliance with those measures.

Member States shall forthwith inform the Commission of the institution of any infringement proceedings.

Article 70

Additives covered by Council Directive 70/524/EEC of 23 November 1970 concerning additives in feedingstuffs (¹), where they are intended to be administered to animals in accordance with that Directive, shall not be considered as veterinary medicinal products for the purposes of this Regulation.

Within three years of the entry into force of this Regulation the Commission shall produce a report on whether the level of harmonization achieved by this Regulation and by Council Directive 90/167/EEC of 26 March 1990 laying down the conditions governing the preparation, placing on the market and use of medicated feedingstuffs in the Community (²) is equivalent to that

provided for in Council Directive 70/524/EEC, accompanied if necessary by the proposals to modify the status of the coccidiostats and other medicinal substances covered by that Directive.

The Council shall decide on the Commission proposal no later than one year after their submission.

Article 71

Within six years of the entry into force of this Regulation, the Commission shall publish a general report on the experience acquired as a result of the operation of the procedures laid down in this Regulation, in Chapter III of Directive 75/319/EEC and in Chapter IV of Directive 81/851/EEC.

Article 72

Where the procedure laid down in this Article is to be followed the Commission shall be assisted by:

— the Standing Committee on Medicinal Products for Human Use, in the case of matters relating to medicinal products for human use,

— the Standing Committee on Veterinary Medicinal Products, in the case of matters relating to veterinary medicinal products.

The representative of the Commission shall submit to the Committee a draft of the measures to be taken. The Committee shall deliver its opinion on the draft within a time limit which the Chairman may lay down according to the urgency of the matter. The opinion shall be delivered by the majority laid down in Article 148 (2) of the Treaty in the case of decisions which the Council is required to adopt on a proposal from the Commission. The votes of the representatives of the Member States within the Committee shall be weighted in the manner set out in that Article. The Chairman shall not vote.

The Commission shall adopt the measures envisaged if they are in accordance with the opinion of the Committee.

If the measures envisaged are not in accordance with the opinion of the Committee, or if no opinion is delivered, the Commission shall, without delay, submit to the Council a proposal relating to the measures to be taken. The Council shall act by a qualified majority.

If on the expiry of a period of three months from the date of referral to the Council, the Council has not acted, the proposed measures shall be adopted by the Commission.

(¹) OJ No L 270, 14. 12. 1970, p. 1. Directive last amended by Commission Directive 92/64/EEC (OJ No L 221, 6. 8. 1992, p. 51).
(²) OJ No L 92, 7. 4. 1990, p. 42.

Article 73

Where the procedure laid down in this Article is to be followed the Commission shall be assisted by:

— the Standing Committee on Medicinal Products for Human Use, in the case of matters relating to medicinal products for human use,

— the Standing Committee on Veterinary Medicinal Products, in the case of matters relating to veterinary medicinal products.

The representative of the Commission shall submit to the Committee a draft of the measures to be taken. The Committee shall deliver its opinion on the draft within a time limit which the Chairman may lay down according to the urgency of the matter. The opinion shall be delivered by the majority laid down in Article 148 (2) of the Treaty in the case of decisions which the Council is required to adopt on a proposal from the Commission. The votes of the representatives of the Member States within the Committee shall be weighted in the manner set out in that Article. The Chairman shall not vote.

The Commission shall adopt the measures envisaged if they are in accordance with the opinion of the Committee.

If the measures envisaged are not in accordance with the opinion of the Committee, or if no opinion is delivered, the Commission shall, without delay, submit to the Council a proposal relating to the measures to be taken. The Council shall act by a qualified majority.

If on the expiry of a period of three months from the date of referral to the Council, the Council has not acted, the proposed measures shall be adopted by the Commission, save where the Council has decided against the said measures by a simple majority.

Article 74

This Regulation shall enter into force on the day following the decision taken by the competent authorities on the headquarters of the Agency.

Subject to the first subparagraph Titles I, II, III and V shall enter into force on 1 January 1995.

This Regulation shall be binding in its entirety and directly applicable in all Member States.

Done at Brussels, 22 July 1993.

For the Council
The President
M. OFFECIERS-VAN DE WIELE

ANNEX

PART A

Medicinal products developed by means of one of the following biotechnological processes:

— recombinant DNA technology,

— controlled expression of genes coding for biologically active proteins in prokaryotes and eukaryotes including transformed mammalian cells,

— hybridoma and monoclonal antibody methods.

Veterinary medicinal products, including those not derived from biotechnology, intended primarily for use as performance enhancers in order to promote the growth of treated animals or to increase yields from treated animals.

PART B

Medicinal products developed by other biotechnological processes which, in the opinion of the Agency, constitute a significant innovation.

Medicinal products administered by means of new delivery systems which, in the opinion of the Agency, constitute a significant innovation.

Medicinal products presented for an entirely new indication which, in the opinion of the Agency, is of significant therapeutic interest.

Medicinal products based on radio-isotopes which, in the opinion of the Agency, are of significant therapeutic interest.

New medicinal products derived from human blood or human plasma.

Medicinal products the manufacture of which employs processes which, in the opinion of the Agency, demonstrate a significant technical advance such as two-dimensional electrophoresis under micro-gravity.

Medicinal products intended for administration to human beings, containing a new active substance which, on the date of entry into force of this Regulation, was not authorized by any Member State for use in a medicinal product intended for human use.

Veterinary medicinal products intended for use in food-producing animals containing a new active substance which, on the date of entry into force of this Regulation, was not authorized by any Member State for use in food-producing animals.

365L0065

65/65/EEC: COUNCIL DIRECTIVE OF 26 JANUARY 1965 ON THE APPROXIMATION OF PROVISIONS LAID DOWN BY LAW, REGULATION OR ADMINISTRATIVE ACTION RELATING TO " MEDICINAL PRODUCTS " [5]

OFFICIAL JOURNAL No 22, 09/02/1965, p. 369; ENGLISH SPECIAL EDITION, VOLUME 1965-66, P. 20
DATE OF NOTIFICATION: 03/02/1965
DATE OF TRANSPOSITION: 31/12/1966; SEE ART. 22
DATE OF TRANSPOSITION: 03/02/1970; SEE ART. 24

AMENDED BY

366L0454
66/454/EEC: COUNCIL DIRECTIVE OF 28 JULY 1966   [1]
OFFICIAL JOURNAL No L 144, 05/08/1966, P. 2658; ENGLISH SPECIAL EDITION, VOLUME 1965-66, P. 168
DATE OF NOTIFICATION: 29/07/1966

375L0319
75/319/EEC: COUNCIL DIRECTIVE OF 20 MAY 1975   [2]
OFFICIAL JOURNAL No L 147, 09/06/1975, P. 13
DATE OF NOTIFICATION: 21/05/1975
DATE OF TRANSPOSITION: 21/11/1976; SEE ART. 38

383L0570
83/570/EEC: COUNCIL DIRECTIVE OF 26 OCTOBER 1983   [3]
OFFICIAL JOURNAL No L 332, 28/11/1983, P. 1
DATE OF NOTIFICATION: 31/10/1983
DATE OF TRANSPOSITION: 31/10/1985; SEE ART. 4

387L0021
87/21/EEC: COUNCIL DIRECTIVE OF 22 DECEMBER 1986   [4]
OFFICIAL JOURNAL No L 15, 17/01/1987, P. 36
DATE OF NOTIFICATION: 23/12/1986
DATE OF TRANSPOSITION: 01/07/1987; SEE ART. 2

389L0341
89/341/EEC: COUNCIL DIRECTIVE OF 3 MAY 1989   [5]
OFFICIAL JOURNAL No L 142, 25/05/1989, P. 11
DATE OF NOTIFICATION: 17/05/1989
DATE OF TRANSPOSITION: 01/01/1992; SEE ART. 4
DATE OF TRANSPOSITION: 31/12/1992; SEE ART. 4

389L0342
89/342/EEC: COUNCIL DIRECTIVE OF 3 MAY 1989   [6]
OFFICIAL JOURNAL No L 142, 25/05/1989, P. 14
DATE OF NOTIFICATION: 17/05/1989
DATE OF TRANSPOSITION: 01/01/1992; SEE ART. 6
DATE OF TRANSPOSITION: 31/12/1992; SEE ART. 6

389L0343
89/343/EEC: COUNCIL DIRECTIVE OF 3 MAY 1989   [7]
OFFICIAL JOURNAL No L 142, 25/05/1989, P. 16
DATE OF NOTIFICATION: 18/05/1989
DATE OF TRANSPOSITION: 01/01/1992; SEE ART. 8
DATE OF TRANSPOSITION: 31/12/1992; SEE ART. 8

392L0027
92/27/EEC: COUNCIL DIRECTIVE OF 31 MARCH 1992   [8]
OFFICIAL JOURNAL No L 113, 30/04/1992, P. 8
DATE OF NOTIFICATION: 13/04/1992
DATE OF TRANSPOSITION: 01/01/1993; SEE ART. 14

392L0073
92/73/EEC: COUNCIL DIRECTIVE OF 22 SEPTEMBER 1992   [9]
OFFICIAL JOURNAL No L 297, 13/10/1992, P. 8
DATE OF NOTIFICATION: 08/10/1992
DATE OF TRANSPOSITION: 31/12/1993; SEE ART. 10

393L0039
93/39/EEC: COUNCIL DIRECTIVE OF 14 JUNE 1993   [10]
OFFICIAL JOURNAL No L 214, 24/08/1993, P. 22
DATE OF TRANSPOSITION: 01/01/1995; SEE ART. 4
DATE OF TRANSPOSITION: 01/01/1998; SEE ART. 4

CHAPTER I

DEFINITIONS AND SCOPE

ARTICLE 1

FOR THE PURPOSES OF THIS DIRECTIVE, THE FOLLOWING SHALL HAVE THE MEANINGS HEREBY ASSIGNED TO THEM;

1. PROPRIETARY MEDICINAL PRODUCT: ANY READY-PREPARED MEDICINAL PRODUCT PLACED ON THE MARKET UNDER A SPECIAL NAME AND IN A SPECIAL PACK.

2. MEDICINAL PRODUCT: ANY SUBSTANCE OR COMBINATION OF SUBSTANCES PRESENTED FOR TREATING OR PREVENTING DISEASE IN HUMAN BEINGS OR ANIMALS.
ANY SUBSTANCE OR COMBINATION OF SUBSTANCES WHICH MAY BE ADMINISTERED TO HUMAN BEINGS OR ANIMALS WITH A VIEW TO MAKING A MEDICAL DIAGNOSIS OR TO RESTORING, CORRECTING OR MODIFYING PHYSIOLOGICAL FUNCTIONS IN HUMAN BEINGS OR IN ANIMALS IS LIKEWISE CONSIDERED A MEDICINAL PRODUCT.

3. SUBSTANCE: ANY MATTER IRRESPECTIVE OF ORIGIN WHICH MAY BE:

- HUMAN, E.G. HUMAN BLOOD AND HUMAN BLOOD PRODUCTS;
- ANIMAL, E.G. MICRO-ORGANISMS, WHOLE ANIMALS, PARTS OF ORGANS, ANIMAL SECRETIONS, TOXINS, EXTRACTS, BLOOD PRODUCTS, ETC;
- VEGETABLE, E.G. MICRO-ORGANISMS, PLANTS, PARTS OF PLANTS, VEGETABLE SECRETIONS, EXTRACTS, ETC;
- CHEMICAL, E.G. ELEMENTS, NATURALLY OCCURRING CHEMICAL MATERIALS AND CHEMICAL PRODUCTS OBTAINED BY CHEMICAL CHANGE OR SYNTHESIS.

" 4. Magistral formula: Any medicinal product prepared in a pharmacy in accordance with a prescription for an individual patient.

5. 'Officinal formula' [R1]: Any medicinal product which is prepared in a pharmacy in accordance with the prescriptions of a pharmacopoeia and is intended to be supplied directly to the patients served by the pharmacy in question. " [5]

[The scope of the Directive has been extended to immunological medicinal products for human use consisting of vaccines, toxins or serums and allergen products [6]; and to radiopharmaceuticals for human use, excluding radionuclides in the form of sealed sources [7]; and to homeopathic medicinal products [9]]

ARTICLE 2

" 1. Chapters II to V shall apply to proprietary medicinal products for human use intended to be placed on the market in Member States.

2. Where a Member State authorizes the placing on the market of industrially produced medicinal products which do not comply with the definition of a proprietary medicinal product, it shall also apply Chapters II to V to them.

3. Chapters II to V shall not apply to:

- medicinal products prepared on the basis of a magistral or official formula,
- medicinal products intended for research and development trials,
- intermediate products intended for further processing by an authorized manufacturer.

4. A Member State may, in accordance with legislation in force and to fulfil special needs, exclude from Chapters II to V medicinal products supplied in response to a bona fide unsolicited order, formulated in accordance with the specifications of an authorized health care professional and for use by his individual patients on his direct personal responsibility. " [5]

CHAPTER II

AUTHORISATION TO PLACE " MEDICINAL PRODUCTS " [5] ON THE MARKET

ARTICLE 3

" No medicinal product may be placed on the market of a Member State unless a marketing authorization has been issued by the competent authorities of that Member State in accordance with this Directive or an authorization has been granted in accordance with Regulation (EEC) No 2309/93 of 22 July 1993 laying down Community procedures for the authorization and supervision of medicinal products for human and veterinary use and establishing a European Agency for the Evaluation of Medicinal Products (1).
The provisions of this Directive shall not affect the powers of the Member States' authorities either as regards the setting of prices for medicinal products or their inclusion in the scope of national health insurance schemes, on the basis of health, economic and social conditions. " [10]

ARTICLE 4

IN ORDER TO OBTAIN AN AUTHORISATION TO PLACE A " MEDICINAL PRODUCT " [5] ON THE MARKET AS PROVIDED FOR IN ARTICLE 3, THE PERSON RESPONSIBLE FOR PLACING THAT

PRODUCT ON THE MARKET SHALL MAKE APPLICATION TO THE COMPETENT AUTHORITY OF THE MEMBER STATE CONCERNED.

" The person responsible for placing medicinal products on the market shall be established in the Community. In respect of medicinal products authorized on the date of implementation of this Directive, the Member State shall if necessary apply this provision at the time of the five-yearly renewal of the marketing authorization provided for in Article 10. " [10]

THE APPLICATION SHALL BE ACCOMPANIED BY THE FOLLOWING PARTICULARS AND DOCUMENTS:

1. NAME OR CORPORATE NAME AND PERMANENT ADDRESS OF THE PERSON RESPONSIBLE FOR PLACING THE PROPRIETARY PRODUCT ON THE MARKET AND, WHERE APPLICABLE, OF THE MANUFACTURER.

2. NAME OF THE PROPRIETARY PRODUCT (BRAND NAME, OR COMMON NAME TOGETHER WITH A TRADE MARK OR NAME OF THE MANUFACTURER, OR SCIENTIFIC NAME TOGETHER WITH A TRADE MARK OR NAME OF THE MANUFACTURER).

3. QUALITATIVE AND QUANTITATIVE PARTICULARS OF ALL THE CONSTITUENTS OF THE PROPRIETARY PRODUCT IN USUAL TERMINOLOGY, BUT EXCLUDING EMPIRICAL CHEMICAL FORMULAE, WITH MENTION OF THE INTERNATIONAL NON-PROPRIETARY NAME RECOMMENDED BY THE WORLD HEALTH ORGANISATION WHERE SUCH NAME EXISTS.

4. BRIEF DESCRIPTION OF THE METHOD OF PREPARATION.

5. THERAPEUTIC INDICATIONS, CONTRA-INDICATIONS AND SIDE-EFFECTS.

6. " Posology, pharmaceutical form, method and route of administration and expected shelf life.
If applicable, reasons for any precautionary and safety measures to be taken for the storage of the medicinal product, its administration to patients and for the disposal of waste products, together with an indication of any potential risks presented by the medicinal product for the environment. " [10]

7. " DESCRIPTION OF THE CONTROL METHODS EMPLOYED BY THE MANUFACTURER (QUALITATIVE AND QUANTITATIVE ANALYSIS OF THE CONSTITUENTS AND OF THE FINISHED PRODUCT, SPECIAL TESTS, E.G. STERILITY TESTS, TESTS FOR THE PRESENCE OF PYROGENIC SUBSTANCES, THE PRESENCE OF HEAVY METALS, STABILITY TESTS, BIOLOGICAL AND TOXICITY TESTS, CONTROLS CARRIED OUT AT AN INTERMEDIATE STAGE OF THE MANUFACTURING PROCESS). " [2]

8. " RESULTS OF:

- PHYSICO-CHEMICAL, BIOLOGICAL OR MICROBIOLOGICAL TESTS,
- PHARMACOLOGICAL AND TOXICOLOGICAL TESTS,
- CLINICAL TRIALS.

HOWEVER, AND WITHOUT PREJUDICE TO THE LAW RELATING TO THE PROTECTION OF INDUSTRIAL AND COMMERCIAL PROPERTY:

(a) THE APPLICANT SHALL NOT BE REQUIRED TO PROVIDE THE RESULTS OF PHARMACOLOGICAL AND TOXICOLOGICAL TESTS OR THE RESULTS OF CLINICAL TRIALS IF HE CAN DEMONSTRATE:

(i) EITHER THAT THE " MEDICINAL PRODUCT " [5] IS ESSENTIALLY SIMILAR TO A PRODUCT AUTHORIZED IN THE COUNTRY CONCERNED BY THE APPLICATION AND THAT THE PERSON RESPONSIBLE FOR THE MARKETING OF THE ORIGINAL " MEDICINAL PRODUCT " [5] HAS CONSENTED TO THE PHARMACOLOGICAL, TOXICOLOGICAL OR CLINICAL REFERENCES CONTAINED IN THE FILE ON THE ORIGINAL " MEDICINAL PRODUCT " [5] BEING USED FOR THE PURPOSE OF EXAMINING THE APPLICATION IN QUESTION;

(ii) OR BY DETAILED REFERENCES TO PUBLISHED SCIENTIFIC LITERATURE PRESENTED IN ACCORDANCE WITH THE SECOND PARAGRAPH OF ARTICLE 1 OF DIRECTIVE 75/318/EEC (2) THAT THE CONSTITUENT OR CONSTITUENTS OF THE " MEDICINAL PRODUCT " [5] HAVE A WELL ESTABLISHED MEDICINAL USE, WITH RECOGNIZED EFFICACY AND AN ACCEPTABLE LEVEL OF SAFETY;

(iii) OR THAT THE " MEDICINAL PRODUCT " **[5]** IS ESSENTIALLY SIMILAR TO A PRODUCT WHICH HAS BEEN AUTHORIZED WITHIN THE COMMUNITY, IN ACCORDANCE WITH COMMUNITY PROVISIONS IN FORCE, FOR NOT LESS THAN SIX YEARS AND IS MARKETED IN THE MEMBER STATE FOR WHICH THE APPLICATION IS MADE; THIS PERIOD SHALL BE EXTENDED TO 10 YEARS IN THE CASE OF HIGH-TECHNOLOGY MEDICINAL PRODUCTS WITHIN THE MEANING OF PART A IN THE ANNEX TO DIRECTIVE 87/22/EEC (3) OR OF A MEDICINAL PRODUCT WITHIN THE MEANING OF PART B IN THE ANNEX TO THAT DIRECTIVE FOR WHICH THE PROCEDURE LAID DOWN IN ARTICLE 2 THEREOF HAS BEEN FOLLOWED; FURTHERMORE, A MEMBER STATE MAY ALSO EXTEND THIS PERIOD TO 10 YEARS BY A SINGLE DECISION COVERING ALL THE PRODUCTS MARKETED ON ITS TERRITORY WHERE IT CONSIDERS THIS NECESSARY IN THE INTEREST OF PUBLIC HEALTH. MEMBER STATES ARE AT LIBERTY NOT TO APPLY THE ABOVEMENTIONED SIX-YEAR PERIOD BEYOND THE DATE OF EXPIRY OF A PATENT PROTECTING THE ORIGINAL PRODUCT.
HOWEVER, WHERE THE " MEDICINAL PRODUCT " **[5]** IS INTENDED FOR A DIFFERENT THERAPEUTIC USE FROM THAT OF THE OTHER " MEDICINAL PRODUCTS " **[5]** MARKETED OR IS TO BE ADMINISTERED BY DIFFERENT ROUTES OR IN DIFFERENT DOSES, THE RESULTS OF APPROPRIATE PHARMACOLOGICAL AND TOXICOLOGICAL TESTS AND/OR OF APPROPRIATE CLINICAL TRIALS MUST BE PROVIDED.

(b) IN THE CASE OF NEW " MEDICINAL PRODUCTS " **[5]** CONTAINING KNOWN CONSTITUENTS NOT HITHERTO USED IN COMBINATION FOR THERAPEUTIC PURPOSES, THE RESULTS OF PHARMACOLOGICAL AND TOXICOLOGICAL TESTS AND OF CLINICAL TRIALS RELATING TO THAT COMBINATION MUST BE PROVIDED, BUT IT SHALL NOT BE NECESSARY TO PROVIDE REFERENCES RELATING TO EACH INDIVIDUAL CONSTITUENT. " **[4]**

9. " A SUMMARY, IN ACCORDANCE WITH ARTICLE 4a, OF THE PRODUCT CHARACTERISTICS, ONE OR MORE SPECIMENS OR MOCK-UPS OF THE SALES PRESENTATION OF THE PROPRIETARY PRODUCT, TOGETHER WITH A PACKAGE LEAFLET WHERE ONE IS TO BE ENCLOSED. " **[3]**

10. A DOCUMENT SHOWING THAT THE MANUFACTURER IS AUTHORISED IN HIS OWN COUNTRY TO PRODUCE PROPRIETARY PRODUCTS.

11. " Copies of any authorization obtained in another Member State or in a third country to place the relevant medicinal product on the market, together with a list of those Member States in which an application for authorization submitted in accordance with this Directive is under examination. Copies of the summary of the product characteristics proposed by the applicant in accordance with Article 4a or approved by the competent authorities of the Member State in accordance with Article 4b. Copies of the package leaflet proposed in accordance with Article 6 of Directive 92/27/EEC or approved by the competent authorities of the Member State in accordance with Article 10 of the same Directive. Details of any decision to refuse authorization, whether in the Community or in a third country, and the reasons for such decision.
This information shall be updated on a regular basis. " **[10]**

" ARTICLE 4a

THE SUMMARY OF THE PRODUCT CHARACTERISTICS REFERRED TO IN POINT 9 OF THE SECOND PARAGRAPH OF ARTICLE 4 SHALL CONTAIN THE FOLLOWING INFORMATION:

1. NAME OF THE PROPRIETARY PRODUCT.

2. QUALITATIVE AND QUANTITATIVE COMPOSITION IN TERMS OF THE ACTIVE INGREDIENTS AND CONSTITUENTS OF THE EXCIPIENT, KNOWLEDGE OF WHICH IS ESSENTIAL FOR PROPER ADMINISTRATION OF THE MEDICINAL PRODUCT; THE INTERNATIONAL NON-PROPRIETARY NAMES RECOMMENDED BY THE WORLD HEALTH ORGANIZATION SHALL BE USED, WHERE SUCH NAMES EXIST, OR FAILING THIS, THE USUAL COMMON NAME OR CHEMICAL DESCRIPTION.

3. PHARMACEUTICAL FORM.

4. PHARMACOLOGICAL PROPERTIES AND, IN SO FAR AS THIS INFORMATION IS USEFUL FOR THERAPEUTIC PURPOSES, PHARMACOKINETIC PARTICULARS.

5. CLINICAL PARTICULARS:

5. 1. THERAPEUTIC INDICATIONS,

5. 2. CONTRA-INDICATIONS,

5. 3. UNDESIRABLE EFFECTS (FREQUENCY AND SERIOUSNESS),

5. 4. SPECIAL PRECAUTIONS FOR USE,

5. 5. USE DURING PREGNANCY AND LACTATION,

5. 6. INTERACTION WITH OTHER MEDICAMENTS AND OTHER FORMS OF INTERACTION,

5. 7. POSOLOGY AND METHOD OF ADMINISTRATION FOR ADULTS AND, WHERE NECESSARY, FOR CHILDREN,

5. 8. OVERDOSE (SYMPTOMS, EMERGENCY PROCEDURES, ANTIDOTES)

5. 9. SPECIAL WARNINGS,

5. 10. EFFECTS ON ABILITY TO DRIVE AND TO USE MACHINES.

6. PHARMACEUTICAL PARTICULARS:

6. 1. INCOMPATIBILITIES (MAJOR),

6. 2. SHELF LIFE, WHEN NECESSARY AFTER RECONSTITUTION OF THE PRODUCT OR WHEN THE CONTAINER IS OPENED FOR THE FIRST TIME,

6. 3. SPECIAL PRECAUTIONS FOR STORAGE,

6. 4. NATURE AND CONTENTS OF CONTAINER,

6. 5. NAME OR STYLE AND PERMANENT ADDRESS OR REGISTERED PLACE OF BUSINESS OF THE HOLDER OF THE MARKETING AUTHORIZATION. " [3]

" 6. 6. special precautions for disposal of unused products or waste materials derived from such products, if appropriate. " [5]

" 7. Full details of internal radiation dosimetry.

8. Additional detailed instructions for extemporaneous preparation and quality control of such preparation and, where appropriate, maximum storage time during which any intermediate preparation such as an eluate or the ready to use pharmaceutical will conform with its specifications. " [7]

" ARTICLE 4b

When the marketing authorization referred to in Article 3 is issued, the person responsible for placing that product on the market shall be informed, by the competent authorities of the Member State concerned, of the summary of the product characteristics as approved by it. The competent authorities shall take all necessary measures to ensure that the information given in the summary is in conformity with that accepted when the marketing authorization is issued or subsequently. The competent authorities shall forward to the European Agency for the Evaluation of Medicinal Products a copy of the authorization together with the summary of the product characteristics referred to in Article 4a.

Furthermore, the competent authorities shall draw up an assessment report and comments on the dossier as regards the results of the analytical and pharmacotoxicological tests and the clinical trials of the medicinal product concerned. The assessment report shall be udapted whenever new information becomes available which is of importance for the evaluation of the quality, safety or efficacy of the medicinal product concerned. " [10]

ARTICLE 5

THE AUTHORISATION PROVIDED FOR IN ARTICLE 3 SHALL BE REFUSED IF, AFTER VERIFICATION OF THE PARTICULARS AND DOCUMENTS LISTED IN ARTICLE 4, IT PROVES THAT THE " MEDICINAL PRODUCT " [5] IS HARMFUL IN THE NORMAL CONDITIONS OF USE, OR THAT ITS THERAPEUTIC EFFICACY IS LACKING OR IS INSUFFICIENTLY SUBSTANTIATED BY THE APPLICANT, OR THAT ITS QUALITATIVE AND QUANTITATIVE COMPOSITION IS NOT AS DECLARED.

AUTHORISATION SHALL LIKEWISE BE REFUSED IF THE PARTICULARS AND DOCUMENTS SUBMITTED IN SUPPORT OF THE APPLICATION DO NOT COMPLY WITH ARTICLE 4.

ARTICLE 6

" This Directive shall not affect the application of national legislation prohibiting or restricting the sale, supply or use of medicinal products as contraceptives or abortifacients. The Member States shall communicate the national legislation concerned to the Commission. " **[10]**

ARTICLE 7

" 1. Member States shall take all appropriate measures to ensure that the procedure for granting an authorization to place a medicinal product on the market is completed within 210 days of the submission of a valid application.

2. Where a Member State notes that an application for authorization submitted after 1 January 1995 is already under active examination in another Member State in respect of that medicinal product, the Member State concerned may decide to suspend the detailed examination of the application in order to await the assessment report prepared by the other Member State in accordance with Article 4b.
The Member State concerned shall inform the other Member State and the applicant of its decision to suspend detailed examination of the application in question. As soon as it has completed the examination of the application and reached a decision, the other Member State shall forward a copy of its assessment report to the Member State concerned.
Within 90 days of the receipt of the assessment report, the Member State concerned shall either recognize the decision of the other Member State and the summary of the product characteristics as approved by it, or, if it considers that there are grounds for supposing that the authorization of the medicinal product concerned may present a risk to public health (4), it shall apply the procedures set out in Articles 10 to 14 of Directive 75/319/EEC. " **[10]**

" Article 7a

With effect from 1 January 1998, where a Member State is informed in accordance with point 11 of the second paragraph of Article 4 that another Member State has authorized a medicinal product which is the subject of an application for authorization in the Member State concerned, that Member State shall forthwith request the authorities of the Member State which has granted the authorization to forward to it the assessment report referred to in the second paragraph of Article 4b.
Within 90 days of the receipt of the assessment report, the Member State concerned shall either recognize the decision of the first Member State and the summary of the product characteristics as approved by it or, if it considers that there are grounds for supposing that the authorization of the medicinal product concerned may present a risk to public health (4), it shall apply the procedures set out in Articles 10 to 14 of Directive 75/319/EEC. " **[10]**

ARTICLE 8

MEMBER STATES SHALL TAKE ALL APPROPRIATE MEASURES TO ENSURE THAT THE HOLDER OF AN AUTHORISATION FURNISHES PROOF THAT THE CONTROLS HAVE BEEN CARRIED OUT ON THE FINISHED PRODUCT IN ACCORDANCE WITH THE METHODS DESCRIBED BY THE APPLICANT PURSUANT TO ITEM 7 OF THE SECOND PARAGRAPH OF ARTICLE 4.

ARTICLE 9

AUTHORISATION SHALL NOT AFFECT THE CIVIL AND CRIMINAL LIABILITY OF THE MANUFACTURER AND, WHERE APPLICABLE, OF THE PERSON RESPONSIBLE FOR PLACING THE "MEDICINAL PRODUCT " [5] ON THE MARKET.

" Article 9a

After an authorization has been issued, the person responsible for placing the product on the market must, in respect of the methods of preparation and control provided for in points 4 and 7 of the second paragraph of Article 4, take account of technical and scientific progress and introduce any changes that may be required to enable that medicinal product to be manufactured and checked by means of generally accepted scientific methods. These changes shall be subject to the approval of the competent authority of the Member State concerned. " [10]

ARTICLE 10

" 1. Authorization shall be valid for five years and shall be renewable for five-year periods, on application by the holder at least three months before the expiry date and after consideration by the competent authority of a dossier containing in particular details of the data on pharmacovigilance and other information relevant to the monitoring of the medicinal product.

2. In exceptional circumstances, and following consultation with the applicant, an authorization may be granted subject to certain specific obligations, including:

- the carrying out of further studies following the granting of authorization,
- the notification of adverse reactions to the medicinal product.

These exceptional decisions may be adopted only for objective and verifiable reasons and shall be based on one of the causes referred to in Part 4 (G) of the Annex to Directive 75/318/EEC. " [10]

CHAPTER III

SUSPENSION AND REVOCATION OF AUTHORISATION TO MARKET " MEDICINAL PRODUCTS " [5]

ARTICLE 11

THE COMPETENT AUTHORITIES OF THE MEMBER STATES SHALL SUSPEND OR REVOKE AN AUTHORISATION TO PLACE A " MEDICINAL PRODUCT " [5] ON THE MARKET WHERE THAT PRODUCT PROVES TO BE HARMFUL IN THE NORMAL CONDITIONS OF USE, OR WHERE ITS THERAPEUTIC EFFICACY IS LACKING, OR WHERE ITS QUALITATIVE AND QUANTITATIVE COMPOSITION IS NOT AS DECLARED. THERAPEUTIC EFFICACY IS LACKING WHEN IT IS ESTABLISHED THAT THERAPEUTIC RESULTS CANNOT BE OBTAINED WITH THE PROPRIETARY PRODUCT.
" AN AUTHORIZATION SHALL ALSO BE SUSPENDED OR REVOKED WHERE THE PARTICULARS SUPPORTING THE APPLICATION AS PROVIDED FOR IN ARTICLES 4 AND 4a ARE INCORRECT OR HAVE NOT BEEN AMENDED IN ACCORDANCE WITH ARTICLE 9a, OR WHEN THE CONTROLS REFERRED TO IN ARTICLE 8 OF THIS DIRECTIVE OR IN ARTICLE 27 OF SECOND COUNCIL DIRECTIVE 75/319/EEC OF 20 MAY 1975 ON THE APPROXIMATION OF PROVISIONS LAID DOWN BY LAW,

REGULATION OR ADMINISTRATIVE ACTION RELATING TO " MEDICINAL PRODUCTS " [5] HAVE NOT BEEN CARRIED OUT. " [3]

ARTICLE 12

ALL DECISIONS TAKEN PURSUANT TO ARTICLES 5, 6 OR 11 SHALL STATE IN DETAIL THE REASONS ON WHICH THEY ARE BASED. A DECISION SHALL BE NOTIFIED TO THE PARTY CONCERNED, WHO SHALL AT THE SAME TIME BE INFORMED OF THE REMEDIES AVAILABLE TO HIM UNDER THE LAWS IN FORCE AND OF THE TIME LIMIT ALLOWED FOR THE EXERCISE OF SUCH REMEDIES.
AUTHORISATIONS TO PLACE A PROPRIETARY PRODUCT ON THE MARKET AND DECISIONS TO REVOKE AUTHORISATIONS SHALL BE PUBLISHED BY EACH MEMBER STATE IN THE APPROPRIATE OFFICIAL PUBLICATION.

CHAPTER IV

LABELLING OF " MEDICINAL PRODUCTS " [5].

Article 13

"..." [8]

Article 14

"..." [8]

Article 15

"..." [8]

Article 16

"..." [8]

Article 17

"..." [8]

Article 18

"..." [8]

Article 19

"..." [8]

Article 20

"..." [8]

CHAPTER V

GENERAL AND FINAL PROVISIONS

ARTICLE 21

AN AUTHORISATION TO MARKET A " MEDICINAL PRODUCT " [5] SHALL NOT BE REFUSED, SUSPENDED OR REVOKED EXCEPT ON THE GROUNDS SET OUT IN THIS DIRECTIVE.

ARTICLE 22

MEMBER STATES SHALL PUT INTO FORCE THE MEASURES NEEDED IN ORDER TO COMPLY WITH THIS DIRECTIVE WITHIN EIGHTEEN MONTHS OF ITS NOTIFICATION AND SHALL INFORM THE COMMISSION FORTHWITH.

[THE TIME LIMIT SHALL BE EXTENDED UNTIL 31 DECEMBER 1966. [1]]

ARTICLE 23

MEMBER STATES SHALL ENSURE THAT THEY COMMUNICATE TO THE COMMISSION THE TEXT OF THE MAIN PROVISIONS OF NATIONAL LAW WHICH THEY ADOPT IN THE FIELD COVERED BY THIS DIRECTIVE.

ARTICLE 24

" WITHIN THE TIME LIMITS AND UNDER THE CONDITIONS LAID DOWN IN ARTICLE 39 (2) AND (3) OF SECOND DIRECTIVE 75/319/EEC, THE RULES LAID DOWN IN THIS DIRECTIVE SHALL BE APPLIED PROGRESSIVELY TO " MEDICINAL PRODUCTS " [5] COVERED BY AN AUTHORIZATION TO PLACE ON THE MARKET BY VIRTUE OF PREVIOUS PROVISIONS. " [2]

ARTICLE 25

THIS DIRECTIVE IS ADDRESSED TO THE MEMBER STATES.

[R1] Corrigendum, OJ No L176, 23/06/1989, p. 55.

(1) OJ No L 214, 24/08/1993, p. 1.
(2) OJ No L 147, 09/06/1975, p. 1.
(3) OJ No L 15, 17/01/1987, p. 38.
(4) The expression "risk to public health" refers to the quality, safety and efficacy of the medicinal product.

375L0319

75/319/EEC: SECOND COUNCIL DIRECTIVE OF 20 MAY 1975 ON THE APPROXIMATION OF PROVISIONS LAID DOWN BY LAW, REGULATION OR ADMINISTRATIVE ACTION RELATING TO PROPRIETARY MEDICINAL PRODUCTS

OFFICIAL JOURNAL No L 147, 09/06/1975, P. 13
DATE OF NOTIFICATION: 21/05/1975
DATE OF TRANSPOSITION: 21/11/1976; SEE ART. 38

AMENDED BY

378L0420
78/420/EEC: COUNCIL DIRECTIVE OF 2 MAY 1975   **[1]**
OFFICIAL JOURNAL No L 123, 11/05/1978, P. 26
DATE OF NOTIFICATION: 03/05/1978

383L0570
83/570/EEC: COUNCIL DIRECTIVE OF 26 OCTOBER 1983   **[2]**
OFFICIAL JOURNAL No L 332, 28/11/1983, P. 1
DATE OF NOTIFICATION: 31/10/1983
DATE OF TRANSPOSITION: 31/10/1985; SEE ART. 4

389L0341
89/341/EEC: COUNCIL DIRECTIVE OF 3 MAY 1989   **[3]**
OFFICIAL JOURNAL No L 142, 25/05/1989, P. 11
DATE OF NOTIFICATION: 17/05/1989
DATE OF TRANSPOSITION: 01/01/1992; SEE ART. 4
DATE OF TRANSPOSITION: 31/12/1992; SEE ART. 4

389L0342
89/342/EEC: COUNCIL DIRECTIVE OF 3 MAY 1989   **[4]**
OFFICIAL JOURNAL No L 142, 25/05/1989, P. 14
DATE OF NOTIFICATION: 17/05/1989
DATE OF TRANSPOSITION: 01/01/1992; SEE ART. 6
DATE OF TRANSPOSITION: 31/12/1992; SEE ART. 6

389L0343
89/343/EEC: COUNCIL DIRECTIVE OF 3 MAY 1989   **[5]**
OFFICIAL JOURNAL No L 142, 25/05/1989, P. 16
DATE OF NOTIFICATION: 18/05/1989
DATE OF TRANSPOSITION: 01/01/1992; SEE ART. 8
DATE OF TRANSPOSITION: 31/12/1992; SEE ART. 8

389L0381
89/381/EEC: COUNCIL DIRECTIVE OF 14 JUNE 1989   **[6]**
OFFICIAL JOURNAL No L 181, 28/06/1989, P. 44
DATE OF TRANSPOSITION: 01/01/1992; SEE ART. 7

392L0027
92/27/EEC: COUNCIL DIRECTIVE OF 31 MARCH 1992   [7]
OFFICIAL JOURNAL No L 113, 30/04/1992, P. 8
DATE OF NOTIFICATION: 13/04/1992
DATE OF TRANSPOSITION: 01/01/1993; SEE ART. 14

392L0073
92/73/EEC: COUNCIL DIRECTIVE OF 22 SEPTEMBER 1992   [8]
OFFICIAL JOURNAL No L 297, 13/10/1992, P. 8
DATE OF NOTIFICATION: 08/10/1992
DATE OF TRANSPOSITION: 31/12/1993; SEE ART. 10

393L0039
93/39/EEC: COUNCIL DIRECTIVE OF 14 JUNE 1993   [9]
OFFICIAL JOURNAL No L 214, 24/08/1993, P. 22
DATE OF TRANSPOSITION: 01/01/1995; SEE ART. 4
DATE OF TRANSPOSITION: 01/01/1998; SEE ART. 4

CHAPTER I

APPLICATION FOR AUTHORIZATION TO PLACE PROPRIETARY MEDICINAL PRODUCTS ON THE MARKET

ARTICLE 1

MEMBER STATES SHALL TAKE ALL APPROPRIATE MEASURES TO ENSURE THAT THE DOCUMENTS AND PARTICULARS LISTED IN POINTS 7 AND 8 OF ARTICLE 4, SECOND PARAGRAPH, OF DIRECTIVE 65/65/EEC (1) ARE DRAWN UP BY EXPERTS WITH THE NECESSARY TECHNICAL OR PROFESSIONAL QUALIFICATIONS BEFORE THEY ARE SUBMITTED TO THE COMPETENT AUTHORITIES. THESE DOCUMENTS AND PARTICULARS SHALL BE SIGNED BY THE EXPERTS.

ARTICLE 2

THE DUTIES OF THE EXPERTS ACCORDING TO THEIR RESPECTIVE QUALIFICATIONS SHALL BE:

(a) TO PERFORM TASKS FALLING WITHIN THEIR RESPECTIVE DISCIPLINES (ANALYSIS, PHARMACOLOGY AND SIMILAR EXPERIMENTAL SCIENCES, CLINICAL TRIALS) AND TO DESCRIBE OBJECTIVELY THE RESULTS OBTAINED (QUALITATIVELY AND QUANTITATIVELY);

(b) TO DESCRIBE THEIR OBSERVATIONS IN ACCORDANCE WITH COUNCIL DIRECTIVE 75/318/EEC OF 20 MAY 1975, ON THE APPROXIMATION OF THE LAWS OF THE MEMBER STATES RELATING TO ANALYTICAL, PHARMACO-TOXICOLOGICAL AND CLINICAL STANDARDS AND PROTOCOLS IN RESPECT OF THE TESTING OF PROPRIETARY MEDICINAL PRODUCTS (2), AND TO STATE, IN PARTICULAR:

- IN THE CASE OF THE ANALYST, WHETHER THE PRODUCT IS CONSISTENT WITH THE DECLARED COMPOSITION, GIVING ANY SUBSTANTIATION OF THE CONTROL METHODS EMPLOYED BY THE MANUFACTURER;
- IN THE CASE OF THE PHARMACOLOGIST OR THE SPECIALIST WITH SIMILAR EXPERIMENTAL COMPETENCE, THE TOXICITY OF THE PRODUCT AND THE PHARMACOLOGICAL PROPERTIES OBSERVED;

- IN THE CASE OF THE CLINICIAN, WHETHER HE HAS BEEN ABLE TO ASCERTAIN EFFECTS ON PERSONS TREATED WITH THE PRODUCT WHICH CORRESPOND TO THE PARTICULARS GIVEN BY THE APPLICANT IN ACCORDANCE WITH ARTICLE 4 OF DIRECTIVE 65/65/EEC, WHETHER THE PATIENT TOLERATES THE PRODUCT WELL, THE POSOLOGY THE CLINICIAN ADVISES AND ANY CONTRA-INDICATIONS AND SIDE-EFFECTS;

(c) WHERE APPLICABLE, TO STATE THE GROUNDS FOR USING THE PUBLISHED REFERENCES MENTIONED IN POINT 8 (a) AND (b) OF ARTICLE 4, SECOND PARAGRAPH, OF DIRECTIVE 65/65/EEC UNDER THE CONDITIONS SET OUT IN DIRECTIVE 75/318/EEC.

DETAILED REPORTS BY THE EXPERTS SHALL FORM PART OF THE PARTICULARS ACCOMPANYING THE APPLICATION WHICH THE APPLICANT SUBMITS TO THE COMPETENT AUTHORITIES.

ARTICLE 3

IN THE EVENT OF ARTICLE 2 OF THIS DIRECTIVE NOT BEING COMPLIED WITH, ARTICLE 5, SECOND PARAGRAPH, OF DIRECTIVE 65/65/EEC SHALL APPLY.

CHAPTER II

EXAMINATION OF THE APPLICATION FOR AUTHORIZATION TO PLACE PROPRIETARY MEDICAL PRODUCTS ON THE MARKET

ARTICLE 4

IN ORDER TO EXAMINE THE APPLICATION SUBMITTED IN ACCORDANCE WITH ARTICLE 4 OF DIRECTIVE 65/65/EEC, THE COMPETENT AUTHORITIES OF THE MEMBER STATES:

(a) MUST VERIFY WHETHER THE PARTICULARS SUBMITTED IN SUPPORT OF THE APPLICATION COMPLY WITH THE SAID ARTICLE 4 AND EXAMINE WHETHER THE CONDITIONS FOR ISSUING AN AUTHORIZATION TO PLACE PROPRIETARY MEDICINAL PRODUCTS ON THE MARKET (MARKETING AUTHORIZATION) ARE COMPLIED WITH;

(b) " may submit the medicinal product, its starting materials and, if need be, its intermediate products or other constituent materials for testing by a State laboratory or by a laboratory designated for that purpose in order to ensure that the control methods employed by the manufacturer and described in the particulars accompanying the application in accordance with the second subparagraph of point 7 of Article 4 of Directive 65/65/EEC are satisfactory. " [3]

(c) MAY, WHERE APPROPRIATE, REQUIRE THE APPLICANT TO SUPPLEMENT THE PARTICULARS ACCOMPANYING THE APPLICATION IN RESPECT OF THE ITEMS LISTED IN THE SECOND PARAGRAPH OF ARTICLE 4 OF DIRECTIVE 65/65/EEC. WHERE THE COMPETENT AUTHORITIES AVAIL THEMSELVES OF THIS OPTION, THE TIME LIMITS LAID DOWN IN ARTICLE 7 OF THE SAID DIRECTIVE SHALL BE SUSPENDED UNTIL SUCH TIME AS THE SUPPLEMENTARY INFORMATION REQUIRED HAS BEEN PROVIDED. LIKEWISE, THESE TIME LIMITS SHALL BE SUSPENDED FOR THE TIME ALLOWED THE APPLICANT, WHERE APPROPRIATE, FOR GIVING ORAL OR WRITTEN EXPLANATION.

ARTICLE 5

MEMBER STATES SHALL TAKE ALL APPROPRIATE MEASURES TO ENSURE THAT:

(a) THE COMPETENT AUTHORITIES VERIFY THAT MANUFACTURERS AND IMPORTERS OF PRODUCTS COMING FROM THIRD COUNTRIES ARE ABLE TO CARRY OUT MANUFACTURE IN COMPLIANCE WITH THE PARTICULARS SUPPLIED PURSUANT TO POINT 4 OF ARTICLE 4, SECOND PARAGRAPH, OF DIRECTIVE 65/65/EEC AND/OR TO CARRY OUT CONTROLS ACCORDING TO THE METHODS DESCRIBED IN THE PARTICULARS ACCOMPANYING THE APPLICATION IN ACCORDANCE WITH POINT 7 OF ARTICLE 4, SECOND PARAGRAPH, OF THAT DIRECTIVE;

(b) THE COMPETENT AUTHORITIES MAY ALLOW MANUFACTURERS AND IMPORTERS OF PRODUCTS COMING FROM THIRD COUNTRIES, IN EXCEPTIONAL AND JUSTIFIABLE CASES, TO HAVE CERTAIN STAGES OF MANUFACTURE AND/OR CERTAIN OF THE CONTROLS REFERRED TO IN (a) CARRIED OUT BY THIRD PARTIES; IN SUCH CASES, THE VERIFICATIONS BY THE COMPETENT AUTHORITIES SHALL ALSO BE MADE IN THE ESTABLISHMENT DESIGNATED.

ARTICLE 6

"..." **[7]**

ARTICLE 7

"..." **[7]**

CHAPTER III

Committee for Proprietary Medicinal Products

" Article 8

1. In order to facilitate the adoption of common decisions by Member States on the authorization of medicinal products for human use on the basis of the scientific criteria of quality, safety and efficacy, and to achieve thereby the free movement of medicinal products within the Community, a Committee for Proprietary Medicinal Products, hereinafter referred to as "the Committee", is hereby set up. The Committee shall be part of the European Agency for the Evaluation of Medicinal Products established by Council Regulation (EEC) No 2309/93 of 22 July 1993 laying down Community procedures for the authorization and supervision of medicinal products for human and veterinary use and establishing a European Agency for the Evaluation of Medicinal Products (3), hereinafter referred to as "the Agency".

2. In addition to the other responsibilities conferred upon it by Community law, the Committee shall examine any question relating to the granting, variation, suspension or withdrawal of marketing authorization for a medicinal product which is submitted to it in accordance with this Directive.

Article 9

1. In order to obtain the recognition according to the procedures laid down in this Chapter in one or more of the Member States of an authorization issued by a Member State in accordance with Article 3 of Directive 65/65/EEC, the holder of the authorization shall submit an application to the competent authorities of the Member State or Member States concerned, together with the information and particulars referred to in Articles 4, 4a and 4b of Directive 65/65/EEC. He shall testify that the dossier is identical to that accepted by the first Member State, or shall identify any additions or amendments it may contain. In the latter case, he shall certify that the summary of the product characteristics proposed by him in accordance with Article 4a of Directive

65/65/EEC is identical to that accepted by the first Member State in accordance with Article 4b of Directive 65/65/EEC. Moreover he shall certify that all the dossiers filed as part of the procedure are identical.

2. The holder of the marketing authorization shall notify the Committee of this application, inform it of the Member States concerned and of the dates of submission of the application and send it a copy of the authorization granted by the first Member State. He shall also send the Committee copies of any such authorization which may have been granted by the other Member States in respect of the medicinal product concerned, and shall indicate whether any application for authorization is currently under consideration in any Member State.

3. Except in cases referred to in Article 7a of Directive 65/65/EEC, before submitting the application, the holder of the authorization shall inform the Member State which granted the authorization on which the application is based that an application is to be made in accordance with this Directive and shall notify it of any additions to the original dossier; that Member State may require the applicant to provide it with all the particulars and documents necessary to enable it to check that the dossiers filed are identical.

In addition the holder of the authorization shall request the Member State which granted the initial authorization to prepare an assessment report in respect of the medicinal product concerned, or, if necessary, to update any existing assessment report. That Member State shall prepare the assessment report, or update it, within 90 days of the receipt of the request.

At the same time as the application is submitted in accordance with paragraph 1 the Member State which granted the initial authorization shall forward the assessment report to the Member State or Member States concerned by the application.

4. Save in the exceptional case provided for in Article 10 (1), each Member State shall recognize the marketing authorization granted by the first Member State within 90 days of receipt of the application and the assessment report. It shall inform the Member State which granted the initial authorization, the other Member States concerned by the application, the Committee, and the person responsible for placing the medicinal product on the market.

Article 10

1. Notwithstanding Article 9 (4), where a Member State considers that there are grounds for supposing that the authorization of the medicinal product concerned may present a risk to public health (4), it shall forthwith inform the applicant, the Member State which granted the initial authorization, any other Member States concerned by the application and the Committee. The Member State shall state its reasons in detail and shall indicate what action may be necessary to correct any defect in the application.

2. All the Member States concerned shall use their best endeavours to reach agreement on the action to be taken in respect of the application. They shall provide the applicant with the opportunity to make his point of view known orally or in writing. However, if the Member States have not reached agreement within the time limit referred to in Article 9 (4) they shall forthwith refer the matter to the Committee for the application of the procedure laid down in Article 13.

3. Within the time limit referred to in paragraph 2, the Member States concerned shall provide the Committee with a detailed statement of the matters on which they have been unable to reach agreement and the reasons for their disagreement. The applicant shall be provided with a copy of this information.

4. As soon as he is informed that the matter has been referred to the Committee, the applicant shall forthwith forward to the Committee a copy of the information and particulars referred to in Article 9 (1).

Article 11

If several applications submitted in accordance with Article 4 and 4a of Directive 65/65/EEC have been made for marketing authorization for a particular medicinal product, and Member States have adopted divergent decisions concerning the authorization of the medicinal product or its suspension or withdrawal from the market, a Member State, or the Commission, or the person responsible for placing the medicinal product on the market may refer the matter to the Committee for application of the procedure laid down in Article 13.

The Member State concerned, the person responsible for placing the medicinal product on the market or the Commission shall clearly identify the question which is referred to the Committee for consideration and, where appropriate, shall inform the aforementioned person thereof.

The Member State and the person responsible for placing the medicinal product on the market shall forward to the Committee all available information relating to the matter in question.

Article 12

The Member States or the Commission or the applicant or holder of the marketing authorization may, in specific cases where the interests of the Community are involved, refer the matter to the Committee for the application of the procedure laid down in Article 13 before reaching a decision on a request for a marketing authorization or on the suspension or withdrawal of an authorization, or on any other variation to the terms of a marketing authorization which appears necessary, in particular to take account of the information collected in accordance with Chapter Va.

The Member State concerned or the Commission shall clearly identify the question which is referred to the Committee for consideration and shall inform the person responsible for placing the medicinal product on the market.

The Member States and the aforementioned person shall forward to the Committee all available information relating to the matter in question.

Article 13

1. When reference is made to the procedure described in this Article, the Committee shall consider the matter concerned and issue a reasoned opinion within 90 days of the date on which the matter was referred to it.

However, in cases submitted to the Committee in accordance with Articles 11 and 12, this period may be extended by 90 days.

In case of urgency, on a proposal from its Chairman, the Committee may agree to impose a shorter deadline.

2. In order to consider the matter, the Committee may appoint one of its members to act as rapporteur. The Committee may also appoint individual experts to advise it on specific questions. When appointing experts, the Committee shall define their tasks and specify the time limit for the completion of these tasks.

3. In the cases referred to in Articles 10 and 11, before issuing its opinion, the Committee shall provide the person responsible for placing the medicinal product on the market with an opportunity to present written or oral explanations.

In the case referred to in Article 12, the person responsible for placing the medicinal product on the market may be asked to explain himself orally or in writing.

If it considers it appropriate, the Committee may invite any other person to provide information relating to the matter before it.

The Committee may suspend the time limit referred to in paragraph 1 in order to allow the person responsible for placing the medicinal product on the market to prepare explanations.

4. Where the opinion of the Committee is that:

- the application does not satisfy the criteria for authorization, or
- the summary of the product characteristics proposed by the applicant in accordance with Article 4a of Directive 65/65/EEC should be amended, or
- the authorization should be granted subject to conditions, with regard to conditions considered essential for the safe and effective use of the medicinal product including pharmacovigilance, or

- a marketing authorization should be suspended, varied or withdrawn,

the Agency shall forthwith inform the person responsible for placing the medicinal product on the market. Within 15 days of the receipt of the opinion, the aforementioned person may notify the Agency in writing of his intention to appeal. In that case, he shall forward the detailed grounds for appeal to the Agency within 60 days of receipt of the opinion. Within 60 days of receipt of the grounds for appeal, the Committee shall consider whether its opinion should be revised, and the conclusions reached on the appeal shall be annexed to the assessment report referred to in paragraph 5.

5. Within 30 days of its adoption, the Agency shall forward the final opinion of the Committee to the Member States, the Commission and the person responsible for placing the medicinal product on the market together with a report describing the assessment of the medicinal product and stating the reasons for its conclusions.
In the event of an opinion in favour of granting or maintaining an authorization to place the medicinal product concerned on the market, the following documents shall be annexed to the opinion:

(a) a draft summary of the product characteristics, as referred to in Article 4a of Directive 65/65/EEC;

(b) any conditions affecting the authorization within the meaning of paragraph 4.

Article 14

1. Within 30 days of the receipt of the opinion, the Commission shall prepare a draft of the decision to be taken in respect of the application, taking into account Community law.
In the event of a draft decision which envisages the granting of marketing authorization, the documents referred to in Article 13 (5)(a) and (b) shall be annexed.
Where, exceptionally, the draft decision is not in accordance with the opinion of the Agency, the Commission shall also annex a detailed explanation of the reasons for the differences.
The draft decision shall be forwarded to the Member States and the applicant.

2. A final decision on the application shall be adopted in accordance with the procedure laid down in Article 37b.

3. The rules of procedure of the Committee referred to in Article 37b shall be adjusted to take account of the tasks incumbent upon it in accordance with this Directive.
These adjustments shall involve the following:

- except in cases referred to in the third subparagraph of paragraph 1, the opinion of the Standing Committee shall be obtained in writing,
- each Member State is allowed at least 28 days to forward written observations on the draft decision to the Commission,
- each Member State is able to require in writing that the draft decision be discussed by the Standing Committee, giving its reasons in detail.

Where, in the opinion of the Commission, the written observations of a Member State raise important new questions of a scientific or technical nature which have not been addressed in the opinion of the Agency, the Chairman shall suspend the procedure and refer the application back to the Agency for further consideration.
The provisions necessary for the implementation of this paragraph shall be adopted by the Commission in accordance with the procedure laid down in Article 37a.

4. A decision adopted in accordance with this Article shall be addressed to the Member States concerned by the matter and to the person responsible for placing the medicinal product on the market. The Member States shall either grant or withdraw marketing authorization, or vary the terms of a marketing authorization as necessary to comply with the decision within 30 days of its notification. They shall inform the Commission and the Committee thereof.

5. The procedure referred to in Articles 8 to 14 shall not apply in the cases provided for in Article 9 (2) of Council Directive 92/73/EEC of 22 September 1992 widening the scope of Directive 65/65/EEC and 75/319/EEC on the approximation of the laws of the Member States on medicinal products and laying down additional provisions on homeopathic medicinal products.

Article 15

Any application by the person responsible for placing the medicinal product on the market to vary a marketing authorization which has been granted in accordance with the provisions of this Chapter shall be submitted to all the Member States which have previously authorized the medicinal product concerned.

The Commission shall, in consultation with the Agency, adopt appropriate arrangements for the examination of variations to the terms of a marketing authorization.

These arrangements shall include a notification system or administration procedures concerning minor variations and define precisely the concept of "a minor variation".

These arrangements shall be adopted by the Commission in the form of an implementing Regulation in accordance with the procedure laid down in Article 37a.

The procedure laid down in Articles 13 and 14 shall apply by analogy to variations made to marketing authorizations for products subject to the Commission's arbitration.

Article 15a

1. Where a Member State considers that the variation of the terms of a marketing authorization which has been granted in accordance with the provisions of this Chapter or its suspension or withdrawal is necessary for the protection of public health, the Member State concerned shall forthwith refer the matter to the Committee for the application of the products laid down in Articles 13 and 14.

2. Without prejudice to the provisions of Article 12, in exceptional cases, where urgent action is essential to protect public health, until a definitive decision is adopted a Member State may suspend the marketing and the use of the medicinal product concerned on its territory. It shall inform the Commission and the other Member States no later than the following working day of the reasons for its action.

Article 15b

Articles 15 and 15a shall apply by analogy to medicinal products authorized by Member States following an opinion of the Committee given in accordance with Article 4 of Directive 87/22/EEC (5) before 1 January 1995.

Article 15c

1. The Agency shall publish an annual report on the operation of the procedures laid down in this chapter and shall forward that report to the European Parliament and the Council for information.

2. By 1 January 2001, the Commission shall publish a detailed review of the operation of the procedures laid down in this chapter and shall propose any amendments which may be necessary to improve these procedures. The Council shall decide, under the conditions provided for in the Treaty, on the Commission proposal within one year of its submission. " [9]

CHAPTER IV

MANUFACTURE AND IMPORTS COMING FROM THIRD COUNTRIES

ARTICLE 16

1. " Member States shall take all appropriate measures to ensure that the manufacture of medicinal products is subject to the holding of an authorization. This manufacturing authorization shall be required notwithstanding that the medicinal products manufactured are intended for export. " [3]

2. THE AUTHORIZATION REFERRED TO IN PARAGRAPH 1 SHALL BE REQUIRED FOR BOTH TOTAL AND PARTIAL MANUFACTURE, AND FOR THE VARIOUS PROCESSES OF DIVIDING UP, PACKAGING OR PRESENTATION.
HOWEVER, SUCH AUTHORIZATION SHALL NOT BE REQUIRED FOR PREPARATION, DIVIDING UP, CHANGES IN PACKAGING OR PRESENTATION WHERE THESE PROCESSES ARE CARRIED OUT, SOLELY FOR RETAIL SUPPLY, BY PHARMACISTS IN DISPENSING PHARMACIES OR BY PERSONS LEGALLY AUTHORIZED IN THE MEMBER STATES TO CARRY OUT SUCH PROCESSES.

3. AUTHORIZATION REFERRED TO IN PARAGRAPH 1 SHALL ALSO BE REQUIRED FOR IMPORTS COMING FROM THIRD COUNTRIES INTO A MEMBER STATE; THIS CHAPTER AND ARTICLE 29 SHALL HAVE CORRESPONDING APPLICATION TO SUCH IMPORTS AS THEY HAVE TO MANUFACTURE.

ARTICLE 17

IN ORDER TO OBTAIN THE AUTHORIZATION REFERRED TO IN ARTICLE 16, THE APPLICANT MUST MEET AT LEAST THE FOLLOWING REQUIREMENTS:

(a) SPECIFY THE PROPRIETARY MEDICINAL PRODUCTS AND PHARMACEUTICAL FORMS WHICH ARE TO BE MANUFACTURED OR IMPORTED AND ALSO THE PLACE WHERE THEY ARE TO BE MANUFACTURED AND/OR CONTROLLED;

(b) HAVE AT HIS DISPOSAL, FOR THE MANUFACTURE OR IMPORT OF THE ABOVE, SUITABLE AND SUFFICIENT PREMISES, TECHNICAL EQUIPMENT AND CONTROL FACILITIES COMPLYING WITH THE LEGAL REQUIREMENTS WHICH THE MEMBER STATE CONCERNED LAYS DOWN AS REGARDS BOTH MANUFACTURE AND CONTROL AND THE STORAGE OF PRODUCTS, IN ACCORDANCE WITH ARTICLE 5 (a).

(c) HAVE AT HIS DISPOSAL THE SERVICES OF AT LEAST ONE QUALIFIED PERSON WITHIN THE MEANING OF ARTICLE 21.

THE APPLICANT MUST PROVIDE PARTICULARS IN SUPPORT OF THE ABOVE IN HIS APPLICATION.

ARTICLE 18

1. THE COMPETENT AUTHORITY OF THE MEMBER STATE SHALL ISSUE THE AUTHORIZATION REFERRED TO IN ARTICLE 16 ONLY AFTER HAVING MADE SURE OF THE ACCURACY OF THE PARTICULARS SUPPLIED PURSUANT TO ARTICLE 17, BY MEANS OF AN INQUIRY CARRIED OUT BY ITS AGENTS.

2. IN ORDER TO ENSURE THAT THE REQUIREMENTS REFERRED TO IN ARTICLE 17 ARE COMPLIED WITH , AUTHORIZATION MAY BE MADE CONDITIONAL ON THE CARRYING OUT OF CERTAIN OBLIGATIONS IMPOSED EITHER WHEN AUTHORIZATION IS GRANTED OR AT A LATER DATE.

3. THE AUTHORIZATION SHALL APPLY ONLY TO THE PREMISES SPECIFIED IN THE APPLICATION AND TO THE PROPRIETARY MEDICINAL PRODUCTS AND PHARMACEUTICAL FORMS SPECIFIED IN THAT SAME APPLICATION.

ARTICLE 19

THE HOLDER OF AN AUTHORIZATION REFERRED TO IN ARTICLE 16 SHALL AT LEAST BE OBLIGED:

(a) TO HAVE AT HIS DISPOSAL THE SERVICES OF STAFF WHO COMPLY WITH THE LEGAL REQUIREMENTS EXISTING IN THE MEMBER STATE CONCERNED BOTH AS REGARDS MANUFACTURE AND CONTROLS;

(b) TO DISPOSE OF THE AUTHORIZED PROPRIETARY MEDICINAL PRODUCTS ONLY IN ACCORDANCE WITH THE LEGISLATION OF THE MEMBER STATES CONCERNED;

(c) TO GIVE PRIOR NOTICE TO THE COMPETENT AUTHORITY OF ANY CHANGES HE MAY WISH TO MAKE TO ANY OF THE PARTICULARS SUPPLIED PURSUANT TO ARTICLE 17; THE COMPETENT AUTHORITY SHALL IN ANY EVENT BE IMMEDIATELY INFORMED IF THE QUALIFIED PERSON REFERRED TO IN ARTICLE 21 IS REPLACED UNEXPECTEDLY;

(d) TO ALLOW THE AGENTS OF THE COMPETENT AUTHORITY OF THE MEMBER STATE CONCERNED ACCESS TO HIS PREMISES AT ANY TIME;

(e) TO ENABLE THE QUALIFIED PERSON REFERRED TO IN ARTICLE 21 TO CARRY OUT HIS DUTIES, FOR EXAMPLE BY PLACING AT HIS DISPOSAL ALL THE NECESSARY FACILITIES.

" (f) to comply with the principles and guidelines of good manufacturing practice for medicinal products as laid down by Community law. " [3]

" Article 19a

The principles and guidelines of good manufacturing practices for medicinal products referred to in Article 19 (f) shall be adopted in the form of a directive addressed to the Member States, in accordance with the procedure laid down in " Article 37a " [9]. Detailed guidelines in line with those principles will be published by the Commission and revised as necessary to take account of technical and scientific progress. " [3]

ARTICLE 20

1. THE MEMBER STATES SHALL TAKE ALL APPROPRIATE MEASURES TO ENSURE THAT THE TIME TAKEN FOR THE PROCEDURE FOR GRANTING THE AUTHORIZATION REFERRED TO IN ARTICLE 16 DOES NOT EXCEED 90 DAYS FROM THE DAY ON WHICH THE COMPETENT AUTHORITY RECEIVES THE APPLICATION.

2. IF THE HOLDER OF THE AUTHORIZATION REQUESTS A CHANGE IN ANY OF THE PARTICULARS REFERRED TO IN ARTICLE 17 (a) AND (b), THE TIME TAKEN FOR THE PROCEDURE RELATING TO THIS REQUEST SHALL NOT EXCEED 30 DAYS. IN EXCEPTIONAL CASES THIS PERIOD OF TIME MAY BE EXTENDED TO 90 DAYS.

3. MEMBER STATES MAY REQUIRE FROM THE APPLICANT FURTHER INFORMATION CONCERNING THE PARTICULARS SUPPLIED PURSUANT TO ARTICLE 17 AND CONCERNING THE QUALIFIED PERSON REFERRED TO IN ARTICLE 21; WHERE THE COMPETENT AUTHORITY CONCERNED EXERCISES THIS RIGHT, APPLICATION OF THE TIME LIMITS REFERRED TO IN PARAGRAPHS 1 AND 2 SHALL BE SUSPENDED UNTIL THE ADDITIONAL DATA REQUIRED HAVE BEEN SUPPLIED.

ARTICLE 21

1. MEMBER STATES SHALL TAKE ALL APPROPRIATE MEASURES TO ENSURE THAT THE HOLDER OF THE AUTHORIZATION REFERRED TO IN ARTICLE 16 HAS PERMANENTLY AND CONTINUOUSLY AT HIS DISPOSAL THE SERVICES OF AT LEAST ONE QUALIFIED PERSON, IN ACCORDANCE WITH THE CONDITIONS LAID DOWN IN ARTICLE 23, RESPONSIBLE IN PARTICULAR FOR CARRYING OUT THE DUTIES SPECIFIED IN ARTICLE 22.

2. IF HE PERSONALLY FULFILS THE CONDITIONS LAID DOWN IN ARTICLE 23, THE HOLDER OF THE AUTHORIZATION MAY HIMSELF ASSUME THE RESPONSIBILITY REFERRED TO IN PARAGRAPH 1.

ARTICLE 22

1. MEMBER STATES SHALL TAKE ALL APPROPRIATE MEASURES TO ENSURE THAT THE QUALIFIED PERSON REFERRED TO IN ARTICLE 21, WITHOUT PREJUDICE TO HIS RELATIONSHIP WITH THE HOLDER OF THE AUTHORIZATION REFERRED TO IN ARTICLE 16, IS RESPONSIBLE, IN THE CONTEXT OF THE PROCEDURES REFERRED TO IN ARTICLE 25, FOR SECURING:

(a) IN THE CASE OF PROPRIETARY MEDICINAL PRODUCTS MANUFACTURED WITHIN THE MEMBER STATES CONCERNED THAT EACH BATCH OF PROPRIETARY MEDICINAL PRODUCTS HAS BEEN MANUFACTURED AND CHECKED IN COMPLIANCE WITH THE LAWS IN FORCE IN THAT MEMBER STATE AND IN ACCORDANCE WITH THE REQUIREMENTS OF THE MARKETING AUTHORIZATION;

(b) IN THE CASE OF PROPRIETARY MEDICINAL PRODUCTS COMING FROM THIRD COUNTRIES, THAT EACH PRODUCTION BATCH HAS UNDERGONE IN THE IMPORTING COUNTRY A FULL QUALITATIVE ANALYSIS , A QUANTITATIVE ANALYSIS OF AT LEAST ALL THE ACTIVE CONSTITUENTS AND ALL THE OTHER TESTS OR CHECKS NECESSARY TO ENSURE THE QUALITY OF PROPRIETARY MEDICINAL PRODUCTS IN ACCORDANCE WITH THE REQUIREMENTS OF THE MARKETING AUTHORIZATION.

THE BATCHES OF PRODUCTS WHICH HAVE UNDERGONE SUCH CONTROLS IN A MEMBER STATE SHALL BE EXEMPT FROM THE ABOVE CONTROLS IF THEY ARE IMPORTED INTO ANOTHER MEMBER STATE, ACCOMPANIED BY THE CONTROL REPORTS SIGNED BY THE QUALIFIED PERSON.
" In the case of medicinal products imported from a third country, where appropriate arrangements have been made by the Community with the exporting country to ensure that the manufacturer of the medicinal product applies standards of good manufacturing practice at least equivalent to those laid down by the Community and to ensure that the controls referred to under (b) have been carried out in the exporting country, the qualified person may be relieved of responsibility for carrying out those controls. " [9]

2. IN ALL CASES AND PARTICULARLY WHERE THE PROPRIETARY MEDICINAL PRODUCTS ARE RELEASED FOR SALE THE QUALIFIED PERSON MUST CERTIFY IN A REGISTER OR EQUIVALENT DOCUMENT PROVIDED FOR THAT PURPOSE THAT EACH PRODUCTION BATCH SATISFIES THE PROVISIONS OF THIS ARTICLE; THE SAID REGISTER OR EQUIVALENT DOCUMENT MUST BE KEPT UP TO DATE AS OPERATIONS ARE CARRIED OUT AND MUST REMAIN AT THE DISPOSAL OF THE AGENTS OF THE COMPETENT AUTHORITY FOR THE PERIOD SPECIFIED IN THE PROVISIONS OF THE MEMBER STATE CONCERNED AND IN ANY EVENT FOR AT LEAST FIVE YEARS.

ARTICLE 23

MEMBER STATES SHALL ENSURE THAT THE QUALIFIED PERSON REFERRED TO IN ARTICLE 21 FULFILS THE FOLLOWING MINIMUM CONDITIONS OF QUALIFICATION:

(a) POSSESSION OF A DIPLOMA, CERTIFICATE OR OTHER EVIDENCE OF FORMAL QUALIFICATIONS AWARDED ON COMPLETION OF A UNIVERSITY COURSE OF STUDY, OR A COURSE RECOGNIZED AS EQUIVALENT BY THE MEMBER STATE CONCERNED, EXTENDING OVER A PERIOD OF AT LEAST FOUR YEARS OF THEORETICAL AND PRACTICAL STUDY IN ONE OF THE FOLLOWING SCIENTIFIC

DISCIPLINES: PHARMACY, MEDICINE, VETERINARY MEDICINE, CHEMISTRY, PHARMACEUTICAL CHEMISTRY AND TECHNOLOGY, BIOLOGY. HOWEVER:

- THE MINIMUM DURATION OF THE UNIVERSITY COURSE MAY BE THREE AND A HALF YEARS WHERE THE COURSE IS FOLLOWED BY A PERIOD OF THEORETICAL AND PRACTICAL TRAINING OF A MINIMUM DURATION OF ONE YEAR AND INCLUDING A TRAINING PERIOD OF AT LEAST SIX MONTHS IN A PHARMACY OPEN TO THE PUBLIC, CORROBORATED BY AN EXAMINATION AT UNIVERSITY LEVEL;
- WHERE TWO UNIVERSITY COURSES OR TWO COURSES RECOGNIZED BY THE STATE AS EQUIVALENT CO-EXIST IN A MEMBER STATE AND WHERE ONE OF THESE EXTENDS OVER FOUR YEARS AND THE OTHER OVER THREE YEARS, THE THREE-YEAR COURSE LEADING TO A DIPLOMA, CERTIFICATE OR OTHER EVIDENCE OF FORMAL QUALIFICATIONS AWARDED ON COMPLETION OF A UNIVERSITY COURSE OR ITS RECOGNIZED EQUIVALENT SHALL BE CONSIDERED TO FULFIL THE CONDITION OF DURATION REFERRED TO IN (a) IN SO FAR AS THE DIPLOMAS, CERTIFICATES OR OTHER EVIDENCE OF FORMAL QUALIFICATIONS AWARDED ON COMPLETION OF BOTH COURSES ARE RECOGNIZED AS EQUIVALENT BY THE STATE IN QUESTION.

THE COURSE SHALL INCLUDE THEORETICAL AND PRACTICAL STUDY BEARING UPON AT LEAST THE FOLLOWING BASIC SUBJECTS:

- APPLIED PHYSICS
- GENERAL AND INORGANIC CHEMISTRY
- ORGANIC CHEMISTRY
- ANALYTICAL CHEMISTRY
- PHARMACEUTICAL CHEMISTRY, INCLUDING ANALYSIS OF MEDICINAL PRODUCTS
- GENERAL AND APPLIED BIOCHEMISTRY (MEDICAL)
- PHYSIOLOGY
- MICROBIOLOGY
- PHARMACOLOGY
- PHARMACEUTICAL TECHNOLOGY
- TOXICOLOGY
- PHARMACOGNOSY (MEDICAL ASPECTS) (STUDY OF THE COMPOSITION AND EFFECTS OF THE ACTIVE PRINCIPLES OF NATURAL SUBSTANCES OF PLANT AND ANIMAL ORIGIN).

STUDIES IN THESE SUBJECTS SHOULD BE SO BALANCED AS TO ENABLE THE PERSON CONCERNED TO FULFIL THE OBLIGATIONS SPECIFIED IN ARTICLE 22.
IN SO FAR AS CERTAIN DIPLOMAS, CERTIFICATES OR OTHER EVIDENCE OF FORMAL QUALIFICATIONS MENTIONED IN (a) DO NOT FULFIL THE CRITERIA LAID DOWN ABOVE, THE COMPETENT AUTHORITY OF THE MEMBER STATE SHALL ENSURE THAT THE PERSON CONCERNED PROVIDES EVIDENCE OF ADEQUATE KNOWLEDGE OF THE SUBJECTS INVOLVED.

(b) PRACTICAL EXPERIENCE FOR AT LEAST TWO YEARS, IN ONE OR MORE UNDERTAKINGS WHICH ARE AUTHORIZED TO MANUFACTURE PROPRIETARY MEDICINAL PRODUCTS, IN THE ACTIVITIES OF QUALITATIVE ANALYSIS OF MEDICINAL PRODUCTS, OF QUANTITATIVE ANALYSIS OF ACTIVE SUBSTANCES AND OF THE TESTING AND CHECKING NECESSARY TO ENSURE THE QUALITY OF PROPRIETARY MEDICINAL PRODUCTS.

THE DURATION OF PRACTICAL EXPERIENCE MAY BE REDUCED BY ONE YEAR WHERE A UNIVERSITY COURSE LASTS FOR AT LEAST FIVE YEARS AND BY A YEAR AND A HALF WHERE THE COURSE LASTS FOR AT LEAST SIX YEARS.

ARTICLE 24

1. A PERSON ENGAGING IN THE ACTIVITIES OF THE PERSON REFERRED TO IN ARTICLE 21 IN A MEMBER STATE AT THE TIME WHEN THIS DIRECTIVE IS BROUGHT INTO FORCE IN THAT STATE BUT WITHOUT COMPLYING WITH THE PROVISIONS OF ARTICLE 23 SHALL BE ELIGIBLE TO CONTINUE TO ENGAGE IN THOSE ACTIVITIES IN THE STATE CONCERNED.

2. THE HOLDER OF A DIPLOMA, CERTIFICATE OR OTHER EVIDENCE OF FORMAL QUALIFICATIONS AWARDED ON COMPLETION OF A UNIVERSITY COURSE - OR A COURSE RECOGNIZED AS

EQUIVALENT BY THE MEMBER STATE CONCERNED - IN A SCIENTIFIC DISCIPLINE ALLOWING HIM TO ENGAGE IN THE ACTIVITIES OF THE PERSON REFERRED TO IN ARTICLE 21 IN ACCORDANCE WITH THE LAWS OF THAT STATE MAY - IF HE BEGAN HIS COURSE PRIOR TO THE NOTIFICATION OF THIS DIRECTIVE - BE CONSIDERED AS QUALIFIED TO CARRY OUT IN THAT STATE THE DUTIES OF THE PERSON REFERRED TO IN ARTICLE 21 PROVIDED THAT HE HAS PREVIOUSLY ENGAGED IN THE FOLLOWING ACTIVITIES FOR AT LEAST TWO YEARS BEFORE THE END OF THE TENTH YEAR FOLLOWING NOTIFICATION OF THIS DIRECTIVE IN ONE OR MORE UNDERTAKINGS AUTHORIZED PURSUANT TO ARTICLE 16: PRODUCTION SUPERVISION AND/OR QUALITATIVE ANALYSIS, QUANTITATIVE ANALYSIS OF ACTIVE SUBSTANCES, AND THE NECESSARY TESTING AND CHECKING UNDER THE DIRECT AUTHORITY OF THE PERSON REFERRED TO IN ARTICLE 21 TO ENSURE THE QUALITY OF THE PROPRIETARY MEDICINAL PRODUCTS.

IF THE PERSON CONCERNED HAS ACQUIRED THE PRACTICAL EXPERIENCE REFERRED TO IN THE FIRST SUBPARAGRAPH MORE THAN 10 YEARS PRIOR TO THE NOTIFICATION OF THIS DIRECTIVE, A FURTHER ONE YEAR'S PRACTICAL EXPERIENCE IN ACCORDANCE WITH THE CONDITIONS REFERRED TO IN THE FIRST SUBPARAGRAPH WILL BE REQUIRED TO BE COMPLETED IMMEDIATELY BEFORE HE ENGAGES IN SUCH ACTIVITIES.

3. A PERSON WHO, AT THE TIME WHEN THIS DIRECTIVE IS BROUGHT INTO FORCE, IS ENGAGED IN DIRECT COLLABORATION WITH A PERSON REFERRED TO IN ARTICLE 21 IN PRODUCTION SUPERVISION ACTIVITIES AND/OR IN QUALITATIVE AND QUANTITATIVE ANALYSIS OF ACTIVE SUBSTANCES AND THE TESTING AND CHECKING NECESSARY TO ENSURE THE QUALITY OF PROPRIETARY MEDICINAL PRODUCTS MAY, FOR A PERIOD OF FIVE YEARS AFTER THIS DIRECTIVE HAS BEEN BROUGHT INTO FORCE, BE CONSIDERED AS QUALIFIED TO TAKE UP IN THAT STATE THE DUTIES OF THE PERSON REFERRED TO IN ARTICLE 21 PROVIDED THAT THAT MEMBER STATE ENSURES THAT THE PERSON SHOWS EVIDENCE OF ADEQUATE THEORETICAL AND PRACTICAL KNOWLEDGE AND HAS ENGAGED IN THE ACTIVITIES MENTIONED FOR AT LEAST FIVE YEARS.

ARTICLE 25

MEMBER STATES SHALL ENSURE THAT THE DUTIES OF QUALIFIED PERSONS REFERRED TO IN ARTICLE 21 ARE FULFILLED, EITHER BY MEANS OF APPROPRIATE ADMINISTRATIVE MEASURES OR BY MAKING SUCH PERSONS SUBJECT TO A PROFESSIONAL CODE OF CONDUCT.
MEMBER STATES MAY PROVIDE FOR THE TEMPORARY SUSPENSION OF SUCH A PERSON UPON THE COMMENCEMENT OF ADMINISTRATIVE OR DISCIPLINARY PROCEDURES AGAINST HIM FOR FAILURE TO FULFIL HIS OBLIGATIONS.

CHAPTER V

SUPERVISION AND SANCTIONS

ARTICLE 26

" The competent authority of the Member State concerned shall ensure, by means of repeated inspections, that the legal requirements governing medicinal products are complied with. " [3]

SUCH INSPECTIONS SHALL BE CARRIED OUT BY OFFICIALS REPRESENTING THE COMPETENT AUTHORITY WHO MUST BE EMPOWERED TO:

(a) INSPECT MANUFACTURING OR COMMERCIAL ESTABLISHMENTS AND ANY LABORATORIES ENTRUSTED BY THE HOLDER OF THE AUTHORIZATION REFERRED TO IN ARTICLE 16 WITH THE TASK OF CARRYING OUT CHECKS PURSUANT TO ARTICLE 5 (b);

(b) TAKE SAMPLES;

(c) EXAMINE ANY DOCUMENTS RELATING TO THE OBJECT OF THE INSPECTION, SUBJECT TO THE PROVISIONS IN FORCE IN THE MEMBER STATES AT THE TIME OF NOTIFICATION OF THIS DIRECTIVE AND WHICH PLACE RESTRICTIONS ON THESE POWERS WITH REGARD TO THE DESCRIPTIONS OF THE METHOD OF PREPARATION.

" After every inspection as referred to in the first subparagraph, the officials representing the competent authority shall report on whether the manufacturer complies with the principles and guidelines of good manufacturing practice laid down by Community law. The content of such reports shall be communicated to the manufacturer who has to undergo the inspection. " [3]

ARTICLE 27

MEMBER STATES SHALL TAKE ALL APPROPRIATE MEASURES TO ENSURE THAT THE PERSON RESPONSIBLE FOR MARKETING A PROPRIETARY MEDICINAL PRODUCT AND, WHERE APPROPRIATE, THE HOLDER OF THE AUTHORIZATION REFERRED TO IN ARTICLE 16, FURNISH PROOF OF THE CONTROLS CARRIED OUT ON THE FINISHED PRODUCT AND/OR THE INGREDIENTS AND OF THE CONTROLS CARRIED OUT AT AN INTERMEDIATE STAGE OF THE MANUFACTURING PROCESS, IN ACCORDANCE WITH THE METHODS LAID DOWN FOR THE PURPOSES OF THE MARKETING AUTHORIZATION.

ARTICLE 28

1. NOTWITHSTANDING THE MEASURES PROVIDED FOR IN ARTICLE 11 OF DIRECTIVE 65/65/EEC, MEMBER STATES SHALL TAKE ALL APPROPRIATE MEASURES TO ENSURE THAT THE SUPPLY OF THE PROPRIETARY MEDICINAL PRODUCT SHALL BE PROHIBITED AND THE PROPRIETARY MEDICINAL PRODUCT WITHDRAWN FROM THE MARKET IF:

(a) THE PROPRIETARY MEDICINAL PRODUCT PROVES TO BE HARMFUL UNDER NORMAL CONDITIONS OF USE;

(b) IT IS LACKING IN THERAPEUTIC EFFICACY;

(c) ITS QUALITATIVE AND QUANTITATIVE COMPOSITION IS NOT AS DECLARED;

(d) THE CONTROLS ON THE FINISHED PRODUCT AND/OR ON THE INGREDIENTS AND THE CONTROLS AT AN INTERMEDIATE STAGE OF THE MANUFACTURING PROCESS HAVE NOT BEEN CARRIED OUT OR IF SOME OTHER REQUIREMENT OR OBLIGATION RELATING TO THE GRANT OF THE AUTHORIZATION REFERRED TO IN ARTICLE 16 HAS NOT BEEN FULFILLED.

2. THE COMPETENT AUTHORITY MAY LIMIT THE PROHIBITION TO SUPPLY THE PRODUCT, OR ITS WITHDRAWAL FROM THE MARKET, TO THOSE BATCHES WHICH ARE THE SUBJECT OF DISPUTE.

" Article 28a

At the request of the manufacturer, the exporter or the authorities of an importing third country, Member States shall certify that a manufacturer of medicinal products is in possession of the authorization referred to in Article 16 (1). When issuing such certificates they shall comply with the following conditions:

1. Member States shall have regard to the prevailing administrative arrangements of the World Health Organization.

2. For medicinal products intended for export which are already authorized on their territory, they shall supply the summary of the product characteristics as approved in accordance with Article 4 (b) of Directive 65/65/EEC.

3. When the manufacturer is not in possession of a marketing authorization he shall provide the authorities responsible for establishing the certificate referred to above with a declaration explaining why no marketing authorization is available. " [3]

ARTICLE 29

1. THE COMPETENT AUTHORITY OF A MEMBER STATE SHALL SUSPEND OR REVOKE THE AUTHORIZATION REFERRED TO IN ARTICLE 16 FOR A CATEGORY OF PREPARATIONS OR ALL PREPARATIONS WHERE ANY ONE OF THE REQUIREMENTS LAID DOWN IN ARTICLE 17 IS NO LONGER MET.

2. IN ADDITION TO THE MEASURES SPECIFIED IN ARTICLE 28, THE COMPETENT AUTHORITY OF A MEMBER STATE MAY SUSPEND MANUFACTURE OR IMPORTS OF PROPRIETARY MEDICINAL PRODUCTS COMING FROM THIRD COUNTRIES, OR SUSPEND OR REVOKE THE AUTHORIZATION REFERRED TO IN ARTICLE 16 FOR A CATEGORY OF PREPARATIONS OR ALL PREPARATIONS WHERE ARTICLES 18, 19, 22 AND 27 ARE NOT COMPLIED WITH.

" CHAPTER Va

Pharmacovigilance

Article 29a

In order to ensure the adoption of appropriate regulatory decisions concerning the medicinal products authorized within the Community, having regard to information obtained about adverse reactions to medicinal products under normal conditions of use, the Member States shall establish a pharmacovigilance system. This system shall be used to collect information useful in the surveillance of medicinal products, with particular reference to adverse reactions in human beings, and to evaluate such information scientifically.
Such information shall be collated with data on consumption of medicinal products.
This system shall also collate information on frequently observed misuse and serious abuse of medicinal products.

Article 29b

For the purpose of this Directive, the following definitions shall apply:

- "adverse reaction" means a reaction which is harmful and unintended and which occurs at doses normally used in man for the prophylaxis, diagnosis or treatment of disease or the modification of physiological function,
- "serious adverse reaction" means an adverse reaction which is fatal, life-threatening, disabling, incapacitating, or which results in or prolongs hospitalization,
- "unexpected adverse reaction" means an adverse reaction which is not mentioned in the summary of product characteristics,
- "serious unexpected adverse reaction" means an adverse reaction which is both serious and unexpected.

Article 29c

The person responsible for placing the medicinal product on the market shall have permanently and continuously at his disposal an appropriately qualified person responsible for pharmacovigilance.
That qualified person shall be responsible for the following:

(a) the establishment and maintenance of a system which ensures that information about all suspected adverse reactions which are reported to the personnel of the company, and to medical representatives, is collected and collated at a single point within the Community;

(b) the preparation for the competent authorities of the reports referred to in Article 29d, in such form as may be laid down by those authorities, in accordance with the relevant national or Community guidelines;

(c) ensuring that any request from the competent authorities for the provision of additional information necessary for the evaluation of the benefits and risks afforded by a medicinal product is answered fully and promptly, including the provision of information about the volume of sales or prescriptions of the medicinal product concerned.

Article 29d

1. The person responsible for placing the medicinal product on the market shall be required to record and to report all suspected serious adverse reactions which are brought to his attention by a health care professional to the competent authorities immediately, and in any case within 15 days of their receipt at the latest.

2. In addition, the person responsible for placing the medicinal product on the market shall be required to maintain detailed records of all other suspected adverse reactions which are reported to him by a health care professional.
Unless other requirements have been laid down as a condition of the granting of authorization, these records shall be submitted to the competent authorities immediately upon request or at least every six months during the first two years following authorization, and once a year for the following three years. Thereafter, the records shall be submitted at five-yearly intervals together with the application for renewal of the authorization, or immediately upon request. These records shall be accompanied by a scientific evaluation.

Article 29e

The Member States shall take all appropriate measures to encourage doctors and other health care professionals to report suspected adverse reactions to the competent authorities.
The Member States may impose specific requirements on medical practitioners, in respect of the reporting of suspected serious or unexpected adverse reactions, in particular where such reporting is a condition of the authorization.

Article 29f

The Member States shall ensure that reports of suspected serious adverse reactions are immediately brought to the attention of the Agency and the person responsible for placing the medicinal product on the market, and in any case within 15 days of their notification, at the latest.

Article 29g

In order to facilitate the exchange of information about pharmacovigilance within the Community, the Commission, in consultation with the Agency, Member States and interested parties, shall draw up guidance on the collection, verification and presentation of adverse reaction reports.

This guidance shall take account of international harmonization work carried out with regard to terminology and classification in the field of pharmacovigilance.

Article 29h

Where as a result of the evaluation of adverse reaction reports a Member State considers that a marketing authorization should be varied, suspended or withdrawn, it shall forthwith inform the Agency and the person responsible for placing the medicinal product on the market.

In case of urgency, the Member State concerned may suspend the marketing of a medicinal product, provided the Agency is informed at the latest on the following working day.

Article 29i

Any amendments which may be necessary to update provisions of this Chapter to take account of scientific and technical progress shall be adopted in accordance with the procedure laid down in Article 37a. " [9]

CHAPTER VI

MISCELLANEOUS PROVISIONS

ARTICLE 30

MEMBER STATES SHALL TAKE ALL APPROPRIATE MEASURES TO ENSURE THAT THE COMPETENT AUTHORITIES CONCERNED COMMUNICATE TO EACH OTHER SUCH INFORMATION AS IS APPROPRIATE TO GUARANTEE THAT THE REQUIREMENTS FOR THE AUTHORIZATIONS REFERRED TO IN ARTICLE 16 OR MARKETING AUTHORIZATIONS ARE FULFILLED.

" Upon reasoned request, Member States shall forthwith communicate the reports referred to in the third subparagraph of Article 26 to the competent authorities of another Member State. If, after considering the reports, the Member State receiving the reports considers that it cannot accept the conclusions reached by the competent authorities of the Member State in which the report was established, it shall inform the competent authorities concerned of its reasons and may request further information. The Member States concerned shall use their best endeavours to reach agreement. If necessary, in the case of serious differences of opinion, the Commission shall be informed by one of the Member States concerned. " [3]

ARTICLE 31

ALL DECISIONS TAKEN PURSUANT TO ARTICLES 18, 28 AND 29 AND ALL NEGATIVE DECISIONS TAKEN PURSUANT TO ARTICLES 5 (b) AND 11 (3) SHALL STATE IN DETAIL THE REASONS ON WHICH THEY ARE BASED. SUCH DECISIONS SHALL BE NOTIFIED TO THE PARTY CONCERNED, WHO SHALL AT THE SAME TIME BE INFORMED OF THE REMEDIES AVAILABLE TO HIM UNDER THE LAWS IN FORCE AND OF THE TIME LIMIT ALLOWED FOR APPLYING FOR SUCH REMEDIES.

ARTICLE 32

NO DECISION CONCERNING SUSPENSION OF MANUFACTURE OR OF IMPORTATION OF PROPRIETARY MEDICINAL PRODUCTS COMING FROM THIRD COUNTRIES, PROHIBITION OF SUPPLY OR WITHDRAWAL FROM THE MARKET OF A PROPRIETARY MEDICINAL PRODUCT MAY BE TAKEN EXCEPT ON THE GROUND SET OUT IN ARTICLES 28 AND 29.

ARTICLE 33

1. EACH MEMBER STATE SHALL TAKE ALL THE APPROPRIATE MEASURES TO ENSURE THAT DECISIONS AUTHORIZING MARKETING, REFUSING OR REVOKING A MARKETING AUTHORIZATION, CANCELLING A DECISION REFUSING OR REVOKING A MARKETING AUTHORIZATION, PROHIBITING SUPPLY, OR WITHDRAWING A PRODUCT FROM THE MARKET, TOGETHER WITH THE REASONS ON WHICH SUCH DECISIONS ARE BASED, ARE BROUGHT TO THE ATTENTION OF THE COMMITTEE FORTHWITH.

" 2. The person responsible for the marketing of a medicinal product shall be obliged to notify the Member States concerned forthwith of any action taken by him to suspend the marketing of a product or to withdraw a product from the market, together with the reasons for such action if the latter concerns the efficacy of the medicinal product or the protection of public health. Member States shall ensure that this information is brought to the attention of the committee.

3. Member States shall ensure that appropriate information about action taken pursuant to paragraphs 1 and 2 which may affect the protection of public health in third countries is forthwith brought to the attention of the World Health Organization, with a copy to the committee.

4. The Commission shall publish annually a list of the medicinal products which are prohibited in the Community. " [3]

ARTICLE 34

" This Directive shall apply to medicinal products for human use within the limits referred to in Article 2 of Directive 65/65/EEC. " [3]
CHAPTERS II TO V OF DIRECTIVE 65/65/EEC AND THIS DIRECTIVE SHALL NOT APPLY TO PROPRIETARY MEDICINAL PRODUCTS CONSISTING OF VACCINES, TOXINS OR SERUMS, TO PROPRIETARY MEDICINAL PRODUCTS BASED ON HUMAN BLOOD OR BLOOD CONSTITUENTS OR RADIOACTIVE ISOTOPES, OR TO HOMEOPATHIC PROPRIETARY MEDICINAL PRODUCTS. A LIST, FOR INFORMATION PURPOSES, OF THESE VACCINES, TOXINS AND SERUMS IS GIVEN IN THE ANNEX.

[This directive has extended its application to: immunological medicinal products for human use consisting of vaccines, toxins or serums and allergen products [4]; radiopharmaceuticals for human use, excluding radionuclides in the form of sealed sources [5]; whole blood, plasma or blood cells of human origin [6]; and homeopathic medicinal products [8]]

ARTICLE 35

THE FOLLOWING SHALL BE SUBSTITUTED FOR POINT 7 OF ARTICLE 4, SECOND PARAGRAPH, OF DIRECTIVE 65/65/EEC: "DESCRIPTION OF THE CONTROL METHODS EMPLOYED BY THE MANUFACTURER (QUALITATIVE AND QUANTITATIVE ANALYSIS OF THE CONSTITUENTS AND OF THE FINISHED PRODUCT, SPECIAL TESTS, E.G. STERILITY TESTS, TESTS FOR THE PRESENCE OF PYROGENIC SUBSTANCES, THE PRESENCE OF HEAVY METALS, STABILITY TESTS, BIOLOGICAL AND

TOXICITY TESTS, CONTROLS CARRIED OUT AT AN INTERMEDIATE STAGE OF THE MANUFACTURING PROCESS)."

ARTICLE 36

THE FOLLOWING SHALL BE SUBSTITUTED FOR ARTICLE 11, SECOND PARAGRAPH, OF DIRECTIVE 65/65/EEC: "AN AUTHORIZATION SHALL ALSO BE SUSPENDED OR REVOKED WHERE THE PARTICULARS SUPPORTING THE APPLICATION AS PROVIDED FOR IN ARTICLE 4 ARE FOUND TO BE INCORRECT, OR WHEN THE CONTROLS REFERRED TO IN ARTICLE 8 OF THIS DIRECTIVE OR IN ARTICLE 27 OF THE SECOND COUNCIL DIRECTIVE 75/319/EEC (1) OF 20 MAY 1975 ON THE APPROXIMATION OF PROVISIONS LAID DOWN BY LAW, REGULATION OR ADMINISTRATIVE ACTION RELATING TO PROPRIETARY MEDICINAL PRODUCTS HAVE NOT BEEN CARRIED OUT." THE FOLLOWING FOOTNOTE SHALL BE ADDED:

"(1) OJ No L 147, 9. 6. 75, p. 13."

ARTICLE 37

THE FOLLOWING SHALL BE SUBSTITUTED FOR ARTICLE 24 OF DIRECTIVE 65/65/EEC: "WITHIN THE TIME LIMITS AND UNDER THE CONDITIONS LAID DOWN IN ARTICLE 39 (2) AND (3) OF SECOND DIRECTIVE 75/319/EEC, THE RULES LAID DOWN IN THIS DIRECTIVE SHALL BE APPLIED PROGRESSIVELY TO PROPRIETARY MEDICINAL PRODUCTS COVERED BY AN AUTHORIZATION TO PLACE ON THE MARKET BY VIRTUE OF PREVIOUS PROVISIONS".

" CHAPTER VIa

Standing Committee procedures

Article 37a

Where the procedure laid down in this Article is to be followed the Commission shall be assisted by the Standing Committee on Medicinal Products for Human Use.
The representative of the Commission shall submit to the Committee a draft of the measures to be taken. The Committee shall deliver its opinion on the draft within a time limit which the Chairman may lay down according to the urgency of the matter. The opinion shall be delivered by the majority laid down in Article 148 (2) of the Treaty in the case of decisions which the Council is required to adopt on a proposal from the Commission. The votes of the representatives of the Member States within the Committee shall be weighted in the manner set out in that Article. The Chairman shall not vote.
The Commission shall adopt the measures envisaged if they are in accordance with the opinion of the Committee.
If the measures envisaged are not in accordance with the opinion of the Committee, or if no opinion is delivered, the Commission shall, without delay, submit to the Council a proposal relating to the measures to be taken. The Council shall act by a qualified majority.
If on the expiry of a period of three months from the date of referral to the Council, the Council has not acted, the proposed measures shall be adopted by the Commission.

Article 37b

Where the procedure laid down in this Article is to be followed the Commission shall be assisted by the Standing Committee on Medicinal Products for Human Use.

The representative of the Commission shall submit to the Committee a draft of the measures to be taken. The Committee shall deliver its opinion on the draft within a time limit which the Chairman may lay down according to the urgency of the matter. The opinion shall be delivered by the majority laid down in Article 148 (2) of the Treaty in the case of decisions which the Council is required to adopt on a proposal from the Commission. The votes of the representatives of the Member States within the Committee shall be weighted in the manner set out in that Article. The Chairman shall not vote.

The Commission shall adopt the measures envisaged if they are in accordance with the opinion of the Committee.

If the measures envisaged are not in accordance with the opinion of the Committee, or if no opinion is delivered, the Commission shall, without delay, submit to the Council a proposal relating to the measures to be taken. The Council shall act by a qualified majority.

If on the expiry of a period of three months from the date of referral to the Council, the Council has not acted, the proposed measures shall be adopted by the Commission, save where the Council has decided against the said measures by a simple majority. " [9]

CHAPTER VII

IMPLEMENTING PROVISIONS AND TRANSITIONAL MEASURES

ARTICLE 38

MEMBER STATES SHALL BRING INTO FORCE THE LAWS, REGULATIONS AND ADMINISTRATIVE PROVISIONS NEEDED IN ORDER TO COMPLY WITH THIS DIRECTIVE WITHIN 18 MONTHS OF ITS NOTIFICATION AND SHALL FORTHWITH INFORM THE COMMISSION THEREOF.

MEMBER STATES SHALL COMMUNICATE TO THE COMMISSION THE TEXT OF THE MAIN PROVISIONS OF NATIONAL LAW WHICH THEY ADOPT IN THE FIELD COVERED BY THIS DIRECTIVE.

ARTICLE 39

1. AS REGARDS THE AUTHORIZATIONS REFERRED TO IN ARTICLE 16 ISSUED BEFORE THE EXPIRY OF THE TIME LIMIT LAID DOWN IN ARTICLE 38, MEMBER STATES MAY GRANT AN ADDITIONAL PERIOD OF ONE YEAR TO THE UNDERTAKINGS CONCERNED TO ENABLE THEM TO COMPLY WITH THE PROVISIONS OF CHAPTER IV.

2. WITHIN 15 YEARS OF THE NOTIFICATION REFERRED TO IN ARTICLE 38, THE OTHER PROVISIONS OF THIS DIRECTIVE SHALL BE APPLIED PROGRESSIVELY TO PROPRIETARY MEDICINAL PRODUCTS PLACED ON THE MARKET BY VIRTUE OF PREVIOUS PROVISIONS.

3. MEMBER STATES SHALL NOTIFY THE COMMISSION, WITHIN THREE YEARS FOLLOWING THE NOTIFICATION OF THIS DIRECTIVE, OF THE NUMBER OF PROPRIETARY MEDICINAL PRODUCTS COVERED BY PARAGRAPH 2, AND, EACH SUBSEQUENT YEAR, OF THE NUMBER OF THESE PRODUCTS FOR WHICH A MARKETING AUTHORIZATION REFERRED TO IN ARTICLE 3 OF DIRECTIVE 65/65/EEC, HAS NOT YET BEEN ISSUED.

ARTICLE 40

THIS DIRECTIVE IS ADDRESSED TO THE MEMBER STATES.

ANNEX

THE EXPRESSION "VACCINES, TOXINS OR SERUMS" USED IN ARTICLE 34 SHALL COVER IN PARTICULAR:

- AGENTS USED TO PRODUCE ACTIVE IMMUNITY (SUCH AS CHOLERA VACCINE, BCG, POLIO VACCINE, SMALLPOX VACCINE);
- AGENTS USED TO DIAGNOSE THE STATE OF IMMUNITY INCLUDING IN PARTICULAR TUBERCULIN AND TUBERCULIN PPD, TOXINS FOR THE SCHICK AND DICK TESTS, BRUCELLIN;
- AGENTS USED TO PRODUCE PASSIVE IMMUNITY (SUCH AS DIPHTHERIA ANTITOXIN, ANTI-SMALLPOX GLOBULIN, ANTILYMPHOCYTIC GLOBULIN).

(1) OJ No 22, 09/02/1965, p. 369.
(2) OJ No L 147, 09/06/1975, p.1.
(3) OJ No L 214, 24/08/1993, p. 1.
(4) The expression "risk to public health" refers to the quality, safety and efficacy of the medicinal product.
(5) OJ No L 15, 17/01/1987, p. 38.

COUNCIL DIRECTIVE

of 22 December 1986

on the approximation of national measures relating to the placing on the market of high-technology medicinal products, particularly those derived from biotechnology

(87/22/EEC)

THE COUNCIL OF THE EUROPEAN COMMUNITIES,

Having regard to the Treaty establishing the European Economic Community, and in particular Article 100 thereof,

Having regard to the proposal from the Commission (¹),

Having regard to the opinion of the European Parliament (²),

Having regard to the opinion of the Economic and Social Committee (³),

Whereas the essential aim of any rules governing the production and distribution of medicinal products must be to safeguard public health;

Whereas high-technology medicinal products requiring lengthy periods of costly research will continue to be developed in Europe only if they benefit from a favourable regulatory environment, particularly identical conditions governing their placing on the market throughout the Community;

Whereas Council Directive 75/319/EEC of 20 May 1975 on the approximation of provisions laid down by law, regulation or administrative action relating to proprietary medicinal products (⁴), as last amended by Directive 83/570/EEC (⁵), makes provision for certain procedures for coordinating national decisions relating to the placing on the market of proprietary medicinal products for human use; whereas pharmaceutical undertakings may, according to these provisions, request a Member State to take due account of an authorization already issued by another Member State;

Whereas Council Directive 81/851/EEC of 28 September 1981 on the approximation of the laws of the Member States relating to veterinary medicinal products (⁶) makes provision for a procedure for coordinating national decisions relating to veterinary medicinal products;

Whereas, however, these procedures are not sufficient to open up to high-technology medicinal products the large Community-wide single market they require;

Whereas, in this technically advanced sector, the scientific expertise available to each of the national authorities is not always sufficient to resolve problems posed by high-technology medicinal products;

Whereas it is consequently important to provide for a Community mechanism for concertation, prior to any national decision relating to a high-technology medicinal product, with a view to arriving at uniform decisions throughout the Community;

Whereas it is desirable to extend this Community concertation to immunological products and substitutes for blood constituents developed by means of new biotechnological processes, and to new products based on radio-isotopes, the development of which in Europe can only take place if a sufficiently large and homogeneous market exists;

Whereas the need for the adoption of new technical rules applying to high-technology medicinal products or for the amendment of existing rules must be examined during a preliminary concertation between the Member States and the Commission within the competent Committees so as not to endanger the advance of pharmaceutical research whilst at the same time ensuring optimum protection of public health within the Community,

HAS ADOPTED THIS DIRECTIVE:

Article 1

Before taking a decision on a marketing authorization or on the withdrawal or, subject to Article 4 (2), suspension of a marketing authorization in respect of the medicinal products listed in the Annex, Member States' authorities shall, in accordance with Articles 2, 3 and 4, refer the matter for an opinion to the Committees referred to in Article 8 of Directive 75/319/EEC and Article 16 of Directive 81/851/EEC.

Article 2

1. As soon as they receive an application for marketing authorization relating to a medicinal product referred to in the Annex (Lists A and B), the competent authorities shall, at the request of the person responsible for placing the product on the market, bring the matter before either

(¹) OJ No C 293, 5. 11. 1984, p. 1.
(²) OJ No C 36, 17. 2. 1986, p. 152.
(³) OJ No C 160, 1. 7. 1985, p. 18.
(⁴) OJ No L 147, 9. 6. 1975, p. 13.
(⁵) OJ No L 332, 28. 11. 1983, p. 1.
(⁶) OJ No L 317, 6. 11. 1981, p. 1.

the Committee for Proprietary Medicinal Products or the Committee for Veterinary Medicinal Products, in accordance with their competence, for an opinion. Any such request shall be submitted in writing to the competent authorities concerned at the same time as the application for marketing authorization and a copy shall be sent to the Committee concerned.

2. As soon as they receive an application for marketing authorization relating to a medicinal product developed by means of new biotechnological processes and referred to in List A in the Annex, the competent authorities shall be required to bring the matter before the Committee for Proprietary Medicinal Products or the Committee for Veterinary Medicinal Products, in accordance with their competence, for an opinion.

3. Paragraph 2 shall not apply if, when submitting the application for marketing authorization, the applicant certifies to the competent authorities of the Member State concerned that :

(i) neither he nor any other natural or legal person with whom he is connected has, during the preceding five years, applied for authorization to place a product containing the same active principle(s) on the market of another Member State ; and

(ii) neither he nor any other natural or legal person with whom he is connected intends, within the five years following the date of the application, to seek authorization to place a product containing the same active principle(s) on the market of another Member State.

In this case, the competent authorities shall notify the appropriate Committee of the application and forward to it a summary of product characteristics as described in Article 4a of Directive 65/65/EEC (¹), as last amended by Directive 87/21/EEC (²) or an equivalent document provided by the applicant if a proprietary medicinal product referred to in the second paragraph of Article 34 of Directive 75/319/EEC or a veterinary medicinal product is involved.

If, within five years of the first application, one or more subsequent applications for authorization to place a product containing the same active principle derived from the same route of synthesis on the market are made to the competent authorities of the other Member States by the person responsible for placing the original product on the market or with his consent, that person shall forthwith inform the competent authorities of the Member State to whom the first application was made and the matter shall be brought before the appropriate Committee for an opinion.

(¹) OJ No 22, 9. 2. 1965, p. 369/65.
(²) See page 36 of this Official Journal.

4. Where the Committee has, in accordance with this Directive, issued a favourable opinion on the placing on the market of a high-technology medicinal product, the competent authorities shall refer the matter to the Committee for a new opinion before deciding on the withdrawal or, subject to Article 4 (2), suspension of the marketing authorization for the medicinal product in question.

5. The competent authorities or the Commission may also consult the Committee for Proprietary Medicinal Products on any technical question concerning the proprietary medicinal products referred to in the second paragraph of Article 34 of Directive 75/319/EEC.

6. The competent authorities or the Commission may also consult the Committee for Veterinary Medicinal Products on any technical question concerning the veterinary medicinal products referred to in the second and third indents of Article 2 (2) of Directive 81/851/EEC.

Article 3

1. The representative of the Member State which initiated the procedure referred to in Article 2 shall act as rapporteur and shall provide all information relevant to the evaluation of the medicinal product. Information thus disclosed shall strictly confidential.

2. The person responsible for placing the medicinal product in question on the market shall immediately be informed of the referral to the Committee. He may, at this own request, provide the Committee with oral or written explanations.

3. When placing the matter before the Committee, the Member State concerned shall ensure that the person responsible for placing the medicinal product on the market transmits to all the members of the Committee an identical summary of the dossier consisting of the summary of the product characteristics together with the reports of the analytical, pharmaco-toxicological and clinical experts.

In addition, a complete and updated copy of the dossier for the application for marketing authorization lodged with the Member State or Member States concerned shall be transmitted to the Committee by the person responsible for placing the product on the market, who shall certify that all the dossiers submitted to the competent authorities and to the Committee in respect of the medicinal product in question are identical.

4. All available evaluation reports and drug-monitoring reports relating to the same medicinal product shall be forwarded to the Committee by the authorities of the Member States and by the person responsible for placing the product in question on the market.

Article 4

1. When the questions referred to it relate to an application for marketing authorization, the Committee shall issue its opinion thirty days before the expiry of the time limits provided for in Article 7 of Directive 65/65/EEC and Article 4 (c) of Directive 75/319/EEC, or in Articles 8 and 9 (3) of Directive 81/851/EEC, as appropriate. To this end, the Member State which referred the matter shall inform the Committee without delay of any extension and of the beginning and end of any suspension of the time limits concerned.

2. When a proposal to suspend or withdraw a marketing authorization is referred to it, the Committee shall fix an appropriate time limit for issuing its reasoned opinion, having regard to the requirements for the protection of public health. However, in cases of urgency, the Member States may suspend the mrketing authorization in question without waiting for the opinion of the Committee provided that they forthwith inform the Committee thereof, indicating the reasons for the suspension and justifying the urgency of this measure.

3. The Committee shall forthwith notify its opinion and, where relevant, any dissenting opinions expressed therein, to the Member State concerned and the person responsible for placing the product on the market.

4. The Member State concerned shall reach a decision on the action it intends to take following the Committee's opinion not later than 30 days after receipt of the information provided for in paragraph 3. It shall forthwith inform the Committee of its decision.

Article 5

Subject to the application of other Community provisions, Member States shall communicate to the Commission in accordance with Articles 8 and 9 of Council Directive 83/189/EEC of 28 March 1983 laying down a procedure for the provision of information in the field of technical standards regulations (¹), draft technical regulations relating to the production and marketing or proprietary medicinal products as defined in Article 1 of Directive 65/65/EEC.

Within one year of adoption of this Directive, the Commission will submit to the Council proposals for Regulations to harmonize, along the lines of Directive 75/319/EEC, the conditions for authorizing the manufacture and placing on the market of the proprietary medicinal products excluded by Article 34 of Directive 75/319/EEC and of the veterinary medicinal products referred to in Article 2 (2) of Directive 81/851/EEC, in view of in particular of the safety problems arising in production and use.

Article 6

Member States shall take the measures necessary to comply with this Directive not later than 1 July 1987. They shall forthwith inform the Commission thereof.

Article 7

This Directive is addressed to the Member States.

Done at Brussels, 22 December 1986.

For the Council
The President
G. SHAW

(¹) OJ No L 109, 26. 4. 1983, p. 8.

ANNEX

LIST OF HIGH-TECHNOLOGY MEDICINAL PRODUCTS

A. **Medicinal products developed by means of the following biotechnological processes:**

— recombinant DNA technology,

— controlled expression of genes coding for biologically active proteins in prokaryotes and eukaryotes, including transformed mammalian cells,

— hybridoma and monoclonal antibody methods.

B. **Other high-technology medicinal products**

— other biotechnological processes which, in the opinion of the competent authority concerned constitute a significant innovation,

— medicinal products administered by means of new delivery systems which, in the opinion of the competent authority concerned, constitute a significant innovation,

— medicinal products containing a new substance or an entirely new indication which, in the opinion of the competent authority concerned, is of significant therapeutic interest,

— new medicinal products based on radio-isotopes which, in the opinion of the competent authority concerned, are of significant therapeutic interest,

— medicinal products the manufacture of which employs processes which, in the opinion of the competent authority concerned, demonstrate a significant technical advance such as two-dimensional electrophoresis under micro-gravity.

COUNCIL DIRECTIVE 93/41/EEC

of 14 June 1993

repealing Directive 87/22/EEC on the approximation of national measures relating to the placing on the market of high-technology medicinal products, particularly those derived from biotechnology

THE COUNCIL OF THE EUROPEAN COMMUNITIES,

Having regard to the Treaty establishing the European Economic Community, and in particular Article 100a thereof,

Having regard to the proposal from the Commission ([1]),

In cooperation with the European Parliament ([2]),

Having regard to the opinion of the Economic and Social Committee ([3]),

Whereas the provisions of Directive 87/22/EEC ([4]) have now been superseded by the provisions of Council Regulation (EEC) No 2309/93 of 22 July 1993 laying down Community procedures for the authorization and supervision of medicinal products for human and veterinary use and establishing a European Agency for the Evaluation of Medicinal Products ([5]) and by Council Directive 88/182/EEC of 22 March 1988 amending Directive 83/189/EEC laying down a procedure for the provision of information in the field of technical standards and regulations ([6]);

Whereas provision has been made in Directive 93/39/EEC ([7]) for the continued management of marketing authorizations ·which have been granted by Member States following the opinion of the Committee for Proprietary Medicinal Products given in accordance with Directive 87/22/EEC;

Whereas, furthermore, provision has been made in Directive 93/40/EEC ([8]) for the continued management of marketing authorization which have been granted by Member States following the opinion of the Committee for Veterinary Medicinal Products given in accordance with Directive 87/22/EEC;

Whereas Directive 87/22/EEC should therefore be repealed;

Whereas in the interests of legal certainty, provision should be made for the continued examination of applications for marketing authorization which have been referred to the Committee for Proprietary Medicinal Products or the. Committee for Veterinary Medicinal Products in accordance with Directive 87/22/EEC before 1 January 1995,

HAS ADOPTED THIS DIRECTIVE:

Article 1

With effect from 1 January 1995, Directive 87/22/EEC is hereby repealed.

Article 2

Applications for marketing authorizations which have been referred to the Committee for Proprietary Medicinal Products or to the Committee for Veterinary Medicinal Products before 1 January 1995 in accordance with Article 2 of Directive 87/22/EEC and in respect of which the Committee concerned has not given an opinion by 1 January 1995 shall be considered in accordance with Regulation (EEC) No 2309/93.

Article 3

Member States shall take all appropriate measures to comply with this Directive with effect from 1 January 1995. They shall forthwith inform the Commission thereof.

When Member States adopt these provisions, they shall contain a reference to this Directive or shall be accompanied by such reference at the time of their official publication. The methods of making such a reference shall be laid down by the Member States.

Article 4

This Directive is addressed to the Member States.

Done at Luxembourg, 14 June 1993.

For the Council
The President
J. TRØJBORG

([1]) OJ No C 58, 8. 3. 1990, p. 1.
([2]) OJ No C 183, 15. 7. 1991, p. 145 and
    OJ No C 150, 31. 5. 1993.
([3]) OJ No C 269, 14. 10. 1991, p. 84.
([4]) OJ No L 15, 17. 1. 1987, p. 38.
([5]) See page 1 of this Official Journal.
([6]) OJ No L 81, 26. 3. 1988, p. 75.
([7]) See page 22 of this Official Journal.
([8]) See page 31 of this Official Journal.

COUNCIL DIRECTIVE

of 3 May 1989

extending the scope of Directives 65/65/EEC and 75/319/EEC and laying down additional provisions for immunological medicinal products consisting of vaccines, toxins or serums and allergens

(89/342/EEC)

THE COUNCIL OF THE EUROPEAN COMMUNITIES,

Hacing regard to the Treaty establishing the European Economic Community, and in particular Article 100a thereof,

Having regard to the proposal from the Commission (¹),

In cooperation with the European Parliament (²),

Having regard to the opinion of the Economic and Social Committee (³),

Whereas disparities in the provisions laid down by law, regulation or administrative action by Member States may hinder trade in immunological products within the Community;

Whereas the essential aim of any rules governing the production, distribution or use of medicinal products must be to safeguard public health;

Whereas Directive 65/65/EEC (⁴), as last amended by Directive 87/21/EEC (⁵), and Second Directive 75/319/EEC (⁶), as last amended by Directive 83/570/EEC (⁷), on the approximation of provisions laid down by law, regulation or administrative action relating to proprietary medicinal products, although appropriate, are inadequate for immunological medicinal products consisting of vaccines, toxins or serums and allergens;

Whereas, in accordance with Article 5 of Council Directive 87/22/EEC of 22 December 1986 on the approximation of national measures relating to the placing on the market of high-technology medicinal products, particularly those derived from biotechnology (⁸), the Commission is required to submit proposals to harmonize, along the lines of Directive 75/319/EEC, the conditions for authorizing the manufacture and placing on the market of immunological medicinal products before 22 December 1987;

Whereas, before an authorization to market an immunological product can be granted, the manufacturer must demonstrate his ability to attain batch-to-batch consistency;

Whereas the Commission should be empowered to adopt any necessary changes in the requirements for the testing of proprietary medicinal products set out in the Annex to Council Directive 75/318/EEC of 20 May 1975 on the approximation of the laws of the Member States relating to analytical, pharmaco-toxicological and clinical standards and protocols in respect of the testing of proprietary medicinal products (⁹), as last amended by Directive 87/19/EEC (¹⁰), to take account of the special nature of immunological medicinal products in close cooperation with the Committee for the Adaptation to Technical Progress of the Directives on the Removal of Technical Barriers to Trade in the Proprietary Medicinal Products Sector, thus ensuring greater quality, safety and efficacy,

HAS ADOPTED THIS DIRECTIVE:

Article 1

1. In derogation from Article 34 of Directive 75/319/EEC, and subject to the provisions of this Directive, Directives 65/65/EEC and 75/319/EEC shall apply to immunological medicinal products for human use consisting of vaccines, toxins or serums and allergen products.

2. For the purposes of this Directive, the following definitions shall apply:

— 'allergen product' shall mean any product which is intended to identify or induce a specific acquired alteration in the immunological response to an allergizing agent,

— vaccines, toxins and serums shall have the meaning assigned to them in the Annex to Directive 75/319/EEC.

Article 2

1. The quantitative particulars of an immunological medicinal product shall be expressed by mass or by international units or by units of biological activity or by specific protein content, where possible, as appropriate to the product concerned.

(¹) OJ No C 36, 8. 2. 1988, p. 25.
(²) OJ No C 290, 14. 11. 1988, p. 131; OJ No C 120, 16. 5. 1989.
(³) OJ No C 208, 8. 8. 1988, p. 64.
(⁴) OJ No 22, 9. 2. 1965, p. 369/65.
(⁵) OJ No L 15, 17. 1. 1987, p. 36.
(⁶) OJ No L 147, 9. 6. 1975, p. 13.
(⁷) OJ No L 332, 28. 11. 1983, p. 1.
(⁸) OJ No L 15, 17. 1. 1987, p. 38.

(⁹) OJ No L 147, 9. 6. 1975, p. 1.
(¹⁰) OJ No L 15, 17. 1. 1987, p. 31.

...pect of immunological products in Directives ...EC and 75/319/EEC the expressions 'qualitative ...quantitative particulars of the constitutents' shall also ...clude particulars relating to biological activity or to protein content and 'qualitative and quantitative composition' shall include the composition of the product expressed in terms of biological activity or of protein content.

3. Whenever the name of an immunological medicinal product is expressed, the common or scientific name of the active constituents shall also be included.

Article 3

In addition to the information referred to in Article 4a of Directive 65/65/EEC the summary of product characteristics referred to in point 9 of the second subparagraph of Article 4 of Directive 65/65/EEC shall contain the following information in respect of immunological products:

— under point 5.4, information regarding any special precautions to be taken by persons handling the immunological medicinal product and persons administering it to patients, together with any precautions to be taken by the patient.

Article 4

1. Member States shall take all appropriate steps to ensure that the manufacturing processes used in the manufacture of immunological products are properly validated and attain batch-to-batch consistency.

2. For the purpose of implementing Article 8 of Directive 65/65/EEC and Article 27 of Directive 75/319/EEC, Member States may require manufacturers of immunological products to submit to a competent authority copies of all the control reports signed by the qualified person in accordance with Article 22 of Directive 75/319/EEC.

3. Where it considers it necessary in the interests of public health, a Member State may require persons responsible for marketing:

— live vaccines,

— immunological medicinal products used in the primary immunization of infants or of other groups at risk,

— immunological medicinal products used in public health immunization programmes,

— new immunological medicinal products or immunological medicinal products manufactured using new or altered kinds of technology or new for a particular manufacturer, during a transitional period normally specified in the marketing authorization,

to submit samples from each batch of the bulk and/or finished product for examination by a State laboratory or a laboratory designated for that purpose before release on to the market unless, in the case of a batch manufactured in another Member State, the competent authority of another Member State has previously examined the batch in question and declared it to be in conformity with the approved specifications. Member States shall ensure that any such examiniation is completed within 60 days of the receipt of the samples.

Article 5

Any amendents which are necesssary in the testing requirements for medicinal products set out in the Annex to Directive 75/318/EEC to take account of the extension of the scope of Directives 65/65/EEC and 75/319/EEC to cover immunological medicinal products shall be adopted in accordance with the procedure laid down in Article 2c of Directive 75/318/EEC.

Article 6

1. Except as provided in paragraph 2, Member States shall take the necessary measures to comply with this Directive not later than 1 January 1992. They shall forthwith inform the Commission thereof.

2. If the amendments to Directive 75/318/EEC referred to in Article 5 have not been adopted by the date referred to in paragraph 1, this Directive shall come into force on the same date as those amendments.

3. Requests for marketing authorizations for products covered by this Directive lodged after the date on which it comes into force must comply with the provisions of this Directive.

4. This Directive shall be progressively extended to existing immunological medicinal products before 31 December 1992.

Article 7

This Directive is addressed to the Member States.

Done at Brussels, 3 May 1989.

For the Council
The President
P. SOLBES

COUNCIL DIRECTIVE

of 3 May 1989

extending the scope of Directives 65/65/EEC and 75/319/EEC and laying down additional provisions for radiopharmaceuticals

(89/343/EEC)

THE COUNCIL OF THE EUROPEAN COMMUNITIES,

Having regard to the Treaty establishing the European Economic Community, and in particular Article 100a thereof,

Having regard to the proposal from the Commission (¹),

In cooperation with the European Parliament (²),

Having regard to the opinion of the Economic and Social Committee (³),

Whereas disparities in the provisions currently laid down by law, regulation or administrative action by Member States may hinder trade in radiopharmaceuticals within the Community;

Whereas the essential aim of any rules governing the production, distributio or use of medicinal products must be to safeguard public health;

Whereas the provisions laid down by Directive 65/65/EEC (⁴), as last amended by Directive 87/21/EEC (⁵), and by Second Directive 75/319/EEC (⁶), as last amended by Directive 83/570/EEC (⁷), on the approximation of provisions laid down by law, regulation or administrative action relating to proprietary medicinal products, although appropriate, are inadequate for radiopharmaceuticals;

Whereas, in accordance with Article 5 of Council Directive 87/22/EEC of 22 December 1986 on the approximation of national provisions relating to the placing on the market of high technology medicinal products, particularly those derived from biotechnology (⁸), the Commission is required to submit proposals to harmonize, along the lines of Directive 75/319/EEC, the conditions for authorizing the manufacture and placing on the market of radiopharmaceuticals before 22 December 1987;

Whereas, in the case of radiopharmaceuticals, generators, kits and precursors, authorization should be required;

whereas, however, a specific authorization should not be required for radiopharmaceuticals in their finished form which are made up exclusively from authorized kits, generators or precursor radiopharmaceuticals in health care establishments;

Whereas the Commission should be empowered to adopt any necessary changes in the requirements for the testing of proprietary medicinal products set out in the Annex to Council Directive 75/318/EEC of 20 May 1975 on the approximation of the laws of the Member States relating to analytical, pharmacotoxicological and clinical standards and protocols in respect of the testing of proprietary medicinal products (⁹), as last amended by Directive 87/19/EEC (¹⁰), to take account of the special nature of radiopharmaceuticals in close cooperation with the Committee for the Adaptation to Technical Progress of the Directives on the Removal of Technical Barriers to Trade in the Proprietary Medicinal Products Sector, thus ensuring the greater quality, safety and efficacy of the medicinal products;

Whereas any rules governing radiopharmaceuticals must take into account the provisions of Council Directive 84/466/Euratom of 3 September 1984 laying down basic measures for the radiation protection of persons undergoing medical examination or treatment (¹¹); whereas account should also be taken of Council Directive 80/836/Euratom of 15 July 1980 amending the Directives laying down the basic safety standards for the health protection of the general public and workers against the dangers of ionizing radiation (¹²), as last amended by Directive 84/467/Euratom (¹³), the objective of which is to prevent the exposure of workers or patients to excessive or unnecessarily high levels of ionizing radiation, and in particular of Article 5c thereof, which requires prior authorization for the addition of radioactive substances to medicinal products as well as for the importation of such medicinal products,

HAS ADOPTED THIS DIRECTIVE:

Article 1

1. In derogation from Article 34 of Directive 75/319/EEC, and subject to the provisions of this Directive,

---

(¹) OJ No C 36, 8. 2. 1988, p. 30.
(²) OJ No C 290, 14. 11. 1988, p. 136; OJ No C 120, 16. 5. 1989.
(³) OJ No C 208, 8. 8. 1988, p. 64.
(⁴) OJ No 22, 9. 2. 1965, p. 369/65.
(⁵) OJ No L 15, 17. 1. 1987, p. 36.
(⁶) OJ No L 147, 9. 6. 1975, p. 13.
(⁷) OJ No L 332, 28. 11. 1983, p. 1.
(⁸) OJ No L 15, 17. 1. 1987, p. 38.

(⁹) OJ No L 147, 9. 6. 1975, p. 1.
(¹⁰) OJ No L 15, 17. 1. 1987, p. 31.
(¹¹) OJ No L 265, 5. 10. 1984, p. 1.
(¹²) OJ No L 246, 17. 9. 1980, p. 1.
(¹³) OJ No L 265, 5. 10. 1984, p. 4.

the provisions of Directives 65/65/EEC and 75/319/EEC shall apply to radiopharmaceuticals for human use, excluding radionuclides in the form of sealed sources.

2. For the purposes of this Directive, the following definitions apply:

— 'radiopharmaceutical' shall mean any medicinal product which, when ready for use, contains one or more radionuclides (radioactive isotopes) included for a medicinal purpose,

— 'generator' shall mean any system incorporating a fixed parent radionuclide from which is produced a daughter radionuclide which is to be removed by elution or by any other method and used in a radiopharmaceutical,

— 'kit' shall mean any preparation to be reconstituted or combined with radionucliedes in the final radiopharmaceutical, usually prior to its administration,

— 'precursor' shall mean any other radionuclide produced for the radio-labelling of another substance prior to administration.

3. Nothing in this Directive shall in any way derogate from the Community rules for the radiation protection of persons undergoing medical examination or treatment or from the Community rules laying down the basic safety standards for the health protection of the general public and workers against the dangers of ionizing radiation.

Article 2

The authorization referred to in Article 3 of Directive 65/65/EEC shall be required for generators, kits, precursor radiopharmaceuticals and industrially prepared radiopharmaceuticals. However, authorization shall not be required for a radiopharmaceutical prepared at the time of use by a person or by an establishment authorized, according to national legislation, to use such medicinal products in an approved health care establishment exclusively from authorized generators, kits or precursor radiopharmaceuticals in accordance with the manufacturer's instructions.

Article 3

In addition to the requirements set out in Article 4 of Directive 65/65/EEC, an application for authorization to market a generator shall also contain the following information and particulars:

— a general description of the system together with a detailed description of the components of the system which may effect the composition or quality of the daughter nucleid preparation,

— qualitative and quantitative particulars of the eluate or the sublimate.

Article 4

For radiopharmaceuticals, in addition to the information referred to in Article 4a of Directive 65/65/EEC, the summary of product characteristics referred to in point 9 of the second paragraph of Article 4 of Directive 65/65/EEC shall contain the following additional points 7 and 8:

'7. Full details of internal radiation dosimetry.

8. Additional detailed instructions for extemporaneous preparation and quality control of such preparation and, where appropriate, maximum storage time during which any intermediate preparation such as an eluate or the ready to use pharmaceutical will conform with its specifications.'

Article 5

The outer carton and the container of medicinal products containing radionuclides shall be labelled in accordance with the regulations for the safe transport of radioactive materials laid down by the International Atomic Energy Agency. Moreover, the labelling shall comply with the following provisions:

(a) The label on the shielding shall include the particulars mentioned in Article 13 of Directive 65/65/EEC. In addition, the labelling on the shielding shall explain in full the codings used on the vial and shall indicate, where necessary, for a given time and date, the amount of radioactivity per dose or per vial and the number of capsules, or, for liquids, the number of millilitres in the container;

(b) The vial shall be labelled with the following information:

— the name or code of the medicinal product, including the name or chemical symbol of the radionuclide;

— the batch identification and expiry date,

— the international symbol for radioactivity,

— the name of the manufacturer,

— the amount of radioactivity as specified under (a).

Article 6

1. Member States shall ensure that a detailed instruction leaflet is enclosed with the packaging of radiopharmaceuticals, generators, kits or precursor radiopharmaceuticals. The text of this leaflet shall be established in accordance with the provisions of Article 6 of Directive 75/319/EEC and shall contain all the information referred to therein. In addition, the leaflet shall include any precautions to be taken by the user and the patient during the

preparation and administration of the product and special precautions for the disposal of the container and its unused contents.

2. Without prejudice to Article 8 of Directive 65/65/EEC and Article 6 of Directive 75/319/EEC, Member States shall permit the use of user information leaflets which have been established in more than one of the languages of the Community provided that the information contained in all the language versions of the leaflet is identical.

Article 7

Any amendments which are necessary in the testing requirements for medicinal products set out in the Annex to Directive 75/318/EEC to take account of the extension of the scope of Directives 65/65/EEC and 75/319/EEC to cover radiopharmaceuticals shall be adopted in accordance with the procedure laid down in Article 2c of Directive 75/318/EEC.

Article 8

1. Save in the case provided for in paragraph 2, Member States shall take the necessary measures to comply with this Directive not later than 1 January 1992. They shall forthwith inform the Commission thereof.

2. If the amendments to Directive 75/318/EEC referred to in Article 7 have not been adopted by the date referred to in paragraph 1, this Directive shall come into force on the same date as those amendments.

3. Requests for marketing authorization for products covered by ths Directive lodged after the date of entry into force must comply with the provisions of this Directive.

4. This Directive shall be progressively extended to existing radiopharmaceutical medicinal products covered by this Directive before 31 December 1992.

Article 9

This Directive is addressed to the Member States.

Done at Brussels, 3 May 1989.

For the Council
The President
P. SOLBES

II

(Acts whose publication is not obligatory)

COUNCIL

COUNCIL DIRECTIVE

of 14 June 1989

extending the scope of Directives 65/65/EEC and 75/319/EEC on the approximation of provisions laid down by law, regulation or administrative action relating to proprietary medicinal products and laying down special provisions for medicinal products derived from human blood or human plasma

(89/381/EEC)

THE COUNCIL OF THE EUROPEAN COMMUNITIES,

Having regard to the Treaty establishing the European Economic Community, and in particular Article 100a thereof,

Having regard to the proposal from the Commission ([1]),

In cooperation with the European Parliament ([2]),

Having regard to the opinion of the Economic and Social Committee ([3]),

Whereas disparities in the laws, regulations or administrative provisions of Member States may hinder trade in medicinal products derived from human blood or human plasma within the Community;

Whereas the essential aim of any rules governing the production, distribution or use of medicinal products must be to ensure a high level of protection of public health;

Whereas the provisions laid down by Directive 65/65/EEC ([4]), as last amended by Directive 87/21/EEC ([5]), and by Directive 75/319/EEC ([6]), as last amended by Directive 83/570/EEC ([7]), both concerning the approximation of provisions laid down by law, regulation or administrative action relating to proprietary medicinal products, although appropriate, are inadequate with regard to medicinal products derived from human blood or human plasma;

Whereas in accordance with Article 5 of Council Directive 87/22/EEC of 22 December 1986 on the approximation of national provisions relating to the placing on the market of high-technology medicinal products, particularly those derived from biotechnology ([8]); the Commission is required to submit proposals to harmonize, along the lines of Directive 75/319/EEC, the conditions for authorizing the manufacture and placing on the market of medicinal products derived from human blood or human plasma;

Whereas the Community entirely supports the efforts of the Council of Europe to promote voluntary unpaid blood and plasma donation to attain self-sufficiency throughout the Community in the supply of blood products, and to ensure respect for ethical principles in trade in therapeutic substances of human origin;

Whereas the rules designed to guarantee the quality, safety and efficacy of medicinal products derived from human blood or human plasma must be applied in the same manner to both public and private establishments, and to blood and plasma imported from third countries;

Whereas, before an authorization to market a medicinal product derived from human blood or human plasma can be granted, the manufacturer must demonstrate his ability to guarantee batch-to-batch consistency and the absence of specific viral contamination, to the extent that the state of technology permits;

([1]) OJ No C 308, 3. 12. 1988, p. 21.
([2]) OJ No C 290, 14. 12. 1988, p. 134 and
   OJ No C 120, 16. 5. 1989.
([3]) OJ No C 208, 8. 8. 1988, p. 64.
([4]) OJ No 22, 9. 2. 1965, p. 369/65.
([5]) OJ No L 15, 17. 1. 1987, p. 36.
([6]) OJ No L 147, 9. 6. 1975, p. 13.
([7]) OJ No L 332, 28. 11. 1983, p. 1.

([8]) OJ No L 15, 17. 1. 1987, p. 38.

Whereas the Commission should be empowered to adopt, in close cooperation with the Committee for the Adaptation to Technical Progress of the Directives on the Removal of Technical Barriers to Trade in Medicinal Products, any necessary changes in the requirements for the testing of proprietary medicinal products set out in the Annex to Council Directive 75/318/EEC of 20 May 1975 on the approximation of the laws of the Member States relating to analytical, pharmaco-toxicological and clinical standards and protocols in respect of the testing of proprietary medicinal products ([1]), as last amended by Directive 87/19/EEC ([2]), to take account of the special nature of medicinal products derived from human blood or human plasma so as to ensure a higher level of quality, safety and efficacy,

HAS ADOPTED THIS DIRECTIVE :

Article 1

1. By way of derogation from Article 34 of Directive 75/319/EEC, and subject to the provisions of this Directive, Directives 65/65/EEC and 75/319/EEC shall aplly to medicinal products based on blood constituents which are prepared industrially by public or private establishments, hereinafter referred to as 'medicinal products derived from human blood or human plasma'; these medicinal products include, in particular albumin, coagulating factors and immunoglobulins of human origin.

2. This Directive shall not apply to whole blood, to plasma or to blood cells of human origin.

3. This Directive shall be without prejudice to Council Decision 86/346/EEC of 25 June 1986 accepting on behalf of the Community the European Agreement relating to the Exchange of Therapeutic Substances of Human Origin ([3]).

Article 2

1. The quantitative particulars of a medicinal product derived from human blood or human plasma shall be expressed by mass or by international units or by units of biological activity as appropriate to the product concerned.

2. In Directives 65/65/EEC and 75/319/EEC the expressions 'qualitative and quantitative particulars of the constituents' shall include particulars relating to biological activity and 'qualitative and quantitative composition' shall include the composition of the product expressed in terms of biological activity.

3. In any document drawn up for the purposes of this Directive, where the name of a medicinal product derived from human blood or human plasma is expressed, the common or scientific name of the active constituents shall also be included at least once ; it may be abbreviated in the remaining references.

Article 3

In respect of the use of human blood or human plasma as a starting material for the manufacture of medicinal products :

1. Member States shall take the necessary measures to prevent the transmission of infectious diseases. Insofar as this is covered by the amendments referred to in Article 6, as well as the application of the monographs of the European Pharmacopoeia regarding blood and plasma, these measures shall comprise those recommended by the Council of Europe and the World Health Organization, particularly with reference to the selection and testing of blood and plasma donors ;

2. Member States shall take the necessary measures to ensure that human blood and human plasma donors and donation centres are always clearly identifiable ;

3. All the safety guarantees referred to in paragraphs 1 and 2 must also be given by importers of human blood or human plasma from third countries ;

4. Member States shall take the necessary measures to promote Community self-sufficiency in human blood or human plasma. For this purpose, they shall encourage the voluntary unpaid donation of blood and plasma and shall take the necessary measures to develop the production and use of products derived from human blood or human plasma coming from voluntary unpaid donations. They shall notify the Commission of such measures.

Article 4

1. Member States shall take all necessary measures to ensure that the manufacturing and purifying processes used in the preparation of medicinal products derived from human blood or human plasma are properly validated, attain batch-to-batch consistency and guarantee, insofar as the state of technology permits, the absence of specific viral contamination. To this end manufacturers shall notify the competent authorities of the method used to reduce or eliminate pathogenic viruses liable to be transmitted by medicinal products derived from human blood or human plasma. The ocmpetent authority may submit samples of the bulk and/or finished product for testing by a State laboratory or a laboratory designated for that purpose, either during the examination of the application pursuant to Article 4 of Directive 75/319/EEC, or after a marketing authorization has been granted.

([1]) OJ No L 147, 9. 6. 1975, p. 1.
([2]) OJ No L 15, 17. 1. 1987, p. 31.
([3]) OJ No L 207, 30. 7. 1986, p. 1.

2. For the purpose of implementing Article 8 of Directive 65/65/EEC and Article 27 of Directive 75/319/EEC, Member States may require manufacturers of medicinal products derived from human blood or human plasma to submit to a competent authority copies of all the control reports signed by the qualified person, in accordance with Article 22 of Directive 75/319/EEC.

3. Where, in the interests of public health, the laws of a Member State so provide, the competent authorities may require persons responsible for marketing medicinal products derived from human blood or human plasma to submit samples from each batch of the bulk and/or finished product for testing by a State laboratory or a laboratory designated for that purpose before being released into free circulation, unless the competent authorities of another Member State have previously examined the batch in question and declared it to be in conformity with the approved specifications. Member States shall ensure that any such examination is completed within sixty days of the receipt of the samples.

Article 5

The procedure laid down in Directive 87/22/EEC shall be extended as necessary to cover medicinal products derived from human blood or human plasma.

Article 6

Any necessary amendments to the testing requirements for medicinal products set out in the Annex to Directive 75/318/EEC to take account of the extension of the scope of Directives 65/65/EEC and 75/319/EEC to cover medicinal products derived from human blood or human plasma shall be adopted in accordance with the procedure laid down in Article 2c of Directive 75/318/EEC.

Article 7

1. Save in the case provided for in paragraph 2, Member States shall take the necessary measures to comply with this Directive before 1 January 1992. They shall forthwith inform the Commission thereof.

2. In the event of the amendments to Directive 75/318/EEC referred to in Article 6 not being adopted by the date referred to in paragraph 1, this date shall be replaced by the date of adoption of the said amendments.

3. Requests for marketing authorization for the products concerned lodged after the date of application of this Directive shall comply with the provisions thereof.

4. This Directive shall be progressively extended, before 31 December 1992, to existing medicinal products derived from human blood or human plasma, referred to in Article 1 (1).

Article 8

This Directive is addressed to the Member States.

Done at Luxembourg, 14 June 1989.

For the Council
The President
P. SOLBES

II

(Acts whose publication is not obligatory)

COUNCIL

COUNCIL DIRECTIVE 92/25/EEC

of 31 March 1992

on the wholesale distribution of medicinal products for human use

THE COUNCIL OF THE EUROPEAN COMMUNITIES,

Having regard to the Treaty establishing the European Economic Community, and in particular Article 100a thereof,

Having regard to the proposal from the Commission (¹),

in cooperation with the European Parliament (²),

Having regard to the opinion of the Economic and Social Committee (³),

Whereas it is important to adopt measures with the aim of progressively establishing the internal market over a period expiring on 31 December 1992; whereas the internal market is to comprise an area without internal frontiers in which the free movement of goods, persons, services and capital is ensured;

Whereas the wholesale distribution of medicinal products is at present subject to different provisions in the various Member States; whereas many operations involving the wholesale distribution of medicinal products for human use may cover several Member States simultaneously;

Whereas it is necessary to exercise control over the entire chain of distribution of medicinal products, from their

manufacture or import into the Community through to supply to the public, so as to guarantee that such products are stored, transported and handled in suitable conditions; whereas the requirements which must be adopted for this purpose will considerably facilitate the withdrawal of defective products from the market and allow more effective efforts against counterfeit products;

Whereas any person involved in the wholesale distribution of medicinal products should be in possession of a special authorization; whereas pharmacists and persons authorized to supply medicinal products directly to the public, and who confine themselves to this activity, should be exempt from obtaining this authorization; whereas it is however necessary, in order to control the complete chain of distribution of medicinal products, that pharmacists and persons authorized to supply medicinal products to the public keep records showing transactions in products received;

Whereas authorization must be subject to certain essential conditions and it is the responsibility of the Member State concerned to ensure that such conditions are met; whereas each Member State must recognize authorizations granted by other Member States;

Whereas certain Member States impose on wholesalers who supply medicinal products to pharmacists and on persons authorized to supply medicinal products to the public certain public service obligations; whereas those Member States must be able to continue to impose those obligations on wholesalers established within their territory; whereas they must also be able to impose them on wholesalers in other Member States on condition that they do not impose any obligation more stringent than those which they impose on their own wholesalers and provided that such obligations may be regarded as

(¹) OJ No C 58, 8. 3. 1990, p. 16 and
OJ No C 207, 8. 8. 1991, p. 11.
(²) OJ No C 183, 15. 7. 1991, p. 139,
and OJ No C 67, 16. 3. 1992.
(³) OJ No C 269, 14. 10. 1991, p. 84.

warranted on grounds of public health protection and are proportionate in relation to the objective of such protection,

HAS ADOPTED THIS DIRECTIVE:

Article 1

1. This Directive covers the wholesale distribution in the Community of medicinal products for human use to which Chapters II to V of Council Directive 65/65/EEC of 26 January 1965 on the approximation of provisions laid down by law, regulation or administrative action relating to medicinal products (¹) apply.

2. For the purposes of this Directive:

— *wholesale distribution of medicinal products* shall mean all activities consisting of procuring, holding, supplying or exporting medicinal products, apart from supplying medicinal products to the public; such activities are carried out with manufacturers or their depositories, importers, other wholesale distributors or with pharmacists and persons authorized or entitled to supply medicinal products to the public in the Member State concerned,

— *public service obligation* shall mean the obligation placed on wholesalers to guarantee permanently an adequate range of medicinal products to meet the requirements of a specific geographical area and to deliver the supplies requested within a very short time over the whole of the area in question.

Article 2

Without prejudice to Article 3 of Directive 65/65/EEC, Member States shall take all appropriate action to ensure that only medicinal products in respect of which a marketing authorization has been granted in accordance with Community law are distributed on their territory.

Article 3

1. Member States shall take all appropriate measures to ensure that the wholesale distribution of medicinal products is subject to the possession of an authorization to engage in activity as a wholesaler in medicinal products, stating the place for which it is valid.

2. Where persons authorized or entitled to supply medicinal products to the public may also, under national law, engage in wholesale business, such persons shall be subject to the authorization provided for in paragraph 1.

3. Possession of an authorization, as mentioned in Article 16 of Second Council Directive 75/319/EEC of 20 May 1975 on the approximation of provisions laid down by law, regulation or administrative action relating to proprietary medicinal products (²), shall include authorization to distribute by wholesale the medicinal products covered by that authorization. Possession of an authorization to engage in activity as a wholesaler in medicinal products shall not give dispensation from the obligation to possess a manufacturing authorization and to comply with the conditions set out in that respect, even where the manufacturing or import business is secondary.

4. At the request of the Commission or any Member State, Member States shall supply all appropriate information concerning the individual authorizations which they have granted under paragraph 1.

5. Checks on the persons and establishments authorized to engage in the activity of wholesaler in medicinal products and the inspection of their premises shall be carried out under the responsibility of the Member State which granted the authorization.

6. The Member State which granted the authorization referred to in paragraph 1 shall suspend or revoke that authorization if the conditions of authorization cease to be met. It shall forthwith inform the other Member States and the Commission thereof.

7. Should a Member State consider that, in respect of a person holding an authorization granted by another Member State under the terms of paragraph 1, the conditions of authorization are not, or are no longer, met, it shall forthwith inform the Commission and the other Member State involved. The latter shall take the measures necessary and shall inform the Commission and the first Member State of the decisions taken and the reasons for those decisions.

Article 4

1. Member States shall ensure that the time taken for the procedure for examining the application for the authorization referred to in Article 3 (1) does not exceed 90 days from the day on which the competent authority of the Member State concerned receives the application.

The competent authority may, if need be, require the applicant to supply all necessary information concerning the conditions of authorization. Where the authority exercises this option, the period laid down in this

---

(¹) OJ No 22, 9. 2. 1965, p. 369/65. Directive last amended by Directive 89/341/EEC (OJ No L 142, 25. 5. 1989, p. 11).

(²) OJ No L 147, 9. 6. 1975, p. 13. Directive last amended by Directive 89/381/EEC (OJ No L 181, 28. 6. 1989, p. 44).

paragraph shall be suspended until the requisite additional data have been supplied.

2. All decisions to refuse, suspend or revoke the authorization referred to in Article 3 (1) shall state in detail the reasons on which they are based. A decision shall be notified to the party concerned, who shall at the same time be informed of the redress available to him under the laws in force and of the time limit allowed for access to such redress.

Article 5

In order to obtain the authorization referred to in Article 3 (1), applicants must fulfil the following minimum requirements:

(a) they must have suitable and adequate premises, installations and equipment so as to ensure proper conservation and distribution of the medicinal products;

(b) they must have staff, and in particular a qualified person designated as responsible, meeting the conditions provided for by the legislation of the Member State concerned;

(c) they must undertake to fulfil the obligations incumbent on them under the terms of Article 6.

Article 6

Holders of the authorization referred to in Article 3 (1) must fulfil the following minimum requirements:

(a) they must make the premises, installations and equipment referred to in Article 5 (a) accessible at all times to the persons responsible for inspecting them;

(b) they must obtain their supplies of medicinal products only from persons who are themselves in possession of the authorization referred to in Article 3 (1) or who are exempt from obtaining such authorization under the terms of Article 3 (3);

(c) they must supply medicinal products only to persons who are themselves in possession of the authorization referred to in Article 3 (1) or who are authorized or entitled to supply medicinal products to the public in the Member State concerned;

(d) they must have an emergency plan which ensures effective implementation of any recall from the market ordered by the competent authorities or carried out in cooperation with the manufacturer or holder of the marketing authorization for the product concerned;

(e) they must keep records either in the form of purchase/sales invoices, or on computer, or in any other form giving for any transaction in medicinal products received or dispatched at least the following information:

— date,

— name of the medicinal product,

— quantity received or supplied,

— name and address of the supplier or consignee, as appropriate;

(f) they must keep the records referred to under (e) available to the competent authorities, for inspection purposes, for a period of five years;

(g) they must comply with the principles and guidelines of good distribution practice for medicinal products as laid down in Article 10.

Article 7

With regard to the supply of medicinal products to pharmacists and persons authorized or entitled to supply medicinal products to the public, Member States shall not impose upon the holder of an authorization referred to in Article 3 (1) which has been granted by another Member State, any obligation, in particular public service obligations, more stringent than those they impose on persons whom they have themselves authorized to engage in equivalent activities.

The said obligations should, moreover, be justified, in keeping with the Treaty, on grounds of public health protection and be proportionate in relation to the objective of such protection.

Article 8

For all supplies of medicinal products to a person authorized or entitled to supply medicinal products to the public in the Member State concerned, the authorized wholesaler must enclose a document that makes it possible to ascertain:

— the date,

— the name and pharmaceutical form of the medicinal product,

— the quantity supplied,

— the name and address of the supplier and consignor.

Member States shall take all appropriate measures to ensure that persons authorized or entitled to supply medicinal products to the public are able to provide information that makes it possible to trace the distribution path of every medicinal product.

Article 9

The provisions of this Directive shall not prevent the application of more stringent requirements laid down by Member States in respect of the wholesale distribution of:

— narcotic or psychotropic substances within their territory,

— medicinal products derived from blood governed by Directive 89/381/EEC [1],

— immunological medicinal products governed by Directive 89/342/EEC [2],

— radiopharmaceuticals governed by Directive 89/343/ EEC [3].

Article 10

The Commission shall publish guidelines on good distribution practice. To this end it shall consult the Committee for Proprietary Medicinal Products and the Pharmaceutical Committee.

Article 11

1. Member States shall bring into force the laws, regulations and administrative provisions necessary to comply with this Directive by 1 January 1993.

They shall forthwith inform the Commission thereof.

2. When these measures are adopted by the Member States, they shall contain a reference to this Directive or shall be accompanied by such reference on the occasion of their official publication. The methods of making such a reference shall be laid down by the Member States.

Article 12

This Directive is addressed to the Member States.

Done at Brussels, 31 March 1992.

For the Council
The President
Vitor MARTINS

---

[1] OJ No L 181, 28. 6. 1989, p. 44.
[2] OJ No L 142, 25. 5. 1989, p. 14.
[3] OJ No L 142, 25. 5. 1989, p. 16.

COUNCIL DIRECTIVE 92/26/EEC

of 31 March 1992

concerning the classification for the supply of medicinal products for human use

THE COUNCIL OF THE EUROPEAN COMMUNITIES,

Having regard to the Treaty establishing the European Economic Community and in particular Article 100a thereof,

Having regard to the proposal from the Commission [1],

In cooperation with the European Parliament [2],

Having regard to the opinion of the Economic and Social Committee [3],

Whereas measures aimed at progressively establishing the internal market over a period expiring on 31 December 1992 need to be taken; whereas the internal market is to comprise an area without internal frontiers in which the free movement of goods, persons, services and capital is ensured;

Whereas the conditions for the supply of medicinal products for human use to the public vary appreciably from one Member State to another; whereas medicinal products sold without prescriptions in certain Member States can be obtained only on medical prescription in other Member States;

Whereas Directive 91/28/EEC [4] specifies what medicinal products may be advertized to the public; whereas, in view of the development of means of communication, the conditions governing the supply of medicinal products to the public should be harmonized.

Whereas, moreover, persons moving around within the Community have the right to carry a reasonable quantity of medicinal products lawfully obtained for their personal use; whereas it must also be possible for a person established in one Member State to receive from another Member State a reasonable quantity of medicinal products intended for his personal use; whereas it is important therefore to harmonize the conditions governing the supply of medicinal products to the public;

Whereas, in addition, under the new system of registration of medicinal products in the Community, certain medicinal products will be the subject of a Community marketing authorization; whereas, in this context, the classification for the supply of medicinal products covered by a Community marketing authorization needs to be established; whereas it is therefore important to set the criteria on the basis of which Community decisions will be taken;

Whereas it is therefore appropriate, as an initial step, to harmonize the basic principles applicable to the classification for the supply of medicinal products in the Community or in the Member State concerned, while taking as a starting point the principles already established on this subject by the Council of Europe as well as the work of harmonization completed within the framework of the United Nations, concerning narcotic and psychotropic substances;

Whereas this Directive is without prejudice to the national social security arrangements for reimbursement or payment for medicinal products on prescription,

HAS ADOPTED THIS DIRECTIVE:

Article 1

1. This Directive concerns the classification for the supply of medicinal products for human use in the Community into:

— medicinal products subject to medical prescription,

— medicinal products not subject to medical prescription.

2. For the purposes of this Directive, the definition of 'medicinal product' in Article 1 of Council Directive 65/65/EEC of 26 January 1965 on the approximation of provisions laid down by law, regulation or administrative action relating to medicinal products [5] as last amended by Directive 89/343/EEC [6], shall apply. In addition, 'medicinal prescription' shall mean any prescription issued by a professional person qualified to prescribe medicinal products.

Article 2

1. When a marketing authorization is granted, the competent authorities shall specify the classification of the medicinal product into:

— a medicinal product subject to medical prescription,

— a medicinal product not subject to medical prescription.

[1] OJ No C 58, 8. 3. 1990, p. 18.
[2] OJ No C 183, 15. 7. 1991, p. 178 and
    OJ No C 67, 16. 3. 1992.
[3] OJ No C 225, 10. 9. 1990, p. 21.
[4] See page 13 of this Official Journal.

[5] OJ No 22, 9. 6. 1965, p. 369/65.
[6] OJ No L 142, 25. 5. 1989, p. 14.

To this end, the criteria laid down in Article 3 (1) shall apply.

2. The competent authorities may fix sub-categories for medicinal products which are available on medical prescription only. In that case, they shall refer to the following classification:

(a) medicinal products on renewable or non-renewable medical prescription;

(b) medicinal products subject to special medical prescription;

(c) medicinal products on restricted medical prescription, reserved for use in certain specialized areas.

Article 3

1. Medicinal products shall be subject to medical prescription where they:

— are likely to present a danger either directly or indirectly, even when used correctly, if utilized without medical supervision, or

— are frequently and to a very wide extent used incorrectly, and as a result are likely to present a direct or indirect danger to human health, or

— contain substances or preparations thereof the activity and/or side effects of which require further investigation, or

— are normally prescribed by a doctor to be administered parenterally.

2. Where Member States provide for the sub-category of medicinal products subject to special medical prescription, they shall take account of the following factors:

— the medicinal product contains, in a non-exempt quantity, a substance classified as a narcotic or a psychotropic substance within the meaning of the international conventions in force (United Nations Conventions of 1961 and 1971), or

— the medicinal product is likely, if incorrectly used, to present a substantial risk of medicinal abuse, to lead to addiction or be misused for illegal purposes, or

— the medicinal product contains a substance which, by reason of its novelty or properties, could be considered as belonging to that group as a precautionary measure.

3. Where Member States provide for the sub-category of medicinal products subject to restricted prescription, they shall take account of the following factors:

— the medicinal product, because of its pharmaceutical characteristics or novelty or in the interests of public health, is reserved for treatments which can only be followed in a hospital environment,

— the medicinal product is used in the treatment of conditions which must be diagnosed in a hospital environment or in institutions with adequate diagnostic facilities, although administration and follow-up may be carried out elsewhere, or

— the medicinal product is intended for outpatients but its use may produce very serious side-effects requiring a prescription drawn up as required by a specialist and special supervision throughout the treatment.

4. A competent authority may waive application of paragraphs 1, 2 and 3 having regard to:

(a) the maximum single dose, the maximum daily dose, the strength, the pharmaceutical form, certain types of packaging; and/or

(b) other circumstances of use which it has specified.

5. If a competent authority does not designate medicinal products into sub-categories referred to in Article 2 (2), it shall nevertheless take into account the criteria referred to in paragraphs 2 and 3 of this Article in determining whether any medicinal product shall be classified as a prescription-only medicine.

Article 4

Medicinal products not subject to prescription shall be those which do not meet the criteria listed in Article 3.

Article 5

1. The competent authorities shall draw up a list of the medicinal products subject on their territory to medical prescription, specifying, if necessary, the category of classification. They shall update this list annually.

2. On the occasion of the five-yearly renewal of the marketing authorization or when new facts are brought to their notice, the competent authorities shall examine and, as appropriate, amend the classification of a medicinal product, by applying the criteria listed in Article 3.

Article 6

1. Within two years of adoption of this Directive, the Member States shall communicate the list referred to in Article 5 (1) to the Commission and to the other Member States, when requested by the latter.

2. Each year, Member States shall communicate to the Commission and to the other Member States the changes that have been made to the list referred to in paragraph 1.

3. Within four years of the adoption of this Directive, the Commission shall submit a report to the Council on the application of this Directive. This report will be accompanied, if necessary, by appropriate proposals.

Article 7

Member States shall bring into force the laws, regulations and administrative provisions necessary to comply with this Directive before 1 January 1993. They shall forthwith inform the Comission thereof.

When Member States adopt these measures, they shall contain a reference to this Directive or shall be accompanied by such reference on the occasion of their official publication. The methods of making such a reference shall be laid down by the Member States.

Article 8

This Directive is addressed to the Member States.

Done at Brussels, 31 March 1992.

For the Council

The President

Vitor MARTINS

COUNCIL DIRECTIVE 92/27/EEC

of 31 March 1992

on the labelling of medicinal products for human use and on package leaflets

THE COUNCIL OF THE EUROPEAN COMMUNITIES,

Having regard to the Treaty establishing the European Economic Community, and in particular Article 100a thereof,

Having regard to the proposal from the Commission (¹),

In cooperation with the European Parliament (²),

Having regard to the opinion of the Economic and Social Committee (³),

Whereas measures aimed a progressively establishing the internal market over a period expiring on 31 December 1992 need to be taken; whereas the internal market is to comprise an area without internal frontiers in which the free movement of goods, persons, services and capital is ensured;

Whereas Council Directive 65/65/EEC of 26 January 1965 on the approximation of provisions laid down by law, regulations or administrative action relating to medicinal products (⁴), as last amended by Directive 89/343/EEC (⁵), establishes a list of particulars to be given on the immediate packaging and the outer packaging of medicinal products for human use; whereas this list should be supplemented and details given of how labelling is to be presented;

Whereas Second Council Directive 75/319/EEC of 20 May 1975 on the approximation of provisions laid down by law, regulation or administrative action relating to proprietary medicinal products (⁶), as last amended by Directive 89/381/EEC (⁷), establishes a non-exhaustive list of particulars to be included in package leaflets; whereas this list should be supplemented and details given of how such leaflets are to be presented;

Whereas the provisions on labelling and on package leaflets should be brought together in a single text;

Whereas the provisions governing the information supplied to users should provide a high degree of consumer protection, in order that medicinal products may be used correctly on the basis of full and comprehensible information;

Whereas the marketing of medicinal products whose labelling and package leaflets comply with this Directive should not be prohibited or impeded on grounds connected with the labelling or package leaflet,

HAS ADOPTED THIS DIRECTIVE:

CHAPTER I

Scope and definitions

Article 1

1. This Directive deals with the labelling of medicinal products for human use and leaflets inserted in packages of such products, to which Chapters II, III, IV and V of Directive 65/65/EEC apply.

2. For the purposes of this Directive:

— *name of the medicinal product* means the name given to a medicinal product, which may be either an invented name or a common or scientific name, together with a trade mark or the name of the manufacturer; the invented name shall not be liable to confusion with the common name,

— *common name* means the international non-proprietary name recommended by the World Health Organization, or, if one does not exist, the usual common name,

— *strength of the medicinal product* means the content of the active ingredient expressed quantitatively per dosage unit, per unit of volume or weight according to the dosage form,

— *immediate packaging* means the container or other form of packaging immediately in contact with the medicinal product,

— *outer packaging* means the packaging into which is placed the immediate packaging,

---

(¹) OJ No C 58, 8. 3. 1990, p. 21.
(²) OJ No C 183, 15. 7. 1991, p. 213.
(³) OJ No C 225, 10. 9. 1990, p. 24.
(⁴) OJ No 22, 9. 2. 1965, p. 369/65.
(⁵) OJ No L 142, 25. 5. 1989, p. 14.
(⁶) OJ No L 147, 9. 6. 1975, p. 13.
(⁷) OJ No L 81, 28. 6. 1989, p. 44.

— *labelling* means information on the immediate or outer packaging,

— *package leaflet* means a leaflet containing information for the user which accompanies the medicinal product,

— *manufacturer* means the holder of the authorization referred to in Article 16 of Directive 75/319/EEC on behalf of whom the qualified person has performed the specific obligations laid down in Article 22 of that Directive.

CHAPTER II

Labelling of medicinal products

Article 2

1. The following particulars shall appear on the outer packaging of medicinal products or, where there is no outer packaging, on the immediate packaging:

(a) the name of the medicinal product followed by the common name where the product contains only one active ingredient and if its name is an invented name; where a medicinal product is available in several pharmaceutical forms and/or several strengths, the pharmaceutical form and/or the strength (baby, child or adult as appropriate) must be include in the name of the medicinal product;

(b) a statement of the active ingredients expressed qualitatively and quantitatively per dosage unit or according to the form of administration for a given volume or weight, using their common names;

(c) the pharmaceutical form and the contents by weight, by volume or by number of doses of the product;

(d) a list of those excipients known to have a recognized action or effect and included in the guidelines published pursuant to Article 12. However, if the product is injectable, or a topical or eye preparation, all excipients must be stated;

(e) the method and, if necessary, the route of administration;

(f) a special warning that the medicinal product must be stored out of reach of children;

(g) a special warning, if this is necessary for the medicinal product concerned;

(h) the expiry date in clear terms (month/year);

(i) special storage procautions, if any;

(j) special precautions for disposal of unused medicinal products or waste materials derived from such products, if appropriate;

(k) the name and address of the holder of the authorization for placing the medicinal product on the market;

(l) the number of the authorization for placing the medicinal product on the market;

(m) the manufacturer's batch number;

(n) in the case of self-medication, instructions on the use of the medicinal products.

2. The outer packaging may include symbols or pictograms designed to clarify certain information mentioned in paragraph 1 and other information compatible with the summary of the product characteristics which is useful for health education, to the exclusion of any element of a promotional nature.

Article 3

1. The particulars laid down in Article 2 shall appear on immediate packagings other than those referred to in paragraphs 2 and 3.

2. The following particulars at least shall appear on immediate packagings which take the form of blister packs and are placed in an outer packaging that complies with the requirements laid down in Article 2:

— the name of the medicinal product as laid down in Article 2 (a),

— the name of the holder of the authorization for placing the product on the market,

— the expiry date,

— the batch number.

3. The following particulars at least shall appear on small immediate packaging units on which the particulars laid down in Article 2 cannot be displayed:

— the name of the medicinal product and, if necessary, the strength and the route of administration,

— the method of administration,

— the expiry date,

— the batch number,

— the contents by weight, by volume or by unit.

Article 4

1. The particulars referred to in Articles 2 and 3 shall be easily legible, clearly comprehensible and indelible.

2. The particulars listed in Article 2 shall appear in the official language or languages of the Member State where the product is placed on the market. This provision shall not prevent these particulars from being indicated in several languages, provided that the same particulars appear in all the languages used.

Article 5

1. Member States may not prohibit or impede the placing on the market of medicinal products within their territory on grounds connected with labelling where such labelling complies with the requirements of this Chapter.

2. Notwithstanding paragraph 1, Member States may require the use of certain forms of labelling making it possible to indicate:

— the price of the medicinal product,

— the reimbursement conditions of social security organizations,

— the legal status for supply to the patient, in accordance with Directive 92/26/EEC (¹),

— identification and authenticity.

CHAPTER III

User package leaflet

Article 6

The inclusion in the packaging of all medicinal products of a package leaflet for the information of users shall be obligatory unless all the information required by Article 7 is directly conveyed on the outer packaging or on the immediate packaging.

Article 7

1. The package leaflet shall be drawn up in accordance with the summary of the product characteristics; it shall include, in the following order:

(a) for the identification of the medicinal product:

— the name of the medicinal product, followed by the common name if the product contains only one active ingredient and if its name is an invented name; where a medicinal product is available in several pharmaceutical forms and/or several strengths, the pharmaceutical form and/or the strength (for example, baby, child, adult) must be included in the name of the medicinal product,

— a full statement of the active ingredients and excipients expressed qualitatively and a statement of the active ingredients expressed quantitatively, using their common names, in the case of each presentation of the product,

— the pharmaceutical form and the contents by weight, by volume or by number of doses of the product, in the case of each presentation of the product,

---

(¹) See page 5 of this Official Journal.

— the pharmaco-therapeutic group, or type of activity in terms easily comprehensible for the patient,

— the name and address of the holder of the authorization for placing the medicinal product on the market and of the manufacturer;

(b) the therapeutic indications;

(c) a list of information which is necessary before taking the medicinal product:

— contra-indications,

— appropriate precautions for use,

— forms of interaction with other medicinal products and other forms of interaction (for example, alcohol, tobacco, foodstuffs) which may affect the action of the medicinal product,

— special warnings.

this list must:

— take into account the particular condition of certain categories of users (e.g. children, pregnant or breastfeeding women, the elderly, persons with specific pathological conditions),

— mention, if appropriate, potential effects on the ability to drive vehicles or to operate machinery,

— detail those excipients, knowledge of which is important for the safe and effective use of the medicinal product and included in the guidelines published pursuant to Article 12;

(d) the necessary and usual instructions for proper use, in particular:

— the dosage,

— the method and, if necessary, route of administration,

— the frequency of administration, specifying if necessary the appropriate time at which the medicinal product may or must be administered,

and, as appropriate, depending on the nature of the product:

— the duration of treatment, where it should be limited,

— the action to be taken in the case of an overdose (for example, symptoms, emergency procedures),

— the course of action to take when one or more doses have not been taken,

— indication, if necessary, of the risk of withdrawal effects;

(e) a description of the undesirable effects which can occur under normal use of the medicinal product and, if necessary, the action to be taken in such a case; the patient should be expressly invited to communicate any undesirable effect which is not mentioned in the leaflet to his doctor or to his pharmacist;

(f) a reference to the expiry date indicated on the label, with:

— a warning against using the product after this date,

— where appropriate, special storage precautions,

— if necessary, a warning against certain visible signs of deterioration;

(g) the date on which the package leaflet was last revised.

2. Notwithstanding paragraph 1 (b), the competent authorities may decide that certain therapeutic indications shall not be mentioned in the package leaflet, where the dissemination of such information might have serious disadvantages for the patient.

3. The package leaflet may include symbols or pictograms designed to clarify certain information mentioned in paragraph 1 and other information compatible with the summary of the product characteristics which is useful for health education, to the exclusion of any element of a promotional nature.

Article 8

The package leaflet must be written in clear and understandable terms for the patient and be clearly legible in the official language or languages of the Member State where the medicinal product is placed on the market. This provision does not prevent the package leaflet being printed in several languages, provided that the same information is given in all the languages used.

Article 9

Member States shall not prohibit or impede the marketing or medicinal products within their territory on grounds relating to the package leaflet if the latter complies with the requirements of this Chapter.

CHAPTER IV

General and final provisions

Article 10

1. One or more specimens or mock-ups of the outer packaging and the immediate packaging of a medicinal product, together with the draft package leaflet, shall be submitted to the authorities competent for authorizing marketing when the authorization for placing the medicinal product on the market is requested.

2. The competent authorities shall refuse the authorization for placing the medicinal product on the market if the labelling or the package leaflet do not comply with the provisions of this Directive or if they are not in accordance with the particulars listed in the summary of product characteristics referred to in Article 4b of Directive 65/65/EEC.

3. All proposed changes to an aspect of the labelling or the package leaflet covered by this Directive and not connected with the summary of characteristics shall be submitted to the authorities competent for authorizing marketing. If the competent authorities have not opposed a proposed change within 90 days following the introduction of the request, the applicant may put the change into effect.

4. The fact that the competent authorities do not refuse an authorization to place the medicinal product on the market pursuant to paragraph 2 or a change to the labelling or the package leaflet pursuant to paragraph 3 does not alter the general legal liability of the manufacturer or as appropriate the holder of the authorization to place the medicinal product on the market.

5. The competent authorities may exempt labels and package leaflets for specific medicinal products from the obligation that certain particulars shall appear and that the leaflet must be in the official language or languages of the Member State where the product is placed on the market, when the product is not intended to be delivered to the patient for self-administration.

Article 11

1. Where the provisions of this Directive are not complied with, and a notice served on the person concerned has remained without effect, the competent authorities of the Member States may suspend the authorization to place the medicinal product on the market, until the labelling and the package leaflet of the medicinal product in question have been made to comply with the requirements of this Directive.

2. All decisions taken pursuant to paragraph 1 shall state in detail the reasons on which they are based. They shall be notified to the party concerned, who shall at the same time be informed of the remedies available to him under the laws in force and of the time limit allowed for the exercise of such remedies.

Article 12

1. As necessary, the Commission shall publish guidelines concerning in particular:

— the formulation of certain special warnings for certain categories of medicinal products,

— the particular information needs relating to self-medication,

— the legibility of particulars on the labelling and package leaflet,

— methods for the identification and authentication of medicinal products,

— the list of excipients which must feature on the labelling of medicinal products and the way these excipients must be indicated.

2. These guidelines shall be adopted in the form of a Directive addressed to the Member States, in accordance with the procedure laid down in Article 2c of Directive 75/318/EEC.

Article 13

Articles 13 to 20 of Directive 65/65/EEC and Articles 6 and 7 of Directive 75/319/EEC are hereby repealed.

Article 14

Member States shall take the measures necessary to comply with this Directive before 1 January 1993. They shall forthwith inform the Commission thereof.

When Member States adopt these measures, they shall contain a reference to this Directive or shall be accompanied by such reference on the occasion of their official publication. The methods of making such a reference shall be laid down by the Member States.

From 1 January 1994, Member States shall refuse an application for authorization to place a medicinal product on the market or for the renewal of an existing authorization, where the labelling and the package leaflet do not comply with the requirements of this Directive.

Article 15

This Directive is addressed to the Member States.

Done at Brussels, 31 March 1992.

For the Council
The President
Vitor MARTINS

COUNCIL DIRECTIVE 92/28/EEC

of 31 March 1992

on the advertising of medicinal products for human use

THE COUNCIL OF THE EUROPEAN COMMUNITIES,

Having regard to the Treaty establishing the European Economic Community, and in particular Article 100a thereof,

Having regard to the proposal from the Commission (1),

In cooperation with the European Parliament (2),

Having regard to the opinion of the Economic and Social Committee (3),

Whereas Directive 84/450/EEC (4) harmonized the laws, regulations and administrative provisions of the Member States concerning misleading advertising; whereas this Directive is without prejudice to the application of measures adopted pursuant to that Directive;

Whereas all Member States have adopted further specific measures concerning the advertising of medicinal products; whereas there are disparities between these measures; whereas these disparities are likely to have an impact on the establishment and functioning of the internal market, since advertising disseminated in one Member State is likely to have effects in other Member States;

Whereas Council Directive 89/552/EEC of 3 October 1989 on the coordination of certain provisions laid down by law, regulation or administrative action in Member States concerning the pursuit of television broadcasting activities (5) prohibits the televisi advertising of medicinal products which are available only on medical prescription in the Member State within whose jurisdiction the television broadcaster is located; whereas this principle should be made of general application by extending it to other media;

Whereas advertising to the general public, even of non-prescription medicinal products, could affect public health, were it to be excessive and ill-considered; whereas advertising of medicinal products to the general public, where it is permitted, ought therefore to satisfy certain essential criteria which ought to be defined;

Whereas, furthermore, distribution of samples free of charge to the general public for promotional ends must be prohibited;

Whereas the advertising of medicinal products to persons qualified to prescribe or supply them contributes to the information available to such persons; whereas, nevertheless, this advertising should be subject to strict conditions and effective monitoring, referring in particular to the work carried out within the framework of the Council of Europe;

Whereas medical sales representatives have an important role in the promotion of medicinal products; whereas, therefore, certain obligations should be imposed upon them, in particular the obligation to supply the person visited with a summary of product characteristics;

Whereas persons qualified to prescribe medicinal products must be able to carry out these functions objectively without being influenced by direct or indirect financial inducements;

Whereas it should be possible within certain restrictive conditions to provide samples of medicinal products free of charge to persons qualified to prescribe or supply them so that they can familiarize themselves with new products and acquire experience in dealing with them;

Whereas persons qualified to prescribe or supply medicinal products must have access to a neutral, objective source of information about products available on the market; whereas it is nevertheless for the Member States to take all measures necessary to this end, in the light of their own particular situation;

Whereas advertising of medicinal products should be subject to effective, adequate monitoring; whereas reference in this regard should be made to the monitoring mechanisms set up by Directive 84/450/EEC;

Whereas each undertaking which manufactures or imports medicinal products should set up a mechanism to ensure that all information supplied about a medicinal product conforms with the approved conditions of use,

(1) OJ No C 163, 4. 7. 1990, p. 10 and
    OJ No C 207, 8. 8. 1991, p. 25.
(2) OJ No C 183, 15. 7. 1991, p. 227 and
    OJ No C 67, 16. 3. 1992.
(3) OJ No C 60, 8. 3. 1991, p. 40.
(4) OJ No L 250, 19. 9. 1984, p. 17.
(5) OJ No L 298, 17. 10. 1989, p. 23.

HAS ADOPTED THIS DIRECTIVE:

CHAPTER I

Scope, definitions and general principles

Article 1

1. This Directive concerns the advertising in the Community of medicinal products for human use covered by Chapters II to V of Council Directive 65/65/EEC of 26 January 1965 on the approximation of provisions laid down by law, regulation or administrative action relating to medicinal products (¹).

2. For the purposes of this Directive:

— the definitions of the name of the medicinal product and of the common name shall be those laid down in Article 1 of Directive 92/27/EEC (²);

— the summary of product characteristics shall be the summary approved by the competent authority which granted the marketing authorization in accordance with Article 4b of Directive 65/65/EEC.

3. For the purposes of this Directive, advertising of medicinal products shall include any form of door-to-door information, canvassing activity or inducement designed to promote the prescription, supply, sale or consumption of medicinal products; it shall include in particular:

— the advertising of medicinal products to the general public,

— advertising of medicinal products to persons qualified to prescribe or supply them,

— visits by medical sales representatives to persons qualified to prescribe medicinal products,

— the supply of samples,

— the provision of inducements to prescribe or supply medicinal products by the gift, offer or promise of any benefit or bonus, whether in money or in kind, except when their intrinsic value is minimal,

— sponsorship of promotional meetings attended by persons qualified to prescribe or supply medicinal products,

— sponsorship of scientific congresses attended by persons qualified to prescribe or supply medicinal products and

in particular payment of their travelling and accommodation expenses in connection therewith.

4. The following are not covered by this Directive:

— the labelling of medicinal products and the accompanying package leaflets, which are subject to the provisions of Directive 92/27/EEC;

— correspondence, possibly accompanied by material of a non-promotional nature, needed to answer a specific question about a particular medicinal product;

— factual, informative announcements and reference material relating, for example, to pack changes, adverse-reaction warnings as part of general drug precautions, trade catalogues and price lists, provided they include no product claims;

— statements relating to human health or diseases, provided there is no reference, even indirect, to medicinal products.

Article 2

1. Member States shall prohibit any advertising of a medicinal product in respect of which a marketing authorization has not been granted in accordance with Community law.

2. All parts of the advertising of a medicinal product must comply with the particulars listed in the summary of product characteristics.

3. The advertising of a medicinal product:

— shall encourage the rational use of the medicinal product, by presenting it objectively and without exaggerating its properties,

— shall not be misleading.

CHAPTER II

Advertising to the general public

Article 3

1. Member States shall prohibit the advertising to the general public of medicinal products which:

— are available on medical prescription only, in accordance with Directive 92/26/EEC (³),

— contain psychotropic or narcotic substances, within the meaning of the international conventions,

---

(¹) OJ No 22, 9. 2. 1965, p. 369/65. Directive last amended by Directive 89/341/EEC (OJ No L 142, 25. 5. 1989, p. 11).
(²) See page 8 of this Official Journal.

(³) See page 5 of this Official Journal.

— may not be advertised to the general public in accordance with paragraph 2.

2. Medicinal products may be advertised to the general public which, by virtue of their composition and purpose, are intended and designed for use without the invervention of a medical practitioner for diagnostic purposes or for the prescription or monitoring of treatment, with the advice of the pharmacist, if necessary.

Member States shall prohibit the mentioning in advertising to the general public of therapeutic indications such as:

— tuberculosis,

— sexually transmitted diseases,

— other serious infectious diseases,

— cancer and other tumoral diseases,

— chronic insomnia,

— diabetes and other metabolic illnesses.

3. Member States shall also be able to ban on their territory advertising to the general public of medicinal products the cost of which may be reimbursed.

4. The prohibition referred to in paragraph 1 shall not apply to vaccination campaigns carried out by the industry and approved by the competent authorities of the Member States.

5. The prohibition referred to in paragraph 1 shall apply without prejudice to Articles 2, 3 and 14 of Directive 89/552/EEC.

6. Member States shall prohibit the direct distribution of medicinal products to the public by the industry for promotional purposes; they may, however, authorize such distribution in special cases for other purposes.

Article 4

1. Without prejudice to Article 3, all advertising to the general public of a medicinal product shall:

(a) be set out in such a way that it is clear that the message is an advertisement and that the product is clearly identified as a medicinal product;

(b) include the following minimum information:

— the name of the medicinal product, as well as the common name if the medicinal product contains only one active ingredient,

— the information necessary for correct use of the medicinal product,

— an express, legible invitation to read carefully the instructions on the package leaflet or on the outer packaging, according to the case.

2. Member States may decide that the advertising of a medicinal product to the general public may, notwithstanding paragraph 1, include only the name of the medicinal product if it is intended solely as a reminder.

Article 5

The advertising of a medicinal product to the general public shall not contain any material which:

(a) gives the impression that a medical consultation or surgical operation is unnecessary, in particular by offering a diagnosis or by suggesting treatment by mail;

(b) suggests that the effects of taking the medicine are guaranteed, are unaccompanied by side effects or are better than, or equivalent to, those of another treatment or medicinal product;

(c) suggests that the health of the subject can be enhanced by taking the medicine;

(d) suggests that the health of the subject could be affected by not taking the medicine; this prohibition shall not apply to the vaccination campaigns referred to in Article 3 (4);

(e) is directed exclusively or principally at children;

(f) refers to a recommendation by scientists, health professionals or persons who are neither of the foregoing but who, because of their celebrity, could encourage the consumption of medicinal products;

(g) suggests that the medicinal product is a foodstuff, cosmetic or other consumer product;

(h) suggests that the safety or efficacy of the medicinal product is due to the fact that it is natural;

(i) could, by a description or detailed representation of a case history, lead to erroneous self diagnosis;

(j) refers, in improper, alarming or misleading terms, to claims of recovery;

(k) uses, in improper, alarming or misleading terms, pictorial representations of changes in the human body caused by disease or injury, or of the action of a medicinal product on the human body or parts thereof;

(l) mentions that the medicinal product has been granted a marketing authorization.

CHAPTER III

Advertising to health professionals

Article 6

1. Any advertising of a medicinal product to persons qualified to prescribe or supply such products shall include:

— essential information compatible with the summary of product characteristics;

— the supply classification of the medicinal product.

Member States may also require such advertising to include the selling price or indicative price of the various presentations and the conditions for reimbursement by social security bodies.

2. Member States may decide that the advertising of a medicinal product to persons qualified to prescribe or supply such products may, notwithstanding paragraph 1, include only the name of the medicinal product, if it is intended solely as a reminder.

Article 7

1. Any documentation relating to a medicinal product which is transmitted as part of the promotion of that product to persons qualified to prescribe or supply it shall include as a minimum the particulars listed in Article 6 (1) and shall state the date on which it was drawn up or last revised.

2. All the information contained in the documentation referred to in paragraph 1 shall be accurate, up-to-date, verifiable and sufficiently complete to enable the recipient to form his or her own opinion of the therapeutic value of the medicinal product concerned.

3. Quotations as well as tables and other illustrative matter taken from medical journals or other scientific works for use in the documentation referred to in paragraph 1 shall be faithfully reproduced and the precise sources indicated.

Article 8

1. Medical sales representatives shall be given adequate training by the firm which employs them and shall have sufficient scientific knowledge to be able to provide information which is precise and as complete as possible about the medicinal products which they promote.

2. During each visit, medical sales representatives shall give the persons visited, or have available for them, summaries of the product characteristics of each medicinal product they present together, if the legislation of the Member State so permits, with details of the price and conditions for reimbursement referred to in Article 6 (1).

3. Medical sales representatives shall transmit to the scientific service referred to in Article 13 (1) any information about the use of the medicinal products they advertise, with particular reference to any adverse reactions reported to them by the persons they visit.

Article 9

1. Where medicinal products are being promoted to persons qualified to prescribe or supply them, no gifts, pecuniary advantages or benefits in kind may be supplied, offered or promised to such persons unless they are inexpensive and relevant to the practice of medicine or pharmacy.

2. Hospitality at sales promotion must always be reasonable in level and secondary to the main purpose of the meeting and must not be extended to other than health professionals.

3. Persons qualified to prescribe or supply medicinal products shall not solicit or accept any inducement prohibited under paragraph 1 or contrary to paragraph 2.

4. Existing measures or trade practices in Member States relating to prices, margins and discounts shall not be affected by this Article.

Article 10

The provisions of Article 9 (1) shall not prevent hospitality being offered, directly or indirectly, at events for purely professional and scientific purposes; such hospitality must always be reasonable in level and remain subordinate to the main scientific objective of the meeting; it must not be extended to persons other than health professionals.

Article 11

1. Free samples shall be provided on an exceptional basis only to persons qualified to prescribe them and on the following conditions:

(a) a limited number of samples for each medicinal product each year on prescription;

(b) any supply of samples must be in response to a written request, signed and dated, from the recipient;

(c) those supplying samples must maintain an adequate system of control and accountability;

(d) each sample shall be identical with the smallest presentation on the market;

(e) each sample shall be marked free medical sample — not for resale or bear another legend of analogous meaning;

(f) each sample shall be accompanied by a copy of the summary of product characteristics;

(g) no samples of medicinal products containing psychotropic or narcotic substances within the meaning of international conventions may be supplied.

2. Member States may also place further restrictions on the distribution of samples of certain medicinal products.

CHAPTER IV

Monitoring of advertising

Article 12

1. Member States shall ensure that there are adequate and effective methods to monitor the advertising of medicinal products. Such methods, which may be based on a system of prior vetting, shall in any event include legal provisions under which persons or organizations regarded under national law as having a legitimate interest in prohibiting any advertisement inconsistent with this Directive may take legal action against such advertisement, or bring such advertisement before an administrative authority competent either to decide on complaints or to initiate appropriate legal proceedings.

2. Under the legal provisions referred to in paragraph 1, Member States shall confer upon the courts or administrative authorities powers enabling them, in cases where they deem such measures to be necessary taking into account all the interests involved and in particular the public interest:

— to order the cessation of, or to institute appropriate legal proceedings for an order for the cessation of, misleading advertising,

or

— if misleading advertising has not yet been published but publication is imminent, to order the prohibition of, or to institute appropriate legal proceedings for an order for the prohibition of, such publication,

even without proof of actual loss or damage or of intention or negligence on the part of the advertiser.

Member States shall also make provision for the measures referred to in the first subparagraph to be taken under an accelerated procedure:

— either with interim effect, or

— with definitive effect,

on the understanding that it is for each Member State to decide which of the two options to select.

Furthermore, Member States may confer upon the courts or administrative authorities powers enabling them, with a view to eliminating the continuing effects of misleading advertising the cessation of which has been ordered by a final decision:

— to require publication of that decision in full or in part and in such form as they deem adequate,

— to require in addition the publication of a corrective statement.

3. Under the legal provisions referred to in paragraph 1, Member States shall ensure that any decision taken in accordance with paragraph 2 shall state in detail the reasons on which it is based and shall be communicated in writing to the person concerned, mentioning the redress available at law and the time limit allowed for access to such redress.

4. This Article shall not exclude the voluntary control of advertising of medicinal products by self-regulatory bodies and recourse to such bodies, if proceedings before such bodies are possible in addition to the judicial or administrative proceedings referred to in paragraph 1.

Article 13

1. The marketing authorization holder shall establish within his undertaking a scientific service in charge of information about the medicinal products which he places on the market.

2. The person responsible for placing the product on the market shall:

— keep available for, or communicate to, the authorities or bodies responsible for monitoring advertising of medicinal products a sample of all advertisements emanating from his undertaking together with a statement indicating the persons to whom it is addressed, the method of dissemination and the date of first dissemination,

— ensure that advertising of medicinal products by his undertaking conforms to the requirements of this Directive,

— verify that medical sales representatives employed by his undertaking have been adequately trained and fulfill the obligations imposed upon them by Article 8 (2) and (3),

— supply the authorities or bodies responsible for monitoring advertising of medicinal products with the information and assistance they require to carry out their responsibilities,

— ensure that the decisions taken by the authorities or bodies responsible for monitoring advertising of medicinal products are immediately and fully complied with.

Article 14

Member States shall take the appropriate measures to ensure that all the provisions of this Directive are applied in full and shall determine in particular what penalties shall be imposed should the provisions adopted in the execution of this Directive be infringed.

Article 15

1. Member States shall take the measures necessary in order to comply with this Directive with effect from 1 January 1993. They shall forthwith inform the Commission thereof.

2. When Member States adopt the said measures, such measures shall contain a reference to this Directive or be accompanied by such reference on the occasion of their official publication. The methods of making such a reference shall be laid down by the Member States.

Article 16

This Directive is addressed to the Member States.

Done at Brussels, 31 March 1992.

For the Council
The President
Vitor MARTINS

COUNCIL DIRECTIVE 92/73/EEC

of 22 September 1992

widening the scope of Directives 65/65/EEC and 75/319/EEC on the approximation of provisions laid down by law, regulation or administrative action relating to medicinal products and laying down additional provisions on homeopathic medicinal products

THE COUNCIL OF THE EUROPEAN COMMUNITIES,

Having regard to the Treaty establishing the European Economic Community, and in particular Article 100a thereof,

Having regard to the proposal from the Commission (¹),

In cooperation with the European Parliament (²),

Having regard to the opinion of the Economic and Social Committee (³),

Whereas differences currently existing between the provisions laid down by law, regulation or administrative action in the Member States may hinder trade in homeopathic medicinal products within the Community and lead to discrimination and distortion of competition between manufacturers of these products;

Whereas the essential aim of any rules governing the production, distribution and use of medicinal products must be to safeguard public health;

Whereas, despite considerable differences in the status of alternative medicines in the Member States, patients should be allowed access to the medicinal products of their choice, provided all precautions are taken to ensure the quality and safety of the said products;

Whereas the anthroposophic medicinal products described in an official pharmacopoeia and prepared by a homeopathic method are to be treated, as regards registration and marketing authorization, in the same way as homeopathic medicinal products;

Whereas the provisions of Directive 65/65/EEC (⁴) and the Second Directive 75/319/EEC (⁵), are not always appropriate for homeopathic medicinal products;

Whereas homeopathic medicine is officially recognized in certain Member States but is only tolerated in other Member States;

Whereas, even if homeopathic medicinal products are not always officially recognized, they are nevertheless prescribed and used in all Member States;

Whereas it is desirable in the first instance to provide users of these medicinal products with a very clear indication of their homeopathic character and with sufficient guarantees of their quality and safety;

Whereas the rules relating to the manufacture, control and inspection of homeopathic medicinal products must be harmonized to permit the circulation throughout the Community of medicinal products which are safe and of good quality;

Whereas, having regard to the particular characteristics of these medicinal products, such as the very low level of active principles they contain and the difficulty of applying to them the conventional statistical methods relating to clinical trials, it is desirable to provide a special, simplified registration procedure for those traditional homeopathic medicinal products which are placed on the market without therapeutic indications in a pharmaceutical form and dosage which do not present a risk for the patient;

Whereas, however, the usual rules governing the authorization to market medicinal products should be applied to homeopathic medicinal products placed on the market with therapeutic indications or in a form which may present risks which must be balanced against the desired therapeutic effect; whereas, in particular, those Member States which have a homeopathic tradition should be able to apply particular rules for the evaluation of the results of tests and trials intended to establish the safety and efficacy of these medicinal products provided that they notify them to the Commission,

HAS ADOPTED THIS DIRECTIVE:

CHAPTER I

Scope

Article 1

1. For the purposes of this Directive, 'homeopathic medicinal product' shall mean any medicinal product

---

(¹) OJ No C 108, 1. 5. 1990, p. 10 and
    OJ No C 244, 19. 9. 1991, p. 8.
(²) OJ No C 183, 15. 7. 1991, p. 322 and
    OJ No C 241, 21. 9. 1992.
(³) OJ No C 332, 31. 12. 1990, p. 29.
(⁴) OJ No 22, 9. 2. 1965, p. 369/65. Directive as last amended by Directive 89/341/EEC (OJ No L 142, 25. 5. 1989, p. 11).
(⁵) OJ No L 147, 9. 6. 1975, p. 13. Directive as last amended by Directive 89/341/EEC (OJ No L 142, 25. 5. 1989, p. 11).

prepared from products, substances or compositions called homeopathic stocks in accordance with a homeopathic manufacturing procedure described by the *European Pharmacopoeia* or, in absence thereof, by the pharmacopoeias currently used officially in the Member States.

2. A homeopathic medicinal product may also contain a number of principles.

Article 2

1. The provisions of this Directive shall apply to homeopathic medicinal products for human use, to the exclusion of homeopathic medicinal products prepared in accordance with a magistral or an officinal formula as defined in Article 1 (4) and (5) of Directive 65/65/EEC and of homeopathic medicinal products which satisfy the criteria laid down in Article 2 (4) of the said Directive.

2. The medicinal products referred to in paragraph 1 shall be identified by a reference on their labels, in clear and legible form, to their homeopathic nature.

CHAPTER II

Manufacture, control and inspection

Article 3

The provisions of Chapter IV of Directive 75/319/EEC shall apply to the manufacture, control, import and export of homeopathic medicinal products.

Article 4

The supervision measures and the sanctions provided for in Chapter V of Directive 75/319/EEC shall apply to homeopathic medicinal products, together with Articles 31 and 32 of the same Directive.

However, the proof of therapeutic efficacy referred to in Article 28 (1) (b) of the same Directive shall not be required for homeopathic medicinal products registered in accordance with Article 7 of this Directive or, where appropriate, admitted in accordance with Article 6 (2).

Article 5

Member States shall communicate to each other all the information necessary to guarantee the quality and safety of homeopathic medicinal products manufactured and marketed within the Community, and in particular the information referred to in Articles 30 and 33 of Directive 75/319/EEC.

CHAPTER III

Placing on the market

Article 6

1. Member States shall ensure that homeopathic medicinal products manufactured and placed on the market within the Community are registered or authorized in accordance with Articles 7, 8 and 9. Each Member State shall take due account of registrations and authorizations previously granted by another Member State.

2. A Member State may refrain from establishing a special, simplified registration procedure for the homeopathic medicinal products referred to in Article 7. A Member State applying this provision shall inform the Commission accordingly. The Member State concerned shall, by 31 December 1995 at the latest, allow the use in its territory of homeopathic medicinal products registered by other Member States in accordance with Articles 7 and 8.

3. Advertising of the homeopathic medicinal products referred to in paragraph 2 of this Article and in Article 7 (1) shall be subject to the provisions of Directive 92/28/EEC of 31 March 1992 on the advertising of medicinal products for human use (¹), with the exception of Article 2 (1) of that Directive.

However, only the information specified in Article 7 (2) may be used in the advertising of such medicinal products.

Moreover, each Member State may prohibit in its territory any advertising of the homeopathic medicinal products referred to in paragraph 2 and in Article 7 (1).

Article 7

1. Only homeopathic medicinal products which satisfy all of the following conditions may be subject to a special, simplified registration procedure:

— they are administered orally of externally,

— no specific therapeutic indication appears on the labelling of the medicinal product or in any information relating thereto,

— there is a sufficient degree of dilution to guarantee the safety of the medicinal product; in particular, the medicinal product may not contain either more than one part per 10 000 of the mother tincture or more than 1/100th of the smallest dose used in allopathy with regard to active principles whose presence in an allopathic medicinal product results in the obligation to submit a doctor's prescription.

At the time of registration, Member States shall determine the classification for the dispensing of the medicinal product.

_____
(¹) OJ No L 113, 30. 4. 1992, p. 13.

2. In addition to the clear mention of the words 'homeopathic medicinal product', the labelling and, where appropriate, package insert for the medicinal products referred to in paragraph 1 shall bear the following, and no other, information:

— the scientific name of the stock or stocks followed by the degree of dilution, making use of the symbols of the pharmacopoeia used in accordance with Article 1 (1),

— name and address of the person responsible for placing the product on the market and, where appropriate, of the manufacturer,

— method of administration and, if necessary, route,

— expiry date, in clear terms (month, year),

— pharmaceutical form,

— contents of the sales presentation,

— special storage precautions, if any,

— a special warning if necessary for the medicinal product,

— manufacturer's batch number,

— registration number,

— 'homeopathic medicinal product without approved therapeutic indications',

— a warning advising the user to consult a doctor if the symptoms persist during the use of the medicinal product.

3. Notwithstanding paragraph 2, Member States may require the use of certain types of labelling in order to show:

— the price of the medicinal product,

— the conditions for refunds by social security bodies.

4. The criteria and rules of procedure provided for in Articles 5 to 12 of Directive 65/65/EEC shall apply by analogy to the special, simplified registration procedure for homeopathic medicinal products, with the exception of the proof of therapeutic efficacy.

Article 8

An application for special, simplified registration submitted by the person responsible for placing the product on the market may cover a series of medicinal products derived from the same homeopathic stock or stocks. The following documents shall be included with the application in order to demonstrate, in particular, the pharmaceutical quality and the batch-to-batch homogeneity of the products concerned:

— scientific name or other name given in a pharmacopoeia of the homeopathic stock or stocks, together with a statement of the various routes of administration, pharmaceutical forms and degree of dilution to be registered,

— dossier describing how the homeopathic stock or stocks is/are obtained and controlled, and justifying its/their homeopathic nature, on the basis of an adequate bibliography,

— manufacturing and control file for each pharamceutical form and a description of the method of dilution and potentization,

— manufacturing authorization for the medicinal product concerned,

— copies of any registrations or authorizations obtained for the same medicinal product in other Member States;

— one or more specimens or mock-ups of the sales presentation of the medicinal products to be registered,

— data concerning the stability of the medicinal product.

Article 9

1. Homeopathic medicinal products other than those referred to in Article 7 of this Directive shall be authorized and labelled in accordance with Articles 4 to 21 of Directive 65/65/EEC including the provisions concerning proof of therapeutic effect and Articles 1 to 7 of Directive 75/319/EEC.

2. A Member State may introduce or retain in its territory specific rules for the pharmacological and toxicological tests and clinical trials of homeopathic medicinal products other than those referred to in Article 7 (1) in accordance with the principles and characteristics of homeopathy as practised in that Member State.

In this case, the Member State concerned shall notify the Commission of the specific rules in force.

CHAPTER IV

Final provisions

Article 10

1. Member States shall take the measures necessary to comply with this Directive by 31 December 1993. They shall forthwith inform the Commission thereof.

When Member States adopt the said measures, they shall contain a reference to this Directive or be accompanied by such reference when they are officially published. The procedure for making such reference shall be adopted by the Member States.

2.   Applications for registration or for marketing authorization for medicinal products covered by this Directive lodged after the date set in paragraph 1 shall comply with the provisions of this Directive.

3.   Not later than 31 December 1995, the Commission shall present a report to the European Parliament and the Council concerning the application of this Directive.

Article 11

This Directive is addressed to the Member States.

Done at Brussels, 22 September 1992.

For the Council
The President
R. NEEDHAM

375L0318

75/318/EEC: COUNCIL DIRECTIVE OF 20 MAY 1975 ON THE APPROXIMATION OF THE LAWS OF MEMBER STATES RELATING TO ANALYTICAL, PHARMACO-TOXICOLOGICAL AND CLINICAL STANDARDS AND PROTOCOLS IN RESPECT OF THE TESTING OF " MEDICINAL PRODUCTS " [3]

OFFICIAL JOURNAL No L 147, 09/06/1975, P. 1
DATE OF NOTIFICATION: 21/05/1975
DATE OF TRANSPOSITION: 21/11/1976; SEE ART. 3

AMENDED BY

383L0570
83/570/EEC: COUNCIL DIRECTIVE OF 26 OCTOBER 1983   [1]
OFFICIAL JOURNAL No L 332, 28/11/1983, P. 1
DATE OF NOTIFICATION: 31/10/1983
DATE OF TRANSPOSITION: 31/10/1985; SEE ART. 4

387L0019
87/19/EEC: COUNCIL DIRECTIVE OF 22 DECEMBER 1986   [2]
OFFICIAL JOURNAL No L 15, 17/01/1987, P. 31
DATE OF NOTIFICATION: 23/12/1986
DATE OF TRANSPOSITION: 01/07/1987; SEE ART. 2

389L0341
89/341/EEC: COUNCIL DIRECTIVE OF 3 MAY 1989   [3]
OFFICIAL JOURNAL No L 142, 25/05/1989, P. 11
DATE OF NOTIFICATION: 17/05/1989
DATE OF TRANSPOSITION: 01/01/1992; SEE ART. 4
DATE OF TRANSPOSITION: 31/12/1992; SEE ART. 4

391L0507
91/507/EEC: COMMISSION DIRECTIVE OF 19 JULY 1991   [4]
OFFICIAL JOURNAL No. L 270, 26/09/1991, P. 32
DATE OF TRANSPOSITION: 01/01/1992; SEE ART. 2
DATE OF TRANSPOSITION: 01/01/1995; SEE ART. 2

393L0039
93/39/EEC: COUNCIL DIRECTIVE OF 14 JUNE 1993   [5]
OFFICIAL JOURNAL No L 214, 24/08/1993, P. 22
DATE OF TRANSPOSITION: 01/01/1995; SEE ART. 4
DATE OF TRANSPOSITION: 01/01/1998; SEE ART. 4

ARTICLE 1

MEMBER STATES SHALL TAKE ALL APPROPRIATE MEASURES TO ENSURE THAT THE PARTICULARS AND DOCUMENTS WHICH MUST ACCOMPANY APPLICATIONS FOR AUTHORIZATION TO PLACE A " MEDICINAL PRODUCT " [3] ON THE MARKET (MARKETING AUTHORIZATION), PURSUANT TO POINTS 3, 4, 6, 7 AND 8 OF ARTICLE 4, SECOND PARAGRAPH, OF DIRECTIVE 65/65/EEC (1), ARE SUBMITTED BY THE PERSONS CONCERNED IN ACCORDANCE WITH THE ANNEX TO THIS DIRECTIVE.
WHERE, PURSUANT TO POINT 8 (a) AND (b) OF ARTICLE 4, SECOND PARAGRAPH, OF THE ABOVEMENTIONED DIRECTIVE, REFERENCES TO PUBLISHED DATA ARE SUBMITTED, THE PROVISIONS OF THIS DIRECTIVE SHALL APPLY IN LIKE MANNER.

ARTICLE 2

NOTWITHSTANDING THE PROVISIONS OF OTHER DIRECTIVES ON " MEDICINAL PRODUCTS " [3], MEMBER STATES SHALL TAKE ALL APPROPRIATE MEASURES TO ENSURE THAT THE COMPETENT AUTHORITIES EXAMINE THE PARTICULARS AND DOCUMENTS SUBMITTED IN SUPPORT OF APPLICATIONS FOR MARKETING AUTHORIZATION IN ACCORDANCE WITH THE CRITERIA OF THE ANNEX TO THIS DIRECTIVE.

" ARTICLE 2a

ANY CHANGES WHICH ARE NECESSARY IN ORDER TO ADAPT THE ANNEX TO TAKE ACCOUNT OF TECHNICAL PROGRESS SHALL BE ADOPTED IN ACCORDANCE WITH THE PROCEDURE LAID DOWN IN ARTICLE 2c.
IF APPROPRIATE, THE COMMISSION SHALL PROPOSE TO THE COUNCIL THAT THE PROCEDURE IN ARTICLE 2c BE REVIEWED IN CONNECTION WITH THE DETAILED RULES SET FOR THE EXERCISE OF THE POWERS OF IMPLEMENTATION GRANTED TO THE COMMISSION.

ARTICLE 2b

1. " The Standing Committee on Medicinal Products for Human Use " [5], HEREINAFTER CALLED "THE COMMITTEE", IS HEREBY SET UP; IT SHALL CONSIST OF REPRESENTATIVES OF THE MEMBER STATES WITH A REPRESENTATIVE OF THE COMMISSION AS CHAIRMAN.

2. THE COMMITTEE SHALL ADOPT ITS OWN RULES OF PROCEDURE.

ARTICLE 2c

1. WHERE THE PROCEDURE LAID DOWN IN THIS ARTICLE IS TO BE FOLLOWED, MATTERS SHALL BE REFERRED TO THE COMMITTEE BY THE CHAIRMAN EITHER ON HIS OWN INITIATIVE OR AT THE REQUEST OF THE REPRESENTATIVE OF A MEMBER STATE.

2. THE REPRESENTATIVE OF THE COMMISSION SHALL SUBMIT TO THE COMMITTEE A DRAFT OF THE MEASURES TO BE ADOPTED. THE COMMITTEE SHALL DELIVER ITS OPINION ON THE DRAFT WITHIN A TIME LIMIT SET BY THE CHAIRMAN, HAVING REGARD TO THE URGENCY OF THE MATTER. IT SHALL ACT BY A QUALIFIED MAJORITY, THE VOTES OF THE MEMBER STATES BEING WEIGHTED AS PROVIDED IN ARTICLE 148 (2) OF THE TREATY. THE CHAIRMAN SHALL NOT VOTE.

3. (a) THE COMMISSION SHALL ADOPT THE MEASURES ENVISAGED WHERE THEY ARE IN ACCORDANCE WITH THE OPINION OF THE COMMITTEE.

(b) WHERE THE MEASURES ENVISAGED ARE NOT IN ACCORDANCE WITH THE OPINION OF THE COMMITTEE, OR IF NO OPINION IS ADOPTED, THE COMMISSION SHALL WITHOUT DELAY PROPOSE TO THE COUNCIL THE MEASURES TO BE ADOPTED. THE COUNCIL SHALL ACT BY A QUALIFIED MAJORITY.

(c) IF, WITHIN THREE MONTHS OF THE PROPOSAL BEING SUBMITTED TO IT, THE COUNCIL HAS NOT ACTED, THE PROPOSED MEASURES SHALL BE ADOPTED BY THE COMMISSION. " [2]

ARTICLE 3

MEMBER STATES SHALL BRING INTO FORCE THE PROVISIONS NEEDED IN ORDER TO COMPLY WITH THIS DIRECTIVE WITHIN 18 MONTHS OF ITS NOTIFICATION AND SHALL FORTHWITH INFORM THE COMMISSION THEREOF.
MEMBER STATES SHALL ENSURE THAT THEY COMMUNICATE TO THE COMMISSION THE TEXT OF THE MAIN PROVISIONS OF NATIONAL LAW WHICH THEY ADOPT IN THE FIELD COVERED BY THIS DIRECTIVE.

ARTICLE 4

THIS DIRECTIVE IS ADDRESSED TO THE MEMBER STATES.

ANNEX

" INTRODUCTION

The particulars and documents accompanying an application for marketing authorization pursuant to Article 4 of Council Directive 65/65/EEC shall be presented in four parts, in accordance with the requirements set out in this Annex and taking account of the guidance published by the Commission in The rules governing medicinal products in the European Community Volume II: Notice to applicants for marketing authorizations for medicinal products for human use in the Member States of the European Community;
In assembling the dossier for application for marketing authorization, applicants shall take into account the Community guidelines relating to the quality, safety and efficacy of medicinal products published by the Commission in The rules governing medicinal products in the European Community, Volume III and its supplements: Guidelines on the quality, safety and efficacy of medicinal products for human use.
All information which is relevant to the evaluation of the medicinal product concerned shall be included in the application, whether favourable or unfavourable to the product. In particular, all relevant details shall be given of any incomplete or abandoned pharmacotoxicological or clinical test or trial relating to the medicinal product. Moreover, in order to monitor the benefit/risk assessment after marketing authorization has been granted, any change to the data in the dossier, any new information not in the original application and all pharmacovigilance reports, shall be submitted to the competent authorities.
The general sections of this Annex give the requirements for all categories of medicinal products; they are supplemented by sections containing additional special requirements for radiopharmaceuticals and for biological medicinal products, such as vaccines, serums, toxins, allergen products, medicinal products derived from human blood or plasma. The additional special requirements for biological medicinal products are also applicable to medicinal products obtained through processes mentioned in List A and the first indent of List B of the Annex to Directive 87/22/EEC (2).
Member States shall also ensure that all tests on animals are conducted in accordance with Council Directive 86/609/EEC (3).

PART I

SUMMARY OF THE DOSSIER

A. Administrative data

The medicinal product which is the subject of the application shall be identified by name and name of the active ingredient(s), together with the pharmaceutical form, the method of administration, the strength and the final presentation, including packaging.

The name and address of the applicant shall be given, together with the name and address of the manufacturers and the sites involved in the different stages of the manufacture (including the manufacturer of the finished product and the manufacturer(s) of the active ingredient(s)), and where relevant the name and address of the importer.

The applicant shall identify the number of volumes of documentation submitted in support of the application and indicate what samples, if any, are also provided.

Annexed to the administrative data shall be copies of the manufacturing authorization as defined in Article 16 of Council Directive 75/319/EEC (4), together with a list of countries in which authorization has been granted, copies of all the summaries of product characteristics in accordance with Article 4a of Directive 65/65/EEC as approved by Member States and a list of countries in which an application has been submitted.

B. Summary of product characteristics

The applicant shall propose a summary of the product characteristics, in accordance with Article 4a of Directive 65/65/EEC.

In addition the applicant shall provide samples or mock-ups of the packaging, labels and package leaflets for the medicinal product concerned.

C. Expert reports

In accordance with Article 2 of Directive 75/319/EEC, expert reports must be provided on the chemical, pharmaceutical and biological documentation, the pharmacotoxicological documentation and the clinical documentation respectively.

The expert report shall consist of a critical evaluation of the quality of the product and the investigations carried out on animals and human beings and bring out all the data relevant for evaluation. It shall be worded so as to enable the reader to obtain a good understanding of the properties, quality, the proposed specifications and control methods, the safety, the efficacy, the advantages and disadvantages of the product.

All important data shall be summarized in an appendix to the expert report, whenever possible including report formats in tabular or in graphic form. The expert report and the summaries shall contain precise cross references to the information contained in the main documentation.

Each expert report shall be prepared by a suitably qualified and experienced person. It shall be signed and dated by the expert, and attached to the report shall be brief information about the educational background, training and occupational experience of the expert. The professional relationship of the expert to the applicant shall be declared.

PART 2

CHEMICAL, PHARMACEUTICAL AND BIOLOGICAL TESTING OF MEDICINAL PRODUCTS

All the test procedures shall correspond to the state of scientific progress at the time and shall be validated procedures; results of the validation studies shall be provided.

All the test procedure(s) shall be described in sufficiently precise detail so as to be reproducible in control tests, carried out at the request of the competent authority; any special apparatus and equipment which may be used shall be described in adequate detail, possibly accompanied by a diagram. The formulae of the laboratory reagents shall be supplemented, if necessary, by the method of preparation. In the case of test procedures included in the European Pharmacopoeia or the pharmacopoeia of a Member State, this description may be replaced by a detailed reference to the pharmacopoeia in question.

A. Qualitative and quantitative particulars of the constituents

The particulars and documents which must accompany applications for marketing authorization, pursuant to point 3 of Article 4 (2) of Directive 65/65/EEC shall be submitted in accordance with the following requirements.

1. Qualitative particulars

1.1. "Qualitative particulars" of all the constituents of the medicinal product shall mean the designation or description of:

- the active ingredient(s),
- the constituent(s) of the excipients, whatever their nature or the quantity used, including colouring matter, preservatives, adjuvants, stabilizers, thickeners, emulsifiers, flavouring and aromatic substances, etc.,
- the constituents, intended to be ingested or otherwise administered to the patient, of the outer covering of the medicinal products - capsules, gelatine capsules, rectal capsules, etc.

These particulars shall be supplemented by any relevant data concerning the container and, where appropriate, its manner of closure, together with details of devices with which the medicinal product will be used or administered and which will be delivered with the product.

1.2. In the context of a radiopharmaceutical kit, which is to be radiolabelled after supply by the manufacturer, the active ingredient is considered to be that part of the formulation which is intended to carry or bind the radionuclide. Details of the source of the radionuclide shall be stated. In addition, any compounds essential for the radiolabelling shall be stated.
In a generator, both mother and daughter radionuclides are to be considered as active ingredients.

2. The "usual terminology", to be used in describing the constituents of medicinal products, shall mean, notwithstanding the application of the other provisions of point 3 of Article 4 (2) of Directive 65/65/EEC:

- in respect of substances which appear in the European Pharmacopoeia or, failing this, in the national pharmacopoeia of one of the Member States, the main title at the head of the monograph in question, with reference to the pharmacopoeia concerned,
- in respect of other substances, the international non-proprietary name recommended by the World Health Organization, which may be accompanied by another non-proprietary name, or, failing these, the exact scientific designation; substances not having an international non-proprietary name or an exact scientific designation shall be described by a statement of how and from what they were prepared, supplemented, where appropriate, by any other relevant details,
- in respect of colouring matter, designation by the "E" code assigned to them in Council Directive 78/25/EEC (5) of 12 December 1977 on the approximation of the rules of the Member States concerning the colouring matters authorized for use in medicinal products.

3. Quantitative particulars

3.1. In order to give "quantitative particulars" of the active ingredients of the medicinal products, it is necessary, depending on the pharmaceutical form concerned, to specify the mass, or the number of units of biological activity, either per dosage-unit or per unit of mass or volume, of each active ingredient.
Units of biological activity shall be used for substances which cannot be defined chemically. Where an International Unit of biological activity has been defined by the World Health Organization, this shall be used. Where no International Unit has been defined, the units of biological activity shall be expressed in such a way as to provide unambiguous information on the activity of the substances.
Whenever possible, biological activity per units of mass shall be indicated.
This information shall be supplemented:

- in respect of injectable preparations, by the mass or units of biological activity of each active ingredient in the unit container, taking into account the usable volume of the product, after reconstitution, where appropriate,
- in respect of medicinal products to be administered by drops, by the mass or units of biological activity of each active ingredient contained in the number of drops corresponding to 1 ml or 1 g of the preparation,
- in respect of syrups, emulsions, granular preparations and other pharmaceutical forms to be administered in measured quantities, by the mass or units of biological activity of each active ingredient per measured quantity.

3.2. Active ingredients present in the form of compounds or derivatives shall be described quantitatively by their total mass, and if necessary or relevant, by the mass of the active entity or entities of the molecule.

3.3. For medicinal products containing an active ingredient which is the subject of an application for marketing authorization in any Member State for the first time, the quantitative statement of an active ingredient which is a salt or hydrate shall be systematically expressed in terms of the mass of the active entity or entities in the molecule. All subsequently authorized medicinal products in the Member States shall have their quantitative composition stated in the same way for the same active ingredient.

3.4. For allergen products, the quantitative particulars shall be expressed by units of biological activity, except for well defined allergen products for which the concentration may be expressed by mass/unit of volume.

3.5. The requirement to express the content of active ingredients in terms of the mass of active entities, as in point 3.3. above, may not apply to radiopharmaceuticals. For radionuclides, radioactivity shall be expressed in becquerels at a given date and, if necessary, time with reference to time zone. The type of radiation shall be indicated.

4. Development pharmaceutics

4.1. An explanation should be provided with regard to the choice of composition, constituents and container and the intended function of the excipients in the finished product. This explanation shall be supported by scientific data on development pharmaceutics. The overage, with justification thereof, should be stated.

4.2. For radiopharmaceuticals, this should include a consideration of chemical/radiochemical purity and its relationship to biodistribution.

B. Description of method of preparation

1. The description of the method of preparation accompanying the application for marketing authorization pursuant to point 4 of Article 4 (2) of Directive 65/65/EEC, shall be drafted in such a way as to give an adequate synopsis of the nature of the operations employed.
For this purpose it shall include at least:

- mention of the various stages of manufacture, so that an assessment can be made of whether the processes employed in producing the pharmaceutical form might have produced an adverse change in the constituents,
- in the case of continuous manufacture, full details concerning precautions taken to ensure the homogeneity of the finished product,
- the actual manufacturing formula, with the quantitative particulars of all the substances used, the quantities of excipients, however, being given in approximate terms in so far as the pharmaceutical form makes this necessary; mention shall be made of any substances that may disappear in the course of manufacture; any overage shall be indicated and justified,
- a statement of the stages of manufacture at which sampling is carried out for in-process control tests, where other data in the documents supporting the application show such tests to be necessary for the quality control of the finished product,
- experimental studies validating the manufacturing process, where a non-standard method of manufacture is used or where it is critical for the product,
- for sterile products, details of the sterilization processes and/or aseptic procedures used.

2. For radiopharmaceutical kits, the description of the method of preparation shall also include details of the manufacture of the kit and details of its recommended final processing to produce the radioactive medicinal product.
For radionuclides, the nuclear reactions involved shall be discussed.

C. Controls of starting materials

1. For the purposes of this paragraph, "starting materials" shall mean all the constituents of the medicinal product and, if necessary, of its container, as referred to in paragraph A, point 1, above.
In the case of:

- an active ingredient not described in the European Pharmacopoeia or in the pharmacopoeia of a Member State, or

- an active ingredient described in the European Pharmacopoeia or in the pharmacopoeia of a Member State when prepared by a method liable to leave impurities not mentioned in the pharmacopoeial monograph and for which the monograph is inappropriate to adequately control its quality,

which is manufactured by a person different from the applicant, the latter may arrange for the detailed description of the manufacturing method, quality control during manufacture and process validation to be supplied directly to the competent authorities by the manufacturer of the active ingredient. In this case, the manufacturer shall however provide the applicant with all the data which may be necessary for the latter to take responsibility for the medicinal product. The manufacturer shall confirm in writing to the applicant that he shall ensure batch to batch consistency and not modify the manufacturing process or specifications without informing the applicant. Documents and particulars supporting the application for such a change shall be supplied to the competent authorities.

The particulars and documents accompanying the application for marketing authorization pursuant to points 7 and 8 of Article 4 (2) of Directive 65/65/EEC shall include the results of the tests, including batch analyses particularly for active ingredients, relating to quality control of all the constituents used. These shall be submitted in accordance with the following provisions.

1.1. Starting materials listed in pharmacopoeias

The monographs of the European Pharmacopoeia shall be applicable to all substances appearing in it.
In respect of other substances, each Member State may require observance of its own national pharmacopoeia with regard to products manufactured in its territory.
Constituents fulfilling the requirements of the European Pharmacopoeia or the pharmacopoeia of one of the Member States shall be deemed to comply sufficiently with point 7 of Article 4 (2) of Directive 65/65/EEC. In this case the description of the analytical methods may be replaced by a detailed reference to the pharmacopoeia in question.
However, where a starting material in the European Pharmacopoeia or in the pharmacopoeia of a Member State has been prepared by a method liable to leave impurities not controlled in the pharmacopoeia monograph, these impurities and their maximum tolerance limits must be declared and a suitable test procedure must be described.
Colouring matter shall, in all cases, satisfy the requirements of Directive 78/25/EEC.
The routine tests carried out on each batch of starting materials must be as stated in the application for marketing authorization. If tests other than those mentioned in the pharmacopoeia are used, proof must be supplied that the starting materials meet the quality requirements of that pharmacopoeia.
In cases where a specification contained in a monograph of the European Pharmacopoeia or in the national pharmacopoeia of a Member State might be insufficient to ensure the quality of the substance, the competent authorities may request more appropriate specifications from the person responsible for placing the product on the market.
The competent authorities shall inform the authorities responsible for the pharmacopoeia in question. The person responsible for placing the product on the market shall provide the authorities of that pharmacopoeia with the details of the alleged insufficiency and the additional specifications applied.
In cases where a starting material is described neither in the European Pharmacopoeia nor in the pharmacopoeia of a Member State, compliance with the monograph of a third country pharmacopoeia can be accepted; in such cases, the applicant shall submit a copy of the monograph accompanied where necessary by the validation of the test procedures contained in the monograph and by a translation where appropriate.

1.2. Starting materials not in a pharmacopoeia

Constituents which are not given in any pharmacopoeia shall be described in the form of a monograph under the following headings:

(a) The name of the substance, meeting the requirements of paragraph A, point 2, shall be supplemented by any trade or scientific synonyms;

(b) the definition of the substance, set down in a form similar to that used in the European Pharmacopoeia, shall be accompanied by any necessary explanatory evidence, especially concerning the molecular structure where appropriate; it must be accompanied by an appropriate description of the method of synthesis. Where substances can only be described by their method of preparation, the description should be sufficiently detailed to characterize a substance which is constant both in its composition and in its effects;

(c) methods of identification may be described in the form of complete techniques as used for production of the substance, and in the form of tests which ought to be carried out as a routine matter;

(d) purity tests shall be described in relation to the sum total of predictable impurities, especially those which may have a harmful effect, and, if necessary, those which, having regard to the combination of substances to which the application refers, might adversely affect the stability of the medicinal product or distort analytical results;

(e) with regard to complex substances of plant or animal/human origin, a distinction must be made between the case where multiple pharmacological effects render chemical, physical or biological control of the principal constituents necessary, and the case of substances containing one or more groups of principles having similar activity, in respect of which an overall method of assay may be accepted;

(f) when materials of animal/human origin are used, measures to ensure freedom from potentially pathogenic agents shall be described;

(g) for radionuclides, the nature of the radionuclide, the identity of the isotope, likely impurities, the carrier, the use and the specific activity shall be given;

(h) any special precautions that may be necessary during storage of the starting material and, if necessary, the maximum period of storage before retesting shall be given.

1.3. Physico-chemical characteristics liable to effect bio-availability

The following items of information concerning active ingredients, whether or not listed in the pharmacopoeias, shall be provided as part of the general description of the active ingredients if the bio-availability of the medicinal product depends on them:

- crystalline form and solubility coefficients,
- particle size, where appropriate after pulverization,
- state of solvation,
- oil/water coefficient of partition (6).

The first three indents are not applicable to substances used solely in solution.

2. For biological medicinal products, such as vaccines, serums, toxins, allergen products and medicinal products derived from human blood or plasma, the requirements of this paragraph shall apply.
For the purposes of this paragraph, starting materials shall mean any substance used in the manufacture of the medicinal product; this includes the constituents of the medicinal product, and, if necessary, of its container, as referred to in paragraph A, point 1 above, as well as source materials such as microorganisms, tissues of either plant or animal origin, cells or fluids (including blood) of human or animal origin, and biotechnological cell constructs. The origin and history of starting materials shall be described and documented.
The description of the starting material shall include the manufacturing strategy, purification/inactivation procedures with their validation and all in-process control procedures designed to ensure the quality, safety and batch to batch consistency of the finished product.

2.1. When cell banks are used, the cell characteristics shall be shown to have remained unchanged at the passage level used for the production and beyond.

2.2. Seed materials, cell banks, pools of serum or plasma and other materials of biological origin and, whenever possible, the source materials from which they are derived shall be tested for adventitious agents.
If the presence of potentially pathogenic adventitious agents is inevitable, the material shall be used only when further processing ensures their elimination and/or inactivation, and this shall be validated.

2.3. Whenever possible, vaccine production shall be based on a seed lot system and on established cell banks; for serums, defined pools of starting materials shall be used.
For bacterial and viral vaccines, the characteristics of the infectious agent shall be demonstrated on the seed. In addition, for live vaccines, the stability of the attenuation characteristics shall be demonstrated on the seed; if this proof is not sufficient, the attenuation characteristics shall also be demonstrated at the production stage.

2.4. For allergen products, the specifications and control methods for the source materials shall be described. The description shall include particulars concerning collection, pretreatment and storage.

2.5. For medicinal products derived from human blood or plasma, the origin and the criteria and procedures for collection, transportation and storage of the source material shall be described and documented.
Defined pools of source material shall be used.

3. For radiopharmaceuticals, starting materials include irradiation target materials.

D. Control tests carried out at intermediate stages of the manufacturing process

1. The particulars and documents accompanying an application for marketing authorization, pursuant to points 7 and 8 of Article 4 (2) of Directive 65/65/EEC, shall include particulars relating to the product control tests that may be carried out at an intermediate stage of the manufacturing process, with a view to ensuring the consistency of the technical characteristics and the production process.
" These tests are essential for checking the conformity of the medicinal product with the formula when, exceptionally, an applicant proposes an analytical method for testing the finished product which does not include the assay of all the active ingredients (or of all the excipient constituents subject to the same requirements as the active ingredients). " [R1]
The same applies where the quality control of the finished product depends on in-process control tests, particularly if the substance is essentially defined by its method or preparation.

2. For biological medicinal products, such as vaccines, serums, toxins, allergen products and medicinal products derived from human blood or plasma, the procedures and the criteria of acceptability published as recommendations of the WHO (Requirements for Biological Substances) shall serve as guidelines for all controls of production stages which are not specified in the European Pharmacopoeia, or falling this, in the national pharmacopoeia of a Member State.
For inactivated or detoxified vaccines, effective inactivation or detoxification shall be verified during each production run, unless this control is dependent upon a test for which the availability of susceptible animals is limited. In this case, the test shall be carried out until consistency of production and correlation with appropriate in process controls have been established and thereafter compensated by appropriate in-process controls.

3. For modified or adsorbed allergens, the allergen products shall be qualitatively and quantitatively characterized at an intermediate stage, as late as possible in the manufacturing process.

E. Control tests on the finished product

1. For the control of the finished product, a batch of a finished product comprises all the units of a pharmaceutical form which are made from the same initial quantity of material and have undergone the same series of manufacturing and/or sterilization operations or, in the case of a continuous production process, all the units manufactured in a given period of time.
The application for marketing authorization shall list those tests which are carried out routinely on each batch of finished product. The frequency of the tests which are not carried out routinely shall be stated. Release limits shall be indicated.
The particulars and documents accompanying the application for marketing authorization pursuant to points 7 and 8 of Article 4 (2) of Directive 65/65/EEC, shall include particulars relating to control tests on the finished product at release. They shall be submitted in accordance with the following requirements.
The provisions of the monographs for pharmaceutical forms, immunosera, vaccines and radiopharmaceutical preparations of the European Pharmacopoeia or failing that, of a Member State, shall be applicable to " all products defined therein. For all controls of biological medicinal products such as vaccines, " [R2] serums, toxins, allergen products and medicinal products derived from human blood or plasma which are not specified in the European Pharmacopoeia or falling this, in the pharmacopoeia of a Member State, the procedures and the criteria of acceptability published as recommendations in the WHO (Requirements for Biological Substances) shall serve as guidelines.
If test procedures and limits other than those mentioned in the monographs of the European Pharmacopoeia, or falling this, in the national pharmacopoeia of a Member State, are used, proof shall be supplied that the finished product would, if tested in accordance with those monographs, meet the quality requirements of that pharmacopoeia for the pharmaceutical form concerned.

1.1. General characteristics of the finished product

Certain tests of the general characteristics of a product shall always be included among the tests on the finished product. These tests shall, wherever applicable, relate to the control of average masses and maximum deviations, to mechanical, physical or microbiological tests, organoleptic characteristics, physical characteristics such as density, pH, refractive index, etc. For each of these characteristics, standards and tolerance limits shall be specified by the applicant in each particular case.

The conditions of the tests, where appropriate, the equipment/apparatus employed and the standards shall be described in precise details whenever they are not given in the European Pharmacopoeia or the pharmacopoeia of the Member States; the same shall apply in cases where the methods prescribed by such pharmacopoeias are not applicable.

Furthermore, solid pharmaceutical forms having to be administered orally shall be subjected to in vitro studies on the liberation and dissolution rate of the active ingredient or ingredients; these studies shall also be carried out where administration is by another means if the competent authorities of the Member State concerned consider this necessary.

1.2. Identification and assay of active ingredient(s)

Identification and assay of the active ingredient(s) shall be carried out either in a representative sample from the production batch or in a number of dosage-units analysed individually.

Unless there is appropriate justification, the maximum acceptable deviation in the active ingredient content of the finished product shall not exceed ± 5% at the time of manufacture.

On the basis of the stability tests, the manufacturer must propose and justify maximum acceptable tolerance limits in the active-ingredient content of the finished product up to the end of the proposed shelf-life.

In certain exceptional cases of particularly complex mixtures, where assay of active ingredients which are very numerous or present in very low amounts would necessitate an intricate investigation difficult to carry out in respect of each production batch, the assay of one or more active ingredients in the finished product may be omitted, on the express condition that such assays are made at intermediate stages in the production process. This relaxation may not be extended to the characterization of the substances concerned. This simplified technique shall be supplemented by a method of quantitative evaluation, enabling the competent authority to have the conformity of the medicinal product with its specification verified after it has been placed on the market.

An in vivo or in vitro biological assay shall be obligatory when physico-chemical methods cannot provide adequate information on the quality of the product. Such an assay shall, whenever possible, include reference materials and statistical analysis allowing calculation of confidence limits. Where these tests cannot be carried out on the finished product, they may be performed at an intermediate stage, as late as possible in the manufacturing process.

Where the particulars given in section B show that a significant overage of an active ingredient is employed in the manufacture of the medicinal product, the description of the control tests on the finished product shall include, where appropriate, the chemical and, if necessary, the toxico-pharmacological investigation of the changes that this substance has undergone, and possibly the characterization and/or assay of the degradation products.

1.3. Identification and assay of excipient constituents

In so far as is necessary, the excipient(s) shall be subject at least to identification tests.

The test procedure proposed for identifying colouring matters must enable a verification to be made that such matters appear in the list annexed to Directive 78/25/EEC.

An upper and lower limit test shall be obligatory in respect of preserving agents and an upper limit test for any other excipient constituent liable to affect adversely physiological functions; an upper and lower limit test shall be obligatory in respect of the excipient if it is liable to affect the bio-availability of an active substance, unless bio-availability is guaranteed by other appropriate tests.

1.4. Safety tests

Apart from the toxico-pharmacological tests submitted with the application for marketing authorization, particulars of safety tests, such as sterility, bacterial endotoxin, pyrogenicity and local tolerance in animals shall be included in the analytical particulars wherever such tests must be undertaken as a matter of routine in order to verify the quality of the product.

2. For all controls of biological medicinal products, such as vaccines, serums, toxins, allergen products and medicinal products derived from human blood or plasma, which are not specified in the European Pharmacopoeia, or failing this, in the national pharmacopoeia of a Member State, the procedures and the criteria of acceptability published as recommendations in the WHO (Requirements for Biological Substances) shall serve as guidelines.

3. For radiopharmaceuticals, radionuclidic purity, radiochemical purity and specific activity shall be described. For content of radioactivity, the deviation from that stated on the label should not exceed ± 10%.

For generators, details on the testing for mother and daughter radionuclides are required. For generator-eluates, tests for mother radionuclides and for other components of the generator system shall be provided.

For kits, the specifications of the finished product shall include tests on performance of products after radiolabelling. Appropriate controls on radiochemical and radionuclidic purity of the radiolabelled compound shall be included. Any material essential for radiolabelling shall be identified and assayed.

F. Stability tests

1. The particulars and documents accompanying the application for marketing authorization pursuant to points 6 and 7 of Article 4 (2) of Directive 65/65/EEC shall be submitted in accordance with the following requirements.

A description shall be given of the investigations by which the shelf life, the recommended storage conditions and the specifications at the end of the shelf-life proposed by the applicant have been determined.

Where a finished product is liable to give rise to degradation products, the applicant must declare these and indicate characterization methods and test procedures.

The conclusions shall contain the results of analyses, justifying the proposed shelf life under the recommended storage conditions and the specifications of the finished product at the end of the shelf-life under these recommended storage conditions.

The maximum acceptable level of degradation products at the end of shelf-life shall be indicated.

A study of the interaction between product and container shall be submitted wherever the risk of such interaction is regarded as possible, especially where injectable preparations or aerosols for internal use are concerned.

2. Where for biological medicinal products, such as vaccines, serums, toxins, allergen products and medicinal products derived from human blood or plasma, stability tests cannot be carried out on the finished products, it is acceptable to carry out stability indicating tests at an intermediate stage of production as late as possible in the manufacturing process. In addition, there should be an evaluation of the stability of the finished product using other secondary tests.

3. For radiopharmaceuticals, information on stability shall be given for generators, kits and radiolabelled products. The stability during use of radiopharmaceuticals in multi-dose vials shall be documented.

PART 3

TOXICOLOGICAL AND PHARMACOLOGICAL TESTS

I. Introduction

1. The particulars and documents accompanying the application for marketing authorization pursuant to point 8 of Article 4, second paragraph, Directive 65/65/EEC shall be given in accordance with the requirements below.

Member States shall ensure that the safety tests are carried out in conformity with the provisions relating to good laboratory practice laid down by Directives 87/18/EEC (7) and 88/320/EEC (8).

The toxicological and pharmacological tests must show:

(a) the potential toxicity of the product and any dangerous or undesirable toxic effects that may occur under the proposed conditions of use in human beings; these should be evaluated in relation to the pathological condition concerned;

(b) the pharmacological properties of the product, in both qualitative and quantitative relationship to the proposed use in human beings. All results must be reliable and of general applicability. Whenever appropriate, mathematical and statistical procedures shall be used in designing the experimental methods and in evaluating the results.

Additionally, it is necessary for clinicians to be given information about the therapeutic potential of the product.

2. Where a medicinal product is intended for topical use, systemic absorption must be investigated, due account also being taken of the possible use of the product on broken skin and absorption through other relevant surfaces. Only if it is proved that " systemic " [R2] absorption under these conditions is negligible may repeated dose " systemic " [R2] toxicity tests, foetal toxicity tests and studies of reproductive function be omitted.

If, however, " systemic " [R2] absorption is demonstrated during therapeutic experimentation, toxicity tests shall be carried out on animals, including where necessary, foetal toxicity tests.

In all cases, tests of local tolerance after repeated application shall be carried out with particular care and include histological examinations; the possibility of sensitization shall be investigated and any carcinogenic potential investigated in the cases referred to in paragraph II E of this Part.

3. For biological medicinal products such as vaccines, serums, toxins, allergen products and medicinal products derived from human blood or plasma, the requirements of this Part may have to be adapted for individual products; therefore the testing programme carried out shall be justified by the applicant.

In establishing the testing programme, the following shall be taken into consideration:

- all tests requiring repeated administration of the product shall be designed to take account of the possible induction of, and interference by, antibodies;
- examination of reproductive function, of embryo/foetal and perinatal toxicity, of mutagenic potential and of carcinogenic potential shall be considered. Where components other than the active ingredient(s) are incriminated, validation of their removal may replace the study.

4. For radiopharmaceuticals, it is appreciated that toxicity may be associated with a radiation dose. In diagnosis, this is a consequence of the use of radiopharmaceuticals; in therapy, it is the wanted property. The evaluation of safety and efficacy of radiopharmaceuticals shall, therefore, address requirements for medicinal products and radiation dosimetry aspects. Organ/tissue exposure to radiation shall be documented. Absorbed radiation dose estimates shall be calculated according to a specified, internationally recognized system by a particular route of administration.

5. The toxicology and pharmacokinetics of an excipient used for the first time in the pharmaceutical field shall be investigated.

6. Where there is a possibility of significant degradation during storage of the medicinal product, the toxicology of degradation products must be considered.

II. Performance of tests

A. Toxicity

1. Single dose toxicity

An acute test is a qualitative and quantitative study of the toxic reactions which may result from a single administration of the active substance or substances contained in the medicinal product, in the proportions and physico-chemical state in which they are present in the actual product.

The acute toxicity test must be carried out in two or more mammalian species of known strain unless a single species can be justified. At least two different routes of administration shall normally be used, one being identical with or similar to that proposed for use in human beings and the other ensuring systemic exposure to the substance.

This study will cover the signs observed, including local reactions. The period during which the test animals are observed shall be fixed by the investigator as being adequate to reveal tissue or organ damage or recovery, usually for a period of 14 days but not less than seven days, but without exposing the animals to prolonged suffering. Animals dying during the observation period should be subject to autopsy as also should all animals surviving to the end of the observation period. Histopathological examinations should be considered on any organ showing macroscopic changes at autopsy. The maximum amount of information should be obtained from the animals used in the study.

The single dose toxicity tests should be conducted in such a way that signs of acute toxicity are revealed and the mode of death assessed as far as reasonably possible. In suitable species a quantitative evaluation of the approximate lethal dose and information on the dose effect relationship should be obtained, but a high level of precision is not required.

These studies may give some indication of the likely effects of acute overdosage in man and may be useful for the design of toxicity studies requiring repeated dosing on the suitable animal species.

In the case of active substances in combination, the study must be carried out in such a way as to check whether or not there is enhancement of toxicity or if novel toxic effects occur.

2. Repeated dose toxicity (sub-acute or chronic toxicity)

Repeated dose toxicity tests are intended to reveal any physiological and/or pathological changes induced by repeated administration of the active substance or combination of active substances under examination, and to determine how these changes are related to dosage.

Generally, it is desirable that two tests be performed: one short-term, lasting two to four weeks, the other long-term. The duration of the latter shall depend on the conditions of clinical use. Its purpose shall be to determine by experiment the non-toxic dose range of the product and normally it shall last three to six months.

In respect of medicinal products to be administered once only to humans, a single test lasting two to four weeks shall be performed.

If however, having regard to the proposed duration of use in human beings, the investigator sees fit to carry out experiments of greater or lesser duration than indicated above, he must give adequate reasons for doing so. Reasons should also be given for the dosages chosen.

Repeated dose toxicity tests shall be carried out on two species of mammals one of which must be a non-rodent. The choice of route(s) of administration employed shall depend on the intended therapeutic use and the possibilities of systemic absorption. The method and frequency of dosage shall be clearly stated.

The maximum dose should be chosen so as to bring harmful effects to light. The lower doses will then enable the animal's tolerance of the product to be determined.

Wherever possible, and always in experiments on small rodents, the design of the experiment and the control procedures must be suited to the scale of the problem being tackled and enable fiducial limits to be determined.

The evaluation of the toxic effects shall be based on observation of behaviour, growth, haematological and biochemical tests, especially those relating to the excretory mechanism, and also on autopsy reports and accompanying histological data. The choice and range of each group of tests will depend on the species of animal used and the state of scientific knowledge at the time.

In the case of new combinations of known substances that have been investigated in accordance with the provisions of this Directive, the long-term tests may, except where acute and sub-acute toxicity tests have demonstrated potentiation or novel toxic effects, " be suitably modified " [R2] by the investigator who shall submit his reasons for such modification.

B. Examination of reproductive function

If the results of other tests reveal anything suggesting harmful effects on progeny or impairment of male or female reproductive function, this shall be investigated by appropriate tests.

C. Embryo/foetal and perinatal toxicity

This investigation comprises a demonstration of the toxic and especially the teratogenic effects observed in the issue of conception when the substance under investigation has been administered to the female during pregnancy.

Although up to the present these tests have had only a limited predictive value in regard to the application of the results to human beings, they are thought to provide important information where the results show effects such as resorptions and other anomalies.

Omission of these tests, either because the medicinal product will not normally be used by women capable of child-bearing or for other reasons, must be adequately justified.

Embryo/foetal toxicity studies shall normally be conducted on two mammalian species, one of which should be other than a rodent. Peri- and postnatal studies shall be conducted in at least one species. Where metabolism of a medicinal product in a particular species is known to be similar to that in man, it is desirable to include this species. Also, it is desirable that one of the species is the same as in the repeated dose toxicity studies.

The details of the test (number of animals, amounts administered, timing of administration and criteria for evaluation of results) shall depend on the state of scientific knowledge at the time when the application is lodged, and the level of statistical significance that the results must attain.

D. Mutagenic potential

The purpose of the study of mutagenic potential is to reveal the changes which a substance may cause in the genetic material of individuals or cells and which have the effect of making successors permanently and hereditarily different from their predecessors. This study is obligatory for any new substance.

The number and types of results and the criteria for their evaluation shall depend on the state of scientific knowledge at the time when the application is lodged.

E. Carcinogenic potential

Tests to reveal carcinogenic effects shall normally be required:

(a) in respect of substances having a close chemical analogy with known carcinogenic or cocarcinogenic compounds;

(b) in respect of substances which have given rise to suspicious changes during the long-term toxicological tests;

(c) in respect of substances which have given rise to suspicious results in the mutagenic-potential tests or in other short-term carcinogenicity tests.

Such tests may also be required in respect of substances to be included in medicinal products likely to be administered regularly over a prolonged period of a patient's life.

The state of scientific knowledge at the time when the application is lodged shall be taken into account when determining the details of the tests.

F. Pharmacodynamics

This heading covers the variations caused by the substance in the functions of the physiological systems, whether these functions are normal or experimentally modified.

This study shall follow two distinct lines of approach.

Firstly, the actions on which the recommended application in therapeutic practice is based shall be adequately described. The results shall be expressed in quantitative terms using, for example, dose-effect curves, time-effect curves etc., and wherever possible, compared with data relating to a substance whose activity is known. Where a higher therapeutic potency is being claimed for a substance, the difference shall be demonstrated and shown to be statistically significant.

Secondly, the investigator shall provide a general pharmacological characterization of the substance, with special reference to collateral effects. In general, the main functions of the physiological systems should be investigated. The depth of this investigation must be increased as the doses liable to produce side-effects approach those producing the main effect for which the substance is being proposed.

The experimental techniques, unless they are standard procedures, must be described in such detail as to allow them to be reproduced, and the investigator must establish their validity. The experimental results shall be set out clearly and, when relevant to the test, their statistical significance quoted.

Unless good reasons are given to the contrary, any quantitative modification of responses resulting from repeated administration of the substance shall be investigated.

Tests on combinations of active substances may be prompted either by pharmacological premises or by indications of therapeutic effect.

In the first case, the pharmacodynamic study shall demonstrate those interactions which might make the combination of value in therapeutic use.

In the second case, where scientific justification for the combination is sought through therapeutic experimentation, the investigation shall determine whether the effects expected from the combination can be demonstrated in animals, and the importance of any collateral effects shall at least be investigated.

If a combination includes a novel active substance, the latter must previously have been studied in depth.

G. Pharmacokinetics

Pharmacokinetics means the study of the fate of the active substance within the organism, and covers the study of the absorption, distribution, biotransformation and excretion of the substance.

The study of these different phases may be carried out both by means of physical, chemical or biological methods, and by observation of the actual pharmacodynamic activity of the substance itself.

Information on distribution and elimination (i.e. biotransformation and excretion) shall be necessary in all cases where such data are indispensable to determine the dosage for humans, and in respect of chemotherapeutic substances (antibiotics, etc.) and substances whose use depends on their non-pharmacodynamic effects (e.g. numerous diagnostic agents, etc.).

Pharmacokinetic investigation of pharmacologically active substances is necessary.

In the case of new combinations of known substances which have been investigated in accordance with the provisions of this Directive pharmacokinetic studies may not be required, if the toxicity tests and therapeutic experimentation justify their omission.

H. Local tolerance

The purpose of local tolerance studies is to ascertain whether medicinal products (both active ingredients and excipients) are tolerated at sites in the body which may come into contact " with the product as a result of " [R2] its administration in clinical use. The testing strategy shall be such that any mechanical effects of administration or purely physico-chemical actions of the product can be distinguished from toxicological or pharmacodynamic ones.

PART 4

CLINICAL DOCUMENTATION

The particulars and documents accompanying applications for marketing authorizations pursuant to point 8 of Article 4 (2) of Directive 65/65/EEC shall be submitted in accordance with the provisions below.

A clinical trial is any systematic study of medicinal products in human subjects whether in patients or non-patient volunteers in order to discover or verify the effects of and/or identify any adverse reaction to investigational products, and/or study their absorption, distribution, metabolism and excretion in order to ascertain the efficacy and safety of the products.

Evaluation of the application for marketing authorization shall be based on clinical trials including clinical pharmacological trials designed to determine the efficacy and safety of the product under normal conditions of use, having regard to the therapeutic indications for use in human beings. Therapeutic advantages must outweigh potential risks.

A. General requirements

The clinical particulars to be provided pursuant to point 8 of Article 4 (2) of Directive 65/65/EEC must enable a sufficiently well-founded and scientifically valid opinion to be formed as to whether the medicinal product satisfies the criteria governing the granting of a marketing authorization. Consequently, an essential requirement is that the results of all clinical trials should be communicated, both favourable and unfavourable.

Clinical trials must always be preceded by adequate pharmacological and toxicological tests, carried out on animals in accordance with the requirements of Part 3 of this Annex. The investigator must acquaint himself with the conclusions drawn from the pharmacological and toxicological studies and hence the applicant must provide him at least with the investigator's brochure, consisting of all the relevant information known prior to the onset of a clinical trial including chemical, pharmaceutical and biological data, toxicological, pharmacokinetic and pharmacodynamic data in animals and the results of earlier clinical trials, with adequate data to justify the nature, scale and duration of the proposed trial; the complete pharmacological and toxicological reports shall be provided on request. For materials of human or animal origin, all available means shall be employed to ensure safety from transmission of infectious agents prior to the commencement of the trial.

B. Conduct of trials

1. Good clinical practice

1.1. All phases of clinical investigation, including bioavailability and bioequivalence studies, shall be designed, implemented and reported in accordance with good clinical practice.

1.2. All clinical trials shall be carried out in accordance with the ethical principles laid down in the current revision of the Declaration of Helsinki. In principle, the freely given informed consent of each trial subject shall be obtained and documented.

The trial protocol, procedures (including statistical design) and documentation shall be submitted by the sponsor and/or investigator for an opinion to the relevant ethics committee. The trials shall not begin before the opinion of this committee has been received in writing.

1.3. Pre-established, systematic written procedures for the organization, conduct, data collection, documentation and verification of clinical trials shall be required.

1.4. In the case of radiopharmaceuticals, clinical trials shall be carried out under the responsibility of a medical doctor authorized to use radionuclides for medical purposes.

2. Archiving

The person responsible for placing the medicinal product on the market shall make arrangements for archiving of documentation.

(a) The investigator shall arrange for the retention of the patient identification codes for at least 15 years after the completion or discontinuation of the trial.

(b) Patient files and other source data shall be kept for the maximum period of time permitted by the hospital, institution or private practice.

(c) The sponsor or other owner of the data shall retain all other documentation pertaining to the trial as long as the product is authorized. These procedures shall include:

- the protocol including the rationale, objectives and statistical design and methodology of the trial, with conditions under which it is performed and managed, and details of the investigational product, the reference medicinal product and/or the placebo used,
- standard operating procedures,
- all written opinions on the protocol and procedures,
- the investigator's brochure,
- case report forms on each trial subject,
- final report,
- audit certificate(s), if available.

(d) The final report shall be retained by the sponsor or subsequent owner, for five years after the product is no longer authorized.

Any change of ownership of the data shall be documented. All data and documents shall be made available if requested by relevant authorities.

C. Presentation of results

1. The particulars of each clinical trial must contain sufficient detail to allow an objective judgement to be made:

- the protocol, including the rationale, objectives and statistical design and methodology of the trial, with conditions under which it is performed and managed, and details of the investigational product used,
- audit certificate(s), if available,
- the list of investigator(s), and each investigator shall give his name, address, appointments, qualifications and clinical duties, state where the trial was carried out and assemble the information in respect of each patient individually, including case report forms on each trial subject,
- final report signed by the investigator and for multicentre trials, by all the investigators or the coordinating (principal) investigator.

2. The particulars of clinical trials referred to above shall be forwarded to the competent authorities. However, in agreement with the competent authorities, the applicant may omit part of this information. Complete documentation shall be provided forthwith upon request.

3. The clinical observations shall be summarized for each trial indicating:

(a) the number and sex of patients treated;

(b) the selection and age-distribution of the groups of patients being investigated and the control groups;

(c) the number of patients withdrawn prematurely from the trials and the reasons for such withdrawal;

(d) where controlled trials were carried out under the above conditions, whether the control group:

- received no treatment,
- received a placebo,
- received another medicinal product of known effect,
- received treatment other than therapy using medicinal products;

(e) the frequency of observed side-effects;

(f) details concerning patients who may be at increased risk, e.g. elderly people, children, women during pregnancy or menstruation, or whose physiological or pathological condition requires special consideration;

(g) parameters or evaluation criteria of efficacy and the results in terms of these parameters;

(h) a statistical evaluation of the results when this is called for by the design of the trials and the variable factors involved.

4. The investigator shall, in his conclusions on the experimental evidence, express an opinion on the safety of the product under normal conditions of use, its compatibility, its efficacy and any useful information relating to indications and contra-indications, dosage and average duration of treatment as well as any special precautions to be taken during treatment and the clinical symptoms of overdosage. In reporting the results of a multi-centre study, the principal investigator shall, in his conclusions, express an opinion on the safety and efficacy of the investigational product on behalf of all centres.

5. In addition, the investigator shall always indicate his observations on:

(a) any signs of habituation, addiction or difficulty in weaning patients from the medicinal product;

(b) any interactions that have been observed with other medicinal products administered concomitantly;

(c) the criteria determining exclusion of certain patients from the trials;

(d) any deaths which occurred during the trial or within the follow-up period.

6. Particulars concerning a new combination of medicinal substances must be identical to those required for new medicinal products and must substantiate the safety and efficacy of the combination.

7. Total or partial omission of data must be explained. Should unexpected results occur during the course of the trials, further preclinical toxicological and pharmacological tests must be undertaken and reviewed.
If the medicinal product is intended for long-term administration, particulars shall be given of any modification of the pharmacological action following repeated administration, as well as the establishment of long-term dosage.

D. Clinical pharmacology

1. Pharmacodynamics

The pharmacodynamic action correlated to the efficacy shall be demonstrated including:

- the dose-response relationship and its time course,
- justification for the dosage and conditions of administration,
- the mode of action, if possible.

The pharmacodynamic action not related to efficacy shall be described.
The demonstration of pharmacodynamic effects in human beings shall not in itself be sufficient to justify conclusions regarding any particular potential therapeutic effect.

2. Pharmacokinetics

The following pharmacokinetic characteristics shall be described:

- absorption (rate and extent),
- distribution,
- metabolism,
- excretion.

Clinically significant features including the implication of the kinetic data for the dosage regimen especially for patients at risk, and differences between man and animal species used in the preclinical studies, shall be described.

3. Interactions

If the product is normally to be administered concomitantly with other medicinal products, particulars shall be given of joint administration tests performed to demonstrate possible modification of the pharmacological action.

If pharmacodynamic/pharmacokinetic interactions exist between the substance and other medical products or substances like alcohol, cafeine, tobacco or nicotine, likely to be taken simultaneously, or if such interactions are likely, they should be described and discussed; particularly from the point of view of clinical relevance and the relationship to the statement concerning interactions in the summary of product characteristics presented in accordance with Article 4a, point 5.6 of Directive 65/65/EEC.

E. Bioavailability/bioequivalence

The assessment of bioavailability must be undertaken in all cases where it is necessary, e.g. where the therapeutic dose is near the toxic dose or where the previous tests have revealed anomalies which may be related to pharmacokinetic properties, such as variable absorption.

In addition, an assessment of bioavailability shall be undertaken where necessary to demonstrate bioequivalence for the medicinal products referred to in Article 4 (2) point 8 (i), (ii) and (iii) of Directive 65/65/EEC.

F. Clinical efficacy and safety

1. In general, clinical trials shall be done as "controlled clinical trials" and if possible, randomized; any other design shall be justified. The control treatment of the trials will vary from case to case and also will depend on ethical considerations; thus it may, in some instances, be more pertinent to compare the efficacy of a new medicinal product with that of an established medicinal product of proven therapeutic value rather than with the effect of a placebo.

As far as possible, and particularly in trials where the effect of the product cannot be objectively measured, steps shall be taken to avoid bias, including methods of randomization and blinding.

2. The protocol of the trial must include a thorough description of the statistical methods to be employed, the number and reasons for inclusion of patients (including calculations of the power of the trial), the level of significance to be used and a description of the statistical unit. Measures taken to avoid bias, particularly methods of randomization, shall be documented. Inclusion of a large number of subjects in a trial must not be regarded as an adequate substitute for a properly controlled trial.

3. Clinical statements concerning the efficacy or safety of a medicinal product under normal conditions of use which are not scientifically substantiated cannot be accepted as valid evidence.

4. The value of data on the efficacy and safety of a medicinal product under normal conditions of use will be very greatly enhanced if such data come from several competent investigators working independently.

5. For vaccines and serums, the immunological status and age of the trial population and the local epidemiology are of critical importance and shall be monitored during the trial and fully described.

For live attenuated vaccines, clinical trials shall be so designed as to reveal potential transmission of the immunizing agent from vaccinated to non-vaccinated subjects. If transmission is possible, the genotypic and phenotypic stability of the immunizing agent shall be studied.

For vaccines and allergen products, follow-up studies shall include appropriate immunological tests, and where applicable, antibody assays.

6. The pertinence of the different trials to the assessment of safety and the validity of methods of evaluation shall be discussed in the expert report.

7. All adverse events including abnormal laboratory values shall be presented individually and discussed, especially:

- in terms of overall adverse experience and

- as a function of the nature, seriousness and causality of effects.

8. A critical assessment of relative safety, taking into account adverse reactions, shall be made in relation to:

- the disease to be treated,
- other therapeutic approaches,
- particular characteristics in sub-groups of patients,
- preclinical data on toxicology and pharmacology.

9. Recommendations shall be made for the conditions of use, with the intention of reducing the incidence of adverse reactions.

G. Documentation for applications in exceptional circumstances

When, in respect of particular therapeutic indications, the applicant can show that he is unable to provide comprehensive data on the quality, efficacy and safety under normal conditions of use, because:

- the indications for which the product in question is intended are encountered so rarely that the applicant cannot reasonably be expected to provide comprehensive evidence, or
- in the present state of scientific knowledge comprehensive information cannot be provided, or
- it would be contrary to generally accepted principles of medical ethics to collect such information,

marketing authorization may be granted on the following conditions:

" (a) the applicant completes on identified programme " [R2] of studies within a time period specified by the competent authority, the results of which shall form the basis of a reassessment of the benefit/risk profile,

(b) the medicinal product in question may be supplied on medical prescription only and may in certain cases be administered only under strict medical supervision, possibly in a hospital and for a radiopharmaceutical, by an authorized person,

(c) the package leaflet and any medical information shall draw the attention of the medical practitioner to the fact that the particulars available concerning the medicinal product in question are as yet inadequate in certain specified respects.

H. Post-marketing experience

1. If the medicinal product is already authorized in other countries, information shall be given in respect of adverse drug reactions of the medicinal product concerned and medicinal products containing the same active ingredient(s), in relation to the usage rates if possible. Information from worldwide studies relevant to the safety of the medicinal product shall be included.
For this purpose, an adverse drug reaction is a reaction which is noxious and unintended and which occurs at doses normally used in man for prophylaxis, diagnosis or therapy of disease or for the modification of physiological function.

2. In the case of vaccines already authorized in other countries, information on the monitoring of vaccinated subjects to evaluate the prevalence of the disease in question as compared to nonvaccinated subjects shall be submitted, when available.

3. For allergen products, response in periods of increased antigen exposure shall be identified. " [4]

[R1] Corrigenda, OJ L No L 299, 30/10/1991, p. 52.
[R2] Corrigenda, OJ L No L 320, 22/11/1991, p. 35.

(1) OJ No 22, 09/02/1965, p. 369.

(2) OJ No L 15, 17/01/1987, p. 38.
(3) OJ No L 358, 18/12/1986, p. 1.
(4) OJ No L 147, 09/06/1975, p. 13.
(5) OJ No L 11, 14/01/1978, p. 18.
(6) The competent authorities may also request the pK and pH values if they think this information is essential.
(7) OJ No L 15, 17/01/1987, p. 29.
(8) OJ No L 145, 11/06/1988, p. 35.

378L0025

78/25/EEC: COUNCIL DIRECTIVE OF 12 DECEMBER 1977 ON THE APPROXIMATION OF THE LAWS OF THE MEMBER STATES RELATING TO THE COLOURING MATTERS WHICH MAY BE ADDED TO MEDICINAL PRODUCTS

OFFICIAL JOURNAL No L 11, 14/01/1978, P. 18
DATE OF NOTIFICATION: 15/12/1977
DATE OF TRANSPOSITION: 15/06/1979; SEE ART. 7

AMENDED BY

179H
ACT CONCERNING THE CONDITIONS OF ACCESSION OF THE HELLENIC REPUBLIC AND THE ADJUSTMENTS TO THE TREATIES   [1]
OFFICIAL JOURNAL No L 291, 19/11/1979, P. 111

381L0464
81/464/EEC: COUNCIL DIRECTIVE OF 24 JUNE 1981   [2]
OFFICIAL JOURNAL No L 183, 04/07/1981, P. 33
DATE OF NOTIFICATION: 02/07/1981
DATE OF TRANSPOSITION: 01/10/1981; SEE ART. 2

185I
ACT CONCERNING THE CONDITIONS OF ACCESSION OF THE KINGDOM OF SPAIN AND THE PORTUGUESE REPUBLIC AND THE ADJUSTMENTS TO THE TREATIES   [3]
OFFICIAL JOURNAL No L 302, 15/11/1985, P. 217

ARTICLE 1

MEMBER STATES SHALL NOT AUTHORIZE, FOR THE COLOURING OF MEDICINAL PRODUCTS FOR HUMAN AND VETERINARY USE AS DEFINED IN ARTICLE 1 OF COUNCIL DIRECTIVE 65/65/EEC OF 26 JANUARY 1965 ON THE APPROXIMATION OF PROVISIONS LAID DOWN BY LAW, REGULATION OR ADMINISTRATIVE ACTION RELATING TO MEDICINAL PRODUCTS (1), ANY COLOURING MATTERS OTHER THAN THOSE COVERED BY ANNEX I, SECTIONS I AND II, TO THE DIRECTIVE OF 23 OCTOBER 1962 AS SUBSEQUENTLY AMENDED. ANY TRANSITIONAL PROVISIONS LAID DOWN FOR CERTAIN OF THESE COLOURING MATTERS SHALL ALSO APPLY.
" HOWEVER, IN THE CASE OF MEDICINAL PRODUCTS, NO DISTINCTION SHALL BE MADE BETWEEN COLOURING MATTER FOR BOTH MASS AND SURFACE COLOURING AND COLOURING MATTER FOR SURFACE COLOURING ONLY. " [2]

ARTICLE 2

MEMBER STATES SHALL TAKE ALL MEASURES NECESSARY TO ENSURE THAT THE COLOURING MATTERS COVERED BY ANNEX I, SECTIONS I AND II, TO THE DIRECTIVE OF 23 OCTOBER 1962 SATISFY THE GENERAL AND SPECIFIC CRITERIA OF PURITY LAID DOWN IN ANNEX III TO THAT DIRECTIVE.

ARTICLE 3

THE METHODS OF ANALYSIS NEEDED TO VERIFY THAT THE GENERAL AND SPECIFIC CRITERIA OF PURITY ADOPTED PURSUANT TO THE DIRECTIVE OF 23 OCTOBER 1962 ARE SATISFIED SHALL ALSO APPLY FOR THE PURPOSE OF THIS DIRECTIVE.

ARTICLE 4

WHERE A COLOURING MATTER IS DELETED FROM ANNEX I TO THE DIRECTIVE OF 23 OCTOBER 1962 BUT THE MARKETING OF FOODSTUFFS CONTAINING THIS COLOURING MATTER IS PERMITTED TO CONTINUE FOR A LIMITED PERIOD, THIS PROVISION SHALL ALSO APPLY TO MEDICINAL PRODUCTS. THIS LIMITED PERIOD OF USE MAY HOWEVER BE AMENDED FOR MEDICINAL PRODUCTS ACCORDING TO THE PROCEDURE LAID DOWN IN ARTICLE 6.

ARTICLE 5

1. A COMMITTEE FOR THE ADAPTATION TO TECHNICAL PROGRESS OF THE DIRECTIVES ON THE ELIMINATION OF TECHNICAL BARRIERS TO TRADE IN THE SECTOR OF COLOURING MATTERS WHICH MAY BE ADDED TO MEDICINAL PRODUCTS, HEREINAFTER CALLED THE "COMMITTEE", IS HEREBY SET UP AND SHALL CONSIST OF REPRESENTATIVES OF THE MEMBER STATES WITH A REPRESENTATIVE OF THE COMMISSION AS CHAIRMAN.

2. THE COMMITTEE SHALL DRAW UP ITS OWN RULES OF PROCEDURE.

ARTICLE 6

1. WHERE THE PROCEDURE LAID DOWN IN THIS ARTICLE IS TO BE FOLLOWED, MATTERS SHALL BE REFERRED TO THE COMMITTEE BY THE CHAIRMAN, EITHER ON HIS OWN INITIATIVE OR AT THE REQUEST OF THE REPRESENTATIVE OF A MEMBER STATE.

2. THE COMMISSION REPRESENTATIVE SHALL SUBMIT A DRAFT OF THE MEASURES TO BE ADOPTED. THE COMMITTEE SHALL DELIVER ITS OPINION ON SUCH MEASURES WITHIN A TIME LIMIT SET BY THE CHAIRMAN ACCORDING TO THE URGENCY OF THE MATTER. OPINIONS SHALL BE DELIVERED BY A MAJORITY OF " fifty-four " [3] VOTES, THE VOTES OF THE MEMBER STATES BEING WEIGHTED AS PROVIDED IN ARTICLE 148 (2) OF THE TREATY. THE CHAIRMAN SHALL NOT VOTE.

3. THE COMMISSION SHALL ADOPT THE PROPOSED MEASURES WHERE THEY ARE IN ACCORDANCE WITH THE OPINION OF THE COMMITTEE.
IF THESE MEASURES ARE NOT IN ACCORDANCE WITH THE OPINION OF THE COMMITTEE, OR IF THE COMMITTEE DOES NOT DELIVER AN OPINION, THE COMMISSION SHALL FORTHWITH SUBMIT TO THE COUNCIL A PROPOSAL REGARDING THE MEASURES TO BE ADOPTED.
THE COUNCIL SHALL ACT BY A QUALIFIED MAJORITY.
IF THE COUNCIL HAS NOT TAKEN A DECISION WITHIN THREE MONTHS OF THE MATTER BEING REFERRED TO IT, THE COMMISSION SHALL ADOPT THE PROPOSED MEASURES.

ARTICLE 7

1. MEMBER STATES SHALL BRING INTO FORCE THE LAWS, REGULATIONS AND ADMINISTRATIVE PROVISIONS NECESSARY TO COMPLY WITH THIS DIRECTIVE WITHIN 18 MONTHS OF ITS NOTIFICATION AND SHALL FORTHWITH INFORM THE COMMISSION THEREOF.

2. HOWEVER, ANY MEMBER STATE MAY PERMIT, ON ITS OWN TERRITORY, UNTIL THE END OF A PERIOD OF FOUR YEARS FROM THE NOTIFICATION OF THIS DIRECTIVE, THE MARKETING OF MEDICINAL PRODUCTS CONTAINING COLOURING MATTERS WHICH DO NOT COMPLY WITH THE REQUIREMENTS OF THIS DIRECTIVE SO LONG AS THESE COLOURING MATTERS WERE AUTHORIZED IN THAT MEMBER STATE BEFORE THE ADOPTION OF THE DIRECTIVE.

3. DEPENDING ON THE OPINION OF THE SCIENTIFIC COMMITTEE FOR FOOD AND OF THE COMMITTEE REFERRED TO IN ARTICLE 5 THE COMMISSION SHALL IF APPROPRIATE SUBMIT TO THE COUNCIL WITHIN TWO YEARS OF THE ADOPTION OF THIS DIRECTIVE A PROPOSAL FOR AMENDMENT OF THE DIRECTIVE TO ALLOW THE USE OF:

- THE COLOURING MATTERS:
-- BRILLIANT BLUE FCF CI 42090,
-- RED 2G CI 18050,
- OTHER COLOURING MATTERS FOR MEDICINAL PRODUCTS FOR EXTERNAL USE ONLY.

THE COUNCIL SHALL TAKE A DECISION ON THE COMMISSION PROPOSAL NO LATER THAN TWO YEARS AFTER ITS SUBMISSION.

4. MEMBER STATES SHALL COMMUNICATE TO THE COMMISSION THE TEXT OF THE MAIN PROVISIONS OF NATIONAL LAW WHICH THEY ADOPT IN THE FIELD COVERED BY THIS DIRECTIVE.

ARTICLE 8

THIS DIRECTIVE IS ADDRESSED TO THE MEMBER STATES.

(1) OJ No 22, 09/02/1965, p. 369.

COMMISSION DIRECTIVE

of 13 June 1991

laying down the principles and guidelines of good manufacturing practice for medicinal products for human use

(91/356/EEC)

THE COMMISSION OF THE EUROPEAN COMMUNITIES,

Having regard to the Treaty establishing the European Economic Community,

Having regard to Council Directive 75/319/EEC of 20 May 1975 on the approximation of provisions laid down by law, regulation or administrative action relating to proprietary medicinal products (¹), as last amended by Directive 89/381/EEC (²), and in particular Article 19a thereof,

Whereas all medicinal products for human use manufactured or imported into the Community, including medicinal products intended for export, should be manufactured in accordance with the principles and guidelines of good manufacturing practice ;

Whereas, in accordance with national legislation, Member States may require compliance with these principles of good manufacturing practice during the manufacture of products intended for use in clinical trials ;

Whereas the detailed guidelines mentioned in Article 19a of Directive 75/319/EEC have been published by the Commission after consultation with the pharmaceutical inspection services of the Member States in the form of a 'Guide to good manufacturing practice for medicinal products';

Whereas it is necessary that all manufacturers should operate an effective quality management of their manufacturing operations, and that this requires the implementation of a pharmaceutical quality assurance system ;

Whereas officials representing the competent authorities should report on whether the manufacturer complies with good manufacturing practice and that these reports should be communicated upon reasoned request to the competent authorities of another Member State ;

Whereas the principles and guidelines of good manufacturing practice should primarily concern personnel, premises and equipment, documentation, production, quality control, contracting out, complaints and product recall, and self inspection ;

Whereas the principles and guidelines envisaged by this Directive are in accordance with the opinion of the Committee for the Adaptation to Technical Progress of the Directives on the Removal of Technical Barriers to Trade in the Proprietary Medicinal Products Sector set up by Article 2b of Council Directive 75/318/EEC of 20 May 1975 on the approximation of the laws of Member States relating to analytical, pharmaco-toxicological and clinical standards and protocols in respect of the testing of proprietary medicinal products (³), as last amended by Directive 89/341/EEC (⁴),

HAS ADOPTED THIS DIRECTIVE :

CHAPTER I

GENERAL PROVISIONS

Article 1

This Directive lays down the principles and guidelines of good manufacturing practice for medicinal products for human use whose manufacture requires the authorization referred to in Article 16 of Directive 75/319/EEC.

Article 2

For the purposes of this Directive, the definition of medicinal products set out in Article 1 (2) of Council Directive 65/65/EEC (⁵), shall apply.

In addition,

— 'manufacturer' shall mean any holder of the authorization referred to in Article 16 of Directive 75/319/EEC,

— 'qualified person' shall mean the person referred to in Article 21 of Directive 75/319/EEC,

— 'pharmaceutical quality assurance' shall mean the sum total of the organized arrangements made with the object of ensuring that medicinal products are of the quality required for their intended use,

— 'good manufacturing practice' shall mean the part of quality assurance which ensures that products are consistently produced and controlled to the quality standards appropriate to their intended use.

(¹) OJ No L 147, 9. 6. 1975, p. 13.
(²) OJ No L 181, 28. 6. 1989, p. 44.

(³) OJ No L 147, 9. 6. 1975, p. 1.
(⁴) OJ No L 142, 25. 5. 1989, p. 11.
(⁵) OJ No 22, 9. 2. 1965, p. 369/65.

Article 3

By means of the repeated inspections referred to in Article 26 of Directive 75/319/EEC, the Member States shall ensure that manufacturers respect the principles and guidelines of good manufacturing practice laid down by this Directive.

For the interpretation of these principles and guidelines of good manufacturing practice, the manufacturers and the agents of the competent authorities shall refer to the detailed guidelines referred to in Article 19a of Directive 75/319/EEC. These detailed guidelines are published by the Commission in the *Guide to good manufacturing practice for medicinal products'* and in its Annexes (Office for Official Publications of the European Communities, *The rules governing medicinal products in the European Community,* Volume IV).

Article 4

The manufacturer shall ensure that the manufacturing operations are carried out in accordance with good manufacturing practice and with the manufacturing authorization.

For medicinal products imported from third countries, the importer shall ensure that the medicinal products have been manufactured by manufacturers duly authorized and conforming to good manufacturing practice standards, at least equivalent to those laid down by the Community.

Article 5

The manufacturer shall ensure that all manufacturing operations subject to an authorization for marketing are carried out in accordance with the information given in the application for marketing authorization as accepted by the competent authorities.

The manufacturer shall regularly review their manufacturing methods in the light of scientific and technical progress. When a modification to the marketing authorization dossier is necessary, the application for modification must be submitted to the competent authorities.

CHAPTER II

PRINCIPLES AND GUIDELINES OF GOOD MANUFACTURING PRACTICE

Article 6

Quality management

The manufacturer shall establish and implement an effective pharmaceutical quality assurance system, involving the active participation of the management and personnel of the different services involved.

Article 7

Personnel

1. At each manufacturing site, the manufacturer shall have competent and appropriately qualified personnel at his disposal in sufficient number to achieve the pharmaceutical quality assurance objective.

2. The duties of managerial and supervisory staff, including the qualified person(s), responsible for implementing and operating good manufacturing practice shall be defined in job descriptions. Their hierarchical relationships shall be defined in an organization chart. Organization charts and job descriptions shall be approved in accordance with the manufacturer's internal procedures.

3. Staff referred to in paragraph 2 shall be given sufficient authority to discharge their responsibilities correctly.

4. Personnel shall receive initial and continuing training including the theory and application of the concept of quality assurance and good manufacturing practice.

5. Hygiene programmes adapted to the activities to be carried out shall be established and observed. These programmes include procedures relating to health, hygiene and clothing of personnel.

Article 8

Premises and equipment

1. Premises and manufacturing equipment shall be located, designed, constructed, adapted and maintained to suit the intended operations.

2. Lay out, design and operation must aim to minimize the risk of errors and permit effective cleaning and maintenance in order to avoid contamination, cross contamination and, in general, any adverse effect on the quality of the product.

3. Premises and equipment intended to be used for manufacturing operations which are critical for the quality of the products shall be subjected to appropriate qualification.

Article 9

Documentation

1. The manufacturer shall have a system of documentation based upon specifications, manufacturing formulae and processing and packaging instructions, procedures and records covering the various manufacturing operations that they perform. Documents shall be clear, free from errors and kept up to date. Pre-established procedures for general manufacturing operations and conditions shall be available, together with specific documents

for the manufacture of each batch. This set of documents shall make it possible to trace the history of the manufacture of each batch. The batch documentation shall be retained for at least one year after the expiry date of the batches to which it relates or at least five years after the certification referred to in Article 22 (2) of Directive 75/319/EEC whichever is the longer.

2. When electronic, photographic or other data processing systems are used instead of written documents, the manufacturer shall have validated the systems by proving that the data will be appropriately stored during the anticipated period of storage. Data stored by these systems shall be made readily available in legible form. The electronically stored data shall be protected against loss or damage of data (e.g. by duplication or back-up and transfer onto another storage system).

Article 10

Production

The different production operations shall be carried out according to pre-established instructions and procedures and in accordance with good manufacturing practice. Adequate and sufficient resources shall be made available for the in-process controls.

Appropriate technical and/or organizational measures shall be taken to avoid cross contamination and mix-ups.

Any new manufacture or important modification of a manufacturing process shall be validated. Critical phases of manufacturing processes shall be regularly revalidated.

Article 11

Quality control

1. The manufacturer shall establish and maintain a quality control department. This department shall be placed under the authority of a person having the required qualifications and shall be independent of the other departments.

2. The quality control department shall have at its disposal one or more quality control laboratories appropriately staffed and equipped to carry out the necessary examination and testing of starting materials, packaging materials and intermediate and finished products testing. Resorting to outside laboratories may be authorized in accordance with Article 12 of this Directive after the

authorization referred to in Article 5b of Directive 75/319/EEC has been granted.

3. During the final control of finished products before their release for sale or distribution, in addition to analytical results, the quality control department shall take into account essential information such as the production conditions, the results of in-process controls, the examination of the manufacturing documents and the conformity of the products to their specifications (including the final finished pack).

4. Samples of each batch of finished products shall be retained for at least one year after the expiry date. Unless in the Member States of manufacture a longer period is required, samples of starting materials (other than solvents, gases and water) used shall be retained for at least two years after the release of the product. This period may be shortened if their stability, as mentioned in the relevant specification, is shorter. All these samples shall be maintained at the disposal of the competent authorities.

For certain medicinal products manufactured individually or in small quantities, or when their storage could raise special problems, other sampling and retaining conditions may be defined in agreement with the competent authority.

Article 12

Work contracted out

1. Any manufacturing operation or operation linked with the manufacture which is carried out under contract, shall be the subject of a written contract between the contract giver and the contract acceptor.

2. The contract shall clearly define the responsibilities of each party and in particular the observance of good manufacturing practice by the contract acceptor and the manner in which the qualified person responsible for releasing each batch shall undertake his full responsibilities.

3. The contract acceptor shall not subcontract any of the work entrusted to him by the contract giver without the written authorization of the contract giver.

4. The contract acceptor shall respect the principles and guidelines of good manufacturing practice and shall submit to inspections carried out by the competent authorities as provided for by Article 26 of Directive 75/319/EEC.

Article 13

Complaints and product recall

The manufacturer shall implement a system for recording and reviewing complaints together with an effective system for recalling promptly and at any time the medicinal products in the distribution network. Any complaint concerning a defect shall be recorded and investigated by the manufacturer. The competent authority shall be informed by the manufacturer of any defect that could result in a recall or abnormal restriction on the supply. In so far as possible, the countries of destination shall also be indicated. Any recall shall be made in accordance with the requirements referred to in Article 33 of Directive 75/319/EEC.

Article 14

Self-inspection

The manufacturer shall conduct repeated self-inspections as part of the quality assurance system in order to monitor the implementation and respect of good manufacturing practice and to propose any necessary corrective measures. Records of such self-inspections and any subsequent corrective action shall be maintained.

CHAPTER III

FINAL PROVISIONS

Article 15

Member States shall bring into force the laws, regulations and administrative provisions necessary to comply with this Directive not later than 1 January 1992. They shall forthwith inform the Commission thereof.

When Member States adopt these provisions, these shall contain a reference to this Directive or shall be accompanied by such reference at the time of their official publication. The procedure for such reference shall be adopted by Member States.

Article 16

This Directive is addressed to the Member States.

Done at Brussels, 13 June 1991.

For the Commission
Martin BANGEMANN
Vice-President

Economic and social environment of medicinal products for human use

COUNCIL DIRECTIVE

of 21 December 1988

relating to the transparency of measures regulating the pricing of medicinal products for human use and their inclusion in the scope of national health insurance systems

(89/105/EEC)

THE COUNCIL OF THE EUROPEAN COMMUNITIES,

Having regard to the Treaty establishing the European Economic Community, and in particular Article 100a thereof,

Having regard to the proposal from the Commission [1],

In cooperation with the European Parliament [2],

Having regard to the opinion of the Economic and Social Committee [3],

Whereas marketing authorizations for proprietary medicinal products issued pursuant to Council Directive 65/65/EEC of 26 January 1965 on the approximation of provisions laid down by law, regulation or administrative action relating to proprietary medicinal products [4], as last amended by Directive 87/21/EEC [5], may be refused only for reasons relating to the quality, safety or efficacy of the proprietary medicinal products concerned;

Whereas Member States have adopted measures of an economic nature on the marketing of medicinal products in order to control public health expenditure on such products; whereas such measures include direct and indirect controls on the prices of medicinal products as a consequence of the inadequacy or absence of competition in the medicinal products market and limitations on the range of products covered by national health insurance systems;

Whereas the primary objective of such measures is the promotion of public health by ensuring the availability of adequate supplies of medicinal products at a reasonable cost; whereas, however, such measures should also be intended to promote efficiency in the production of medicinal products and to encourage research and development into new medicinal products, on which the maintenance of a high level of public health within the Community ultimately depends;

Whereas disparities in such measures may hinder or distort intra-Community trade in medicinal products and thereby directly affect the functioning of the common market in medicinal products;

Whereas the objective of this Directive is to obtain an overall view of national pricing arrangements, including the manner in which they operate in individual cases and all the criteria on which they are based, and to provide public access to them for all those involved in the market in medicinal products in the Member States; whereas this information should be public;

Whereas, as a first step towards the removal of these disparites, it is urgently necessary to lay down a series of requirements intended to ensure that all concerned can verify that the national measures do not constitute quantitative restrictions on imports or exports or measures having equivalent effect thereto; whereas, however, these requirements do not effect the policies of those Member States which rely primarily upon free competition to determine the price of medicinal products; whereas these requirements also do not affect national policies on price setting and on the determination of social security schemes, except as far as it is necessary to attain transparency within the meaning of this Directive;

Whereas the further harmonization of such measures must take place progressively,

HAS ADOPTED THIS DIRECTIVE:

Article 1

1. Member States shall ensure that any national measure, whether laid down by law, regulation or administrative action, to control the prices of medicinal products for human use or to restrict the range of medicinal products covered by their national health insurance systems complies with the requirements of this Directive.

2. The definition of 'medicinal products' laid down in Article 1 of Directive 65/65/EEC shall apply to this Directive.

3. Nothing in this Directive shall permit the marketing of a proprietary medicinal product in respect of which the authorization provided for in Article 3 of Directive 65/65/EEC has not been issued.

---

[1] OJ No C 17, 23. 1. 1987, p. 6 and OJ No C 129, 18. 5. 1988, p. 14.
[2] OJ No C 94, 11. 4. 1988, p. 62 and OJ No C 326, 19. 12. 1988.
[3] OJ No C 319, 30. 11. 1987, p. 47.
[4] OJ No 22, 9. 2. 1965, p. 369/65.
[5] OJ No L 15, 17. 1. 1987, p. 36.

Article 2

The following provisions shall apply if the marketing of a medicinal product is permitted only after the competent authorities of the Member State concerned have approved the price of the product:

1. Member States shall ensure that a decision on the price which may be charged for the medicinal product concerned is adopted and communicated to the applicant within 90 days of the receipt of an application submitted, in accordance with the requirements laid down in the Member State concerned, by the holder of a marketing authorization. The applicant shall furnish the competent authorities with adequate information. If the information supporting the application is inadequate, the competent authorities shall forthwith notify the applicant of what detailed additional information is required and take their final decision within 90 days of receipt of this additional information. In the absence of such a decision within the abovementioned period or periods, the applicant shall be entitled to market the product at the price proposed.

2. Should the competent authorities decide not to permit the marketing of the medicinal product concerned at the price proposed by the applicant, the decision shall contain a statement of reasons based on objective and verifiable criteria. In addition, the applicant shall be informed of the remedies available to him under the laws in force and the time limits allowed for applying for such remedies.

3. At least once a year, the competent authorities shall publish in an appropriate publication, and communicate to the Commission, a list of the medicinal products the price of which has been fixed during the relevant period, together with the prices which may be charged for such products.

Article 3

Without prejudice to Article 4, the following provisions shall apply if an increase in the price of a medicinal product is permitted only after prior approval has been obtained from the competent authorities:

1. Member States shall ensure that a decision is adopted on an application submitted, in accordance with the requirements laid down in the Member State concerned, by the holder of a marketing authorization to increase the price of a medicinal product and communicated to the applicant within 90 days of its receipt. The applicant shall furnish the competent authorities with adequate information including details of those events intervening since the price of the medicinal product was last determined which in his opinion justify the price increase requested. If the information supporting the application is inadequate, the competent authorities shall forthwith notify the applicant of what detailed additional

information is required and take their final decision within 90 days of receipt of this additional information.

In case of an exceptional number of applications, the period may be extended once only for a further 60 days. The applicant shall be notified of such extension before the expiry of the period.

In the absence of such a decision within the abovementioned period or periods, the applicant shall be entitled to apply in full the price increase requested.

2. Should the competent authorities decide not to permit the whole or part of the price increase requested, the decision shall contain a statement of reasons based on objective and verifiable criteria and the applicant shall be informed of the remedies available to him under the laws in force and the time limits allowed for applying for such remedies.

3. At least once a year, the competent authorities shall publish in an appropriate publication and communicate to the Commission, a list of the medicinal products for which price increases have been granted during the relevant period, together with the new price which may be charged for such products.

Article 4

1. In the event of a price freeze imposed on all medicinal products or on certain categories of medicinal products by the competent authorities of a Member State, that Member State shall carry out a review, at least once a year, to ascertain whether the macro-economic conditions justify that the freeze be continued unchanged. Within 90 days of the start of this review, the competent authorities shall announce what increases or decreases in prices are being made, if any.

2. In exceptional cases, a person who is the holder of a marketing authorization for a medicinal product may apply for a derogation from a price freeze if this is justified by particular reasons. The application shall contain an adequate statement of these reasons. Member States shall ensure that a reasoned decision on any such application is adopted and communicated to the applicant within 90 days. If the information supporting the application is inadequate, the competent authorities shall forthwith notify the applicant of what detailed additional information is required and take their final decision within 90 days of receipt of this additional information. Should the derogation be granted, the competent authorities shall forthwith publish an announcement of the price increase allowed.

Should there be an exceptional number of applications, the period may be extended once only for a further 60 days. The applicant shall be notified of such extension before the expiry of the initial period.

Article 5

Where a Member State adopts a system of direct or indirect controls on the profitability of persons responsible for placing medicinal products on the market, the Member State concerned shall publish the following information in an appropriate publication and communicate it to the Commission:

(a) the method or methods used in the Member State concerned to define profitability: return on sales and/or return on capital;

(b) the range of target profit currently permitted to persons responsible for placing medicinal products on the market in the Member State concerned;

(c) the criteria according to which target rates of profit are accorded to an individual responsible for placing medicinal products on the market, together with the criteria according to which they will be allowed to retain profits above their given targets in the Member State concerned;

(d) the maximum percentage profit which any person responsible for placing medicinal products on the market is allowed to retain above his target in the Member State concerned.

This information shall be updated once a year or when significant changes are made.

Where, in addition to operating a system of direct or indirect controls on profits, a Member State operates a system of controls on the prices of certain types of medicinal products which are excluded from the scope of the profit control scheme, Articles 2, 3 and 4 shall, where relevant, apply to such price controls. However, the said Articles shall not apply where the normal operation of a system of direct or indirect controls on profits results exceptionally in a price being fixed for an individual medicinal product.

Article 6

The following provisions shall apply if a medicinal product is covered by the national health insurance system only after the competent authorities have decided to include the medicinal product concerned in a positive list of medicinal products covered by the national health insurance system.

1. Member States shall ensure that a decision on an application submitted, in accordance with the requirements laid down in the Member State concerned, by the holder of a marketing authorization to include a medicinal product in the list of medicinal products covered by the health insurance systems is adopted and communicated to the applicant within 90 days of its receipt. Where an application under this Article may be made before the competent authorities have agreed the price to be charged for the product pursuant to Article 2, or where a decision on the price of a medicinal product

and a decision on its inclusion within the list of products covered by the health insurance system are taken after a single administrative procedure, the time limit shall be extended for a further 90 days. The applicant shall furnish the competent authorities with adequate information. If the information supporting the application is inadequate, the time limit shall be suspended and the competent authorities shall forthwith notify the applicant of what detailed additional information is required.

Where a Member State does not permit an application to be made under this Article before the competent authorities have agreed the price to be charged for the product pursuant to Article 2, the Member State concerned shall ensure that the overall period of time taken by the two procedures does not exceed 180 days. This time limit may be extended in accordance with Article 2 or suspended in accordance with the provisions of the preceding subparagraph.

2. Any decision not to include a medicinal product in the list of products covered by the health insurance system shall contain a statement of reasons based upon objective and verifiable criteria, including, if appropriate, any expert opinions or recommendations on which the decision is based. In addition, the applicant shall be informed of the remedies available to him under the laws in force and of the time limits allowed for applying for such remedies.

3. Before the date referred to in Article 11 (1), Member States shall publish in an appropriate publication and communicate to the Commission the criteria which are to be taken into account by the competent authorities in deciding whether or not to include medicinal products on the lists.

4. Within one year of the date referred to in in Article 11 (1), Member States shall publish in an appropriate publication and communicate to the Commission a complete list of the products covered by their health insurance system, together with their prices fixed by the national competent authorities. This information shall be updated at least once every year.

5. Any decision to exclude a product from the list of products covered by the health insurance system shall contain a statement of reasons based on objective and verifiable criteria. Such decisions, including, if appropriate, any expert opinions or recommendations on which the decisions are based, shall be communicated to the person responsible, who shall be informed of the remedies available to him under the laws in force and the time limits allowed for applying for such remedies.

6. Any decision to exclude a category of medicinal products from the list of products covered by the health insurance system shall contain a statement of reasons based on objective and verifiable criteria and be published in an appropriate publication.

Article 7

The following provisions shall apply if the competent authorities of a Member State are empowered to adopt decisions to exclude individual or categories of medicinal products from the coverage of its national health insurance system (negative lists).

1. Any decision to exclude a category of medicinal products from the coverage of the national health insurance system shall contain a statement of reasons based upon objective and verifiable criteria and be published in an appropriate publication.

2. Before the date referred to in Article 11 (1), Member States shall publish in an appropriate publication and communicate to the Commission the criteria which are to be taken into account by the competent authorities in deciding whether or not to exclude an individual medicinal product from the coverage of the national health insurance system.

3. Any decision to exclude an individual medicinal product from the coverage of the national health insurance system shall contain a statement of reasons based on objective and verifiable criteria. Such decisions, including, if appropriate, any expert opinions or recommendations on which the decisions are based, shall be communicated to the person responsible, who shall be informed of the remedies available to him under the laws in force and the time limits allowed for applying for such remedies.

4. Within one year of the date referred to in Article 11 (1), the competent authorities shall publish in an appropriate publication and communicate to the Commission a list of the individual medicinal products which have been excluded from the scope of its health insurance system. This information shall be updated at least every six months.

Article 8

1. Before the date referred to in Article 11 (1), Member States shall communicate to the Commission any criteria concerning the therapeutic classification of medicinal products which are used by the competent authorities for the purposes of the national social security system.

2. Before the date referred to in Article 11 (1), Member States shall communicate to the Commission any criteria which are used by the competent authorities in verifying the fairness and transparency of the prices charged for transfers within a group of companies of active principles or intermediate products used in the manufacture of medicinal products or finished medicinal products.

Article 9

1. In the light of experience, the Commission shall, not later than two years after the date referred to in Article 11 (1), submit to the Council a proposal containing appropriate measures leading towards the abolition of any remaining barriers to, or distortions of, the free movement of proprietary medicinal products, so as to bring this sector closer into line within the normal conditions of the internal market.

2. The Council shall decide on the Commission proposal not later than one year after its submission.

Article 10

1. A Committee called the 'Consultative Committee for the implementation of Directive 89/105/EEC relating to the transparency of measures regulating the pricing of medicinal products for human use and their inclusion in the scope of national health insurance systems' shall be set up and attached to the Commission.

2. The tasks of the committee shall be to examine any question relating to the application of this Directive which is brought up by the Commission or at the request of a Member State.

3. The committee shall consist of one representative from each Member State. There shall be one deputy for each representative. This deputy shall be entitled to participate in meetings of the committee.

4. A representative of the Commission shall chair the committee.

5. The committee shall adopt its rules of procedure.

Article 11

1. Member States shall bring into force the laws, regulations and administrative provisions necessary to comply with this Directive by 31 December 1989 at the latest. They shall forthwith inform the Commission thereof.

2. Before the date referred to in paragraph 1, Member States shall communicate to the Commission the texts of any laws, regulations or administrative provisions relating to the pricing of medicinal products, the profitability of manufacturers of medicinal products and the coverage of medicinal products by the national health insurance system. Amendments and modifications to these laws, regulations or administrative provisions shall be communicated to the Commission forthwith.

Article 12

This Directive is addressed to the Member States.

Done at Brussels, 21 December 1988.

For the Council
The President
V. PAPANDREOU

Communication from the Commission on the compatibility with Article 30 of the EEC Treaty of measures taken by Member States relating to price controls and reimbursement of medicinal products

(86/C 310/08)

I. INTRODUCTION

Elimination of unjustified barriers has traditionally been done through individual infringement proceedings. In its 'White Paper on completing the internal market' (COM(85) 310), however, the Commission announced that it would also take more systematic action, by publishing general communications setting out the legal situation, particularly in regard to Articles 30 to 36 of the EEC Treaty, for the whole of an economic sector or in relation to a particular type of barrier (paragraph 155). Amongst the priority sectors quoted in this respect is the pharmaceutical sector (paragraph 156).

II. GENERAL REMARKS

The market for medicinal products has certain characteristics that distinguish it very clearly from the markets for other consumer products. Firstly, the final consumer of a medicinal product has scarcely any influence on the choice of medicinal product, at least in the case of those prescribed by a doctor. Moreover, the demand for a medicinal product is normally related to the treatment of a particular complaint, and medicinal products cannot readily be substituted for others. Secondly, the market for medicinal products is characterized by the payment of medical expenses by social security institutions instead of by consumers.

In these circumstances, it is understandable that Member States should try to limit expenditure on pharmaceuticals, since the community bears the greater part of it. To this end, most Member States have taken measures to control prices of medicinal products and reimbursements of medicinal products by social security: these measures form part of the health policy of the Member States and aim to offer the best possible treatment to all citizens, without excessive cost to the public purse.

Such measures are in principle compatible with Community law, provided that their restrictive effect on the free movement of goods is not disproportionate in relation to the legitimate interest which it is sought to protect. It is important, in particular, that such measures should not involve any difference in treatment that places products imported from other Member States at a disadvantage, and that they should not render the sale of imported products economically unviable or more difficult than that of domestic products, or make certain import routes impossible or more costly than others.

The Court of Justice has had occasion to restate these principles, notably in two judgments handed down recently in references for preliminary rulings (judgments of the Court of 29. November 1983 in Case 181/82 'Roussel' (1983), ECR 3849 to 3871, and of 7 February 1984 in Case 238/82 'Duphar' (1984), ECR 523 to 545). These judgments offer the Commission interpretative guidelines which enable it to exercise stricter control of the application of the rules of the EEC Treaty on the free movement of goods, in particular Articles 30 to 36 thereof.

As announced in its White Paper on the completion of the internal market (COM(85) 310), in 1986 the Commission will be transmitting to the Council a proposal for a directive on the transparency of prices for pharmaceutical products and reimbursements by social security. The communication does not prejudge proposals which the Commission may make on that occasion: it sets out Member States' obligations under the rules of the EEC Treaty itself, as interpreted by the Court of Justice, and as the Commission intends to apply them, under its own responsibility, in order to achieve a unified internal market in the Community.

III. PRICE CONTROL FOR MEDICINAL PRODUCTS

A. General

In the absence of Community provisions, Member States are free, each within their own territories, to adopt legislation to control prices of pharmaceutical products, provided that such legislation does not hinder the free movement of goods within the Community.

Article 30 of the EEC Treaty prohibits all measures having an effect equivalent to a quantitative restriction on trade between Member States. According to the well-established case-law of the Court, any measures which are capable of hindering, directly or indirectly, actually or potentially, trade between Member States are to be regarded as measures having such effect (see judgment of the Court of 11 July 1974 in Case 8/74 'Dassonville' (1974), ECR 837 to 865).

The Court had occasion to state that these principles apply to price control systems. It stressed in this aspect that whilst rules controlling prices applicable equally to domestic and imported products do not in themselves amount to a measure having an effect equivalent to a quantitative restriction, they may in fact produce such an effect when prices are fixed at such a level that the marketing of imported products becomes either impossible or more difficult than the marketing of national products (see judgment of the Court of 6 November 1979 in Cases 16 to 20/79 'Danis' (1979), ECR 3327 to 3342).

On the other hand, in the case of price controls providing for separate or different systems for imported and domestic products, the Court has indicated that such rules must be considered as a measure having an effect equivalent to a quantitative restriction wherever it is capable of hindering the sale of imported products in any way (see the abovementioned judgment 181/82 'Roussel').

Furthermore, in Directive 70/50/EEC of 22 December 1969 (OJ No L 13 of 19 January 1970) the Commission points out the incompatibility with Article 30 of measures which:

— lay down, for imported products only, minimum or maximum prices below or above which imports are prohibited, reduced or made subject to conditions liable to hinder importation,

— lay down less favourable prices for imported products than for domestic products,

— preclude any increase in the price of the imported product corresponding to the supplementary costs and charges inherent in importation,

— fix the prices of products solely on the basis of the cost price or the quality of domestic products at such a level as to create a hindrance to import.

B. Determination of prices

The general principles to be observed here are grouped around two main aspects: realistic prices and transparency of prices. Each product must be able to have its own price, calculated on the basis of its real cost using a transparent method of calculation.

It is generally for manufacturers and importers to determine the prices of each of their products, which are then assessed by the authorities in accordance with measures designed to control the prices of proprietary pharmaceuticals.

If, when new products are placed on the market, Member States can justify asking firms for information to enable them to assess the components of the prices that such firms propose to charge, they must then allow pharmaceutical firms to take account of the various elements making up the cost of the products (research, raw materials, processing, advertising, transport, expenses and charges inherent in importing, etc.).

In any case, the marketing authorization (within the meaning of Council Directive 65/65/EEC of 26 January 1965 — OJ No L 22 of 9 February 1965) for a pharmaceutical product may not in any circumstances be refused, suspended or revoked save on grounds relating to public health. This means, in particular, that a Member State may not refuse, suspend or revoke a marketing authorization simply because it considers the price of a pharmaceutical product to be excessive (see judgment of the Court of 26 January 1984 in Case 301/82 'Clin-Midy' (1984), ECR 251 to 260).

C. Price freezes

1. Differentiated price freezes

Firstly, it is clear that Member States may not introduce price controls that are applicable solely to imported products; such measures always contravene Article 30 of the EEC Treaty in so far as they can be a hindrance to imported products, particularly when the prices fixed are not sufficient to cover the price of the product.

In the abovementioned judgment 181/82 'Roussel', the Court ruled on a price control system that differentiated between domestic and imported products. After noting that 'the legislation in question does not apply to domestic products and imported products alike but consists of different sets of rules for the two groups of products, laid down by different decrees and different also as regards their substantive content', the Court ruled that 'legislation of that kind, which differentiates between the two groups of products, must be regarded as a measure having an effect equivalent to a quantitative restriction where it is capable of making more difficult, in any manner whatever, the sale of imported products'. Article 30 of the EEC Treaty therefore precludes a Member State from introducing specific legislation which refers to the manufacturer's basic prices usually charged for pharmaceutical products intended for consumption within the territory of the Member State in which they are produced, where the legislation applicable to domestic production is based solely on a freeze of the level of prices at a given reference date (see the abovementioned judgment 181/182 'Roussel').

On the other hand, according to the Commission, a system that freezes the prices of domestic pharmaceutical products and margins on the importation and distribution of imported products should not in itself be regarded as incompatible with Article 30 of the EEC Treaty, in as much as such a system would enable importers either to increase the prices of their products in line with increases in costs in the Member State in which they were manufactured, or not to increase them in order to maintain their competitive position in relation to domestic products whose prices have been frozen.

2. Non-differentiated price freezes

According to the case-law of the Court, whilst rules imposing a price freeze which are applicable equally to domestic products and imported products do not amount in themselves to a measure having an effect equivalent to a quantitative restriction, they may in fact produce such an effect when prices are at such a level that the marketing of imported products becomes either impossible or more difficult than the marketing of national products (see the abovementioned judgment 'Danis').

This is especially the case, according to the Court, where national rules, while preventing the increased prices of imported products from being passed on in sale prices, freeze prices at a level so low that — taking into account the general situation of imported products in relation to that of domestic products — traders wishing to import the products in question into the Member State concerned can do so only at a loss, or, having regard to the level at which prices for national products are frozen, are impelled to give preference to the latter products (see the same judgment).

This is the case where measures fix the price of products solely on the basis of the cost price of domestic products, at such a level as to create a hindrance to importation or preclude any increase in the price of the imported product corresponding to the supplementary costs and charges inherent in import (see Commissie Directive 70/50/EEC).

The Court of Justice has nevertheless acknowledged that Member States have the possibility of 'combating inflation and adopting measures intended to control increases in the price of medicines, whatever their origin, on condition that they do so by means of measures which do not place imported medicines at a disadvantage' (see the abovementioned judgment 181/82 'Roussel'). In this respect, the Commission reserves the right to verify the real nature of such aims in the public interest and to take action against measures which have other objectives or place imported products at a disadvantage.

Finally, the Commission considers that a Member State may not freeze prices of pharmaceutical products so a to preclude any influence, on the prices of imported products, of an increase in costs in the Member State in which they are produced or of a change in exchange rates.

3. Freezing of margins

On the one hand, the Commission would point out that in its Directive 70/50/EEC it considered that national measures which 'fix profit margins or any other price components for imported products only or fix these differently for domestic products and for imported products, to the detriment of the latter', constitute measures having an effect equivalent to quantitative restrictions.

On the other hand, the fixing of maximum margins for the distribution and retail sale of both domestic and imported pharmaceutical products is not, in principle, likely to hinder the free movement of goods in the Community, whether the margin is calculated on the price of the product or corresponds to a fixed amount.

Maximum margins fixed for the distribution and retail sale of pharmaceutical products may not, however, include import costs in the case of pharmaceutical products imported from another Member State. Such a system would tend to discourage imports from other Member States and encourage wholesalers and retailers to obtain supplies on the national market (see judgment of the Court of June 1985 in Case 116/84 'Roelstraete', not yet reported in the ECR).

According to the Commission, the freezing of importers' margins on imports is compatible with Article 30 of the EEC Treaty only on the dual condition that the measure allows importers to cover the costs and charges inherent in import (see the abovementioned Directive 70/50/EEC) and that it is accompanied by a price freezing system for domestic products.

4. Revision of prices and derogations from freezes

The Commission would point out to Member States that fixed or frozen prices must be revised when economic conditions so require, following any changes in the market. However, when authorizing price rises for domestic or imported pharmaceutical products, Member States may not base the change solely on the cost price of national products. In any case, the various components of the cost must be taken into consideration with a view to establishing prices that are sufficiently remunerative.

Finally, Member States may not link the grant of price rises or derogations from price freezes to conditions that can be met only by firms established within the territory of the State in question, such as conditions or undertakings relating to the development of research, job creation, investments within the territory of the State concerned or growth of exports and recovery of the trade balance.

IV. REIMBURSEMENTS FOR MEDICINAL PRODUCTS

A. General

According to the Court of Justice, measures adopted within the framework of a compulsory national health-care scheme with the object of refusing insured persons the right to be supplied, at the expense of the insurance institution, with specifically named medicinal preparations are compatible with Article 30 of the EEC Treaty if the determination of the excluded medicinal preparations involves no discrimination regarding the origin of the products and is carried out on the basis of objective and verifiable criteria, such as the existence on the market of other, less expensive products having the same therapeutic effect, the fact that the preparations in question are freely marketed without the need for any medical prescription, or are products excluded from reimbursement for reasons of a pharmaco-therapeutic nature justified by the protection of public health, and provided that it is possible to amend the lists whenever compliance with the specified criteria so requires (see the abovementioned judgment 'Duphar').

These principles, set out for a negative list (listing medicinal products which are ineligible for reimbursement), apply *mutatis mutandis* to positive lists (listing medicinal products which are approved for reimbursement).

B. Application of objective criteria

The Court has essentially laid down a fundamental condition to be satisfied by the Member States to ensure that their reimbursement systems for medicinal products are compatible with Article 30: the determination of medicinal products excluded in the case of a negative list or included in the case of a positive list must be carried out in accordance with objective criteria regardless of the origin of the products.

The Court has given three examples of objective criteria which could justify a decision to exclude a product from reimbursement:

— the existence on the market of other, less expensive products having the same therapeutic effect,

— the fact that the preparations in question are freely marketed without the need for any medical prescription,

— reasons of a pharmaco-therapeutic nature justified by the protection of public health.

These examples enable the Commission to state the conditions under which Member States may exclude certain medicinal products from reimbursement.

Medicinal products may be excluded from the list of reimbursable products on a group basis or individually, subject to certain conditions in each case.

1. *Exclusion of categories of products*

The definition of groups or categories of products which are approved or ineligible for reimbursement must be based on objective, general criteria of a therapeutic nature. When therapeutic classes are defined, for reimbursement purposes, they may not therefore be reduced to a single product or single active substance, which, by the approval of one class, would allow the reimbursement of a particular product and, by the prohibition of another class, would prevent another product having an equivalent therapeutic effect from being reimbursed.

When a therapeutic class is approved for reimbursement, all products in that class need not necessarily be reimbursable: in this case, individual products may not be excluded except as indicated below.

2. *Exclusion of individual products*

The exclusion from reimbursement or the refusal to allow reimbursement of specifically named medicinal products must be based on an assessment of the cost (financial) and benefit (therapeutic) of the treatment, in comparison with other treatments. The assessment may lead to the exclusion from reimbursement of medicinal products whose efficacy has not been proven in application of Community directives or whose cost is excessive, and to the exclusion of certain indications which could lead to unjustified social security expenditure.

In general, the Commission considers that the only financial criterion that may be taken into account to approve a particular medicinal product for reimbursement or to exclude it from reimbursement is the cost of treatment. Thus a medicinal product may be excluded from reimbursement owing to the existence on the market of one or more medicinal products having an equivalent therapeutic effect, provided that, for the assessment of the therapeutic effect, account is taken of the indications and side effects of each medicinal product. Account should be taken, when comparing treatment costs, of the dosage and presumed duration of the treatment until the therapeutic effect in question is achieved.

3. *Notes*

The exclusion from reimbursement of products freely marketed without a medical prescription is in line with the principles set out above (see the abovementioned judgment 238/82 'Duphar').

The Commission regards the following as incompatible with the principles set out above:

— the exclusion from reimbursement, for one or more therapeutic classes, of proprietary products only, regardless of price, or the approval for reimbursement of unbranded products only, regardless of proce,

— the exclusive approval for reimbursement, for each therapeutic class or for all therapeutic classes, of a predetermined number of medicinal products.

C. Procedural questions

According to the Court of Justice, the criteria used by Member States to exclude certain medicinal products from reimbursement must be verifiable by any importer. Furthermore, it must be possible to amend the lists of medicinal products approved for reimbursement or ineligible for reimbursement whenever compliance with the specified criteria so requires. Decisions relating to approval for reimbursement or exclusion from reimbursement must therefore satisfy certain formal and procedural conditions. In this connection also, a distinction should be made between the exclusion of classes of products and individual decisions relating to certain products.

1. *Exclusion of categories of products*

Decisions relating to the exclusion of certain categories of products, defined as set out above, must be published officially. If all products belonging to the categories of products for which reimbursement is approved are not reimbursed, the criteria used to determine which products are excluded or which are approved must likewies be published.

2. *Exclusion of certain products*

(a) Time limits

When they receive an application for the approval of a medicinal product for reimbursement, Member States are bound to make a decision within a reasonable period. In the Commission's view, this period should in no case exceed 120 days as allowed for the granting of a marketing authorization (see Article 7 of the abovementioned Directive 65/65/EEC).

(b) Grounds

Reasons must be given for decisions by virtue of which certain products are not approved for reimbursement. When the reason given for exclusion from reimbursement relates to the existence on the market of other products having an equivalent therapeutic effect, the decision must name these products, give their prices and details of the dosage and duration of treatment used to compare prices.

(c) Notification and means of redress

Decisions by virtue of which certain products are not approved for reimbursement must be notified to the firms concerned with an indication of the means of redress against such decisions and the time limits within which appeals must be made.

3. *Revision of lists*

As the Court has stated, Member States are bound to amend the lists of medicinal products ineligible for reimbursement whenever compliance with the specified criteria so requires. To this end, Member States must arrange for periodic revision of the positive and negative lists.

V. CONCLUSION

The Commission invites the Member States to examine their rules and administrative practices in the light of the principles set out in this Communication and, where necessary, to bring them into line with these principles. Without prejudice to its intention, mentioned above, to put to the Council in the near future a proposal for a Directive on transparency of prices for pharmaceutical products and reimbursements by social security schemes, the Commission reserves the right to commence proceedings under Article 169 of the EEC Treaty, or to pursue such proceedings which have already been opened, against Member States which in its view have failed to fulfil the obligations incumbent upon them in this sector under the EEC Treaty.

COUNCIL REGULATION (EEC) No 1768/92

of 18 June 1992

concerning the creation of a supplementary protection certificate for medicinal products

(See below, page 285)

II

(Preparatory Acts)

COMMISSION

Commission communication on parallel imports of proprietary medicinal products for which marketing authorizations have already been granted

In order progressively to establish the free movement of proprietary medicinal products, the Council has adopted four Directives (¹) essentially relating to the conditions in which the Member States deliver marketing authorizations for these products.

Furthermore, in the 'De Peijper' case (²), the Court of Justice of the European Communities, to which the matter was referred under Article 177 of the EEC Treaty, has delivered a judgment on parallel imports of medicinal products. This judgment gives the Commission interpretative rulings enabling it to exercise more stringent checks on the application of the rules of the Treaty on free movement of goods, in particular the provision of Articles 30 to 36 of the EEC Treaty.

Following this judgment, the Commission considered it necessary to supplement the existing Directives by transmitting to the Council on 2 June 1980 a proposal for a Directive (³) relating to parallel imports of proprietary medicinal products.

The Commission has taken note of the objections raised by the Economic and Social Committee to the proposal relating to parallel imports and the negative vote taken on that proposal by the European Parliament on 16 October 1981.

The Commission has therefore decided to withdraw its proposal, especially as its adoption by the Council appears improbable in the present circumstances.

The Commission is not, however, abandoning its responsibility to ensure that full effect is given to the provisions of the Treaty relating to the free movement of goods. The Parliament stressed during its discussion and in the text of its resolution its attachment to the principle of free movement. This is why the Commission wishes to indicate, on the occasion of this withdrawal, the way in which it intends to apply, under its own responsibility, the rules embodied in the Treaty as interpreted by the Court of Justice, in order to preserve the unity of the Community's internal market.

In case 104/75, the Court had to give a ruling on a set of health regulations relating to the marketing of medicinal products that prevented the marketing of a medicinal product introduced as a parallel import.

The Court first of all established that national rules or practices which result in imports being channelled in such a way that only certain traders can effect these imports, whereas others are prevented from doing so, are caught by the prohibition set out in Article 30 of the EEC Treaty.

The Court went on to reaffirm the Member States' right, in pursuance of Article 36 of the EEC Treaty, to decide, subject to the limitations imposed by the Treaty, on the level of protection they wish to afford for the health and life of persons, in particular the stringency of the checks to be carried out.

(¹) Directive 65/65/EEC of 26 January 1965, OJ No 22, 9. 2. 1965; Directive 75/318/EEC of 20 May 1975, OJ No L 147, 9. 6. 1975; Directive 75/319/EEC of 20 May 1975, OJ No L 147, 9. 6. 1975; Directive 78/25/EEC of 12 December 1977, OJ No L 11, 14. 1. 1978.

(²) CJEC 20 May 1976, Case 104/75, 1976 Report, p. 613.

(³) Proposal dated 2 June 1980 for a Directive amending Directives 65/65/EEC and 75/319/EEC (OJ No C 143, 12. 6. 1980).

It nevertheless immediately stressed the general context in which this competence of the Member States was to be exercised:

'National rules or practices which do restrict imports of pharmaceutical products or are capable of doing so are only compatible with the Treaty to the extent to which they are necessary for the effective protection of health and life of humans.

National rules or practices do not fall within the exception specified in Article 36 if the health and life of humans can be as effectively protected by measures which do not restrict intra-Community trade so much.

In particular Article 36 cannot be relied on to justify rules or practices which, even though they are beneficial, contain restrictions which are explained primarily by a concern to lighten the administration's burden or reduce public expenditure, unless, in the absence of the said rules or practices, this burden or expenditure clearly would exceed the limits of what can reasonably be required.'

In the case in point the competent national authorities intended to prevent a parallel importer from marketing a medicinal product that was similar to a medicinal product which had already been authorized and was produced by the same manufacturer for two reasons.

First, the parallel manufacturer was not able to provide the authorities with the complete file (¹) relating to the quality, efficacy and safety of the product in general, which the manufacturer's authorized importer had already supplied to those same authorities with a view to obtaining a marketing authorization for that medicinal product.

Secondly, the parallel importer could not, unlike the authorized importer, obtain from the manufacturer the reports on checks made on each manufacturing batch.

In the judgment on the 'De Peijper' case, the Court ruled that 'national rules or practices which make it possible for a manufacturer of the pharmaceutical product in question and his duly appointed representative, simply by refusing to produce the documents relating to the medicinal preparation in general or to a specific batch of that preparation, to enjoy a monopoly of the importing and marketing of the product, must be regarded as being unnecessarily restrictive, unless it is clearly proved that any other rules or practices would obviously be beyond the means which can be reasonably expected of an administration operating in a normal manner ...'

'It is only if the information or documents to be produced by the manufacturer or his duly appointed importer show that there are several variants of the medicinal preparation and that the differences between these variants have a therapeutic effect that there would be any justification for treating the variants as different medicinal preparations, for the purpose of authorizing them to be placed on the market and as regards producing the relevant documents ...'

The Commission, in its role as guardian of the Treaty, will ensure that the rules and practices applied by Member States to parallel imports of medicinal products, and in particular proprietary medicinal products which account for the majority of intra-Community trading operations in medicinal products, will remain within limits compatible with Articles 30 to 36.

In particular, such measures must:

— be strictly necessary from the health standpoint,

— obstruct intra-Community trade as little as possible,

— require the Member States to adopt an active and vigilant atittude towards pharmaceutical companies.

The Commission points out that the competent authorities in the Member States are not entitled to oppose the marketing of any medicinal product, the subject of parallel importation, that already has a marketing authorization, on the grounds that the parallel importer is not able to obtain documents which only the manufacturer or his approved representative can have at their disposal.

In the absence of any harmonized rules governing the system of parallel imports, it is up to the Commission, in accordance with the procedure under Article 169, and to the interested parties, in accordance with the means of redress which they have at their disposal, to ensure that parallel imports of medicinal products are made possible under the conditions laid down by the rulings of the Court.

(¹) This file comprises *inter alia* a description of the manufacturer's production and control methods and the results of the analytical, toxico-pharmacological and clinical tests conducted on the medicinal product in general.

After consulting senior experts in public health matters from the Member States' administrations meeting in the Pharmaceutical Committee ('), the Commission had proposed a uniform system for parallel imports of proprietary medicinal products. Despite the withdrawal of its proposal, the Commission considers it useful to indicate safe ways of monitoring parallel imports which, subject to the rulings of the Court, seem to it to be justified for the purpose of protecting the health and life of humans pursuant to Article 36 of the Treaty.

The Commission points out that the competent authorities of the Member States already have at their disposal two important safeguards for health in the case of parallel imports of proprietary medicinal products.

On the one hand, the national rules governing the activities of importers, wholesalers and, where applicable, manufacturers of proprietary medicinal products apply equally to parallel importers. These rules usually cover professional competence and responsibilities, the technical premises and equipment required and the rules for the operation of such establishments, in particular the procedures relating to the preservation of documents to facilitate official checks and inspections.

On the other hand, the authorities competent to issue marketing authorizations for proprietary medicinal products already, as a rule, possess the dossier relating to the quality, efficacy and safety of the medicinal product in general, which has been supplied by the manufacturer or his approved importer and which states, in pursuance of Article 4 (11) of Directive 65/65/EEC, the authorizations already obtained for the product in any other Member State. According to the Court, the competent administration of the importing Member State is clearly entitled to require the manufacturer, or his duly appointed importer, to state whether the manufacturer, or the group of manufacturers to which he belongs, produces several variants of the same medicinal product for different Member States. It this is so, it is only if the documents submitted by the manufacturer show that there are differences having a therapeutic effect that there would be any justification for treating the variants as different medicinal products for the purpose of marketing authorization.

In addition to these safeguards, the authorities have a legitimate interest in being able to verify, at all times

and beyond doubt, whether the batches of imported medicinal products are in conformity with the particulars contained in the dossier.

The Commission concedes that the parallel importer may be required to supply the competent authorities in the Member State into which the product is imported with certain information readily accessible to him when he wants to market for the first time a proprietary medicinal product already marketed by the manufacturer or his duly appointed representative.

This information must allow the competent authorities in the Member State into which the product is imported to check, within a reasonable period, that the proprietary medicinal product that is the subject of parallel importation is effectively covered by the marketing authorization already granted to the manufacturer or his duly appointed representative. In the Commission's view, this period should not exceed 45 days from the time the parallel importer gives the following information to the competent authorities:

(a) name of the proprietary medicinal product in the Member State into which it is imported and in the Member State from which it comes;

(b) name or corporate name and permanent address of the person responsible for placing the product on the market in the Member State into which it is imported and in the Member State from which it comes, and where appropriate, of the manufacturer(s);

(c) name or corporate name and permanent address of the parallel importer;

(d) numbers of the marketing authorizations in the Member State into which the product is imported and in the Member State from which it comes;

(e) any other general information useful for the marketing of the proprietary medicinal product in the Member State into which it is imported, i.e.

— qualitative and quantitative composition in terms of active principles, by dosage unit or in percentage, using the international non-proprietary names recommended by the World Health Organization where such names exist,

— pharmaceutical form and route of administration,

— therapeutic indications and normal dosage,

— contra-indications and main side-effects,

— storage precautions, if any;

('') Set up by Council Decision 75/320/EEC of 20 May 1975, OJ No L 147, 9. 6. 1975.

(f) one or more specimens or mock-ups of the proprietary product in the form in which it will be marketed in the Member State into which it is imported, including the package leaflet, if any.

To enable the authorities to be effectively informed of the marketing of each batch of the product imported, the parallel importer should, in the Commission's view, register the origin, quantity and batch numbers of the imported medicinal products whenever he imports them, and hold this information at the disposal of the competent authorities.

The Commission points out that pursuant to Chapter IV of Directive 75/319/EEC each batch of proprietary medicinal products manufactured in a Member State is checked by the manufacturer who makes out a certificate and registers the operations carried out in documents that remain at the disposal of the agents of the competent authority for at least five years. Because these control reports are sent to him by the manufacturer, the duly appointed importer is exempt from repeating the controls in the Member State into which the product is imported.

Since the parallel importer does not have access to these control reports, the national authorities have to adopt a more active policy when they wish to verify the controls carried out by the manufacturer on a given batch. They can choose for this purpose one of the four approaches given in the De Peijper judgment, i.e.:

— they can obtain the manufacturing control reports by taking legislative or administrative measures compelling the manufacturer himself, or his duly appointed representative, to supply them;

— they can obtain these reports through the authorities in the country of manufacture;

— they can, whenever possible, lay down a presumption of conformity with the specifications of the medicament and it would be up to them, in appropriate cases, to rebut this presumption after verification of the conformity;

— as far as this presumption is fully impracticable, they can allow the parallel importer to provide proof of conformity by any means other than by documents to which he has no access.

The parallel importer is liable, in the same way as the person responsible for marketing, to the measures taken by the Member States to withdraw the product, to suspend or revoke the authorization or to prohibit supply of the product, pursuant to Article 28 of Directive 75/319/EEC.

By appropriate cooperation between the Member State authorities, it would be possible to supplement, if necessary, the monitoring measures compatible with Article 36 of the Treaty, designed to check the conformity of medicinal products imported in parallel.

In the De Peijper judgment, the Court held that simple cooperation between the authorities of the Member States would enable them to obtain on a reciprocal basis the documents necessary for checking certain largely standardized and widely distributed products.

In addition to the obligations resulting from Article 5 of the EEC Treaty, the obligation for the competent authorities to communicate to each other such information as is appropriate to guarantee that the requirements for the marketing or manufacturing authorizations are fulfilled is specifically spelled out in Article 30 of Directive 75/319/EEC.

The Commission for its part is prepared to do everything it can to assist the Member States in exchanging the information they consider necessary to check the conformity of parallel imports of proprietary medicinal products.

The Commission considers that the Committee for Proprietary Medicinal Products, set up by Directive 75/319/EEC, provides a suitable forum for any exchanges of information between the representatives of the Member States responsible for marketing authorizations for proprietary medicinal products. The Commission also holds at the disposal of Member States a continuously updated list of the persons appointed by the competent authorities to supply at short notice any necessary information on marketing or manufacturing authorizations in application of Articles 30 and 33 of Directive 75/319/EEC.

Texts relating to
marketing authorizations
for veterinary medicinal products

COUNCIL REGULATION (EEC) No 2309/93

of 22 July 1993

laying down Community procedures for the authorization and supervision of medicinal products for human and veterinary use and establishing a European Agency for the Evaluation of Medicinal Products

(See above, page 19)

381L0851

81/851/EEC: COUNCIL DIRECTIVE OF 28 SEPTEMBER 1981 ON THE APPROXIMATION OF THE LAWS OF THE MEMBER STATES RELATING TO VETERINARY MEDICINAL PRODUCTS

OFFICIAL JOURNAL No L 317, 06/11/1981, P. 1
DATE OF NOTIFICATION: 09/10/1981
DATE OF TRANSPOSITION: 09/10/1983; SEE ART. 51

AMENDED BY

390L0676
90/676/EEC: COUNCIL DIRECTIVE OF 13 DECEMBER 1990   [1]
OFFICIAL JOURNAL No L 373, 31/12/1990, P. 15
DATE OF NOTIFICATION: 18/12/1990
DATE OF TRANSPOSITION: 01/01/1992; SEE ART. 2

390L0677
90/677/EEC: COUNCIL DIRECTIVE OF 13 DECEMBER 1990   [2]
OFFICIAL JOURNAL No L 373, 31/12/1990, P. 26
DATE OF NOTIFICATION: 18/12/1990
DATE OF TRANSPOSITION: 01/01/1992; SEE ART. 6

392L0074
92/74/EEC: COUNCIL DIRECTIVE OF 22 SEPTEMBER 1992   [3]
OFFICIAL JOURNAL No L 297, 13/10/1992, P. 12
DATE OF NOTIFICATION: 08/10/1992
DATE OF TRANSPOSITION: 31/12/1993; SEE ART. 10

393L0040
93/40/EEC: COUNCIL DIRECTIVE OF 14 JUNE 1993   [4]
OFFICIAL JOURNAL No L 214, 24/08/1993, P. 31
DATE OF TRANSPOSITION: 01/01/1995; SEE ART. 3
DATE OF TRANSPOSITION: 01/01/1998; SEE ART. 3

CHAPTER I

DEFINITIONS AND SCOPE

ARTICLE 1

1. THE DEFINITIONS LAID DOWN IN ARTICLE 1 OF COUNCIL DIRECTIVE 65/65/EEC OF 26 JANUARY 1965 ON THE APPROXIMATION OF PROVISIONS LAID DOWN BY LAW, REGULATION OR ADMINISTRATIVE ACTION RELATING TO PROPRIETARY MEDICINAL PRODUCTS (1) SHALL APPLY TO THIS DIRECTIVE.

2. FOR THE PURPOSES OF THIS DIRECTIVE, THE FOLLOWING DEFINITIONS SHALL APPLY:

- "VETERINARY MEDICINAL PRODUCT" SHALL MEAN ANY MEDICINAL PRODUCT INTENDED FOR ANIMALS,

- "READY-MADE VETERINARY MEDICINAL PRODUCT" SHALL MEAN ANY VETERINARY MEDICINAL PRODUCT PREPARED IN ADVANCE WHICH DOES NOT COMPLY WITH THE DEFINITION OF PROPRIETARY MEDICINAL PRODUCTS AND WHICH IS MARKETED IN A PHARMACEUTICAL FORM WHICH MAY BE USED WITHOUT FURTHER PROCESSING,
- "PRE-MIX FOR MEDICATED FEEDINGSTUFFS" SHALL MEAN ANY VETERINARY MEDICINAL PRODUCT PREPARED IN ADVANCE WITH A VIEW TO THE SUBSEQUENT MANUFACTURE OF MEDICATED FEEDINGSTUFFS,
- "MEDICATED FEEDINGSTUFFS" SHALL MEAN ANY MIXTURE OF A VETERINARY MEDICINAL PRODUCT OR PRODUCTS AND FEED OR FEEDS WHICH IS READY PREPARED FOR MARKETING AND INTENDED TO BE FED TO ANIMALS WITHOUT FURTHER PROCESSING, BECAUSE OF ITS CURATIVE OR PREVENTIVE PROPERTIES OR OTHER PROPERTIES AS A MEDICINAL PRODUCT COVERED BY ARTICLE 1 (2) OF DIRECTIVE 65/65/EEC.

3. UNTIL COMMUNITY RULES ARE ADOPTED FOR MEDICATED FEEDINGSTUFFS, MEMBER STATES MAY LAY DOWN THAT THIS TERM SHALL INCLUDE SEMI-FINISHED PRODUCTS WHICH ARE MANUFACTURED FROM A PRE-MIX FOR MEDICATED FEEDINGSTUFFS FOR WHICH AN AUTHORIZATION PURSUANT TO ARTICLE 4 OF THIS DIRECTIVE HAS BEEN ISSUED AND FEEDINGSTUFFS, WHERE SUCH SEMI-FINISHED PRODUCTS ARE INTENDED TO BE PROCESSED BY FURTHER MIXING WITH FEEDINGSTUFFS TO BECOME MEDICATED FEEDINGSTUFFS READY FOR USE. MEMBER STATES SHALL ENSURE THAT SUCH SEMI-FINISHED PRODUCTS ARE SUBJECT TO THE CONTROL OF THE COMPETENT AUTHORITIES AND THAT THEY ARE USED EXCLUSIVELY FOR THE MANUFACTURE OF MEDICATED FEEDINGSTUFFS UNDER THE CONDITIONS WHICH GOVERNED THE MARKETING AUTHORIZATION FOR THE PRE-MIX FOR MEDICATED FEEDINGSTUFFS.

4. ADDITIVES COVERED BY COUNCIL DIRECTIVE 70/524/EEC OF 23 NOVEMBER 1970 CONCERNING ADDITIVES IN FEEDINGSTUFFS (2), AS SUBSEQUENTLY AMENDED, WHERE THEY ARE INCORPORATED IN ANIMAL FEEDINGSTUFFS AND SUPPLEMENTARY ANIMAL FEEDINGSTUFFS IN ACCORDANCE WITH THAT DIRECTIVE, SHALL NOT BE CONSIDERED AS VETERINARY MEDICINAL PRODUCTS FOR THE PURPOSES OF THIS DIRECTIVE.

5. " Member States shall take all measures necessary to ensure that only persons empowered under their national legislation in force possess or have under their control veterinary medicinal products or substances which may be used as veterinary medicinal products that have anabolic, anti-infectious, anti-parasitic, anti-inflammatory, hormonal or psychotropic properties.
Member States shall maintain a register of producers and dealers permitted to be in possession of active substances which may be used in the manufacture of veterinary medicinal products having the properties referred to in the first subparagraph. Such persons must maintain detailed records of all dealings in substances which may be used in the manufacture of veterinary medicinal products and keep these records available for inspection by the competent authorities for a period of at least three years.
Any amendments to be made to the list of substances referred to in the first subparagraph shall be adopted in accordance with the procedure referred to in " Article 42j " [4]. " [1]

ARTICLE 2

1. THE PROVISIONS OF THIS DIRECTIVE SHALL APPLY TO VETERINARY MEDICINAL PRODUCTS OFFERED FOR SALE INTER ALIA IN THE FORM OF PROPRIETARY MEDICINAL PRODUCTS, READY-MADE VETERINARY MEDICINAL PRODUCTS OR PRE-MIXES FOR MEDICATED FEEDINGSTUFFS.
" This Directive shall apply to veterinary medicinal products used in order to produce active or passive immunity or to diagnose the state of immunity, in accordance with the provisions of Directive 90/676/EEC which widens the scope of this Directive. " [1]

[The scope of this Directive has been extended to immunological veterinary medicinal products [2]; and to homeopathic veterinary medicinal products [3]]

2. THE PROVISIONS OF THIS DIRECTIVE SHALL NOT APPLY TO:

- MEDICATED FEEDINGSTUFFS,
- "..." [1]
- VETERINARY MEDICINAL PRODUCTS BASED ON RADIOACTIVE ISOTOPES,
- "..." [1]

- HOMEOPATHIC MEDICINAL PRODUCTS.

3. HOWEVER, MEDICATED FEEDINGSTUFFS MAY BE PREPARED ONLY FROM PRE-MIXES WHICH HAVE BEEN AUTHORIZED UNDER THIS DIRECTIVE. WITHIN TWO YEARS OF THE NOTIFICATION OF THIS DIRECTIVE, THE COUNCIL SHALL, ON THE BASIS OF A COMMISSION REPORT ACCOMPANIED IF NECESSARY BY APPROPRIATE PROPOSALS, DELIBERATE ON A LIST OF PHARMACOLOGICAL MOLECULES WHICH MAY BE USED FOR PREPARING PRE-MIXES AND ON THE PROCEDURE FOR DRAWING UP THIS LIST.

ARTICLE 3

MEMBER STATES MAY PERMIT EXEMPTIONS FROM THE PROVISIONS OF ARTICLE 4 (1) ON THEIR TERRITORY IN RESPECT OF VETERINARY MEDICINAL PRODUCTS INTENDED SOLELY FOR AQUARIUM FISH, CAGE BIRDS, HOMING PIGEONS, TERRARIUM ANIMALS AND SMALL RODENTS, PROVIDED THAT SUCH PRODUCTS DO NOT CONTAIN SUBSTANCES THE USE OF WHICH REQUIRES VETERINARY CONTROL AND THAT ALL POSSIBLE MEASURES HAVE BEEN TAKEN TO PREVENT UNAUTHORIZED USE OF THE PRODUCTS FOR OTHER ANIMALS.

CHAPTER II

APPLICATION FOR MARKETING AUTHORIZATION FOR VETERINARY MEDICINAL PRODUCTS

ARTICLE 4

" 1. " No veterinary medicinal product may be placed on the market of a Member State unless a marketing authorization has been issued by the competent authorities of that Member State in accordance with this Directive or a marketing authorization has been granted in accordance with Council Regulation (EEC) 2309/93 of 22 July 1993 laying down Community procedures for the authorization and supervision of medicinal products for human and veterinary use and establishing an European Agency for the evaluation of medicinal products (3). " [4]
However, where the health situation so requires, a Member State may authorize the placing on the market or administration to animals of veterinary medicinal products which have been authorized by another Member State in accordance with this Directive.
In the event of a serious disease epidemic the States may provisionally allow the use of immunological veterinary medicinal products without an authorization for placing on the market, in the absence of a suitable medicinal product and after informing the Commission of the detailed conditions of use.

2. A Member State shall not authorize the placing on the market of a veterinary medicinal product intended for administration to food-producing animals whose flesh or products are intended for human consumption, unless:

(a) the active substance or substances capable of pharmacological action contained in the veterinary medicinal product were authorized for use in other veterinary medicinal products in the Member State concerned on the date of entry into force of Council Regulation (EEC) No 2377/90 of 26 June 1990 laying down a Community procedure for the fixing of maximum levels of residues of veterinary medicinal products in foodstuffs of animal origin (4);

(b) the active substance or substances capable of pharmacological action is or are mentioned in Annex I, II or III to the aforementioned Regulation.

" From 1 January 1997 the Member States shall not permit foodstuffs for human consumption to be taken from test animals unless maximum residue limits have been established by the Community in accordance with the provisions of Regulation (EEC) No 2377/90 and an appropriate withdrawal period has been established to ensure that this maximum limit will not be exceeded in the foodstuffs. " [4]

3. No veterinary medicinal product may be administered to animals unless the authorization referred to above has been issued, except for the tests of veterinary medicinal products referred to in point 10 of Article 5 which have been accepted by the competent national authorities, following notification or authorization, in accordance with the national rules in force.

The Member States shall permit the placing on the market of foodstuffs obtained from animals treated during these tests only if they are satisfied that the foodstuffs do not contain residues which may present a risk for human health.

Without prejudice to stricter Community or national rules relating to dispensing veterinary medicinal products and to protect human and animal health, a prescription shall be required for dispensing to the public the following veterinary medicinal products;

(a) those products subject to official restrictions on supply or use, such as:

- the restrictions resulting from the implementation of the relevant United Nations conventions on narcotic and psychotropic substances,
- the restrictions on the use of veterinary medicinal products resulting from Community law;

(b) those products in respect of which special precautions must be taken by the veterinarian in order to avoid any unnecessary risk to:

- the target species,
- the person administering the products to the animal,
- the consumer of foodstuffs obtained from the treated animal,
- the environment;

(c) those products intended for treatments or pathological processes which require a precise prior diagnosis or the use of which may cause effects which impede or interfere with subsequent diagnostic or therapeutic measures;

(d) magistral formulae intended for animals.

In addition, a prescription shall be required for new veterinary medicinal products containing an active ingredient which has been authorized for use in a veterinary medicinal product for less than five years unless, having regard to the information and particulars provided by the applicant, or experience acquired in the practical use of the product, the competent authorities are satisfied that none of the criteria referred to in (a) to (d) of the third subparagraph apply.

4. However, where there exists no authorized medicinal product for a condition, Member States may exceptionally, in particular in order to avoid causing unacceptable suffering to the animals concerned, permit the administration by a veterinarian or under his/her direct personal responsibility to an animal or to a small number of animals on a particular holding (5):

(a) of a veterinary medicinal product authorized in the Member State concerned for use in another animal species, or for another condition in the same species; or

(b) if there is no product such as referred to in point (a), of a medicinal product authorized for use in the Member State concerned in human beings in accordance with Directive 65/65/EEC of 26 January 1965; or

(c) if there is no product such as referred to in point (b) and within the limits of the law of the Member State concerned, of a veterinary medicinal product prepared extemporaneously by a person authorized to do so under national legislation in accordance with the terms of a veterinary prescription,

provided that the medicinal product, where administered to animals whose flesh or products are intended for human consumption, contains only substances to be found in a veterinary medicinal product authorized for such animals in the Member State concerned and that in the case of food-producing animals the veterinarian responsible specifies an appropriate withdrawal period to ensure that food produced from the treated animals does not contain residues harmful to consumers.

Unless the product used indicates a withdrawal period for the species concerned, the specified withdrawal period shall not be less than:

7 days: eggs,
7 days: milk,
28 days: meat from poultry and mammals including fat and offal,

500 degree days: meat from fish.

The veterinarian shall keep adequate records of the date of examination of the animals, details of the owner, the number of animals treated, the diagnosis, the medicinal products prescribed, the dosages administered, the duration of treatment and the withdrawal periods recommended, and make these records available for inspection by the competent authorities for a period of at least three years. This requirement may be extended by the Member States to animals whose flesh or products are not intended for human consumption.

5. Notwithstanding paragraph 3, Member States shall ensure that veterinarians providing services in another Member State can take with them and administer to animals small quantities of ready-made veterinary medicinal products not exceeding daily requirements other than immunological veterinary medicinal products which are not authorized for use in the Member State in which the services are provided (host Member State), providing that the following conditions are satisfied:

(a) the authorization to place the product on the market provided for in paragraph 1 has been issued by the competent authorities of the Member State in which the veterinarian is established;

(b) the veterinary medicinal products are transported by the veterinarian in the original manufacturer's packaging;

(c) the veterinary medicinal products intended for administration to food-producing animals have the same qualitative and quantitative composition in terms of active principles as the medicinal products authorized in accordance with paragraph 1 in the host Member State;

(d) a veterinarian providing services in another Member State shall acquaint himself with the good veterinary practices applied in that Member State. He shall ensure that the withdrawal period specified on the labelling of the veterinary medicinal product concerned is complied with, unless he could reasonably be expected to know that a longer withdrawal period should be specified to comply with these good veterinary practices;

(e) the veterinarian shall not furnish any veterinary medicinal product to the owner or keeper of the animals treated in the host Member State unless this is permissible on the basis of the rules of the host Member State; in this case he shall, however, supply only in relation to animals under his care and only the minimum quantities of veterinary medicinal product necessary to complete the treatment of animals concerned on that occasion;

(f) the veterinarian shall be required to keep detailed records of the animals treated, the diagnosis, the veterinary medicinal products administered, the dosage administered, the duration of treatment and the withdrawal period applied. These records shall be available for inspection by the competent authorities of the host State for a period of at least three years;

(g) the overall range and quantity of veterinary medicinal products carried by the veterinarian shall not exceed that generally required for the daily needs of good veterinary practice. " [1]

ARTICLE 5

" For the purpose of obtaining the authorization for placing a product on the market provided for in Article 4, the person responsible for placing the product on the market shall lodge an application with the competent authority of the Member State.
" The person responsible for placing veterinary medicinal products on the market shall be established in the Community. In respect of veterinary medicinal products authorized on the date of implementation of this Directive, the Member States shall if necessary apply this provision at the time of the five-yearly renewal of the marketing authorization provided for in Article 15. " [4]
The following particulars and documents shall accompany such application:

1. name or business name and permanent address or registered place of business of the person responsible for placing the product on the market and, if different, of the manufacturer or manufacturers involved and of the sites of manufacture;

2. name of the veterinary medicinal product (brand name, non-proprietary name, with or without a trademark, or name of the manufacturer or scientific name or formula, with or without a trademark, or the name of the manufacturer);

3. qualitative and quantitative particulars of all the constituents of the veterinary medicinal product, using the usual terminology but not empirical chemical formula and giving the international non-proprietary name recommended by the World Health Organization, where such a name exists;

4. description of the method of preparation;

5. therapeutic indications, contra-indications and side-effects;

6. dosage for the various species of animal for which the veterinary medicinal product is intended, its pharmaceutical form, method and route of administration and proposed shelf life;

7. if applicable, explanations of the precautionary and safety measures to be taken when the product is stored, when it is administered to animals and when waste therefrom is disposed of, together with an indication of any potential risks the medicinal product might pose to the environment and the health of humans, animals or plants;

8. indication of the withdrawal period necessary between the last administration of the veterinary medicinal product to animals under normal conditions of use and the production of foodstuffs from such animals in order to ensure that such foodstuffs do not contain residues in quantities in excess of the maximum limits laid down. Where necessary, the applicant shall propose and justify a tolerance level for residues which may be accepted in foodstuffs without risk for the consumer, together with routine analysis methods which could by used by the competent authorities to trace residues;

9. description of the control testing methods employed by the manufacturer (qualitative and quantitative analysis of the constituents and the finished product, specific tests, e.g. sterility tests, test for the presence of pyrogens, for the presence of heavy metals, stability tests, biological and toxicity tests, tests on intermediate products);

10. results of:

- physico-chemical, biological or microbiological tests,
- toxicological and pharmacological tests,
- clinical trials.

However, and without prejudice to the law relating to the protection of industrial and commercial property:

(a) the applicant shall not be required to provide the results of toxicological and pharmacological tests and clinical trials if he can demonstrate:

(i) either that the veterinary medicinal product is essentially similar to a medicinal product authorized in the Member State concerned by the application and that the person responsible for placing the original veterinary medicinal product on the market has agreed that the toxicological, pharmacological or clinical references contained in the file on the original veterinary medicinal product may be used for the purpose of examining the application in question;

(ii) or by detailed references to the scientific literature presented in accordance with the second paragraph of Article 1 of Directive 81/852/EEC (6), as amended by Directive 87/20/EEC (7), that the constituent or constituents of the veterinary medicinal product have a well-established medicinal use, with recognized efficacy and an acceptable level of safety;

(iii) or that the veterinary medicinal product is essentially similar to a product which has been authorized within the Community, in accordance with Community provisions in force, for not less than six years and is marketed in the Member State for which the application is made; this period shall be extended to 10 years in the case of high-technology medicinal products appearing on the list in Part A of the Annex to Directive 87/22/EEC (9) or of a medicinal product appearing on the list in Part B of the Annex to that Directive for which the procedure laid down in Article 2 of that Directive has been followed. Furthermore, a Member State may also extend this period to 10 years by a single Decision covering all the products marketed in its territory where it considers this necessary in the interest of public health. Member States are at liberty not to apply the abovementioned six-year period beyond the date of expiry of a patent protecting the original product;

(b) in the case of new veterinary medicinal products containing known constituents not hitherto used in combination for therapeutic purposes, the results of toxicological and pharmacological tests and of clinical trials relating to that combination must be provided, but it shall not be necessary to provide references relating to each individual constituent:

11. a summary in accordance with Article 5a of the product characteristics, one or more specimens or mock-ups of the sales presentation of the veterinary medicinal product together with the package insert referred to in Article 48 (1);

12. a document showing that the manufacturer is authorized in his own country to produce veterinary medicinal products;

13. " copies of any authorization obtained in another Member State or in a third country to place the relevant veterinary medicinal product on the market, together with a list of those Member States in which an application for authorization submitted in accordance with this Directive is under examination. Copies of the summary of the product characteristics proposed by the applicant in accordance with Article 5a or approved by the competent authority of the Member State in accordance with Article 5b and copies of the package insert proposed, details of any decision to refuse authorization, whether in the Community or a third country and the reasons for that decision.
This information shall be updated on a regular basis; " **[4]**

14. in the case of medicinal products containing new active ingredients which are not mentioned in Annex I, II or III to Regulation (EEC) No 2377/90, a copy of the documents submitted to the Commission in accordance with Annex V to the Regulation. " **[1]**

" Article 5a

The summary of the product characteristics referred to in point 11 of point 2 of the second paragraph of Article 5 shall contain the following information:

1. name of the veterinary medicinal product;

2. qualitative and quantitative composition in terms of the active ingredients and constituents of the excipient, knowledge of which is essential for proper administration of the medicinal product; the international non-proprietary names recommended by the World Health Organization shall be used, where such names exist, or failing this, the usual non-proprietary name or chemical description;

3. pharmaceutical form;

4. pharmacological properties and, in so far as this information is useful for therapeutic purposes, pharmacokinetic particulars;

5. clinical particulars:

5.0 target species,
5.1 indications for use, specifying the target species,
5.2 contra-indications,
5.3 undesirable effects (frequency and seriousness),
5.4 special precautions for use,
5.5 use during pregnancy and lactation,
5.6 interaction with other medicaments and other forms of interaction,
5.7 posology and method of administration,
5.8 overdose (symptoms, emergency procedures, antidotes) (if necessary),
5.9 special warnings for each target species,
5.10 withdrawal periods,
5.11 special precautions to be taken by the person administering the product to animals;

6. pharmaceutical particulars:

6.1 incompatibilities (major),
6.2 shelf life, when necessary after reconstitution of the product or when the container is opened for the first time,

6.3 special precautions for storage,

6.4 nature and contents of container,

6.5 name or style and permanent address or registered place of business of the holder of the authorization to place the product on the market,

6.6 special precautions for the disposal of unused product or waste materials, if any. " [1]

" Article 5b

When the marketing authorization referred to in Article 4 (1) is issued, the person responsible for placing that veterinary medicinal product on the market shall be informed, by the competent authorities of the Member State concerned, of the summary of the product characteristics as approved by it. The competent authorities shall take all necessary measures to ensure that the information given in the summary is in conformity with that accepted when the marketing authorization is issued or subsequently. The competent authorities shall forward to the European Agency for the Evaluation of Medicinal Products a copy of the authorization together with the summary of the product characteristics referred to in Article 5a.

Furthermore, the competent authorities shall draw up an assessment report and comments on the dossier as regards the results of the analytical and pharmacotoxicological tests and the clinical trials of the veterinary medicinal product concerned. The assessment report shall be updated whenever new information becomes available which is of importance for the evaluation of the quality, safety or efficacy of the veterinary medicinal product concerned. " [4]

ARTICLE 6

MEMBER STATES SHALL MAKE ALL NECESSARY ARRANGEMENTS TO ENSURE THAT THE DOCUMENTS AND PARTICULARS LISTED IN POINTS 8, 9 AND 10 OF THE SECOND PARAGRAPH OF ARTICLE 5 ARE DRAFTED BY EXPERTS WITH THE REQUISITE TECHNICAL OR PROFESSIONAL QUALIFICATIONS BEFORE BEING SUBMITTED TO THE COMPETENT AUTHORITIES.

THESE DOCUMENTS AND PARTICULARS SHALL BE SIGNED BY THE EXPERTS IN QUESTION.

ARTICLE 7

ACCORDING TO THEIR PARTICULAR QUALIFICATIONS, THE ROLE OF THE EXPERTS SHALL BE:

1. TO CARRY OUT SUCH WORK AS FALLS WITHIN THEIR PARTICULAR DISCIPLINE (ANALYSIS, PHARMACOLOGY AND SIMILAR EXPERIMENTAL SCIENCES, CLINICAL TRIALS) AND TO DESCRIBE OBJECTIVELY THE RESULTS OBTAINED IN BOTH QUANTITATIVE AND QUALITATIVE TERMS;

2. TO DESCRIBE THEIR FINDINGS IN ACCORDANCE WITH COUNCIL DIRECTIVE 81/852/EEC OF 28 SEPTEMBER 1981 ON THE APPROXIMATION OF THE LAWS OF THE MEMBER STATES RELATING TO ANALYTICAL, PHARMACO-TOXICOLOGICAL AND CLINICAL STANDARDS AND PROTOCOLS IN RESPECT OF THE TESTING OF VETERINARY MEDICINAL PRODUCTS, AND IN PARTICULAR TO STATE:

(a) IN THE CASE OF ANALYSTS, WHETHER THE PRODUCT CONFORMS WITH THE STATED COMPOSITION, PROVIDING ANY REASONS FOR THE CONTROL TESTING METHODS WHICH THE MANUFACTURER IS TO USE;

(b) IN THE CASE OF PHARMACOLOGISTS AND APPROPRIATELY QUALIFIED SPECIALISTS:

- THE TOXICITY OF THE PRODUCT AND THE PHARMACOLOGICAL PROPERTIES OBSERVED,
- WHETHER, AFTER ADMINISTRATION OF THE VETERINARY MEDICINAL PRODUCT UNDER NORMAL CONDITIONS OF USE AND OBSERVANCE OF THE RECOMMENDED WITHDRAWAL PERIOD, FOODSTUFFS OBTAINED FROM THE TREATED ANIMALS CONTAIN RESIDUES WHICH MIGHT CONSTITUTE A HEALTH HAZARD TO THE CONSUMER;

(c) IN THE CASE OF CLINICIANS, WHETHER THEY HAVE FOUND IN ANIMALS TREATED WITH THE PRODUCT EFFECTS CORRESPONDING TO THE INFORMATION FURNISHED BY THE MANUFACTURER PURSUANT TO ARTICLE 5, WHETHER THE PRODUCT IS WELL TOLERATED, WHAT DOSAGE THEY RECOMMEND AND WHAT ARE THE CONTRA-INDICATIONS AND SIDE-EFFECTS, IF ANY;

3. TO GIVE REASONS FOR THE USE OF THE REFERENCES TO PUBLISHED DATA REFERRED TO IN POINT 10 (a) AND (b) OF THE SECOND PARAGRAPH OF ARTICLE 5, ACCORDING TO THE CONDITIONS LAID DOWN BY COUNCIL DIRECTIVE 81/852/EEC.

" The experts' detailed reports shall form part of the documentation which the applicant shall lodge with the competent authorities. A brief curriculum vitae of the expert shall be appended to each report. " [1]

CHAPTER III

EXAMINATION OF APPLICATIONS FOR AUTHORIZATION - AUTHORIZATION - RENEWAL OF AUTHORIZATION

ARTICLE 8

" 1. Member States shall take all appropriate measures to ensure that the procedure for granting an authorization to place a veterinary medicinal product on the market is completed within 210 days of the submission of a valid application.

2. Where a Member State notes that an application for authorization submitted after 1 January 1995 is already under active examination in another Member State in respect of that veterinary medicinal product, the Member State concerned may decide to suspend the detailed examination of the application in order to await the assessment report prepared by the other Member State in accordance with Article 5b.
The Member State concerned shall inform the other Member State and the applicant of its decision to suspend detailed examination of the application in question. As soon as it has completed the examination of the application and reached a decision, the other Member State shall forward a copy of its assessment report to the Member State concerned.
Within 90 days of the receipt of the assessment report, the Member State concerned shall either recognize the decision of the other Member State and the summary of the product characteristics as approved by it or, if it considers that there are grounds for supposing that the authorization of the veterinary medicinal product concerned may present a risk to human or animal health or the environment (9), it shall apply the procedures set out in Articles 18 to 22 of this Directive. " [4]

" Article 8a

With effect from 1 January 1998, where a Member State is informed in accordance with point 13 of the second paragraph of Article 5 that another Member State has authorized a veterinary medicinal product which is the subject of an application for authorization in the Member State concerned, that Member State shall forthwith request the authorities of the Member State which has granted the authorization to forward to it the assessment report referred to in the second paragraph of Article 5b.
Within 90 days of the receipt of the assessment report, the Member State concerned shall either recognize the decision of the first Member State and the summary of the product characteristics as approved by it or, if it considers that there are grounds for supposing that the authorization of the veterinary medicinal product concerned may present a risk to human or animal health or the environment (9), it shall apply the procedures set out in Articles 18 to 22 of this Directive. " [4]

ARTICLE 9

IN ORDER TO EXAMINE THE APPLICATION SUBMITTED PURSUANT TO ARTICLE 4, THE COMPETENT AUTHORITIES OF THE MEMBER STATES:

1. SHALL CHECK THAT THE DOCUMENTATION SUBMITTED IN SUPPORT OF THE APPLICATION COMPLIES WITH ARTICLE 5 AND, ON THE BASIS OF THE REPORTS DRAWN UP BY THE EXPERTS PURSUANT TO ARTICLE 7, ASCERTAIN WHETHER THE CONDITIONS FOR THE ISSUE OF THE MARKETING AUTHORIZATION HAVE BEEN FULFILLED;

2. " may submit the medicinal product, its active principles and if necessary intermediate products or other constituent materials for testing by a State laboratory or by a laboratory designated for that purpose, in order to ensure that the testing methods employed by the manufacturer and described in the application documents, in accordance with point 9 of the second paragraph of Article 5, are satisfactory. " [1]

3. MAY, WHERE APPROPRIATE, REQUIRE THE APPLICANT TO PROVIDE FURTHER INFORMATION AS REGARDS THE ITEMS LISTED IN ARTICLE 5. WHERE THE COMPETENT AUTHORITIES TAKE THIS COURSE OF ACTION, THE TIME LIMITS SPECIFIED IN ARTICLE 8 SHALL BE SUSPENDED UNTIL THE FURTHER DATA REQUIRED HAVE BEEN PROVIDED. SIMILARLY, THESE TIME LIMITS SHALL BE SUSPENDED FOR ANY PERIOD WHICH THE APPLICANT MAY BE GIVEN TO PROVIDE ORAL OR WRITTEN EXPLANATIONS.

" 4. may require the applicant to submit substances in the quantities necessary to verify the analytical detection method proposed by the applicant in accordance with point 8 of the second paragraph of Article 5 and to put it into effect as part of routine checks to reveal the presence of residues of the veterinary medicinal products concerned ". [1]

ARTICLE 10

MEMBER STATES SHALL TAKE ALL APPROPRIATE MEASURES TO ENSURE THAT:

1. THE COMPETENT AUTHORITIES ASCERTAIN THAT THE MANUFACTURERS AND IMPORTERS OF VETERINARY MEDICINAL PRODUCTS FROM THIRD COUNTRIES ARE ABLE TO MANUFACTURE THEM IN COMPLIANCE WITH THE DETAILS SUPPLIED PURSUANT TO POINT 4 OF THE SECOND PARAGRAPH OF ARTICLE 5 AND/OR TO CARRY OUT CONTROL TESTS IN ACCORDANCE WITH THE METHODS DESCRIBED IN THE APPLICATION DOCUMENTS UNDER POINT 9 OF THE SECOND PARAGRAPH OF ARTICLE 5;

2. THE COMPETENT AUTHORITIES MAY AUTHORIZE MANUFACTURERS AND IMPORTERS OF VETERINARY MEDICINAL PRODUCTS FROM THIRD COUNTRIES, WHERE CIRCUMSTANCES SO JUSTIFY, TO HAVE CERTAIN STAGES OF MANUFACTURE AND/OR CERTAIN OF THE CONTROL TESTS REFERRED TO IN PARAGRAPH 1 CARRIED OUT BY THIRD PARTIES; IN SUCH CASES CHECKS BY THE COMPETENT AUTHORITIES SHALL ALSO BE CARRIED OUT IN THE ESTABLISHMENTS CONCERNED.

ARTICLE 11

THE AUTHORIZATION PROVIDED FOR IN ARTICLE 4 SHALL BE WITHHELD IF EXAMINATION OF THE DOCUMENTS AND PARTICULARS LISTED IN ARTICLE 5 ESTABLISHES THAT:

1. THE VETERINARY MEDICAL PRODUCT IS HARMFUL UNDER THE CONDITIONS OF USE STATED AT THE TIME OF APPLICATION FOR AUTHORIZATION, HAS NO THERAPEUTIC EFFECT OR THE APPLICANT HAS NOT PROVIDED SUFFICIENT PROOF OF SUCH EFFECT AS REGARDS THE SPECIES OF ANIMAL WHICH IS TO BE TREATED, OR ITS QUALITATIVE OR QUANTITATIVE COMPOSITION IS NOT AS STATED;

2. THE WITHDRAWAL PERIOD RECOMMENDED BY THE APPLICANT IS NOT LONG ENOUGH TO ENSURE THAT FOODSTUFFS OBTAINED FROM THE TREATED ANIMAL DO NOT CONTAIN RESIDUES WHICH MIGHT CONSTITUTE A HEALTH HAZARD TO THE CONSUMER, OR IS INSUFFICIENTLY SUBSTANTIATED;

3. THE VETERINARY MEDICINAL PRODUCT IS OFFERED FOR SALE FOR A USE PROHIBITED UNDER OTHER COMMUNITY PROVISIONS. HOWEVER, PENDING COMMUNITY RULES, THE COMPETENT AUTHORITIES MAY REFUSE TO GRANT AUTHORIZATION FOR A VETERINARY MEDICINAL PRODUCT WHERE SUCH ACTION IS NECESSARY FOR THE PROTECTION OF PUBLIC HEALTH, CONSUMER OR ANIMAL HEALTH.

AUTHORIZATION SHALL ALSO BE WITHHELD IF THE APPLICATION DOCUMENTS SUBMITTED TO THE COMPETENT AUTHORITIES DO NOT COMPLY WITH ARTICLES 5, 6 AND 7.

ARTICLE 12

THE AUTHORIZATION PROVIDED FOR IN ARTICLE 4 MAY REQUIRE THE PERSON RESPONSIBLE FOR MARKETING TO INDICATE ON THE CONTAINER AND/OR THE OUTER WRAPPING AND THE PACKAGE INSERT, WHERE THE LATTER IS REQUIRED, OTHER PARTICULARS ESSENTIAL FOR SAFETY OR HEALTH PROTECTION, INCLUDING ANY SPECIAL PRECAUTIONS RELATING TO USE AND ANY OTHER WARNINGS RESULTING FROM THE CLINICAL AND PHARMACOLOGICAL TRIALS PRESCRIBED IN POINT 10 OF ARTICLE 5 OR FROM EXPERIENCE GAINED DURING THE USE OF THE VETERINARY MEDICINAL PRODUCT ONCE IT HAS BEEN MARKETED.
THE AUTHORIZATION MAY ALSO REQUIRE THE INCLUSION OF A TRACER SUBSTANCE IN THE VETERINARY MEDICINAL PRODUCT.

ARTICLE 13

THE GRANTING OF AUTHORIZATION SHALL NOT DIMINISH THE GENERAL LEGAL LIABILITY OF THE MANUFACTURER AND, WHERE APPROPRIATE, OF THE PERSON RESPONSIBLE FOR MARKETING.

ARTICLE 14

" 1. " After an authorization has been issued, the person responsible for placing the veterinary medicinal product on the market must, in respect of the methods of preparation and control provided for in points 4 and 9 of the second subparagraph of Article 5, take account of technical and scientific progress and introduce any changes that may be required to enable that veterinary medicinal product to be manufactured and checked by means of generally accepted scientific methods. These changes shall be subject to the approval of the competent authority of the Member State concerned. " [4]
Upon request from the competent authorities, the person responsible for placing the product on the market shall also review the analytical detection methods provided for in point 8 of the second paragraph of Article 5 and propose any changes which may be necessary to take account of scientific and technical progress.

2. The person responsible for placing the product on the market shall forthwith inform the competent authorities of any new information which might entail the amendment of the particulars and documents referred to in Article 5 or the approved summary of the product characteristics referred to in Article 5b. In particular, he shall forthwith inform the competent authorities of any prohibition or restriction imposed by the competent authorities of any country in which the veterinary medicinal product is marketed and of any serious unexpected reaction occurring in the animals concerned or human beings.

3. The person responsible for placing the product on the market shall be required to maintain records of all undesirable effects observed in animals or human beings. The records so established shall be kept for at least five years and shall be made available to the competent authorities upon request.

4. The person responsible for placing the product on the market shall immediately inform the competent authorities, with a view to authorization, of any alteration he proposes to make to the particulars and documents referred to in Article 5. " [1]

ARTICLE 15

" 1. Authorization shall be valid for five years and shall be renewable for five-year periods, on application by the holder at least three months before the expiry date and after consideration of a dossier updating the information previously submitted.

2. In exceptional circumstances, and following consultation with the applicant, an authorization may be granted subject to certain specific obligations, and subject to annual review, including:

- the carrying out of further studies following the granting of authorization,
- the notification of adverse reactions to the veterinary medicinal product.

These exceptional decisions may only be adopted for objective and verifiable reasons. " [4]

" CHAPTER IV

Committee for Veterinary Medicinal Products

Article 16

1. In order to facilitate the adoption of common decisions by Member States on the authorization of veterinary medicinal products on the basis of the scientific criteria of quality, safety and efficacy, and to achieve thereby the free movement of veterinary medicinal products within the Community, a Committee for Veterinary Medicinal Products, hereinafter referred to as "the Committee", is hereby set up. The Commission shall be part of the European Agency for the Evaluation of Medicinal Products established by Regulation (EEC) No 2309/93, hereinafter referred to as "the Agency".

2. In addition to the other responsibilities conferred upon it by Community law, the Committee shall examine any question relating to the granting, variation, suspension or withdrawal of authorization for a veterinary medicinal product which is submitted to it in accordance with the provisions of this Directive.

3. The Committee shall adopt own rules of procedure.

Article 17

1. In order to obtain the recognition according to the procedure laid down in this Chapter in one or more of the Member States of an authorization issued by a Member State in accordance with Article 4, the holder of the authorization shall submit an application to the competent authorities of the Member State or Member States concerned, together with the information and particulars referred to in Articles 5, 5a and 5b. He shall testify that the dossier is identical to that accepted by the first Member State, or shall identify any additions or amendments it may contain. In the latter case, he shall certify that the summary of the product characteristics proposed by him in accordance with Article 5a is identical to that accepted by the first Member State in accordance with Article 5b. Moreover, he shall certify that all the dossiers filed as part of this procedure are identical.

2. The holder of the marketing authorization shall notify the Committee of this application, inform it of the Member States concerned and of the dates of submission of the application and send it a copy of the authorization granted by the first Member State. He shall also send the Committee copies of any such

authorization which may have been granted by the other Member States in respect of the veterinary medicinal product concerned, and shall indicate whether any application for authorization is currently under consideration in any Member State.

3. Except in cases referred to in Article 8a, before submitting the application, the holder of the authorization shall inform the Member State which granted the authorization on which the application is based that an application is to be made in accordance with this Directive and shall notify it of any additions to the original dossier; that Member State may require the applicant to provide it with all the particulars and documents necessary to enable it to check that the dossiers filed are identical.

In addition the holder of the authorization shall request the Member State which granted the initial authorization to prepare an assessment report in respect of the veterinary medicinal product concerned, or, if necessary, to update any existing assessment report. That Member State shall prepare the assessment report, or update it, within 90 days of the receipt of the request.

At the same time as the application is submitted in accordance with paragraph 1 the Member State which granted the initial authorization shall forward the assessment report to the Member State or Member States concerned by the application.

4. Save in the exceptional case provided for in Article 18 (1), each Member State shall recognize the marketing authorization granted by the first Member State within 90 days of receipt of the application and the assessment report. It shall inform the Member State which granted the initial authorization, the other Member States concerned by the application, the Committee, and the person responsible for placing the veterinary medicinal product on the market.

Article 18

1. Notwithstanding Article 17 (4), where a Member State considers that there are grounds for supposing that the authorization of the veterinary medicinal product concerned may present a risk to human or animal health or the environment (9), it shall forthwith inform the applicant, the Member State which granted the initial authorization, any other Member States concerned by the application and the Committee. The Member State shall state its reason in detail and shall indicate what action may be necessary to correct any defect in the application.

2. All the Member States concerned shall use their best endeavours to reach agreement on the action to be taken in respect of the application. They shall provide the applicant with the opportunity to make his point of view known orally or in writing. However, if the Member States have not reached agreement within the time limit referred to in Article 17 (4) they shall forthwith refer the matter to the Committee for the application of the procedure laid down in Article 21.

3. Within the time limit referred to in paragraph 2, the Member States concerned shall provide the Committee with a detailed statement of the matters on which they have been unable to reach agreement and the reasons for their disagreement. The applicant shall be provided with a copy of this information.

4. As soon as he is informed that the matter has been referred to the Committee, the applicant shall forthwith forward to the Committee a copy of the information and particulars referred to in Article 17 (1).

Article 19

If several applications submitted in accordance with Articles 5 and 5a have been made for marketing authorization for a particular veterinary medicinal product and Member States have adopted divergent decisions concerning the authorization of that veterinary medicinal product, or its suspension or withdrawal from the market, a Member State, or the Commission, or the person responsible for placing the aforementioned product on the market may refer the matter to the Committee for application of the procedure laid down in Article 21.

The Member State concerned, the person responsible for placing the veterinary medicinal product on the market or the Commission shall clearly identify the question which is referred to the Committee for consideration and, if appropriate, shall inform the aforementioned person thereof.

The Member States and the person responsible for placing the veterinary medicinal product on the market shall forward to the Committee all available information relating to the matter in question.

Article 20

The Member States or the Commission or the applicant or holder of the marketing authorization may, in specific cases where the interests of the Community are involved, refer the matter to the Committee for the application of the procedure laid down in Article 21 before reaching a decision on a request for a marketing authorization or on the suspension or withdrawal of an authorization, or on any other variations to the terms of a marketing authorization which appears necessary, in particular to take account of the information collected in accordance with Chapter VIa.

The Member State concerned or the Commission shall clearly identify the question which is referred to the Committee for consideration and shall inform the person responsible for placing the veterinary medicinal product on the market.

The Member States and the aforementioned person shall forward to the Committee all available information relating to the matter in question.

Article 21

1. When reference is made to the procedure described in this Article, the Committee shall consider the matter concerned and issue a reasoned opinion within 90 days of the date on which the matter was referred to it.

However, in cases submitted to the Committee in accordance with Articles 19 and 20, this period may be extended by 90 days.

In case of urgency, on a proposal from its Chairman, the Committee may agree to impose a shorter deadline.

2. In order to consider the matter, the Committee may appoint one of its Members to act as rapporteur. The Committee may also appoint individual experts to advise it on specific questions. When appointing experts, the Committee shall define their tasks and specify the time limit for the completion of these tasks.

3. In the cases referred to in Articles 18 and 19, before issuing its opinion, the Committee shall provide the person responsible for placing the veterinary medicinal product on the market with an opportunity to present written or oral explanations.

In the case referred to in Article 20, the person responsible for placing the veterinary medicinal product on the market may be asked to explain himself orally or in writing.

If it considers it appropriate, the Committee may invite any other person to provide information relating to the matter before it.

The Committee may suspend the time limit referred to in paragraph 1 in order to allow the person responsible for placing the veterinary medicinal product on the market to prepare explanations.

4. Where the opinion of the Committee is that:

- the application does not satisfy the criteria for authorization, or
- the summary of the product characteristics proposed by the applicant in accordance with Article 5a should be amended, or
- the authorization should be granted subject to conditions, with regard to conditions considered essential for the safe and effective use of the veterinary medicinal product including pharmacovigilance, or
- a marketing authorization should be suspended, varied or withdrawn,

the Agency shall forthwith inform the person responsible for placing the veterinary medicinal product on the market. Within 15 days of the receipt of the opinion, the aforementioned person may notify the Agency in writing of his intention to appeal. In that case, he shall forward the detailed grounds for appeal to the Agency within 60 days of receipt of the opinion. Within 60 days of receipt of the grounds for appeal, the Committee shall consider whether its opinion should be revised, and the conclusions reached on the appeal shall be annexed to the assessment report referred to in paragraph 5.

5. Within 30 days of its adoption, the Agency shall forward the final opinion of the Committee to the Member States, the Commission and the person responsible for placing the veterinary medicinal product on the market

together with a report describing the assessment of the veterinary medicinal product and the reasons for its conclusions.

In the event of an opinion in favour of granting or maintaining an authorization to place the veterinary medicinal product concerned on the market, the following documents shall be annexed to the opinion:

(a) a draft summary of the product characteristics, as referred to in Article 5a; where necessary this will reflect differences in the veterinary conditions pertaining in the Member States.

(b) any conditions affecting the authorization within the meaning of paragraph 4.

Article 22

1. Within 30 days of the receipt of the opinion, the Commission shall prepare a draft of the decision to be taken in respect of the application, taking into account Community law.

In the event of a draft decision which envisages the granting of marketing authorization, the documents referred to in Article 21 (5)(a) and (b) shall be annexed.

Where, exceptionally, the draft decision is not in accordance with the opinion of the Agency, the Commission shall also annex a detailed explanation of the reasons for the differences.

The draft decision shall be forwarded to the Member States and the applicant.

2. A final decision on the application shall be adopted in accordance with the procedure laid down in Article 42k.

3. The rules of procedure of the Committee referred to in Article 42k shall be adjusted to take account of the tasks incumbent upon it in accordance with this Directive.

These adjustments shall involve the following:

- except in cases referred to in the third subparagraph of paragraph 1, the opinion of the Standing Committee shall be obtained in writing,
- each Member State is allowed at least 28 days to forward written observations on the draft decision to the Commission,
- each Member State is able to require in writing that the draft decision be discussed by the Standing Committee, giving its reasons in detail.

Where, in the opinion of the Commission, the written observations of a Member State raise important new questions of a scientific or technical nature which have not been addressed in the opinion of the Agency, the Chairman shall suspend the procedure and refer the application back to the Agency for further consideration.

The provisions necessary for the implementation of this paragraph shall be adopted by the Commission in accordance with the procedure laid down in Article 42j.

4. A decision adopted in accordance with this Article shall be addressed to the Member States concerned by the matter and to the person responsible for placing the veterinary medicinal product on the market. The Member States shall either grant or withdraw marketing authorization, or vary the terms of a marketing authorization as necessary to comply with the decision within 30 days of its notification. They shall inform the Commission and the Committee thereof.

5. The procedure referred to in Articles 16 to 22 shall not apply in the cases provided for in Article 9 (2) of Council Directive 92/74/EEC of 22 September 1992 widening the scope of Directive 81/851/EEC on the approximation of the laws of the Member States on veterinary medicinal products and laying down additional provisions on homeopathic veterinary medicinal products.

Article 23

Any application by the person responsible for placing the veterinary medicinal product on the market to vary a marketing authorization which has been granted in accordance with the provisions of this Chapter shall be submitted to all the Member States which have previously authorized the veterinary medicinal product concerned.

The Commission shall, in consultation with the Agency, adopt appropriate arrangements for the examination of variations to the terms of a marketing authorization.

These arrangements shall include a notification system or administration procedures concerning minor variations and define precisely the concept of "a minor variation".

These arrangements shall be adopted by the Commission in the form of an implementing Regulation in accordance with the procedure laid down in Article 42j.

The procedure laid down in Articles 21 and 22 shall apply by analogy to variations made to marketing authorizations for products subject to the Commission's arbitration.

Article 23a

1. Where a Member State considers that the variation of the terms of a marketing authorization which has been granted in accordance with the provisions of this Chapter or its suspension or withdrawal is necessary for the protection of human or animal health or the environment, the Member State concerned shall forthwith refer the matter to the Committee for the application of the procedures laid down in Articles 21 and 22.

2. Without prejudice to the provisions of Article 20, in exceptional cases, where urgent action is essential to protect human or animal health or the environment, until a definitive decision is adopted, a Member State may suspend the marketing and the use of the veterinary medicinal product concerned on its territory. It shall inform the Commission and the other Member States no later than the following working day of the reasons for its action.

Article 23b

Articles 23 and 23a shall apply by analogy to veterinary medicinal products authorized by Member States following an opinion of the Committee given in accordance with Article 4 of Directive 87/22/EEC before 1 January 1995.

Article 23c

1. The Agency shall publish an annual report on the operation of the procedures laid down in this Chapter and shall forward that report to the European Parliament and the Council for information.

2. By 1 January 2001, the Commission shall publish a detailed review of the operation of the procedures laid down in this Chapter and shall propose any amendments which may be necessary to improve these procedures. The Council shall decide, under the conditions provided for in the Treaty, on the Commission proposal within one year of its submission. " [4]

CHAPTER V

MANUFACTURE OF VETERINARY MEDICINAL PRODUCTS - IMPORTS FROM THIRD COUNTRIES

ARTICLE 24

" 1. Member States shall take all appropriate measures to ensure that the manufacture of veterinary medicinal products is subject to the holding of an authorization. This manufacturing authorization shall likewise be required for veterinary medicinal products intended for export. " [1]

2. THE AUTHORIZATION REFERRED TO IN PARAGRAPH 1 SHALL BE REQUIRED BOTH FOR TOTAL AND PARTIAL MANUFACTURE AND FOR THE VARIOUS PROCESSES OF DIVIDING UP, PACKAGING OR PRESENTATION.
HOWEVER, SUCH AUTHORIZATION SHALL NOT BE REQUIRED FOR PREPARATION, DIVIDING UP, CHANGES IN PACKAGING OR PRESENTATION WHERE THESE PROCESSES ARE CARRIED OUT SOLELY FOR RETAIL SUPPLY BY PHARMACISTS IN DISPENSING PHARMACIES OR BY PERSONS LEGALLY AUTHORIZED IN THE MEMBER STATES TO CARRY OUT SUCH PROCESSES.

3. THE AUTHORIZATION REFERRED TO IN PARAGRAPH 1 SHALL ALSO BE REQUIRED FOR IMPORTS FROM THIRD COUNTRIES INTO A MEMBER STATE; THIS CHAPTER AND ARTICLE 36 SHALL APPLY TO SUCH IMPORTS IN THE SAME WAY AS TO MANUFACTURE. " Member States shall take all appropriate measures to ensure that veterinary medicinal products brought into their territory from a third country and destined for another Member State are accompanied by a copy of the authorization referred to in paragraph 1. " [1]

" Article 24a

At the request of the manufacturer of veterinary medicinal products, the exporter thereof or the authorities of an importing third country, Member States shall certify that such manufacturer is in possession of the authorization referred to in Article 24. When issuing such certificates, Member States shall comply with the following conditions:

1. Member States shall have regard to the prevailing administrative arrangements of the World Health Organization;

2. for veterinary medicinal products intended for export which are already authorized in their territory, they shall supply the summary of the product characteristics as approved in accordance with Article 5b or, in the absence thereof, an equivalent document.

Where the manufacturer is not in possession of an authorization to place the product on the market, he shall provide the authorities responsible for establishing the certificate referred to in the first paragraph with a declaration explaining why such authorization is not available. " [1]

ARTICLE 25

IN ORDER TO OBTAIN THE AUTHORIZATION REFERRED TO IN ARTICLE 24, THE APPLICANT SHALL MEET AT LEAST THE FOLLOWING REQUIREMENTS:

(a) HE SHALL SPECIFY THE VETERINARY MEDICINAL PRODUCTS AND PHARMACEUTICAL FORMS WHICH ARE TO BE MANUFACTURED OR IMPORTED AND ALSO THE PLACE WHERE THEY ARE TO BE MANUFACTURED AND/OR CONTROLLED;

(b) HE SHALL HAVE AT HIS DISPOSAL, FOR THE MANUFACTURE OR IMPORT OF THE ABOVE, SUITABLE AND SUFFICIENT PREMISES, TECHNICAL EQUIPMENT AND CONTROL FACILITIES COMPLYING WITH THE LEGAL REQUIREMENTS WHICH THE MEMBER STATE CONCERNED LAYS DOWN AS REGARDS BOTH MANUFACTURE AND CONTROL AND THE STORAGE OF PRODUCTS, IN ACCORDANCE WITH ARTICLE 10 (1);

(c) HE SHALL HAVE AT HIS DISPOSAL THE SERVICES OF AT LEAST ONE QUALIFIED PERSON WITHIN THE MEANING OF ARTICLE 29.

THE APPLICANT SHALL PROVIDE PARTICULARS IN HIS APPLICATION TO ESTABLISH HIS COMPLIANCE WITH THE ABOVE REQUIREMENTS.

ARTICLE 26

1. THE COMPETENT AUTHORITY OF THE MEMBER STATE SHALL NOT ISSUE THE AUTHORIZATION REFERRED TO IN ARTICLE 24 UNTIL IT HAS ESTABLISHED THE ACCURACY OF THE PARTICULARS SUPPLIED PURSUANT TO ARTICLE 25 BY MEANS OF AN INQUIRY CARRIED OUT BY ITS REPRESENTATIVES.

2. IN ORDER TO ENSURE THAT THE REQUIREMENTS REFERRED TO IN ARTICLE 25 ARE COMPLIED WITH, AUTHORIZATION MAY BE MADE CONDITIONAL ON THE FULFILMENT OF CERTAIN OBLIGATIONS IMPOSED EITHER WHEN AUTHORIZATION IS GRANTED OR AT A LATER DATE.

3. THE AUTHORIZATION SHALL APPLY ONLY TO THE PREMISES SPECIFIED IN THE APPLICATION AND TO THE VETERINARY MEDICINAL PRODUCTS AND PHARMACEUTICAL FORMS SPECIFIED IN THAT APPLICATION.

ARTICLE 27

THE HOLDER OF AN AUTHORIZATION REFERRED TO IN ARTICLE 24 SHALL AT LEAST BE OBLIGED TO:

(a) HAVE AT HIS DISPOSAL THE SERVICES OF STAFF COMPLYING WITH THE LEGAL REQUIREMENTS EXISTING IN THE MEMBER STATE CONCERNED AS REGARDS BOTH MANUFACTURE AND CONTROLS;

(b) DISPOSE OF THE AUTHORIZED VETERINARY MEDICINAL PRODUCTS ONLY IN ACCORDANCE WITH THE LEGISLATION OF THE MEMBER STATES CONCERNED;

(c) GIVE PRIOR NOTICE TO THE COMPETENT AUTHORITY OF ANY CHANGES WHICH HE MAY WISH TO MAKE TO ANY OF THE PARTICULARS SUPPLIED PURSUANT TO ARTICLE 25; THE COMPETENT AUTHORITY SHALL, IN ANY EVENT, BE IMMEDIATELY INFORMED IF THE QUALIFIED PERSON REFERRED TO IN ARTICLE 29 IS REPLACED UNEXPECTEDLY;

(d) ALLOW THE REPRESENTATIVES OF THE COMPETENT AUTHORITY OF THE MEMBER STATE CONCERNED ACCESS TO HIS PREMISES AT ANY TIME;

(e) ENABLE THE QUALIFIED PERSON REFERRED TO IN ARTICLE 29 TO CARRY OUT HIS DUTIES, PARTICULARLY BY PLACING AT HIS DISPOSAL ALL THE NECESSARY FACILITIES.

" (f) comply with the principles and the guidelines of good manufacturing practice for medicinal products laid down by Community law;

(g) keep detailed records of all veterinary medicinal products supplied by him, including samples, in accordance with the laws of the countries of destination. The following information at least shall be recorded in respect of each transaction, whether or not it is made for payment:

- date,
- name of the veterinary medicinal product,
- quantity supplied,
- name and address of the recipient,
- batch number.

These records shall be available for inspection by the competent authorities for a period of at least three years. "
[1]

" Article 27a

The principles and guidelines of good manufacturing practice for veterinary medicinal products referred to in Article 27 (f) shall be adopted in the form of a Directive addressed to the Member States in accordance with the procedure laid down in " Article 42j " [4], taking account of the specific nature of the veterinary medicinal product. Detailed guidelines shall be published by the Commission and revised as appropriate to take account of scientific and technical progress. " [1]

ARTICLE 28

1. THE MEMBER STATES SHALL TAKE ALL APPROPRIATE MEASURES TO ENSURE THAT THE TIME TAKEN FOR THE PROCEDURE FOR GRANTING THE AUTHORIZATION REFERRED TO IN ARTICLE 24 DOES NOT EXCEED 90 DAYS FROM THE DAY ON WHICH THE COMPETENT AUTHORITY RECEIVES THE APPLICATION.

2. IF THE HOLDER OF THE AUTHORIZATION REQUESTS A CHANGE IN ANY OF THE PARTICULARS REFERRED TO IN ARTICLE 25 (a) AND (b), THE TIME TAKEN FOR THE PROCEDURE RELATING TO THIS REQUEST SHALL NOT EXCEED 30 DAYS. IN EXCEPTIONAL CASES, THIS PERIOD OF TIME MAY BE EXTENDED TO 90 DAYS.

3. MEMBER STATES MAY REQUIRE FROM THE APPLICANT FURTHER INFORMATION CONCERNING BOTH THE PARTICULARS SUPPLIED PURSUANT TO ARTICLE 25 AND THE QUALIFIED PERSON REFERRED TO IN ARTICLE 29; WHERE THE COMPETENT AUTHORITY CONCERNED EXERCISES THIS RIGHT, APPLICATION OF THE TIME LIMITS REFERRED TO IN PARAGRAPHS 1 AND 2 SHALL BE SUSPENDED UNTIL THE ADDITIONAL DATA REQUIRED HAVE BEEN SUPPLIED.

ARTICLE 29

1. MEMBER STATES SHALL TAKE ALL APPROPRIATE MEASURES TO ENSURE THAT THE HOLDER OF THE AUTHORIZATION REFERRED TO IN ARTICLE 24 HAS PERMANENTLY AND CONTINUOUSLY AT HIS DISPOSAL THE SERVICES OF AT LEAST ONE QUALIFIED PERSON WHO FULFILS THE CONDITIONS LAID DOWN IN ARTICLE 31 AND IS RESPONSIBLE, IN PARTICULAR, FOR CARRYING OUT THE DUTIES SPECIFIED IN ARTICLE 30.

2. IF HE PERSONALLY FULFILS THE CONDITIONS LAID DOWN IN ARTICLE 31, THE HOLDER OF THE AUTHORIZATION MAY HIMSELF ASSUME THE RESPONSIBILITY REFERRED TO IN PARAGRAPH 1.

ARTICLE 30

1. MEMBER STATES SHALL TAKE ALL APPROPRIATE MEASURES TO ENSURE THAT THE QUALIFIED PERSON REFERRED TO IN ARTICLE 29 IS, WITHOUT PREJUDICE TO HIS RELATIONSHIP WITH THE HOLDER OF THE AUTHORIZATION REFERRED TO IN ARTICLE 24, RESPONSIBLE, IN THE CONTEXT OF THE PROCEDURES REFERRED TO IN ARTICLE 33, FOR ENSURING THAT:

(a) IN THE CASE OF VETERINARY MEDICINAL PRODUCTS MANUFACTURED WITHIN THE MEMBER STATE CONCERNED, EACH BATCH OF VETERINARY MEDICINAL PRODUCTS HAS BEEN MANUFACTURED AND CHECKED IN COMPLIANCE WITH THE LAWS IN FORCE IN THAT MEMBER STATE AND IN ACCORDANCE WITH THE REQUIREMENTS OF THE MARKETING AUTHORIZATION;

(b) IN THE CASE OF VETERINARY MEDICINAL PRODUCTS COMING FROM THIRD COUNTRIES, EACH PRODUCTION BATCH IMPORTED HAS UNDERGONE IN THE IMPORTING COUNTRY A FULL QUALITATIVE ANALYSIS, A QUANTITATIVE ANALYSIS OF AT LEAST ALL THE ACTIVE INGREDIENTS AND ALL THE OTHER TESTS OR CHECKS NECESSARY TO ENSURE THE QUALITY OF VETERINARY MEDICINAL PRODUCTS IN ACCORDANCE WITH THE REQUIREMENTS OF THE MARKETING AUTHORIZATION.

BATCHES OF VETERINARY MEDICINAL PRODUCTS WHICH HAVE UNDERGONE SUCH CONTROLS IN A MEMBER STATE SHALL BE EXEMPT FROM THE ABOVE CONTROLS IF THEY ARE IMPORTED INTO ANOTHER MEMBER STATE, ACCOMPANIED BY THE CONTROL REPORTS SIGNED BY THE QUALIFIED PERSON.

" In the case of veterinary medicinal products imported from a third country, where appropriate arrangements have been made by the Community with the exporting country to ensure that the manufacturer of the veterinary medicinal product applies standards of good manufacturing practice at least equivalent to those laid down by the Community and to ensure that the controls referred to under (b) have been carried out in the exporting country, the qualified person may be relieved of responsibility for carrying out those controls. " [4]

2. IN ALL CASES, AND PARTICULARLY WHERE THE VETERINARY MEDICINAL PRODUCTS ARE RELEASED FOR SALE, THE QUALIFIED PERSON SHALL CERTIFY, IN A REGISTER OR EQUIVALENT DOCUMENT PROVIDED FOR THE PURPOSE, THAT EACH PRODUCTION BATCH SATISFIES THE PROVISIONS OF THIS ARTICLE; THE SAID REGISTER OR EQUIVALENT DOCUMENT SHALL BE KEPT UP TO DATE AS OPERATIONS ARE CARRIED OUT AND SHALL REMAIN AT THE DISPOSAL OF THE REPRESENTATIVES OF THE COMPETENT AUTHORITY FOR THE PERIOD SPECIFIED IN THE PROVISIONS OF THE MEMBER STATE CONCERNED AND, IN ANY EVENT, FOR AT LEAST FIVE YEARS.

ARTICLE 31

MEMBER STATES SHALL ENSURE THAT THE QUALIFIED PERSON REFERRED TO IN ARTICLE 29 FULFILS THE FOLLOWING MINIMUM CONDITIONS OF QUALIFICATION.

(a) POSSESSION OF A DIPLOMA, CERTIFICATE OR OTHER EVIDENCE OF FORMAL QUALIFICATIONS AWARDED ON COMPLETION OF A UNIVERSITY COURSE OF STUDY, OR A COURSE RECOGNIZED AS EQUIVALENT BY THE MEMBER STATE CONCERNED, EXTENDING OVER A PERIOD OF AT LEAST FOUR YEARS OF THEORETICAL AND PRACTICAL STUDY IN ONE OF THE FOLLOWING SCIENTIFIC DISCIPLINES: PHARMACY, MEDICINE, VETERINARY SCIENCE, CHEMISTRY, PHARMACEUTICAL CHEMISTRY AND TECHNOLOGY, BIOLOGY. HOWEVER:

- THE MINIMUM DURATION OF THE UNIVERSITY COURSE MAY BE THREE AND A HALF YEARS WHERE THE COURSE IS FOLLOWED BY A PERIOD OF THEORETICAL AND PRACTICAL TRAINING OF AT LEAST ONE YEAR AND INCLUDES A TRAINING PERIOD OF AT LEAST SIX MONTHS IN A PHARMACY OPEN TO THE PUBLIC, CORROBORATED BY AN EXAMINATION AT UNIVERSITY LEVEL,
- WHERE TWO UNIVERSITY OR RECOGNIZED EQUIVALENT COURSES CO-EXIST IN A MEMBER STATE AND WHERE ONE OF THESE EXTENDS OVER FOUR YEARS AND THE OTHER OVER THREE YEARS, THE DIPLOMA, CERTIFICATE OR OTHER EVIDENCE OF FORMAL QUALIFICATIONS AWARDED ON COMPLETION OF THE THREE-YEAR UNIVERSITY COURSE OR ITS RECOGNIZED EQUIVALENT SHALL BE CONSIDERED TO FULFIL THE CONDITION OF DURATION REFERRED TO IN (a) IN SO FAR AS THE DIPLOMAS, CERTIFICATES OR OTHER EVIDENCE OF FORMAL QUALIFICATIONS AWARDED ON COMPLETION OF BOTH COURSES ARE RECOGNIZED AS EQUIVALENT BY THE STATE IN QUESTION.

THE COURSE SHALL INCLUDE THEORETICAL AND PRACTICAL TUITION BEARING UPON AT LEAST THE FOLLOWING BASIC SUBJECTS:

- EXPERIMENTAL PHYSICS,
- GENERAL AND INORGANIC CHEMISTRY,
- ORGANIC CHEMISTRY,
- ANALYTICAL CHEMISTRY,
- PHARMACEUTICAL CHEMISTRY, INCLUDING ANALYSIS OF MEDICINAL PRODUCTS,
- GENERAL AND APPLIED BIOCHEMISTRY (MEDICAL),
- PHYSIOLOGY,
- MICROBIOLOGY,

- PHARMACOLOGY,
- PHARMACEUTICAL TECHNOLOGY,
- TOXICOLOGY,
- PHARMACOGNOSY (STUDY OF THE COMPOSITION AND EFFECTS OF THE ACTIVE PRINCIPLES OF NATURAL SUBSTANCES OF PLANT AND ANIMAL ORIGIN).

TUITION IN THESE SUBJECTS SHOULD BE SO BALANCED AS TO ENABLE THE PERSON CONCERNED TO FULFIL THE OBLIGATIONS SPECIFIED IN ARTICLE 30.

IN SO FAR AS CERTAIN DIPLOMAS, CERTIFICATES OR OTHER EVIDENCE OF FORMAL QUALIFICATIONS MENTIONED IN (a) DO NOT FULFIL THE CRITERIA LAID DOWN ABOVE, THE COMPETENT AUTHORITY OF THE MEMBER STATE SHALL ENSURE THAT THE PERSON CONCERNED PROVIDES EVIDENCE THAT HE HAS, IN THE SUBJECTS INVOLVED, THE KNOWLEDGE REQUIRED FOR THE MANUFACTURE AND CONTROL OF VETERINARY MEDICINAL PRODUCTS.

(b) PRACTICAL EXPERIENCE FOR AT LEAST TWO YEARS, IN ONE OR MORE UNDERTAKINGS WHICH ARE AUTHORIZED MANUFACTURERS, IN THE ACTIVITIES OF QUALITATIVE ANALYSIS OF MEDICINAL PRODUCTS, OF QUANTITATIVE ANALYSIS OF ACTIVE PRINCIPLES AND OF THE TESTING AND CHECKING NECESSARY TO ENSURE THE QUALITY OF VETERINARY MEDICINAL PRODUCTS.

THE DURATION OF PRACTICAL EXPERIENCE MAY BE REDUCED BY ONE YEAR WHERE A UNIVERSITY COURSE LASTS FOR AT LEAST FIVE YEARS AND BY A YEAR AND A HALF WHERE THE COURSE LASTS FOR AT LEAST SIX YEARS.

ARTICLE 32

1. A PERSON ENGAGING IN THE ACTIVITIES OF THE PERSON REFERRED TO IN ARTICLE 29 IN A MEMBER STATE AT THE TIME WHEN THIS DIRECTIVE IS BROUGHT INTO FORCE IN THAT STATE BUT NOT COMPLYING WITH THE PROVISIONS OF ARTICLE 31 SHALL BE ELIGIBLE TO CONTINUE TO ENGAGE IN THOSE ACTIVITIES IN THE STATE CONCERNED.

2. THE HOLDER OF A DIPLOMA, CERTIFICATE OR OTHER EVIDENCE OF FORMAL QUALIFICATIONS AWARDED ON COMPLETION OF A UNIVERSITY COURSE - OR A COURSE RECOGNIZED AS EQUIVALENT BY THE MEMBER STATE CONCERNED - IN A SCIENTIFIC DISCIPLINE ALLOWING HIM TO ENGAGE IN THE ACTIVITIES OF THE PERSON REFERRED TO IN ARTICLE 29 IN ACCORDANCE WITH THE LAWS OF THAT STATE MAY - IF HE BEGAN HIS COURSE PRIOR TO THE NOTIFICATION OF THIS DIRECTIVE - BE CONSIDERED AS QUALIFIED TO CARRY OUT IN THAT STATE THE DUTIES OF THE PERSON REFERRED TO IN ARTICLE 29, PROVIDED THAT HE HAS PREVIOUSLY ENGAGED IN THE FOLLOWING ACTIVITIES FOR AT LEAST TWO YEARS BEFORE THE END OF THE 10TH YEAR FOLLOWING NOTIFICATION OF THIS DIRECTIVE IN ONE OR MORE UNDERTAKINGS AUTHORIZED PURSUANT TO ARTICLE 24: PRODUCTION SUPERVISION AND/OR QUALITATIVE ANALYSIS, QUANTITATIVE ANALYSIS OF ACTIVE PRINCIPLES, AND THE NECESSARY TESTING AND CHECKING UNDER THE DIRECT AUTHORITY OF A PERSON AS REFERRED TO IN ARTICLE 29 TO ENSURE THE QUALITY OF VETERINARY MEDICINAL PRODUCTS.

IF THE PERSON CONCERNED HAS ACQUIRED THE PRACTICAL EXPERIENCE REFERRED TO IN THE FIRST SUBPARAGRAPH MORE THAN 10 YEARS PRIOR TO THE NOTIFICATION OF THIS DIRECTIVE, A FURTHER ONE YEAR'S PRACTICAL EXPERIENCE IN ACCORDANCE WITH THE CONDITIONS REFERRED TO IN THE FIRST SUBPARAGRAPH SHALL BE COMPLETED BY HIM IMMEDIATELY BEFORE HE ENGAGES IN SUCH ACTIVITIES.

3. A PERSON WHO, AT THE TIME THIS DIRECTIVE IS BROUGHT INTO FORCE, IS ENGAGED IN DIRECT COLLABORATION WITH A PERSON REFERRED TO IN ARTICLE 29 IN PRODUCTION SUPERVISION ACTIVITIES AND/OR IN QUALITATIVE ANALYSIS, QUANTITATIVE ANALYSIS OF ACTIVE PRINCIPLES, AND THE TESTING AND CHECKING NECESSARY TO ENSURE THE QUALITY OF MEDICINAL PRODUCTS MAY, FOR A PERIOD OF FIVE YEARS THEREAFTER, BE CONSIDERED AS QUALIFIED TO TAKE UP IN THAT STATE THE DUTIES OF THE PERSON REFERRED TO IN ARTICLE 29, PROVIDED THAT THE MEMBER STATE ENSURES THAT THE PERSON SHOWS EVIDENCE OF ADEQUATE THEORETICAL AND PRACTICAL KNOWLEDGE AND HAS ENGAGED IN THE ACTIVITIES MENTIONED FOR AT LEAST FIVE YEARS.

ARTICLE 33

MEMBER STATES SHALL ENSURE THAT THE OBLIGATIONS OF QUALIFIED PERSONS REFERRED TO IN ARTICLE 29 ARE FULFILLED, EITHER BY MEANS OF APPROPRIATE ADMINISTRATIVE MEASURES OR BY MAKING SUCH PERSONS SUBJECT TO A PROFESSIONAL CODE OF CONDUCT.
MEMBER STATES MAY PROVIDE FOR THE TEMPORARY SUSPENSION OF SUCH A PERSON UPON THE COMMENCEMENT OF ADMINISTRATIVE OR DISCIPLINARY PROCEEDINGS AGAINST HIM FOR FAILURE TO FULFIL HIS OBLIGATIONS.

CHAPTER VI

SUPERVISION AND SANCTIONS

ARTICLE 34

" The competent authority of the Member State concerned shall ensure by means of repeated inspection that the legal requirements relating to veterinary medicinal products are complied with. " [1]
SUCH INSPECTIONS SHALL BE CARRIED OUT BY AUTHORIZED REPRESENTATIVES OF THE COMPETENT AUTHORITY WHO SHALL BE EMPOWERED TO:

1. INSPECT MANUFACTURING OR TRADING ESTABLISHMENTS AND ANY LABORATORIES ENTRUSTED BY THE HOLDER OF THE AUTHORIZATION REFERRED TO IN ARTICLE 24 (1), WITH THE TASK OF CARRYING OUT CONTROL TESTS PURSUANT TO ARTICLE 10 POINT 2;

2. TAKE SAMPLES;

3. EXAMINE ANY DOCUMENTS RELATING TO THE OBJECT OF THE INSPECTION, SUBJECT TO CURRENT PROVISIONS IN THE MEMBER STATES AT THE TIME OF NOTIFICATION OF THIS DIRECTIVE WHICH PLACE RESTRICTIONS ON THESE POWERS WITH REGARD TO THE DESCRIPTION OF THE METHOD OF PREPARATION.
" The officials representing the competent authority shall report after each of the inspections mentioned in the first paragraph on whether the manufacturer complies with the principles and guidelines of good manufacturing practice referred to in Article 27a. The inspected manufacturer shall be informed of the content of such reports. " [1]

ARTICLE 35

MEMBER STATES SHALL TAKE ALL APPROPRIATE MEASURES TO ENSURE THAT THE PERSON RESPONSIBLE FOR MARKETING AND, WHERE APPROPRIATE, THE HOLDER OF THE AUTHORIZATION REFERRED TO IN ARTICLE 24 (1) FURNISH PROOF OF THE CONTROL TESTS CARRIED OUT ON THE FINISHED PRODUCT AND/OR ON THE CONSTITUENTS AND INTERMEDIATE PRODUCTS OF THE MANUFACTURING PROCESS, IN ACCORDANCE WITH THE METHODS LAID DOWN FOR THE PURPOSES OF MARKETING AUTHORIZATION.

ARTICLE 36

THE COMPETENT AUTHORITIES OF THE MEMBER STATES SHALL SUSPEND OR WITHDRAW MARKETING AUTHORIZATION WHEN IT IS CLEAR THAT:

1. THE VETERINARY MEDICINAL PRODUCT PROVES TO BE HARMFUL UNDER THE CONDITIONS OF USE STATED AT THE TIME OF APPLICATION FOR AUTHORIZATION OR SUBSEQUENTLY, THE VETERINARY MEDICINAL PRODUCT DOES NOT HAVE ANY THERAPEUTIC EFFECT OR ITS QUALITATIVE AND QUANTITATIVE COMPOSITION IS NOT AS STATED;

2. THE RECOMMENDED WITHDRAWAL PERIOD IS INADEQUATE TO ENSURE THAT FOODSTUFFS OBTAINED FROM THE TREATED ANIMAL DO NOT CONTAIN RESIDUES WHICH MIGHT CONSTITUTE A HEALTH HAZARD TO THE CONSUMER;

3. THE VETERINARY MEDICINAL PRODUCT IS OFFERED FOR SALE FOR A USE WHICH IS PROHIBITED BY OTHER COMMUNITY PROVISIONS. HOWEVER, PENDING COMMUNITY RULES, THE COMPETENT AUTHORITIES MAY REFUSE TO GRANT AUTHORIZATION FOR A VETERINARY MEDICINAL PRODUCT WHERE SUCH ACTION IS NECESSARY FOR THE PROTECTION OF PUBLIC, CONSUMER OR ANIMAL HEALTH;

4. THE INFORMATION GIVEN IN THE APPLICATION DOCUMENTS PURSUANT TO ARTICLE 5 AND 14 IS INCORRECT;

5. THE CONTROL TESTS REFERRED TO IN ARTICLE 35 HAVE NOT BEEN CARRIED OUT;

6. THE OBLIGATION REFERRED TO IN THE SECOND PARAGRAPH OF ARTICLE 12 HAS NOT BEEN FULFILLED.

THE VETERINARY MEDICINAL PRODUCT SHALL BE DEEMED TO HAVE NO THERAPEUTIC EFFECT IF IT IS ESTABLISHED THAT IT DOES NOT PRODUCE THERAPEUTIC RESULTS IN THE SPECIES OF ANIMAL FOR WHICH THE TREATMENT IS INTENDED.
AUTHORIZATION MAY ALSO BE SUSPENDED, OR WITHDRAWN WHERE IT IS ESTABLISHED THAT:

- THE PARTICULARS SUPPORTING THE APPLICATION, AS PROVIDED FOR IN ARTICLE 5, HAVE NOT BEEN AMENDED IN ACCORDANCE WITH THE FIRST AND THIRD PARAGRAPHS OF ARTICLE 14,
- ANY NEW INFORMATION AS REFERRED TO IN THE SECOND PARAGRAPH OF ARTICLE 14 HAS NOT BEEN COMMUNICATED TO THE COMPETENT AUTHORITIES.

ARTICLE 37

1. WITHOUT PREJUDICE TO ARTICLE 36, MEMBER STATES SHALL TAKE ALL NECESSARY MEASURES TO ENSURE THAT SUPPLY OF A VETERINARY MEDICINAL PRODUCT IS PROHIBITED AND THAT THE MEDICINAL PRODUCT CONCERNED IS WITHDRAWN FORM THE MARKET WHERE:

(a) IT IS CLEAR THAT THE VETERINARY MEDICINAL PRODUCT IS HARMFUL UNDER THE CONDITIONS OF USE STATED AT THE TIME OF THE APPLICATION FOR AUTHORIZATION OR SUBSEQUENTLY, PURSUANT TO THE THIRD PARAGRAPH OF ARTICLE 14;

(b) THE VETERINARY MEDICINAL PRODUCT HAS NO THERAPEUTIC EFFECT ON THE SPECIES OF ANIMAL FOR WHICH THE TREATMENT WAS INTENDED;

(c) THE QUALITATIVE AND QUANTITATIVE COMPOSITION OF THE VETERINARY MEDICINAL PRODUCT IS NOT AS STATED;

(d) THE RECOMMENDED WITHDRAWAL PERIOD IS INADEQUATE TO ENSURE THAT FOODSTUFFS OBTAINED FROM THE TREATED ANIMAL DO NOT CONTAIN RESIDUES WHICH MIGHT CONSTITUTE A HEALTH HAZARD TO THE CONSUMER;

(e) THE CONTROL TESTS REFERRED TO IN ARTICLE 35 HAVE NOT BEEN CARRIED OUT, OR ANY OTHER REQUIREMENT OR OBLIGATION RELATING TO THE GRANT OF THE AUTHORIZATION REFERRED TO IN ARTICLE 24 (1) HAS NOT BEEN COMPLIED WITH.

2. THE COMPETENT AUTHORITY MAY CONFINE THE PROHIBITION ON SUPPLY AND WITHDRAWAL FROM THE MARKET SOLELY TO THE CONTESTED PRODUCTION BATCHES.

ARTICLE 38

1. THE COMPETENT AUTHORITY OF A MEMBER STATE SHALL SUSPEND OR WITHDRAW THE AUTHORIZATION REFERRED TO IN ARTICLE 24 FOR A CATEGORY OF PREPARATIONS OR FOR ALL PREPARATIONS IF ANY OF THE REQUIREMENTS LAID DOWN FOR OBTAINING THIS AUTHORIZATION IS NO LONGER MET.

2. THE COMPETENT AUTHORITY OF A MEMBER STATE MAY, IN ADDITION TO THE MEASURES PROVIDED FOR IN ARTICLE 37, EITHER SUSPEND MANUFACTURE OR IMPORTS OF VETERINARY MEDICINAL PRODUCTS FROM THIRD COUNTRIES OR SUSPEND OR WITHDRAW THE AUTHORIZATION REFERRED TO IN ARTICLE 24 FOR A CATEGORY OF PREPARATIONS OR FOR ALL PREPARATIONS IN THE EVENT OF NON-COMPLIANCE WITH THE PROVISIONS REGARDING MANUFACTURE OR IMPORTS FROM THIRD COUNTRIES.

" Article 38a

Member States shall take appropriate measures to encourage veterinarians and other professionals concerned to report to the competent authorities any undesirable effect of veterinary medicinal products. " [1]

ARTICLE 39

" Member States shall take all measures necessary to ensure that the competent authorities concerned communicate the appropriate information to each other, in particular regarding compliance with the requirements adopted for authorization as referred to in Article 24 (1), or for authorization to place products on the market, for the purpose of verifying compliance with the provisions of Chapter VIII.
Upon reasoned request, Member States shall forthwith communicate the reports referred to in the third paragraph of Article 34 to the competent authorities of another Member State. If, after considering the reports, the Member State receiving the reports considers that it cannot accept the conclusions reached by the competent authority of the Member State in which the report was established, it shall inform the competent authorities concerned of its reasons and may request further information. The Member States concerned shall attempt to reach agreement. If necessary, in the event of serious differences of opinion, one of the Member States concerned shall inform the Commission. " [1]

ARTICLE 40

ALL DECISIONS TAKEN PURSUANT TO ARTICLES 11, 36, 37 AND 38, ALL NEGATIVE DECISIONS TAKEN PURSUANT TO ARTICLE 10 POINT 2 AND ARTICLE 19 (3) OF THIS DIRECTIVE AND ALL DECISIONS TO WITHHOLD AUTHORIZATION TO MANUFACTURE OR TO IMPORT FROM THIRD COUNTRIES OR TO SUSPEND OR WITHDRAW MANUFACTURING AUTHORIZATION SHALL STATE IN DETAIL THE REASONS ON WHICH THEY ARE BASED. SUCH DECISIONS SHALL BE NOTIFIED TO THE PARTY CONCERNED WHO SHALL AT THE SAME TIME BE INFORMED OF THE REMEDIES AVAILABLE TO HIM UNDER CURRENT LEGISLATION AND THE TIME ALLOWED FOR SEEKING SUCH REMEDIES. MARKETING AUTHORIZATIONS AND REVOCATIONS OF SUCH AUTHORIZATIONS SHALL BE PUBLISHED BY EACH MEMBER STATE IN ITS OFFICIAL GAZETTE.

ARTICLE 41

NO DECISION TO:

- WITHHOLD, WITHDRAW OR SUSPEND MARKETING AUTHORIZATION,
- PROHIBIT THE SUPPLY OF A VETERINARY MEDICINAL PRODUCT OR HAVE IT WITHDRAWN FROM THE MARKET,
- WITHHOLD, WITHDRAW OR SUSPEND AUTHORIZATION TO MANUFACTURE OR TO IMPORT VETERINARY MEDICINAL PRODUCTS FROM THIRD COUNTRIES,
- SUSPEND MANUFACTURE OF IMPORTS OF VETERINARY MEDICINAL PRODUCTS FROM THIRD COUNTRIES,

MAY BE TAKEN ON GROUNDS OTHER THAN THOSE SET OUT IN THIS DIRECTIVE.

ARTICLE 42

" 1. Each Member State shall take all appropriate measures to ensure that the Committee is informed immediately of decisions granting marketing authorization and of all decisions refusing or withdrawing marketing authorization, cancelling a decision refusing or withdrawing marketing authorization, prohibiting supply or withdrawing a product from the market, together with the reasons on which such decisions are based.

2. The person responsible for placing a veterinary medicinal product on the market shall be obliged to notify the Member States forthwith of any action taken by him to suspend the marketing of a product or to withdraw a product from the market, together with the reasons for such action if it concerns the effectiveness of the veterinary medicinal product or the protection of public health. Member States shall ensure that this information is brought to the attention of the Committee.

3. Member States shall ensure that appropriate information about actions taken pursuant to paragraphs 1 and 2 which may affect the protection of health in third countries is forthwith brought to the attention of the relevant international organizations, with a copy to the Committee. " [1]

" CHAPTER VIa

Pharmacovigilance

Article 42a

In order to ensure the adoption of appropriate regulatory decisions concerning the veterinary medicinal products authorized within the Community, having regard to information obtained about suspected adverse reactions to medicinal products under normal conditions of use, the Member States shall establish a pharmacovigilance system. This system shall be used to collect information useful in the surveillance of veterinary medicinal products, with particular reference to adverse reactions in animals, and to evaluate such information scientifically.
Such information shall be collated with data on consumption of veterinary medicinal products.
This system shall also collate information on frequently observed misuse and serious abuse of veterinary medicinal products.

Article 42b

For the purpose of this Directive, the following definitions shall apply:

- "adverse reaction" means a reaction which is harmful and unintended and which occurs at doses normally used in animals for the prophylaxis, diagnosis or treatment of disease or the modification of physiological function.
- "serious adverse reaction" means an adverse reaction which is fatal, life-threatening, lesion-producing, disabling, incapacitating, or which results in permanent or prolonged symptoms in the animals treated,
- "unexpected adverse reaction" means an adverse reaction which is not mentioned in the summary of the product characteristics,
- "serious unexpected adverse reaction" means an adverse reaction which is both serious and unexpected.

Article 42c

The person responsible for placing the veterinary medicinal product on the market shall have permanently and continuously at his disposal an appropriately qualified person responsible for pharmacovigilance.
That qualified person shall be responsible for the following:

(a) the establishment and maintenance of a system which ensures that information about all suspected adverse reactions which are reported to the personnel of the company, including its representatives, is collected and collated at a single point;

(b) the preparation for the competent authorities of the reports referred to in Article 42d, in such form as may be laid down by those authorities, in accordance with the relevant national or Community guidelines;

(c) ensuring that any request from the competent authorities for the provision of additional information necessary for the evaluation of the benefits and risks afforded by a veterinary medicinal product is answered fully and promptly, including the provision of information about the volume of sales or prescriptions of the veterinary medicinal product concerned.

Article 42d

1. The person responsible for placing the veterinary medicinal product on the market shall be required to record and to report all suspected serious adverse reactions which are brought to his attention to the competent authorities immediately, and in any case within 15 days of their receipt at the latest.

2. In addition, the person responsible for placing the veterinary medicinal product on the market shall be required to maintain detailed records of all other suspected adverse reactions which are reported to him.
Unless other requirements have been laid down as a condition of the granting of authorization, these records shall be submitted to the competent authorities immediately upon request or at least every six months during the first two years following authorization, and once a year for the following three years. Thereafter, the records shall be submitted at five-yearly intervals together with the application for renewal of the authorization, or immediately upon request. These records shall be accompanied by a scientific evaluation.

Article 42e

The Member States shall take all appropriate measures to encourage the reporting of suspected adverse reactions to the competent authorities.

Article 42f

The Member States shall ensure that reports of suspected serious adverse reactions are immediately brought to the attention of the Agency and the person responsible for placing the veterinary medicinal product on the market, and in any case within 15 days of their notification, at the latest.

Article 42g

In order to facilitate the exchange of information about pharmacovigilance within the Community, the Commission, in consultation with the Agency, Member States and interested parties, shall draw up guidance on the collection, verification and presentation of adverse reaction reports.

This guidance shall take account of international harmonization work carried out with regard to terminology and classification in the field of pharmacovigilance when use of such work can be made in the field of the veterinary medicinal product concerned.

Article 42h

Where as a result of the evaluation of adverse reaction reports a Member State considers that a marketing authorization should be varied, suspended or withdrawn, it shall forthwith inform the Agency and the person responsible for placing the veterinary medicinal product on the market.

In case of urgency, the Member State concerned may suspend the marketing of a veterinary medicinal product, provided the Agency is informed no later than on the following working day.

Article 42i

Any amendments which may be necessary to update the provisions of this Chapter to take account of scientific and technical progress shall be adopted in accordance with the procedure laid down in Article 42j. " [4]

" Chapter VIb

Standing Committee procedure

Article 42j

Where the procedure laid down in this Article is to be followed the Commission shall be assisted by the Standing Committee on Veterinary Medicinal Products.

The representative of the Commission shall submit to the Committee a draft of the measures to be taken. The Committee shall deliver its opinion on the draft within a time limit which the Chairman may lay down according to the urgency of the matter. The opinion shall be delivered by the majority laid down in Article 148 (2) of the Treaty in the case of decisions which the Council is required to adopt on a proposal from the Commission. The votes of the representatives of the Member States within the Committee shall be weighted in the manner set out in that Article. The Chairman shall not vote.

The Commission shall adopt the measures envisaged if they are in accordance with the opinion of the Committee.

If the measures envisaged are not in accordance with the opinion of the Committee, or if no opinion is delivered, the Commission shall, without delay, submit to the Council a proposal relating to the measures to be taken. The Council shall act by a qualified majority.

If on the expiry of a period of three months from the date of referral to the Council, the Council has not acted, the proposed measures shall be adopted by the Commission.

Article 42k

Where the procedure laid down in this Article is to be followed the Commission shall be assisted by the Standing Committee on Veterinary Medicinal Products.

The representative of the Commission shall submit to the Committee a draft of the measures to be taken. The Committee shall deliver its opinion on the draft within a time limit which the Chairman may lay down according to the urgency of the matter. The opinion shall be delivered by the majority laid down in Article 148 (2) of the Treaty in the case of decisions which the Council is required to adopt on a proposal from the Commission. The votes of the representatives of the Member States within the Committee shall be weighted in the manner set out in that Article. The Chairman shall not vote.

The Commission shall adopt the measures envisaged if they are in accordance with the opinion of the Committee.

If the measures envisaged are not in accordance with the opinion of the Committee, or if no opinion is delivered, the Commission shall, without delay, submit to the Council a proposal relating to the measures to be taken. The Council shall act by a qualified majority.

If on the expiry of a period of three months from the date of referral to the Council, the Council has not acted, the proposed measures shall be adopted by the Commission, save where the Council has decided against the said measures by a simple majority. " [4]

CHAPTER VII

LABELLING AND PACKAGE INSERTS OF VETERINARY MEDICINAL PRODUCTS

ARTICLE 43

THE FOLLOWING INFORMATION, WHICH SHALL CONFORM WITH THE PARTICULARS AND DOCUMENTS PROVIDED PURSUANT TO ARTICLE 5 AND BE APPROVED BY THE COMPETENT AUTHORITIES, SHALL APPEAR IN LEGIBLE CHARACTERS ON CONTAINERS AND OUTER PACKAGES OF MEDICINAL PRODUCTS:

" 1. Name of the veterinary medicinal product, which may be a brand name or a non-proprietary name accompanied by a trade mark or the name of the manufacturer, or a scientific name or formula, with or without a trade mark, or the name of the manufacturer.

Where the special name of a medicinal product containing only one active ingredient is a brand name, this name must be accompanied in legible characters by the international non-propriety name recommended by the World Health Organization, where such names exist or, where no such name exists, by the usual non-proprietary name.

2. A statement of the active ingredients expressed qualitatively and quantitatively per dosage unit or according to the form of administration for a particular volume or weight, using the international non-proprietary names recommended by the World Health Organization, where such names exist or, where no such names exist, the usual non-proprietary names. " [1]

3. REFERENCE NUMBER FOR PRODUCTION IDENTIFICATION (MANUFACTURER'S BATCH NUMBER);

4. MARKETING AUTHORIZATION NUMBER;

5. NAME OR CORPORATE NAME AND PERMANENT ADDRESS OR REGISTERED PLACE OF BUSINESS OF THE PERSON RESPONSIBLE FOR MARKETING AND OF THE MANUFACTURER, IF DIFFERENT;

6. THE SPECIES OF ANIMAL FOR WHICH THE VETERINARY MEDICINAL PRODUCT IS INTENDED; THE METHOD AND ROUTE OF ADMINISTRATION;

" 7. The withdrawal period, even if nil, in the case of veterinary medicinal products administered to food-producing animals.

8. Expiry date, in plain language. " [1]

9. SPECIAL STORAGE PRECAUTIONS, IF ANY;

" 9a. Special precautions for disposal of unused product or waste material, if any. " [1]

10. PARTICULARS REQUIRED TO BE INDICATED PURSUANT TO THE FIRST PARAGRAPH OF ARTICLE 12, IF ANY;

11. THE WORDS "FOR ANIMAL TREATMENT ONLY".

THE PHARMACEUTICAL FORM AND THE CONTENTS BY WEIGHT, VOLUME OR NUMBER OF DOSE-UNITS NEED ONLY BE SHOWN ON THE OUTER PACKAGE.
THE PROVISIONS OF PART 1, A OF THE ANNEX TO COUNCIL DIRECTIVE 81/852/EEC, IN SO FAR AS THEY CONCERN THE QUALITATIVE AND QUANTITATIVE COMPOSITION OF VETERINARY MEDICINAL PRODUCTS IN RESPECT OF ACTIVE INGREDIENTS, SHALL APPLY TO THE PARTICULARS PROVIDED FOR IN POINT 2.

ARTICLE 44

AS REGARDS AMPOULES, THE PARTICULARS LISTED IN THE FIRST PARAGRAPH OF ARTICLE 43 SHALL BE GIVEN ON THE OUTER PACKAGE. ON THE CONTAINERS, HOWEVER, ONLY THE FOLLOWING PARTICULARS SHALL BE NECESSARY:

- NAME OF VETERINARY MEDICINAL PRODUCT,
- QUANTITY OF THE ACTIVE INGREDIENTS,
- ROUTE OF ADMINISTRATION,
- REFERENCE NUMBER FOR PRODUCTION IDENTIFICATION (MANUFACTURER'S BATCH NUMBER),
- DATE OF EXPIRY,
- THE WORDS "FOR ANIMAL TREATMENT ONLY".

ARTICLE 45

AS REGARDS SMALL SINGLE-DOSE CONTAINERS, OTHER THAN AMPOULES, ON WHICH IT IS IMPOSSIBLE TO GIVE THE PARTICULARS MENTIONED IN ARTICLE 44, THE REQUIREMENTS OF ARTICLE 43 SHALL APPLY ONLY TO THE OUTER PACKAGE.

ARTICLE 46

WHERE THERE IS NO OUTER PACKAGE, ALL THE PARTICULARS WHICH SHOULD FEATURE ON SUCH PACKAGE PURSUANT TO THE PRECEDING ARTICLES SHALL BE SHOWN ON THE CONTAINER.

ARTICLE 47

THE PARTICULARS MENTIONED IN POINTS 6, 7, 8, 9, 10 AND 11 OF THE FIRST PARAGRAPH OF ARTICLE 43 AND IN THE THIRD AND SIXTH INDENTS OF ARTICLE 44 SHALL APPEAR ON THE OUTER

PACKAGE AND ON THE CONTAINER OF THE MEDICINAL PRODUCTS IN THE LANGUAGE OR LANGUAGES OF THE COUNTRY IN WHICH THEY ARE PLACED ON THE MARKET.

ARTICLE 48

" The inclusion of a package insert in the packaging of veterinary medicinal products shall be obligatory unless all the information required by this Article can be conveyed on the container and the external packaging. Member States shall take all appropriate measures to ensure that the insert relates solely to the veterinary medicinal product with which it is included. The insert shall be in the official language or languages of the Member State in which the medicinal product is marketed. " [1]

THE PACKAGE INSERT SHALL CONTAIN AT LEAST THE FOLLOWING INFORMATION, WHICH SHALL CONFORM WITH THE PARTICULARS AND DOCUMENTS PROVIDED PURSUANT TO ARTICLE 5 AND BE APPROVED BY THE COMPETENT AUTHORITIES:

(a) NAME OR CORPORATE NAME AND PERMANENT ADDRESS OR REGISTERED PLACE OF BUSINESS OF THE PERSON RESPONSIBLE FOR MARKETING AND OF THE MANUFACTURER, IF DIFFERENT;

(b) NAME OF THE VETERINARY MEDICINAL PRODUCT AND A STATEMENT OF ITS ACTIVE INGREDIENTS EXPRESSED QUALITATIVELY AND QUANTITATIVELY.
THE INTERNATIONAL NON-PROPRIETARY NAMES RECOMMENDED BY THE WORLD HEALTH ORGANIZATION SHALL BE USED WHEREVER THEY EXIST;

(c) THE MAIN THERAPEUTIC INDICATIONS, CONTRA-INDICATIONS AND SIDE-EFFECTS IN SO FAR AS THESE PARTICULARS ARE NECESSARY FOR THE USE OF THE VETERINARY MEDICINAL PRODUCT;

(d) THE SPECIES OF ANIMAL FOR WHICH THE VETERINARY MEDICINAL PRODUCT IS INTENDED, THE DOSAGE FOR EACH SPECIES, THE METHOD AND ROUTE OF ADMINISTRATION AND ADVICE ON CORRECT ADMINISTRATION, IF NECESSARY;

(e) " the withdrawal period, even if this is nil, in the case of veterinary medicinal products administered to food-producing animals; " [1]

(f) SPECIAL STORAGE PRECAUTIONS, IF ANY;

(g) PARTICULARS REQUIRED TO BE INDICATED PURSUANT TO THE FIRST PARAGRAPH OF ARTICLE 12, IF ANY.

" (h) special precautions for the disposal of unused product or waste materials, if any. " [1]

SUCH PARTICULARS MUST APPEAR IN THE LANGUAGE OR LANGUAGES OF THE COUNTRY IN WHICH THE PRODUCT IS MARKETED. THE OTHER INFORMATION SHALL BE CLEARLY SEPARATE FROM THE ABOVEMENTIONED PARTICULARS.
"..." [1]

ARTICLE 49

WHERE THE PROVISIONS OF THIS CHAPTER ARE NOT OBSERVED AND A FORMAL NOTICE ADDRESSED TO THE PERSON CONCERNED HAS BEEN INEFFECTUAL, THE COMPETENT AUTHORITIES OF THE MEMBER STATES MAY SUSPEND OR WITHDRAW MARKETING AUTHORIZATION.
ALL DECISIONS TAKEN BY VIRTUE OF THE PRECEDING PARAGRAPH SHALL STATE IN DETAIL THE REASONS ON WHICH THEY ARE BASED. A DECISION SHALL BE NOTIFIED TO THE PARTY CONCERNED, ALONG WITH THE REMEDIES AVAILABLE TO HIM UNDER CURRENT LEGISLATION AND THE TIME ALLOWED FOR SEEKING SUCH REMEDIES.

ARTICLE 50

THE REQUIREMENTS OF MEMBER STATES CONCERNING CONDITIONS OF SUPPLY TO THE PUBLIC, THE MARKING OF PRICES ON MEDICINAL PRODUCTS FOR VETERINARY USE AND INDUSTRIAL PROPERTY RIGHTS SHALL NOT BE AFFECTED BY THE PROVISIONS OF THIS CHAPTER.

" CHAPTER VIIIa

Distribution of veterinary medicinal products

Article 50a

1. Member States shall take all appropriate measures to ensure that wholesale dealing in veterinary medicinal products is subject to the holding of an authorization and to ensure that the time taken for the procedure for granting this authorisation does not exceed 90 days from the date on which the competent authority receives the application.
For the purposes of this Directive, wholesale dealing shall include the purchase, sale, import, export, or any other commercial transaction in veterinary medicinal products, whether or not for profit, except for:

- the supply by a manufacturer of veterinary medicinal products manufactured by himself,
- retail supplies of veterinary medicinal products by persons permitted to carry out such supplies in accordance with Article 50b.

Member States may also exclude supplies of small quantities of veterinary medicinal products from one retailer to another.

2. In order to obtain the authorization referred to in paragraph 1, the applicant shall have at his disposal technically competent staff and suitable and sufficient premises complying with the requirements laid down in the Member State concerned as regards the storage and handling of products.

3. The holder of the authorization referred to in paragraph 1 shall be required to keep detailed records. The following minimum information shall be recorded in respect of each incoming or outgoing transaction:

(a) date;

(b) precise identity of the veterinary medicinal product;

(c) manufacturer's batch number, expiry date;

(d) quantity received or supplied;

(e) name and address of the supplier or recipient.

At least once a year a detailed audit shall be carried out to compare incoming and outgoing supplies with supplies currently held in stock, any discrepancies being recorded.
These records shall be available for inspection by the competent authorities for a period of at least three years.

4. Member States shall take all appropriate measures to ensure that wholesalers supply veterinary medicinal products only to persons permitted to carry out retail activities in accordance with Article 50b, or to other persons who are lawfully permitted to receive veterinary medicinal products from wholesalers.

Article 50b

1. Member States shall take all appropriate measures to ensure that the retail supply of veterinary medicinal products is conducted only by persons who are permitted to carry out such operations by the legislation of the Member State concerned.

2. Any person permitted under the preceding paragraph to sell veterinary medicinal products shall be required to keep detailed records. The following information shall be recorded in respect of each incoming or outgoing transaction:

(a) date;

(b) precise identity of the veterinary medicinal product;

(c) manufacturer's batch number;

(d) quantity received or supplied;

(e) name and address of the supplier or recipient;

(f) where relevant, name and address of the prescribing veterinarian and a copy of the prescription.

At least once a year a detailed audit shall be carried out, and incoming and outgoing products shall be reconciled with products currently held in stock, any discrepancies being recorded.
These records shall be available for inspection by the competent authorities for a period of three years.

3. Member States may limit the scope of the record-keeping requirements referred to in paragraph 2. However, these requirements shall always be applied in case of veterinary medicinal products intended for administration to animals whose flesh or products are intended for human consumption and which are available only on veterinary prescription or in respect of which a withdrawal period must be observed.

4. Not later that 1 January 1992, Member States shall communicate to the Commission a list of the veterinary medicinal products which are available without prescription. After having taken note of the communication from the Member States, the Commission shall examine whether suitable measures should be proposed for drawing up a Community list of such products.

Article 50c

Member States shall ensure that the owners or keepers of food-producing animals can provide proof of purchase, possession and administration of veterinary medicinal products containing the substances set out in Article 1 (5); Member States may extend the scope of this obligation to other medicinal veterinary products.
In particular, Member States may require the maintenance of a record giving at least the following information:

(a) date;

(b) identity of the veterinary medicinal product;

(c) quantity;

(d) name and address of the supplier of the medicinal product;

(e) identification of the animals treated. " [1]

CHAPTER VIII

IMPLEMENTING PROVISIONS AND TRANSITIONAL MEASURES

ARTICLE 51

MEMBER STATES SHALL BRING INTO FORCE THE LAWS, REGULATIONS AND ADMINISTRATIVE PROVISIONS NECESSARY TO COMPLY WITH THIS DIRECTIVE WITHIN 24 MONTHS OF ITS NOTIFICATION AND SHALL FORTHWITH INFORM THE COMMISSION THEREOF.
MEMBER STATES SHALL ENSURE THAT THE MAIN PROVISIONS OF NATIONAL LAW WHICH THEY ADOPT IN THE FIELD GOVERNED BY THIS DIRECTIVE ARE COMMUNICATED TO THE COMMISSION.

ARTICLE 52

1. AS REGARDS THE AUTHORIZATIONS REFERRED TO IN ARTICLE 24 WHICH ARE ISSUED BEFORE THE EXPIRY OF THE TIME LIMIT LAID DOWN IN ARTICLE 51, MEMBER STATES MAY GRANT AN ADDITIONAL PERIOD OF ONE YEAR FOR THE UNDERTAKINGS CONCERNED TO COMPLY WITH THE PROVISIONS OF CHAPTER V.

2. THE OTHER PROVISIONS OF THIS DIRECTIVE SHALL BE APPLIED PROGRESSIVELY, WITHIN 10 YEARS OF THE NOTIFICATION REFERRED TO IN ARTICLE 51, TO VETERINARY MEDICINAL PRODUCTS PLACED ON THE MARKET BY VIRTUE OF EARLIER PROVISIONS.

3. MEMBER STATES SHALL NOTIFY THE COMMISSION, WITHIN THREE YEARS FOLLOWING THE NOTIFICATION OF THIS DIRECTIVE, OF THE NUMBER OF VETERINARY MEDICINAL PRODUCTS COVERED BY PARAGRAPH 2 AND, IN EACH SUBSEQUENT YEAR, OF THE NUMBER OF SUCH PRODUCTS FOR WHICH THE MARKETING AUTHORIZATION REFERRED TO IN ARTICLE 4 HAS NOT YET BEEN ISSUED.

ARTICLE 53

THIS DIRECTIVE IS ADDRESSED TO THE MEMBER STATES.

(1) OJ No 22, 09/12/1965, p. 369.
(2) OJ No L 270, 14/12/1970, p. 1.
(3) OJ No L 214, 24/08/1993, p. 1.
(4) OJ No L 224, 18/08/1990, p.1.
(5) The phrase "an animal or a small number of animals on a particular holding" also covers pets, and should be interpreted more flexibly for minor or exotic animal species which do not produce food.
(6) OJ No L 317, 06/11/1981, p. 16.
(7) OJ No L 15, 17/01/1987, p. 34.
(8) OJ No L 15, 17/01/1987, p. 38.
(9) The expression "risk to human or animal health or the environment" refers to the quality, safety and efficacy of the veterinary medicinal product.

COUNCIL DIRECTIVE

of 22 December 1986

on the approximation of national measures relating to the placing on the market of high-technology medicinal products, particularly those derived from biotechnology

(87/22/EEC)

repealed with effect from 1 January 1995
by Directive 93/41/EEC

(See above, page 75)

COUNCIL DIRECTIVE 93/41/EEC

of 14 June 1993

repealing Directive 87/22/EEC on the approximation of national measures relating to the placing on the market of high-technology medicinal products, particularly those derived from biotechnology

(See above, page 79)

COUNCIL DIRECTIVE

of 13 December 1990

extending the scope of Directive 81/851/EEC on the approximation of the laws of the Member States relating to veterinary medicinal products and laying down additional provisions for immunological veterinary medicinal products

(90/677/EEC)

THE COUNCIL OF THE EUROPEAN COMMUNITIES,

Having regard to the Treaty establishing the European Economic Community, and in particular Article 100a thereof,

Having regard to the proposal from the Commission [1],

In cooperation with the European Parliament [2],

Having regard to the opinion of the Economic and Social Committee [3],

Whereas disparities in the provisions laid down by law, regulation or administrative action by Member States may hinder trade in immunological veterinary medicinal products within the Community;

Whereas the essential aim of any rules governing the production, distribution or use of veterinary medicinal products must be to ensure a high level of protection of public health;

Whereas the provisions of Directive 81/851/EEC [4] as last amended by Directive 90/676/EEC [5], although appropriate, are not adequate for veterinary medicinal products used in order to produce active immunity, to diagnose the state of immunity or to produce passive immunity (immunological veterinary medicinal products);

Whereas in accordance with Article 5 of Council Directive 87/22/EEC of 22 December 1986 on the approximation of national provisions relating to the placing on the market of high-technology medicinal products, particularly those derived from biotechnology [6], the Commission is required to submit proposals to harmonize the conditions for authorizing the manufacture and placing on the market of immunological veterinary medicinal products;

Whereas, before an authorization to market an immunological veterinary medicinal product can be granted, the manufacturer must demonstrate his ability to attain batch-to-batch consistency;

Whereas the competent authorities should also be empowered to prohibit the use of an immunological veterinary medicinal product when the immunological responses of the treated animal will interfere with a national or Community programme for the diagnosis, eradication or control of animal disease;

Whereas changes will be required to the requirements for the testing of veterinary medicinal products laid down in Annex I to Council Directive 81/852/EEC of 28 September 1981 on the approximation of the laws of the Member States relating to analytical, pharmaco-toxicological and clinical standards and protocols in respect of the testing of veterinary medicinal products [7], as amended by Directive 87/20/EEC [8], to take account of the special nature of immunological veterinary medicinal products; whereas the Commission should be empowered to adopt the necessary changes in close cooperation with the Committee for the Adaptation to Technical Progress of the Directives on the Removal of Technical Barriers to Trade in the Veterinary Medicinal Products Sector, thus ensuring greater quality, safety and effectiveness,

HAS ADOPTED THIS DIRECTIVE:

Article 1

1. Subject to the provisions of this Directive, Directive 81/851/EEC shall apply to immunological veterinary medicinal products.

2. For the purposes of this Directive 'immunological veterinary medicinal product' means a veterinary medicinal product administered to animals in order to produce active or passive immunity or to diagnose the state of immunity.

3. This Directive and Directive 81/851/EEC shall not apply to inactivated immunological veterinary medicinal products which are manufactured from pathogens and antigens obtained from an animal or animals from a holding and used for the treatment of that animal or the animals of that holding in the same locality.

4. Member States may provide that this Directive does not apply to non-activated immunological veterinary medicinal products of the type referred to in paragraph 3.

---

[1] OJ No C 61, 10. 3. 1989, p. 20 and
     OJ No C 131, 30. 5. 1990, p. 20.
[2] OJ No C 96, 17. 4. 1990, p. 111 and
     Decision of 21 November 1990 (not yet published in the Official
     Journal).
[3] OJ No C 201, 7. 8. 1989, p. 1.
[4] OJ No L 317, 6. 11. 1981, p. 1.
[5] See page 15 of this Official Journal.
[6] OJ No L 15, 17. 1. 1987, p. 38.
[7] OJ No L 317, 6. 11. 1981, p. 16.
[8] OJ No L 15, 17. 1. 1987, p. 34.

Article 2

1.   The quantitative particulars of an immunological veterinary medicinal product shall be expressed by mass or by international units or by units of biological activity or by the number of germs or by specific protein content where possible, as appropriate to the product concerned.

2.   In respect of immunological veterinary medicinal products, in Directive 81/851/EEC the expression 'qualitative and quantitative composition of the constituents' shall include particulars relating to biological activity or to protein content and the expression 'qualitative and quantitative composition' shall include the composition of the product expressed in terms of the biological activity or of protein content.

3.   In any document established in accordance with Directive 81/851/EEC in which the name of an immunological veterinary medicinal product is expressed, the full common or scientific name of the active constituents shall also be included at least once.

Article 3

1.   Member States shall take all appropriate measures to ensure that the manufacturing processes used in the manufacture of immunological veterinary medicinal products are completely validated and batch-to-batch consistency is ensured, in accordance with Article 34 of Directive 81/851/EEC.

2.   For the purpose of implementing Article 35 of Directive 81/851/EEC, Member States may require persons responsible for placing immunological veterinary medicinal products on the market to submit to the competent authorities copies of all the control reports signed by the qualified person in accordance with Article 30 of Directive 81/851/EEC.

The person responsible for placing immunological veterinary medicinal products on the market shall ensure that an adequate number of representative samples of each batch of finished products is held in stock at least up to the expiry date, and provide samples promptly to the competent authorities on request.

3.   Where it considers it necessary, a Member State may require persons responsible for placing immunological veterinary medicinal products on the market to submit samples from the batches of the bulk and/or finished product for examination by a State laboratory or an approved laboratory before entry in free circulation. In the case of a batch manufactured in another Member State, examined by the competent authority of another Member State and declared to be in conformity with national specifications, such a control may be carried out only after the control reports of the batch in question have been examined, after the Commission has been informed, and where the difference in veterinary conditions between the two Member States concerned justifies it. Except where the Commission has been informed that a longer period is necessary to complete the analyses, Member States shall ensure that any such examination is completed within 60 days of receipt of the samples. The person responsible for placing the product on the market shall be notified of the results of the examination within the same time limit. Before 1 January 1992, the Member States shall notify the Commission of the immunological veterinary medicinal products subject to compulsory official control before being placed on the market.

Article 4

In the absence of specific Community legislation concerning the use of immunological veterinary medicinal products for the eradication or control of animal disease, a Member State may, in accordance with its national legislation, prohibit the manufacture, import, possession, sale, supply and/or use of immunological veterinary medicinal products on the whole or part of its territory if it is established that:

(a)   the administration of the product to animals will interfere with the implementation of a national programme for the diagnosis, control or eradication of animal disease, or will cause difficulties in certifying the absence of contamination in live animals or in foodstuffs or other products obtained from treated animals;

(b)   the disease to which the product is intended to confer immunity is largely absent from the territory in question.

The competent authorities of the Member States shall inform the Commission of all instances in which the provisions of this Article are applied.

Article 5

The amendments which need to be made to the testing requirements for veterinary medicinal products set out in the Annex to Directive 81/852/EEC to take account of the extension of the scope of Directive 81/851/EEC to cover immunological veterinary medicinal products shall be adopted in accordance with the procedure laid down in Article 2c of Directive 81/852/EEC.

Article 6

1.   Member States shall take the necessary measures to comply with this Directive not later than 1 January 1992. They shall forthwith inform the Commission thereof.

In the event of the amendments referred to in Article 5 not being adopted by 1 January 1991, the date indicated in the first subparagraph shall be put back to one year after the date of adoption of those amendments.

2.   When Member States adopt the measures referred to in paragraph 1, they shall contain a reference to this Directive

or shall be accompanied by such reference on the occasion of their official publication. The methods of making such a reference shall be laid down by the Member States.

3. Requests for marketing authorization for products covered by this Directive lodged after the date indicated in paragraph 1 must comply with the provisions of this Directive.

4. Within five years of the date indicated in the first subparagraph of paragraph 1, this Directive shall apply to existing immunological veterinary medicinal products.

Article 7

This Directive is addressed to the Member States.

Done at Brussels, 13 December 1990.

For the Council
The President
P. ROMITA

COUNCIL DIRECTIVE 92/74/EEC

of 22 September 1992

widening the scope of Directive 81/851/EEC on the approximation of provisions laid down by law, regulation or administrative action relating to veterinary medicinal products and laying down additional provisions on homeopathic veterinary medicinal products

THE COUNCIL OF THE EUROPEAN COMMUNITIES,

Having regard to the Treaty establishing the European Economic Community, and in particular Article 100a thereof,

Having regard to the proposal from the Commission [1],

In cooperation with the European Parliament [2],

Having regard to the opinion of the Economic and Social Committee [3],

Whereas differences currently existing between the provisions laid down by law, regulation or administrative action in the Member States may hinder trade in homeopathic veterinary medicinal products within the Community and lead to discrimination and distortion of competition between manufacturers of these products;

Whereas the essential aim of any rules governing the production, distribution and use of veterinary medicinal products must be to safeguard human and animal health;

Whereas, despite considerable differences in the status of alternative medicines in the Member States, free choice of treatment should be guaranteed, provided all precautions are taken to ensure the quality of products;

Whereas the provisions of Directive 81/851/EEC [4] are not always appropriate for homeopathic veterinary medicinal products;

Whereas homeopathic medicine is officially recognized in certain Member States but is only tolerated in other Member States;

Whereas, even if homeopathic medicinal products are not always officially recognized, they are nevertheless prescribed and used in most Member States;

Whereas it is desirable in the first instance to provide users of these medicinal products with a very clear indication of their homeopathic character and with sufficient guarantees of their quality and safety;

Whereas the rules relating to the manufacture, control and inspection of homeopathic veterinary medicinal products must be harmonized to permit the circulation throughout the Community of medicinal products which are safe and of good quality;

Whereas, having regard to the particular characteristics of these medicinal products, such as the very low level of active principles they contain and the difficulty of applying to them the conventional statistical methods relating to clinical trials, it is desirable to provide a special, simplified registration procedure for those traditional homeopathic medicinal products which are placed on the market without specific therapeutic indications in a pharmaceutical form and dosage which do not present a risk for the animal;

Whereas in the light of current knowledge it appears difficult to allow according to a special, simplified registration procedure the marketing of medicinal products intended to be administered to animals whose flesh or products are intended for human consumption; whereas, however, this question should be re-examined during the preparation of the overall report on the application of this Directive which has to be submitted by the Commission not later than 31 December 1995;

Whereas, however, the usual rules governing the authorization to market veterinary medicinal products must be applied to homeopathic veterinary medicinal products marketed with therapeutic indications or in a form which may present risks which must be balanced against the desired therapeutic effect; whereas Member States should be able to apply particular rules for the evaluation of the results of tests and trials intended to establish the safety and efficacy of these medicinal products for pet animals and exotic species, provided that they notify them to the Commission,

HAS ADOPTED THIS DIRECTIVE:

CHAPTER I

Scope

Article 1

1. For the purposes of this Directive, 'homeopathic veterinary medicinal product' shall mean any veterinary

---

[1] OJ No C 108, 1. 5. 1990, p. 13.
[2] OJ No C 183, 15. 7. 1991, p. 323 and
OJ No C 241, 21. 9. 1992.
[3] OJ No C 332, 31. 12. 1990, p. 32.
[4] OJ No L 317, 6. 11. 1981, p. 1. Directive as amended by Directive 90/676/EEC (OJ No L 373, 31. 12. 1990, p. 15).

medicinal product prepared from products, substances or compositions called homeopathic stocks in accordance with a homeopathic manufacturing procedure described by the *European Pharmacopoeia* or, in absence thereof, by the pharmacopoeias currently used officially in the Member States.

2.   A homeopathic veterinary medicinal product may also contain a number of principles.

Article 2

1.   The provisions of this Directive shall apply to homeopathic medicinal products for veterinary use.

This Directive shall not apply to homeopathic veterinary medicinal products which meet the conditions of Article 4 (4) of Directive 81/851/EEC; however, the withdrawal period referred to in the second subparagraph of that Article 4 (4) shall not apply with regard to homeopathic veterinary medicinal products in which the level of active principles is equal to or less than one part per million.

2.   Without prejudice to Article 7 (2), the medicinal products referred to in paragraph 1 shall be identified by the inclusion on their labels, in clearly legible form, of the words 'homeopathic medicinal product for veterinary use'.

3.   This Directive shall not apply to immunological homeopathic veterinary medicinal products, which shall be authorized by Member States in accordance with the provisions of Council Directive 90/677/EEC of 13 December 1990 extending the scope of Directive 81/851/EEC on the approximation of the laws of the Member States relating to veterinary medicinal products and laying down additional provisions for immunological veterinary medicinal products (¹).

CHAPTER II

Manufacture, control and inspection

Article 3

The provisions of Chapter V of Directive 81/851/EEC shall apply to the manufacture, control, import and export of homeopathic veterinary medicinal products.

Article 4

The supervision measures and the sanctions provided for in Chapter VI of Directive 81/851/EEC shall apply to homeopathic veterinary medicinal products.

However, the proof of therapeutic effect referred to in Article 37 (1) (b) of the same Directive shall not be required

(¹) OJ No L 373, 31. 12. 1990, p. 26.

for homeopathic veterinary medicinal products registered in accordance with Article 7 of this Directive or, where appropriate, admitted in accordance with Article 6 (2).

Article 5

Member States shall communicate to each other all the information necessary to guarantee the quality and safety of homeopathic veterinary medicinal products manufactured and marketed within the Community, and in particular the information referred to in Articles 39 and 42 of Directive 81/851/EEC.

CHAPTER III

Placing on the market

Article 6

1.   Member States shall ensure that homeopathic veterinary medicinal products manufactured and marketed within the Community are registered or authorized in accordance with the provisions of Articles 7, 8 and 9. Each Member State shall take due account of registrations and authorizations previously granted by another Member State.

2.   A Member State may refrain from establishing a special, simplified registration procedure for the homeopathic veterinary medicinal products referred to in Article 7. A Member State applying this provision shall inform the Commission accordingly. The Member State concerned shall, by 31 December 1995 at the latest, allow the use in its territory of homeopathic veterinary medicinal products registered by other Member States in accordance with Articles 7 and 8.

Article 7

1.   Only homeopathic veterinary medicinal products which satisfy all of the following conditions may be subject to a special, simplified registration procedure:

— they are intended for administration to pet animals or exotic species whose flesh or products are not intended for human consumption,

— they are administered by a route described in the *European Pharmacopoeia* or, in absence thereof, by the pharmacopoeias currently used officially in the Member States,

— no specific therapeutic indication appears on the labelling of the veterinary medicinal product or in any information relating thereto,

— there is a sufficient degree of dilution to guarantee the safety of the medicinal product; in particular, the medicinal product may not contain either more than one part per 10 000 of the mother tincture or more than 1/100th of the smallest dose used in allopathy with regard to active principles whose presence in an allopathic medicinal product results in the obligation to submit a veterinary prescription.

At the time of registration, Member States shall determine the classification for the dispensing of the medicinal product.

2. In addition to the clear mention of the words 'homeopathic veterinary medicinal product without approved therapeutic indications', the labelling and, where appropriate, package insert for the medicinal products referred to in paragraph 1 shall bear the following information and no other information:

— the scientific name of the stock or stocks followed by the degree of dilution, using the symbols of the pharmacopoeia used in accordance with Article 1 (1),

— name and address of the person responsible for marketing and, where appropriate, of the manufacturer,

— method of administration and, if necessary, route,

— expiry date, in clear terms (month, year),

— pharmaceutical form,

— contents of the sales presentation,

— special storage precautions, if any,

— target species,

— a special warning if necessary for the medicinal product,

— manufacturer's batch number,

— registration number.

3. The criteria and rules of procedure provided for in Articles 8 to 15 of Directive 81/851/EEC shall apply by analogy to the special, simplified registration procedure for homeopathic veterinary medicinal products, with the exception of the proof of therapeutic effect.

Article 8

A special, simplified application for registration submitted by the person responsible for marketing may cover a series of medicinal products derived from the same homeopathic stock or stocks. The following documents shall be included with the application in order to demonstrate, in particular, the pharmaceutical quality and the batch-to-batch homogeneity of the products concerned:

— scientific name or other name given in a pharmacopoeia of the homeopathic stock or stocks, together with a statement of the various routes of administration, pharmaceutical forms and degree of dilution to be registered,

— dossier describing how the homeopathic stock or stocks is/are obtained and controlled, and justifying its/their homeopathic nature, on the basis of an adequate

homeopathic bibliography; in the case of homeopathic veterinary medicinal products containing biological substances, a description of the measures taken to ensure the absence of pathogens,

— manufacturing and control file for each pharmaceutical form and a description of the method of dilution and potentiation,

— manufacturing authorization for the medicinal products concerned,

— copies of any registrations or authorizations obtained for the same medicinal products in other Member States,

— one or more specimens or mock-ups of the sales presentation of the medicinal products to be registered,

— data concerning the stability of the medicinal product.

Article 9

1. Homeopathic veterinary medicinal products other than those referred to in Article 7 shall be authorized in accordance with the provisions of Articles 5 to 15 of Directive 81/851/EEC, including the provisions concerning proof of therapeutic effect, and labelled in accordance with Articles 43 to 50 of the same Directive.

2. A Member State may introduce or retain in its territory specific rules for the pharmacological and toxicological tests and clinical trials of homeopathic veterinary medicinal products intended for pet animals and exotic species whose flesh or products are not intended for human consumption, other than those referred to in Article 7 (1), in accordance with the principles and characteristics of homeopathy as practised in that Member State.

In this case, the Member State concerned shall notify the Commission of the specific rules in force.

CHAPTER IV

Final provisions

Article 10

1. Member States shall take the measures necessary to comply with this Directive by 31 December 1993. They shall forthwith inform the Commission thereof.

When Member States adopt these measures, they shall contain a reference to this Directive or shall be accompanied by such reference on the occasion of their official publication. The methods of making such a reference shall be laid down by the Member States.

2. Applications for registration or for marketing authorization for products covered by this Directive lodged after the date set in paragraph 1 shall comply with the provisions of this Directive.

3. Not later than 31 December 1995, the Commission shall present a report to the Council and to the European Parliament concerning the implementation of this Directive.

Article 11

This Directive is addressed to the Member States.

Done at Brussels, 22 September 1992.

For the Council
The President
R. NEEDHAM

381L0852

81/852/EEC: COUNCIL DIRECTIVE OF 28 SEPTEMBER 1981 ON THE APPROXIMATION OF THE LAWS OF THE MEMBER STATES RELATING TO ANALYTICAL, PHARMACO-TOXICOLOGICAL AND CLINICAL STANDARDS AND PROTOCOLS IN RESPECT OF THE TESTING OF VETERINARY MEDICINAL PRODUCTS

OFFICIAL JOURNAL No L 317, 06/11/1981, P. 16
DATE OF NOTIFICATION: 09/10/1981
DATE OF TRANSPOSITION: 09/10/1983; SEE ART. 3

AMENDED BY

387L0020
87/20/EEC: COUNCIL DIRECTIVE OF 22 DECEMBER 1986 [1]
OFFICIAL JOURNAL No L 15, 17/01/1987, P. 34
DATE OF NOTIFICATION: 23/12/1986
DATE OF TRANSPOSITION: 01/07/1987; SEE ART. 2

392L0018
92/18/EEC: COMMISSION DIRECTIVE OF 20 MARCH 1992 [2]
OFFICIAL JOURNAL No L 97, 10/04/1992, P. 1
DATE OF TRANSPOSITION: 01/04/1993; SEE ART. 2.

393L0040
93/40/EEC: COUNCIL DIRECTIVE OF 14 JUNE 1993 [3]
OFFICIAL JOURNAL No L 214, 24/08/1993, P. 31
DATE OF TRANSPOSITION: 01/01/1995; SEE ART. 3
DATE OF TRANSPOSITION: 01/01/1998; SEE ART. 3

ARTICLE 1

MEMBER STATES SHALL TAKE ALL APPROPRIATE MEASURES TO ENSURE THAT THE PARTICULARS AND DOCUMENTS WHICH SHALL ACCOMPANY APPLICATIONS FOR AUTHORIZATION TO PLACE A VETERINARY MEDICINAL PRODUCT ON THE MARKET, PURSUANT TO POINTS 3, 4, 6, 8, 9 AND 10 OF THE SECOND PARAGRAPH OF ARTICLE 5 OF DIRECTIVE 81/851/EEC (1), ARE SUBMITTED BY THE PERSONS CONCERNED IN ACCORDANCE WITH THE ANNEX TO THIS DIRECTIVE.
WHERE, PURSUANT TO POINT 10 (a) OR (b) OF THE SECOND PARAGRAPH OF ARTICLE 5 OF THE ABOVEMENTIONED DIRECTIVE, REFERENCES TO PUBLISHED DATA ARE SUBMITTED, THE PROVISIONS OF THIS DIRECTIVE SHALL APPLY IN LIKE MANNER.

ARTICLE 2

THE COMMITTEE FOR VETERINARY MEDICINAL PRODUCTS REFERRED TO IN ARTICLE 16 OF DIRECTIVE 81/851/EEC MAY EXAMINE ANY QUESTION RELATING TO THE APPLICATION OF THIS DIRECTIVE.

" ARTICLE 2a

ANY CHANGES WHICH ARE NECESSARY IN ORDER TO ADAPT THE ANNEX TO TAKE ACCOUNT OF TECHNICAL PROGRESS SHALL BE ADOPTED IN ACCORDANCE WITH THE PROCEDURE LAID DOWN IN ARTICLE 2c.
IF APPROPRIATE, THE COMMISSION SHALL PROPOSE TO THE COUNCIL THAT THE PROCEDURE IN ARTICLE 2c BE REVIEWED IN CONNECTION WITH THE DETAILED RULES SET FOR THE EXERCISE OF THE POWERS OF IMPLEMENTATION GRANTED TO THE COMMISSION.

ARTICLE 2b

1. A " Standing Committee on Veterinary Medicinal Products " [3], HEREINAFTER CALLED "THE COMMITTEE", IS HEREBY SET UP; IT SHALL CONSIST OF REPRESENTATIVES OF THE MEMBER STATES WITH A REPRESENTATIVE OF THE COMMISSION AS CHAIRMAN.

2. THE COMMITTEE SHALL ADOPT ITS OWN RULES OF PROCEDURE.

ARTICLE 2c

1. WHERE THE PROCEDURE LAID DOWN IN THIS ARTICLE IS TO BE FOLLOWED, MATTERS SHALL BE REFERRED TO THE COMMITTEE BY THE CHAIRMAN, EITHER ON HIS OWN INITIATIVE OR AT THE REQUEST OF THE REPRESENTATIVE OF A MEMBER STATE.

2. THE REPRESENTATIVE OF THE COMMISSION SHALL SUBMIT TO THE COMMITTEE A DRAFT OF THE MEASURES TO BE ADOPTED. THE COMMITTEE SHALL DELIVER ITS OPINION ON THE DRAFT WITHIN A TIME LIMIT SET BY THE CHAIRMAN HAVING REGARD TO THE URGENCY OF THE MATTER. IT SHALL ACT BY A QUALIFIED MAJORITY, THE VOTES OF THE MEMBER STATES BEING WEIGHTED AS PROVIDED IN ARTICLE 148 (2) OF THE TREATY. THE CHAIRMAN SHALL NOT VOTE.

3. (a) THE COMMISSION SHALL ADOPT THE MEASURES ENVISAGED WHERE THEY ARE IN ACCORDANCE WITH THE OPINION OF THE COMMITTEE.

(b) WHERE THE MEASURES ENVISAGED ARE NOT IN ACCORDANCE WITH THE OPINION OF THE COMMITTEE, OR IF NO OPINION IS ADOPTED, THE COMMISSION SHALL WITHOUT DELAY PROPOSE TO THE COUNCIL THE MEASURES TO BE ADOPTED. THE COUNCIL SHALL ACT BY A QUALIFIED MAJORITY.

(c) IF, WITHIN THREE MONTHS OF THE PROPOSAL BEING SUBMITTED TO IT, THE COUNCIL HAS NOT ACTED, THE PROPOSED MEASURES SHALL BE ADOPTED BY THE COMMISSION. " [1]

ARTICLE 3

MEMBER STATES SHALL BRING INTO FORCE THE PROVISIONS NECESSARY TO COMPLY WITH THIS DIRECTIVE WITHIN 24 MONTHS FOLLOWING ITS NOTIFICATION AND SHALL FORTHWITH INFORM THE COMMISSION THEREOF.
MEMBER STATES SHALL ENSURE THAT THE TEXTS OF THE MAIN PROVISIONS OF NATIONAL LAW WHICH THEY ADOPT IN THE FIELD COVERED BY THIS DIRECTIVE ARE COMMUNICATED TO THE COMMISSION.

ARTICLE 4

THIS DIRECTIVE IS ADDRESSED TO THE MEMBER STATES.

" ANNEX

INTRODUCTION

The particulars and documents accompanying an application for marketing authorization pursuant to Article 5 of Council Directive 81/851/EEC shall be presented in accordance with the requirements set out in this Annex and taking account of the guidance contained in the "Notice to applicants for marketing authorizations for veterinary medicinal products in the Member States of the European Community", published by the Commission in The rules governing medicinal products in the European Community, volume V: Veterinary Medicinal Products.

In assembling the dossier for application for marketing authorization, applicants shall take into account the Community guidelines relating to the quality, safety and efficacy of veterinary medicinal products published by the Commission in The rules governing medicinal products in the European Community.

All information which is relevant to the evaluation of the medicinal product concerned shall be included in the application, whether favourable or unfavourable to the product. In particular, all relevant details shall be given of any incomplete or abandoned test or trial relating to the veterinary medicinal product. Moreover, after marketing authorization, any information not in the original application, pertinent to the benefit/risk assessment, shall be submitted forthwith to the competent authorities.

Member States ensure that all experiments on animals are conducted in accordance with Council Directive 86/609/EEC of 24 November 1986 on the approximation of laws, regulations and administrative provisions of the Member States regarding the protection of animals used for experimental and other scientific purposes (2).

The provisions of Title I of this Annex shall apply to veterinary medicinal products other than immunological veterinary medicinal products intended for administration to animals in order to produce active or passive immunity or to diagnose the state of immunity.

The provisions of Title II of this Annex shall apply to veterinary medicinal products intended for administration to animals to produce active or passive immunity or to diagnose the state of immunity, hereinafter referred to as "immunological veterinary medicinal products".

TITLE I

REQUIREMENTS FOR VETERINARY MEDICINAL PRODUCTS OTHER THAN IMMUNOLOGICAL VETERINARY MEDICINAL PRODUCTS

PART 1

SUMMARY OF THE DOSSIER

A. ADMINISTRATIVE DATA

The veterinary medicinal product which is the subject of the application shall be identified by name and by name of the active ingredient(s), together with the strength and pharmaceutical form, the method and route of administration and a description of the final sales presentation of the product.

The name and address of the applicant shall be given, together with the name and address of the manufacturers and the sites involved in the different stages of the manufacture (including the manufacturer of the finished product and the manufacturer(s) of the active ingredient(s)), and where relevant the name and address of the importer.

The applicant shall identify the number and titles of volumes of documentation submitted in support of the application and indicate what samples, if any, are also provided.

Annexed to the administrative data shall be a document showing that the manufacturer is authorized to produce the veterinary medicinal products concerned, as defined in Article 24 of Directive 81/851/EEC, together with a list of countries in which authorization has been granted, copies of all the summaries of product characteristics in accordance with Article 5a of Directive 81/851/EEC as approved by Member States and a list of countries in which an application has been submitted.

B. SUMMARY OF PRODUCT CHARACTERISTICS

The applicant shall propose a summary of the product characteristics, in accordance with Article 5a of Directive 81/851/EEC.

In addition the applicant shall provide one or more specimens or mock-ups of the sales presentation of the veterinary medicinal product, together with a package insert where one is required.

C. EXPERT REPORTS

In accordance with Article 7 of Directive 81/851/EEC, expert reports must be provided on the analytical documentation, the pharmacotoxicological documentation, the residues documentation and the clinical documentation.

Each expert report shall consist of a critical evaluation of the various tests and/or trials which have been carried out in accordance with this Directive, and bring out all the data relevant for evaluation. The expert shall give his opinion as to whether sufficient guarantees have been provided as to the quality, safety and efficacy of the product concerned. A factual summary is not sufficient.

All important data shall be summarized in an appendix to the expert report, whenever possible in tabular or graphic form. The expert report and the summaries shall contain precise cross references to the information contained in the main documentation.

Each expert report shall be prepared by a suitably qualified and experienced person. It shall be signed and dated by the expert, and attached to the report shall be brief information about the educational background, training and occupational experience of the expert. The professional relationship of the expert to the applicant shall be declared.

PART 2

ANALYTICAL (PHYSICO-CHEMICAL, BIOLOGICAL OR MICROBIOLOGICAL) TESTS OF VETERINARY MEDICINAL PRODUCTS OTHER THAN IMMUNOLOGICAL VETERINARY MEDICINAL PRODUCTS

All test procedures shall correspond to the state of scientific progress at the time and shall be validated procedures; results of the validation studies shall be provided.

All the test procedure(s) shall be described in sufficiently precise detail so as to be reproducible in control tests, carried out at the request of the competent authority; any special apparatus and equipment which may be used shall be described in adequate detail, possibly accompanied by a diagram. The formulae of the laboratory reagents shall be supplemented, if necessary, by the method of preparation. In the case of test procedures included in the European Pharmacopoeia or the pharmacopoeia of a Member State, this description may be replaced by a detailed reference to the pharmacopoeia in question.

A. QUALITATIVE AND QUANTITATIVE PARTICULARS OF THE CONSTITUENTS

The particulars and documents which must accompany applications for marketing authorization, pursuant to point 3 of Article 5, second paragraph, of Directive 81/851/EEC shall be submitted in accordance with the following requirements.

1. Qualitative particulars

"Qualitative particulars" of all the constituents of the medicinal product shall mean the designation or description of:

- the active ingredient(s),
- the constituent(s) of the excipients, whatever their nature or the quantity used, including colouring matter, preservatives, adjuvants, stabilizers, thickeners, emulsifiers, flavouring and aromatic substances, etc,
- the constituents, intended to be ingested or otherwise administered to animals, of the outer covering of the medicinal products - capsules, gelatine capsules, etc.

These particulars shall be supplemented by any relevant data concerning the container and, where appropriate, its manner of closure, together with details of devices with which the medicinal product will be used or administered and which will be delivered with the product.

2. The "usual terminology", to be used in describing the constituents of medicinal products, shall mean, notwithstanding the application of the other provisions of point 3 of Article 5, second paragraph, of Directive 81/851/EEC:

- in respect of substances which appear in the European Pharmacopoeia or, failing this, in the national pharmacopoeia of one of the Member States, the main title at the head of the monograph in question, with reference to the pharmacopoeia concerned,
- in respect of other substances, the international non-proprietary name recommended by the World Health Organization (WHO), which may be accompanied by another non-proprietary name, or, failing these, the exact scientific designation; substances not having an international non-proprietary name or an exact scientific designation shall be described by a statement of how and from what they were prepared, supplemented, where appropriate, by any other relevant details,
- in respect of colouring matter, designation by the "E" code assigned to them in Council Directive 78/25/EEC of 12 December 1977 on the approximation of the rules of the Member States concerning the colouring matters authorized for use in medicinal products (3).

3. Quantitative particulars

3.1. In order to give "quantitative particulars" of the active ingredients of the medicinal products, it is necessary, depending on the pharmaceutical form concerned, to specify the mass, or the number of units of biological activity, either per dosage-unit or per unit of mass or volume, of each active ingredient.
Units of biological activity shall be used for substances which cannot be defined chemically. Where an International Unit of biological activity has been defined by the World Health Organization, this shall be used. Where no International Unit has been defined, the units of biological activity shall be expressed in such a way as to provide unambiguous information on the activity of the substances.
Whenever possible, biological activity per units of mass or volume shall be indicated.
This information shall be supplemented:

- in respect of injectable preparations, by the mass or units of biological activity of each active ingredient in the unit container, taking into account the usable volume of the product, after reconstitution, where appropriate,
- in respect of medicinal products to be administered by drops, by the mass or units of biological activity of each active ingredient contained in the number of drops corresponding to 1 ml or 1 g of the preparation,
- in respect of syrups, emulsions, granular preparations and other pharmaceutical forms to be administered in measured quantities, by the mass or units of biological activity of each active ingredient per measured quantity.

3.2. Active ingredients present in the form of compounds or derivatives shall be described quantitatively by their total mass, and if necessary or relevant, by the mass of the active entity or entities of the molecule.

3.3. For medicinal products containing an active ingredient which is the subject of an application for marketing authorization in any Member State for the first time, the quantitative statement of an active ingredient which is a salt or hydrate shall be systematically expressed in terms of the mass of the active entity or entities in the molecule. All subsequently authorized medicinal products in the Member States shall have their quantitative composition stated in the same way for the same active ingredient.

4. Development pharmaceutics

An explanation shall be provided with regard to the choice of composition, constituents and container and the intended function of the excipients in the finished product. This explanation shall be supported by scientific data on development pharmaceutics. The overage, with justification thereof, shall be stated.

B. DESCRIPTION OF METHOD OF PREPARATION

The description of the method of preparation accompanying the application for marketing authorization pursuant to point 4 of Article 5, second paragraph, of Directive 81/851/EEC, shall be drafted in such a way as to give an adequate synopsis of the nature of the operations employed.
For this purpose it shall include at least:

- mention of the various stages of manufacture, so that an assessment can be made of whether the processes employed in producing the pharmaceutical form might have produced an adverse change in the constituents,
- in the case of continuous manufacture, full details concerning precautions taken to ensure the homogeneity of the finished product,
- the actual manufacturing formula, with the quantitative particulars of all the substances used, the quantities of excipients, however, being given in approximate terms in so far as the pharmaceutical form makes this necessary; mention shall be made of any substances that may disappear in the course of manufacture; any overage shall be indicated and justified,
- a statement of the stages of manufacture at which sampling is carried out for in-process control tests, where other data in the documents supporting the application show such tests to be necessary for the quality control of the finished product,
- experimental studies validating the manufacturing process, where a non-standard method of manufacture is used or where it is critical for the product,
- for sterile products, details of the sterilization processes and/or aseptic procedures used.

C. CONTROL OF STARTING MATERIALS

1. For the purposes of this paragraph, "starting materials" shall mean all the constituents of the medicinal product and, if necessary, of its container, as referred to in paragraph A, point 1, above.
In the case of:

- an active ingredient not described in the European Pharmacopoeia or in the pharmacopoeia of a Member State,
or
- an active ingredient described in the European Pharmacopoeia or in the pharmacopoeia of a Member State when prepared by a method liable to leave impurities not mentioned in the pharmacopoeial monograph and for which the monograph is inappropriate adequately to control its quality,

which is manufactured by a person different from the applicant, the latter may arrange for the detailed description of the manufacturing method, quality control during manufacture and process validation to be supplied directly to the competent authorities by the manufacturer of the active ingredient. In this case, the manufacturer shall however provide the applicant with all the data which may be necessary for the latter to take responsibility for the medicinal product. The manufacturer shall confirm in writing to the applicant that he shall ensure batch to batch consistency and not modify the manufacturing process or specifications without informing the applicant. Documents and particulars supporting the application for such a change shall be supplied to the competent authorities.
The particulars and documents accompanying the application for marketing authorization pursuant to points 9 and 10 of Article 5, second paragraph, of Directive 81/851/EEC shall include the results of the tests, including batch analyses particularly for active ingredients, relating to quality control of all the constituents used. These shall be submitted in accordance with the following provisions.

1.1. Starting materials listed in pharmacopoeias

The monographs of the European Pharmacopoeia shall be applicable to all substances appearing in it.
In respect of other substances, each Member State may require observance of its own national pharmacopoeia with regard to products manufactured in its territory.
Constituents fulfilling the requirements of the European Pharmacopoeia or the pharmacopoeia of one of the Member States shall be deemed to comply sufficiently with point 9 of Article 5, second paragraph, of Directive 81/851/EEC. In this case the description of the analytical methods may be replaced by a detailed reference to the pharmacopoeia in question.
However, where a starting material in the European Pharmacopoeia or in the pharmacopoeia of a Member State has been prepared by a method liable to leave impurities not controlled in the pharmacopoeia monograph these impurities and their maximum tolerance limits must be declared and a suitable test procedure must be described.
Colouring matter shall, in all cases, satisfy the requirements of Council Directive 78/25/EEC.

The routine tests carried out on each batch of starting materials must be as stated in the application for marketing authorization. If tests other than those mentioned in the pharmacopoeia are used, proof must be supplied that the starting materials meet the quality requirements of that pharmacopoeia.

In cases where a specification contained in a monograph of the European Pharmacopoeia or in the national pharmacopoeia of a Member State might be insufficient to ensure the quality of the substance, the competent authorities may request more appropriate specifications from the person responsible for placing the product on the market.

The competent authorities shall inform the authorities responsible for the pharmacopoeia in question. The person responsible for placing the product on the market shall provide the authorities of that pharmacopoeia with the details of the alleged insufficiency and the additional specifications applied.

In cases where a starting material is described neither in the European Pharmacopoeia nor in the pharmacopoeia of a Member State, compliance with the monograph of a third country pharmacopoeia can be accepted; in such cases, the applicant shall submit a copy of the monograph accompanied where necessary by the validation of the test procedures contained in the monograph and by a translation where appropriate.

1.2. Starting materials not in a pharmacopoeia

Constituents which are not given in any pharmacopoeia shall be described in the form of a monograph under the following headings:

(a) the name of the substance, meeting the requirements of paragraph A point 2, shall be supplemented by any trade or scientific synonyms;

(b) the definition of the substance, set down in a form similar to that used in the European Pharmacopoeia, shall be accompanied by any necessary explanatory evidence, especially concerning the molecular structure where appropriate; it must be accompanied by an appropriate description of the method of synthesis. Where substances can only be described by their method of preparation, the description shall be sufficiently detailed to characterize a substance which is constant both on its composition and in its effects;

(c) methods of identification may be described in the form of complete techniques as used for production of the substance, and in the form of tests which ought to be carried out as a routine matter;

(d) purity tests shall be described in relation to the sum total of predictable impurities, especially those which may have a harmful effect, and, if necessary, those which, having regard to the combination of substances to which the application refers, might adversely affect the stability of the medicinal product or distort analytical results;

(e) with regard to complex substances of plant or animal origin, a distinction must be made between the case where multiple pharmacological effects render chemical, physical or biological control of the principal constituents necessary, and the case of substances containing one or more groups of principles having similar activity, in respect of which an overall method of assay may be accepted;

(f) when materials of animal origin are used, measures to ensure freedom from potentially pathogenic agents shall be described;

(g) any special precautions that may be necessary during storage of the starting material and, if necessary, the maximum period of storage before retesting shall be given.

1.3. Physico-chemical characteristics liable to affect bioavailability

The following items of information concerning active ingredients, whether or not listed in the pharmacopoeias, shall be provided as part of the general description of the active ingredients if the bio-availability of the medicinal product depends on them:

- crystalline form and solubility coefficients,
- particle size, where appropriate after pulverization,
- state of solvation,
- oil/water coefficient of partition (4).

The first three indents are not applicable to substances used solely in solution.

2. Where source materials such as micro-organisms, tissues of either plant or animal origin, cells or fluids (including blood) of human or animal origin or biotechnological cell constructs are used in the manufacture of veterinary medicinal products, the origin and history of starting materials shall be described and documented. The description of the starting material shall include the manufacturing strategy, purification/inactivation procedures with their validation and all in-process control procedures designed to ensure the quality, safety and batch to batch consistency of the finished product.

2.1. When cell banks are used, the cell characteristics shall be shown to have remained unchanged at the passage level used for the production and beyond.

2.2. Seed materials, cell banks, pools of serum and other materials of biological origin and, whenever possible, the source materials from which they are derived shall be tested for adventitious agents.

If the presence of potentially pathogenic adventitious agents is inevitable, the material shall be used only when further processing ensures their elimination and/or inactivation, and this shall be validated.

D. CONTROL TESTS CARRIED OUT AT INTERMEDIATE STAGES OF THE MANUFACTURING PROCESS

The particulars and documents accompanying an application for marketing authorization, pursuant to points 9 and 10 of Article 5, second paragraph, of Directive 81/851/EEC, shall include particulars relating to the product control tests that may be carried out at an intermediate stage of the manufacturing process, with a view to ensuring the consistency of the technical characteristics and the production process.

These tests are essential for checking the conformity of the medicinal product with the formula when, exceptionally, an applicant proposes an analytical method for testing the finished product which does not include the assay of all the active ingredients (or of all the excipient constituents subject to the same requirements as the active ingredients).

The same applies where the quality control of the finished product depends on in-process control tests, particularly if the substance is essentially defined by its method of preparation.

E. CONTROL TESTS ON THE FINISHED PRODUCT

1. For the control of the finished product, a batch of a finished product comprises all the units of a pharmaceutical form which are made from the same initial quantity of material and have undergone the same series of manufacturing and/or sterilization operations or, in the case of a continuous production process, all the units manufactured in a given period of time.

The application for marketing authorization shall list those tests which are carried out routinely on each batch of finished product. The frequency of the tests which are not carried out routinely shall be stated. Release limits shall be indicated.

The particulars and documents accompanying the application for marketing authorization pursuant to points 9 and 10 of Article 5, second paragraph, of Directive 81/851/EEC, shall include particulars relating to control tests on the finished product at release. They shall be submitted in accordance with the following requirements.

The provisions of the general monographs of the European Pharmacopoeia, or failing that, of a Member State, shall be applicable to all products defined therein.

If test procedures and limits other than those mentioned in the general monographs of the European Pharmacopoeia, or failing this, in the national pharmacopoeia of a Member State, are used, proof shall be supplied that the finished product would, if tested in accordance with those monographs, meet the quality requirements of that pharmacopoeia for the pharmaceutical form concerned.

1.1. General characteristics of the finished product

Certain tests of the general characteristics of a product shall always be included among the tests on the finished product. These tests shall, wherever applicable, relate to the control of average masses and maximum deviations, to mechanical, physical or microbiological tests, organoleptic characteristics, physical characteristics such as density, pH, refractive index, etc. For each of these characteristics, standards and tolerance limits shall be specified by the applicant in each particular case.

The conditions of the tests, where appropriate, the equipment/apparatus employed and the standards shall be described in precise details whenever they are not given in the European Pharmacopoeia or the pharmacopoeia of the Member States; the same shall apply in cases where the methods prescribed by such pharmacopoeias are not applicable.

Furthermore, solid pharmaceutical forms having to be administered orally shall be subjected to in vitro studies on the liberation and dissolution rate of the active ingredient or ingredients; these studies shall also be carried out where administration is by another means if the competent authorities of the Member State concerned consider this necessary.

1.2. Identification and assay of active ingredient(s)

Identification and assay of the active ingredient(s) shall be carried out either in a representative sample from the production batch or in a number of dosage-units analysed individually.

Unless there is appropriate justification, the maximum acceptable deviation in the active-ingredient content of the finished product shall not exceed ± 5% at the time of manufacture.

On the basis of the stability tests, the manufacturer must propose and justify maximum acceptable tolerance limits in the active-ingredient content of the finished product up to the end of the proposed shelf-life.

In certain exceptional cases of particularly complex mixtures, where assay of active ingredients which are very numerous or present in very low amounts would necessitate an intricate investigation difficult to carry out in respect of each production batch, the assay of one or more active ingredients in the finished product may be omitted, on the express condition that such assays are made at intermediate stages in the production process. This relaxation may not be extended to the characterization of the substances concerned. This simplified technique shall be supplemented by a method of quantitative evaluation, enabling the competent authority to have the conformity of the medicinal product with its specification verified after it has been placed on the market.

An in vivo or in vitro biological assay shall be obligatory when physico-chemical methods cannot provide adequate information on the quality of the product. Such an assay shall, whenever possible, include reference materials and statistical analysis allowing calculation of confidence limits. Where these tests cannot be carried out on the finished product, they may be performed at an intermediate stage, as late as possible in the manufacturing process.

Where the particulars given in section B show that a significant overage of an active ingredient is employed in the manufacture of the medicinal product, the description of the control tests on the finished product shall include, where appropriate, the chemical and, if necessary, the toxico-pharmacological investigation of the changes that this substance has undergone, and possibly the characterization and/or assay of the degradation products.

1.3. Identification and assay of excipient constituents

In so far as is necessary, the excipient(s) shall be subject at least to identification tests.

The test procedure proposed for identifying colouring matters must enable a verification to be made that such matters appear in the list annexed to Directive 78/25/EEC.

An upper and lower limit test shall be obligatory in respect of preserving agents and an upper limit test for any other excipient constituent liable to affect adversely physiological functions; an upper and lower limit test shall be obligatory in respect of the excipient if it is liable to affect the bio-availability of an active substance, unless bio-availability is guaranteed by other appropriate tests.

1.4. Safety tests

Apart from the toxico-pharmacological tests submitted with the application for marketing authorization, particulars of safety tests, such as sterility, bacterial endotoxin, pyrogenicity and local tolerance in animals shall be included in the analytical particulars wherever such tests must be undertaken as a matter of routine in order to verify the quality of the product.

F. STABILITY TEST

The particulars and documents accompanying the application for marketing authorization pursuant to points 6 and 9 of Article 5, second paragraph, of Directive 81/851/EEC shall be submitted in accordance with the following requirements.

A description shall be given of the investigations by which the shelf life, the recommended storage conditions and the specifications at the end of the shelf life proposed by the applicant have been determined.

In the case of pre-mixes for medicated feedingstuffs, information shall also be given as necessary on the shelf life of the medicated feedingstuffs manufactured from these pre-mixes in accordance with the recommended instructions for use.

Where a finished product requires reconstitution prior to administration, details of the proposed shelf life for the reconstituted product are required, supported by relevant stability data.

In the case of multi-dose vials, stability data shall be presented to justify a shelf life for the vial after it has been punctured for the first time.

Where a finished product is liable to give rise to degradation products, the applicant must declare these and indicate characterization methods and test procedures.

The conclusions shall contain the results of analyses, justifying the proposed shelf life under the recommended storage conditions and the specifications of the finished product at the end of the shelf life of the finished product under these recommended storage conditions.

The maximum acceptable level of degradation products at the end of shelf life shall be indicated.

A study of the interaction between product and container shall be submitted wherever the risk of such interaction is regarded as possible, especially where injectable preparations or aerosols for internal use are concerned.

PART 3

SAFETY AND RESIDUES TESTING

The particulars and documents which shall accompany the application for marketing authorization pursuant to point 10 of the second paragraph of Article 5 of Directive 81/851/EEC shall be submitted in accordance with the requirements below.

Member States shall ensure that the tests are carried out in accordance with the provisions relating to good laboratory practice laid down by Council Directives 87/18/EEC (5) and 88/320/EEC (6).

A. Safety testing

CHAPTER I

PERFORMANCE OF TESTS

1. Introduction

The safety documentation shall show:

1. the potential toxicity of the medicinal product and any dangerous or undesirable effects which may occur under the proposed conditions of use in animals; these should be evaluated in relation to the severity of the pathological condition concerned;

2. the potential harmful effects to man of residues of the veterinary medicinal product or substance in foodstuffs obtained from treated animals and what difficulties these residues may create in the industrial processing of foodstuffs;

3. the potential risks which may result from the exposure of human beings to the medicinal product, for example during its administration to the animal;

4. the potential risks for the environment resulting from the use of the medicinal product.

All results shall be reliable and valid generally. Whenever appropriate, mathematical and statistical procedures shall be used in designing the experimental methods and in evaluating the results. Additionally, clinicians shall be given information about the therapeutic potential of the product and about the hazards connected with its use.

In some cases it may be necessary to test the metabolites of the parent compound where these represent the residues of concern.

An excipient used in the pharmaceutical field for the first time shall be treated like an active ingredient.

2. Pharmacology

Pharmacological studies are of fundamental importance in clarifying the mechanisms by which the medicinal product produces its therapeutic effects and therefore pharmacological studies conducted in experimental and target species of animal should be included in Part 4.

However, pharmacological studies may also assist in the understanding of toxicological phenomena. Moreover, where a medicinal product produces pharmacological effects in the absence of a toxic response, or at doses lower than those required to elicit toxicity, these pharmacological effects shall be taken into account during the evaluation of the safety of the product.

Therefore the safety documentation shall always be preceded by details of pharmacological investigations undertaken in laboratory animals and all relevant information observed during clinical studies in the target animal.

3. Toxicology

3.1. Single-dose toxicity

Single-dose toxicity studies can be used to predict:

- the possible effects of acute overdosage in the target species,
- the possible effects of accidental administration to humans,
- the doses which may usefully be employed in the repeat dose studies.

Single dose toxicity studies should reveal the acute toxic effects of the substance and the time course for their onset and remission.

These studies should normally be carried out in at least two mammalian species. One mammalian species may be replaced, if appropriate, by an animal species for which the medicinal product is intended. At least two different routes of administration should normally be studied. One of these may be the same as, or similar to, that proposed for the target species. If substantial exposure of the user of the medicinal product is anticipated, for example by inhalation or dermal contact, these routes should be studied.

In order to reduce the number and suffering of the animals involved, new protocols for single dose toxicity testing are continually being developed. Studies carried out in accordance with these new procedures when properly validated will be accepted, as well as studies carried out in accordance with established internationally recognized guidelines.

3.2. Repeated-dose toxicity

Repeated-dose toxicity tests are intended to reveal any physiological and/or pathological changes induced by repeated administration of the active substance or combination of active substances under examination, and to determine how these changes are related to dosage.

In the case of substances or medicinal products intended solely for use in animals which do not produce food for human consumption, a repeated dose toxicity study in one species of experimental animal will normally be sufficient. This study may be replaced by a study conducted in the target animal. The frequency and route of administration, and the duration of the study should be chosen having regard to the proposed conditions of clinical use. The investigator shall give his reasons for the extent and duration of the trials and the dosages chosen.

In the case of substances or medicinal products intended for use in food producing animals, the study should be conducted in at least two species, one of which should be a non-rodent. The investigator shall give his reasons for the choice of species, having regard to the available knowledge of the metabolism of the product in animals and man. The test substance shall be administered orally. The duration of the test shall be at least 90 days. The investigator shall clearly state and give his reasons for the method and frequency of administration and the length of the trials.

The maximum dose should normally be selected so as to bring harmful effects to light. The lowest dose level should not produce any evidence of toxicity.

Evaluation of the toxic effects shall be based on observation of behaviour, growth, haematology and physiological tests, especially those relating to the excretory organs, and also on autopsy reports and accompanying histological data. The choice and range of each group of tests depends on the species of animal used and the state of scientific knowledge at the time.

In the case of new combinations of known substances which have been investigated in accordance with the provisions of this Directive, the repeated-dose tests may, except where toxicity tests have demonstrated potentiation or novel toxic effects, be suitably modified by the investigator, who shall submit his reasons for such modifications.

3.3. Tolerance in the target species

Details should be provided of any signs of intolerance which have been observed during studies conducted in the target species in accordance with the requirements of Part 4, Chapter I, Section B. The studies concerned, the dosages at which the intolerance occurred and the species and breeds concerned should be identified. Details of any unexpected physiological changes should also be provided.

3.4. Reproductive toxicity including teratogenicity

3.4.1. Study of the effects on reproduction

The purpose of this study is to identify possible impairment of male or female reproductive function or harmful effects on progeny resulting from the administration of the medicinal products or substance under investigation.

In the case of substances or medicinal products intended for use in food-producing animals, the study of the effects on reproduction shall be carried out in the form of a two-generation study on at least one species, usually a rodent. The substance or product under investigation shall be administered to males and females at an appropriate time prior to mating. Administration should continue until the weaning of the F2 generation. At least three dose levels shall be used. The maximum dose should be selected so as to bring harmful effects to light. The lowest dose level should not produce any evidence of toxicity.

Evaluation of the effects on reproduction shall be based upon fertility, pregnancy and maternal behaviour; the suckling, growth and development of the F1 offspring from conception to maturity; the development of the F2 offspring to weaning.

3.4.2. Study of embryotoxic/fetotoxic effects including teratogenecity

In the case of substances or medicinal products intended for use in food producing animals, studies of embryotoxic/fetotoxic effects, including teratogenicity, shall be carried out. These studies shall be carried out in at least two mammalian species, usually a rodent and the rabbit. The details of the test (number of animals, doses, time at which administered and criteria for the evaluation of results) shall depend on the state of scientific knowledge at the time the application is lodged and the level of statistical significance which the results should attain. The rodent study may be combined with the study of effects on reproductive function.

In the case of substances or medicinal products which are not intended for use in food producing animals, a study of embryotoxic/fetotoxic effects, including teratogenicity, shall be required in at least one species, which may be the target species, if the product is intended for use in animals which might be used for breeding.

3.5. Mutagenicity

Mutagenicity tests are intended to assess the potential of substances to cause transmissible changes in the genetic material of cells.

Any new substance intended for use in veterinary medicinal products must be assessed for mutagenic properties.

The number and types of tests and the criteria for the evaluation of the results shall depend on the state of scientific knowledge when the application is submitted.

3.6. Carcinogenicity

Long term animal carcinogenicity studies will usually be required for substances to which human beings will be exposed

- which have a close chemical analogy with known carcinogens,
- which during mutagenicity testing produced results indicating a possibility of carcinogenic effects,
- which have given rise to suspect signs during toxicity testing.

The state of scientific knowledge at the time the application is submitted shall be taken into account when designing carcinogenicity studies and evaluating their results.

3.7. Exceptions

Where a medicinal product is intended for topical use, systemic absorption shall be investigated in the target species of animal. If it is proved that systemic absorption is negligible, the repeated dose toxicity tests, the tests for reproductive toxicity and the carcinogenicity tests may be omitted, unless:

- under the conditions of use laid down, oral ingestion of the medicinal product by the animal is to be expected, or
- the medicinal particular may enter foodstuffs obtained from the treated animal (intramammary preparations).

4. Other requirements

4.1. Immunotoxicity

Where the effects observed during repeated dose studies in animals include specific changes in lymphoid organ weights and/or histology and changes in the cellularity of lymphoid tissues, bone marrow or peripheral leukocytes, the investigator shall consider the need for additional studies of the effects of the product on the immune system.

The state of scientific knowledge at the time the application is submitted shall be taken into account when designing such studies and evaluating their results.

4.2. Microbiological properties of residues

4.2.1. Potential effects on the human gut flora

The microbiological risk presented by residues of anti-microbial compounds for the human intestinal flora shall be investigated in accordance with the state of scientific knowledge at the time the application is submitted.

4.2.2. Potential effects on the microorganisms used for industrial food processing

In certain cases, it may be necessary to carry out tests to determine whether residues cause difficulties affecting technological processes in industrial foodstuff processing.

4.3. Observations in humans

Information shall be provided showing whether the constituents of the veterinary medicinal product are used as medicinal products in human therapy; if this is so, a report should be made on all the effects observed (including side-effects) in humans and on their cause, to the extent that they may be important for the assessment of the veterinary medicinal product, where appropriate in the light of trial results of bibliographical documents; where constituents of the veterinary medicinal products are themselves not used or are no longer used as medicinal products in human therapy, the reasons should be stated.

5. Ecotoxicity

5.1. The purpose of the study of the ecotoxicity of a veterinary medicinal product is to assess the potential harmful effects which the use of the product may cause to the environment and to identify any precautionary measures which may be necessary to reduce such risks.

5.2. An assessment of ecotoxicity shall be compulsory for any application for marketing authorization for a veterinary medicinal product other than applications submitted in accordance with point 10 of Article 5, second paragraph, of Directive 81/851/EEC.

5.3. This assessment shall normally be conducted in two phases.

In the first phase, the investigator shall assess the potential extent of exposure to the environment of the product, its active ingredients or relevant metabolites, taking into account:

- the target species, and the proposed pattern of use (for example, mass-medication or individual animal medication),
- the method of administration, in particular the likely extent to which the product will enter directly into environmental systems,
- the possible excretion of the product, its active ingredients or relevant metabolites into the environment by treated animals; persistence in such excretia,
- the disposal of unused or waste product.

5.4. In a second phase, having regard to the extent of exposure of the product to the environment, and the available information about the physical/chemical, pharmacological and/or toxicological properties of the compound which has been obtained during the conduct of the other tests and trials required by this Directive, the investigator shall then consider whether further specific investigation of the effects of the product on particular eco-systems is necessary.

5.5. As appropriate, further investigation may be required of:

- fate and behaviour in soil,
- fate and behaviour in water and air,
- effects on aquatic organisms,
- effects on other non-target organisms.

These further investigations shall be carried out in accordance with the test protocols laid down in Annex V of Directive 67/548/EEC (7), as last amended by Commission Directive 91/632/EEC (8), or where an end point is not adequately covered by these protocols, in accordance with other internationally recognized protocols on the veterinary medicinal product and/or the active substance(s) and/or the excreted metabolites as appropriate. The number and types of tests and the criteria for their evaluation shall depend upon the state of scientific knowledge at the time the application is submitted.

CHAPTER II

PRESENTATION OF PARTICULARS AND DOCUMENTS

As in any scientific work, the dossier of safety tests shall include the following:

(a) an introduction defining the subject, accompanied by any useful bibliographical references;

(b) the detailed identification of the substance under review, including:

- international non-proprietary name (INN),
- International Union of Pure and Applied Chemistry Name (IUPAC),
- Chemical Abstract Service (CAS) number,
- therapeutical and pharmacological classification,
- synonyms and abbreviations,
- structural formula,
- molecular formula,
- molecular weight,
- degree of impurity,
- qualitative and quantitative composition of impurities,
- description of physical properties,
- melting point,
- boiling point,
- vapour pressure,
- solubility in water and organic solvents expressed in g/l, with indication of temperature,
- density,
- spectra of refraction, rotation, etc;

(c) a detailed experimental protocol giving the reasons for any omission of certain tests listed above, a description of the methods, apparatus and materials used, details of the species, breed or strain of animals, where they were obtained, their number and the conditions under which they were housed and fed, stating inter alia whether they were free from specific pathogens (SPF);

(d) all the results obtained, whether favourable or unfavourable. The original data should be described in sufficient detail to allow the results to be critically evaluated independently of their interpretation by the author. By way of explanation, the results may be accompanied by illustrations;

(e) a statistical analysis of the results, where such is called for by the test programme, and variance within the data;

(f) an objective discussion of the results obtained, leading to conclusions on the safety of the substance, on its safety margin in the test animal and the target animal and its possible side-effects, on its fields of application, on its active dose levels and any possible incompatibilities;

(g) a detailed description and a thorough discussion of the results of the study of the safety of residues in food, and its relevance for the evaluation of potential risks presented by residues to humans. This discussion shall be followed by proposals to ensure that any danger to man is eliminated by applying internationally recognized assessment criteria, for example: no observed effect level in animals, proposals for a choice of safety factor and for acceptable daily intake (ADI);

(h) a thorough discussion of any risks for persons preparing the medicinal product or administering it to animals, followed by proposals for appropriate measures to reduce such risks;

(i) a thorough discussion of the risks which use of the veterinary medicinal product under the practical conditions proposed may represent for the environment followed by appropriate proposals to reduce such risks;

(j) all information necessary to acquaint the clinician as fully as possible with the utility of the proposed product. The discussion will be supplemented by suggestions as to side-effects and possible treatment for acute toxic reactions in animals to which the product is to be administered;

(k) a concluding expert report which provides a detailed critical analysis of the information referred to above in the light of the state of scientific knowledge at the time the application is submitted together with a detailed summary of all the results of the relevant safety tests and precise bibliographical references.

B. Residue testing

CHAPTER I

PERFORMANCE OF TESTS

1. Introduction

For the purposes of this Directive, "residues" means all active ingredients or metabolites thereof which remain in meat or other foodstuffs produced from the animal to which the medicinal product in question has been administered.
The purpose of studying residues is to determine whether, and if so under what conditions and to what extent, residues persist in foodstuffs produced from treated animals and to ascertain the withdrawal periods to be adhered to in order to obviate any hazard to human health and/or difficulties in the industrial processing of foodstuffs.
Assessment of the hazard due to residues entails establishing whether residues are present in the animals treated under recommended conditions of use and investigating the effects of those residues.
In the case of veterinary medicinal products intended for use in food-producing animals, the residue documentation shall show:

1. to what extent, and how long, do residues of the veterinary medicinal product or its metabolites persist in the tissues of the treated animal or foodstuffs obtained therefrom;

2. that in order to prevent any risk to the health of the consumer of foodstuffs of treated animals, or difficulties in the industrial processing of foodstuffs, it is possible to establish realistic withdrawal periods which can be observed under practical farming conditions;

3. that practical analytical methods suitable for routine use are available to verify compliance with the withdrawal period.

2. Metabolism and residue kinetics

2.1. Pharmacokinetics (absorption, distribution, biotransformation, excretion)

The purpose of pharmacokinetic studies with respect to residues of veterinary medicinal products is to evaluate the absorption, distribution, biotransformation and excretion of the product in the target species.
The final product, or a formulation which is bioequivalent, shall be administered to the target species at the maximum recommended dose.
Having regard to the method of administration, the extent of absorption of the medicinal product shall be fully described. If it is demonstrated that systemic absorption of products for topical application is negligible, further residue studies will not be required.
The distribution of the medicinal product in the target animal shall be described; the possibility of plasma protein binding, or passage into milk or eggs and of the accumulation of lipophilic compounds shall be considered.
The pathways for the excretion of the product from the target animal shall be described. The major metabolites shall be identified and characterized.

2.2. Depletion of residues

The purposes of these studies, which measure the rate at which residues deplete in the target animal after the last administration of the medicinal product, is to permit the determination of withdrawal periods.

At varying times after the test animal has received the final dose of the medicinal product, the quantities of residues present shall be determined by appropriate physical, chemical or biological methods; the technical procedures and the reliability and sensitivity of the methods employed shall be specified.

3. Routine analytical method for the detection of residues

Analytical procedures shall be proposed which can be carried out in the course of a routine examination and which have a level of sensitivity such as to enable violations of legally permitted maximum residue limits to be detected with certainty.

The analytical method proposed shall be described in detail. It shall be validated and shall be sufficiently rugged for use under normal conditions of routine monitoring for residues.

The following characteristics shall be described:

- specificity,
- accuracy, including sensitivity,
- precision,
- limit of detection,
- limit of quantitation,
- practicability and applicability under normal laboratory conditions,
- susceptibility to interference.

The suitability of the analytical method proposed shall be evaluated in the light of the state of scientific and technical knowledge at the time the application is submitted.

CHAPTER II

PRESENTATION OF PARTICULARS AND DOCUMENTS

As in any scientific work, the dossier of residue tests shall include the following:

(a) an introduction defining the subject, accompanied by any useful bibliographical references;

(b) a detailed identification of the product, including:

- composition,
- purity,
- batch identification,
- relationship to the final product,
- specific activity and radio-purity of labelled substances,
- position of labelled atoms in the molecule;

(c) a detailed experimental protocol giving the reasons for any omission of certain tests listed above, a description of the methods, apparatus and materials used, details of the species, breed or strain of animals, where they were obtained, their number and the conditions under which they were housed and fed;

(d) all the results obtained, whether favourable or unfavourable. The original data should be described in sufficient detail to allow the results to be critically evaluated independently of their interpretation by the author. The results may be accompanied by illustrations;

(e) a statistical analysis of the results, where such is called for by the test programme, and variance within the data;

(f) an objective discussion of the results obtained, followed by proposals for maximum residue limits for the active substances contained in the product, specifying the marker residue and target tissues concerned, and proposals concerning the withdrawal periods necessary to ensure that no residues which might constitute a hazard for consumers are present in foodstuffs obtained from treated animals;

(g) a concluding expert report which provides a detailed critical analysis of the information referred to above in the light of the state of scientific knowledge at the time the application is submitted together with a detailed summary of the results of the residue tests and precise bibliographical references.

PART 4

PRE-CLINICAL AND CLINICAL TESTING

The particulars and documents which shall accompany applications for marketing authorizations pursuant to point 10 of the second paragraph of Article 5 of Directive 81/851/EEC shall be submitted in accordance with the provisions of Chapters I, II and III below.

CHAPTER I

PRE-CLINICAL REQUIREMENTS

Pre-clinical studies are required to establish the pharmacological activity and the tolerance of the product.

A. Pharmacology

A.1. PHARMACODYNAMICS

The study of pharmacodynamics shall follow two distinct lines of approach:
First, the mechanism of action and the pharmacological effects on which the recommended application in practice is based shall be adequately described. The results shall be expressed in quantitative terms (using, for example, dose-effect curves, time-effect curves, etc.) and, wherever possible, in comparison with a substance the activity of which is well known. Where a higher efficacy is being claimed for an active ingredient, the difference shall be demonstrated and shown to be statistically significant.
Secondly, the investigator shall give an overall pharmacological assessment of the active ingredient, with special reference to the possibility of side-effects. In general, the main functions shall be investigated.
The investigator shall identify the effect of the route of administration, formulation, etc, on the pharmacological activity of the active ingredient.
The investigations shall be intensified where the recommended dose approaches that liable to produce effects.
The experimental techniques, unless they are standard procedures, shall be described in such detail as to allow them to be reproduced, and the investigator shall establish their validity. The experimental results shall be set out clearly and, for certain types of tests, their statistical significance quoted.
Unless good reasons are given to the contrary, any quantitative modification of responses resulting from repeated administration of the substance shall also be investigated.
Medicinal combinations may be prompted either on pharmacological grounds or by clinical indications. In the first case, the pharmacodynamic and/or pharmacokinetic studies shall demonstrate those interactions which might make the combination itself of value in clinical use. In the second case, where scientific justification for the medicinal combination is sought through clinical experimentation, the investigation shall determine whether the effects expected from the combination can be demonstrated in animals and, at least, the importance of any side-effects shall be checked. If a combination includes a novel active substance, the latter shall have been previously studied in depth.

A.2. Pharmacokinetics

Basic pharmacokinetic information concerning a new active substance is generally useful in the clinical context. Pharmacokinetic objectives can be divided into two main areas:

(i) descriptive pharmacokinetics leading to the evaluation of basic parameters such as body clearance, volume(s) of distribution, mean residence time, etc;

(ii) use of these parameters to investigate the relationships between dosage regimen, plasma and tissue concentration and pharmacologic, therapeutic or toxic effects.

In target species, pharmacokinetic studies are, as a rule, necessary in order to employ drugs with the greatest possible efficacy and safety. Such studies are especially useful to assist the clinician in establishing dosage regimens (route and site of administration, dose, dosing interval, number of administrations, etc.) and to adopt dosage regimens according to certain population variables (e.g. age, disease). Such studies can be more efficient in number of animals and generally provide more information than classical dose titration studies.

In the case of new combinations of known substances which have been investigated in accordance with the provisions of this Directive, pharmacokinetic studies of the fixed combination are not required if it can be justified that the administration of the active ingredients as a fixed combination does not change their pharmacokinetic properties.

A.2.1. Bioavailability/bioequivalence

Appropriate bioavailability studies shall be undertaken to establish bioequivalence:

- when comparing a reformulated product with the existing one,
- when comparing a new method or route of administration with an established one,
- in all cases referred to in Article 5 second paragraph point 10 (i), (ii), and (iii) of Directive 81/851/EEC.

B. Tolerance in the target species of animal

The purpose of this study, which shall be carried out with all animal species for which the medicinal product is intended, is to carry out in all such animal species local and general tolerance trials designed to establish a tolerated dosage wide enough to allow an adequate safety margin and the clinical symptoms of intolerance using the recommended route or routes, in so far as this may be achieved by increasing the therapeutic dose and/or the duration of treatment. The report on the trials shall contain as many details as possible of the expected pharmacological effects and the adverse side-effects; the latter shall be assessed with due regard to the fact that the animals used may be of very high value.

The medicinal product shall be administered at least via the recommended route of administration.

C. Resistance

Data on the emergence of resistant organisms are necessary in the case of medicinal products used for the prevention or treatment of infectious diseases or parasitic infestations in animals.

CHAPTER II

CLINICAL REQUIREMENTS

1. General principles

The purposes of clinical trials are to demonstrate or substantiate the effect of the veterinary medicinal product after administration of the recommended dosage, to specify its indications and contra-indications according to species, age, breed and sex, its directions for use, any side-effects which it may have and its safety and tolerance under normal conditions of use.

Unless justified, clinical trials shall be carried out with control animals (controlled clinical trials). The effect obtained should be compared with a placebo or with absence of treatment and/or with the effect of an authorized medicinal product known to be of therapeutic value. All the results obtained, whether positive or negative, shall be reported.

The methods used to make the diagnosis shall be specified. The results shall be set out by making use of quantitative or conventional clinical criteria. Adequate statistical methods shall be used and justified.

In the case of a veterinary medicinal product intended primarily for use as a performance enhancer, particular attention shall be given to:

- the yield of animal produce,
- the quality of animal produce (organoleptic, nutritional, hygienic and technological qualities)
- nutritional efficiency and growth of animal,
- the general status of health of the animal.

Experimental data shall be confirmed by data obtained under practical field conditions.

Where, in respect of particular therapeutic indications, the applicant can show that he is unable to provide comprehensive data on therapeutic effect because:

(a) the indications for which the medicinal product in question is intended are encountered so rarely that the applicant cannot reasonably be expected to provide comprehensive evidence;

(b) in the present state of scientific knowledge, comprehensive information cannot be provided;

the marketing authorization may only be granted subject to the following conditions;

(a) the medicinal product in question is to be supplied on veterinary prescription only and may, in certain cases, be administered only under strict veterinary supervision;

(b) the package insert and any other information must draw the attention of the veterinary practitioner to the fact that, in certain specified respects, the particulars available concerning the medicinal product in question are as yet incomplete.

2. Performance of trials

All veterinary clinical trials shall be conducted in accordance with a fully considered detailed trial protocol which shall be recorded in writing prior to commencement of the trial. The welfare of the trial animals shall be subject to veterinary supervision and shall be taken fully into consideration during the elaboration of any trial protocol and throughout the conduct of the trial.

Pre-established systematic written procedures for the organization, conduct, data collection, documentation and verification of clinical trials shall be required.

Before the commencement of any trial, the informed consent of the owner of the animals to be used in the trial shall be obtained and documented. In particular, the animal owner shall be informed in writing of the consequences of participation in the trial for the subsequent disposal of treated animals or for the taking of foodstuffs from treated animals. A copy of this notification, countersigned and dated by the animal owner, shall be included in the trial documentation.

Unless the trial is conducted with a blind design, the provisions of Articles 43 to 47 of Directive 81/851/EEC concerning the labelling of veterinary medicinal products shall apply by analogy to the labelling of formulations intended for use in veterinary clinical trials. In all cases, the words "for veterinary clinical trial use only" shall appear prominently and indelibly upon the labelling.

CHAPTER III

PARTICULARS AND DOCUMENTS

As in any scientific work, the dossier on efficacy shall include an introduction defining the subject accompanied by any useful bibliographical documentation.

All pre-clinical and clinical documentation must be sufficiently detailed to enable an objective judgement to be made. All studies and trials must be reported, whether favourable or unfavourable to the applicant.

1. Records of pre-clinical observations

Wherever possible, particulars shall be given of the results of:

(a) tests demonstrating pharmacological actions;

(b) tests demonstrating the pharmacological mechanisms underlying the therapeutic effect;

(c) tests demonstrating the main pharmacokinetic processes.

Should unexpected results occur during the course of the tests, these should be detailed.
Additionally the following particulars shall be provided in all pre-clinical studies:

(a) a summary;

(b) a detailed experimental protocol giving a description of the methods, apparatus and materials used, details such as species, age, weight, sex, number, breed or strain of animals, identification of animals, dose, route and schedule of administration;

(c) a statistical analysis of the results where relevant;

(d) an objective discussion of the results obtained, leading to conclusions on the safety and efficacy of the product.

Total or partial omission of these data must be explained.

2.1. Records of clinical observations

All the particulars shall be supplied by each of the investigators on individual record-sheets in the case of individual treatment and collective record-sheets in the case of collective treatment.
The particulars supplied shall take the following form:

(a) name, address, function and qualifications of investigator in charge;

(b) place and date of treatment; name and address of owner of the animals;

(c) details of the trial protocol giving a description of the methods used, including methods of randomization and blinding, details such as the route of administration, schedule of administration, the dose, identification of trial animals, species, breeds or strains, age, weight, sex, physiological status;

(d) method of rearing and feeding, stating the composition of the feed and the nature and quantity of any additives contained in the feed;

(e) case history (as full as possible), occurrence and course of any inter-current diseases;

(f) diagnosis and means used to make it;

(g) symptoms and severity of the disease, if possible according to conventional criteria;

(h) the precise identification of the clinical trial formulation used in the trial;

(i) dosage of the medicinal product, method, route and frequency of administration and precautions, if any, taken during administration (duration of injection, etc.);

(j) duration of treatment and period of subsequent observation;

(k) all details concerning medicinal products (other than that under study) which have been administered during the period of examination, either prior to or concurrently with the test product and, in the latter case, details of the interactions observed;

(l) all results of the clinical trials (including unfavourable or negative results) with a full statement of the clinical observations and the results of the objective tests of activity (laboratory analyses, physiological tests), required to evaluate the application; the techniques used must be specified, and the significance of any variations in the results explained (for example, variance in method, variance between individuals or the effects of the medication); demonstration of the pharmacodynamic effect in animals shall not in itself suffice to justify conclusions concerning any therapeutic effect;

(m) all particulars of any unintended effects, whether harmful or not, and of any measures taken in consequence; the cause-and-effect relationship shall be investigated if possible;

(n) effect of animals' performance (for example: egg-laying, milk production and reproductive function);

(o) effects on the quality of foodstuffs obtained from treated animals, particularly in the case of medicinal products intended for use as performance enhancers;

(p) a conclusion on each individual case or, where collective treatment is concerned, on each collective case.

Omission of one or more items (a) to (p) shall be justified.
The person responsible for placing the veterinary medicinal product on the market shall make all necessary arrangements to ensure that the original documents, which formed the basis of the data supplied, are kept for at least five years after the product is no longer authorized.

2.2. Summary and conclusions of clinical observations

In respect of each clinical trial, the clinical observations shall be summarized in a synopsis of the trials and the results thereof, indicating in particular:

(a) the number of controls, the number of animals treated either individually or collectively, with a breakdown according to species, breed or strain, age and sex;

(b) the number of animals withdrawn prematurely from the trials and the reasons for such withdrawal;

(c) in the case of control animals, whether they have:

- received no treatment;
- received a placebo,
- received another authorized medicinal product of known effect,
- received the active ingredient under investigation in a different formulation or by a different route;

(d) the frequency of observed side-effect;

(e) observations as to the effect on performance (for example, egg-laying, milk production, reproductive function and food quality);

(f) details concerning test animals which may be at increased risk owing to their age, their mode of rearing or feeding, or the purpose for which they are intended, or animals the physiological or pathological condition of which requires special consideration;

(g) a statistical evaluation of the results, when this is called for by the test programme.

Finally, the investigator shall draw general conclusions from the experimental evidence, expressing his opinion on the harmlessness of the medicinal product under the proposed conditions of use, its therapeutic effect and any useful information relating to indications and contra-indications, dosage and average duration of treatment and where appropriate, any interactions observed with other medicinal products or feed additives as well as any special precautions to be taken during treatment and the clinical symptoms of overdosage.

In the case of fixed combination products, the investigator shall also draw conclusions concerning the safety and the efficacy of the product when compared with the separate administration of the active ingredients involved.

3. Concluding expert report

The concluding expert report shall provide a detailed critical analysis of all the pre-clinical and clinical documentation in the light of the state of scientific knowledge at the time the application is submitted together with a detailed summary of the results of the tests and trials submitted and precise bibliographic references.

TITLE II

REQUIREMENTS FOR IMMUNOLOGICAL VETERINARY MEDICINAL PRODUCTS

Without prejudice to the specific requirements laid down by Community legislation for the control and eradication of animal disease, the following requirements shall apply to immunological veterinary medicinal products.

PART 5

SUMMARY OF THE DOSSIER

A. ADMINISTRATIVE DATA

The immunological veterinary medicinal product which is the subject of the application shall be identified by name and by name of the active ingredients, together with the strength and pharmaceutical form, the method and route of administration, and a description of the final sales presentation of the product.

The name and address of the applicant shall be given, together with the name and address of the manufacturer and the sites involved in the different stages of manufacture (including the manufacturer of the finished product and the manufacturer(s) of the active ingredient(s)) and where relevant the name and address of the importer.

The applicant shall identify the number and titles of volumes of documentation submitted in support of the application and indicate what samples, if any, are also provided.

Annexed to the administrative data shall be copies of a document showing that the manufacturer is authorized to produce immunological veterinary medicinal products, as defined in Article 24 of Directive 81/851/EEC (with a brief description of the production site). Moreover, the list of organisms handled at the production site shall be given.

The applicant shall submit a list of countries in which authorization has been granted, copies of all the summaries of product characteristics in accordance with Article 5a of Directive 81/851/EEC as approved by Member States and a list of countries in which an application has been submitted.

B. SUMMARY OF PRODUCT CHARACTERISTICS

The applicant shall propose a summary of the product characteristics, in accordance with Article 5a of Directive 81/851/EEC.

In addition the applicant shall provide one or more specimens or mock-ups of the sales presentation of the immunological veterinary medicinal product, together with a package insert, where one is required.

C. EXPERT REPORTS

In accordance with Article 7 of Directive 81/851/EEC, expert reports must be provided on all aspects of the documentation.

Each expert report shall consist of a critical evaluation of the various tests and/or trials, which have been carried out in accordance with this Directive, and bring out all the data relevant for evaluation. The expert shall give his opinion as to whether sufficient guarantees have been provided as to the quality, safety and efficacy of the product concerned. A factual summary is not sufficient.

All important data shall be summarised in an appendix to the expert report, whenever possible in tabular or graphic form. The expert report and the summaries shall contain precise cross references to the information contained in the main documentation.

Each expert report shall be prepared by a suitably qualified and experienced person. It shall be signed and dated by the expert, and attached to the report shall be brief information about the educational background, training and occupational experience of the expert. The professional relationship of the expert to the applicant shall be declared.

PART 6

ANALYTICAL (PHYSICO-CHEMICAL, BIOLOGICAL OR MICROBIOLOGICAL) TESTS OF IMMUNO-LOGICAL VETERINARY MEDICINAL PRODUCTS

All test procedures used shall correspond to the state of scientific progress at the time and shall be validated procedures; results of the validation studies shall be provided.

All the test procedure(s) shall be described in sufficiently precise detail so as to be reproducible in control tests, carried out at the request of the competent authority; any special apparatus and equipment which may be used shall be described in adequate detail, possibly accompanied by a diagram. The formulae of the laboratory reagents shall be supplemented, if necessary, by the method of preparation. In the case of test procedures included in the European Pharmacopoeia or the pharmacopoeia of a Member State, this description may be replaced by a detailed reference to the pharmacopoeia in question.

A. QUALITATIVE AND QUANTITATIVE PARTICULARS OF THE CONSTITUENTS

The particulars and documents which must accompany applications for marketing authorization, pursuant to point 3 of Article 5, second paragraph, of Directive 81/851/EEC shall be submitted in accordance with the following requirements.

1. Qualitative particulars

"Qualitative particulars" of all the constituents of the immunological veterinary medicinal product shall mean the designation or description of:

- the active ingredient(s),
- the constituents of the adjuvants,
- the constituent(s) of the excipients, whatever their nature or the quantity used, including preservatives, stabilizers, emulsifiers, colouring matter, flavouring, aromatic substances, markers, etc.,
- the constituents of the pharmaceutical form administered to animals.

These particulars shall be supplemented by any relevant data concerning the container and, where appropriate, its manner of closure, together with details of devices with which the immunological veterinary medicinal product will be used or administered and which will be delivered with the product.

2. The "usual terminology", to be used in describing the constituents of immunological veterinary medicinal products, shall mean, notwithstanding the application of the other provisions of point 3 of Article 5, second paragraph, of Directive 81/851/EEC:

- in respect of substances which appear in the European Pharmacopoeia or, failing this, in the national pharmacopoeia of one of the Member States, the main title of the monograph in question, which will be obligatory for all such substances, with reference to the pharmacopoeia concerned,
- in respect of other substances, the international non-proprietary name recommended by the World Health Organization, which may be accompanied by another non-proprietary name or, failing these, the exact scientific designation; substances not having an international non-proprietary name or an exact scientific designation shall be described by a statement of how and from what they were prepared, supplemented, where appropriate, by any other relevant details,
- in respect of colouring matter, designation by the "E" code assigned to them in Council Directive 78/25/EEC.

3. Quantitative particulars

In order to give the "quantitative particulars" of the active ingredients of an immunological veterinary medicinal product, it is necessary to specify whenever possible the number of organisms, the specific protein content, the mass, the number of International Units (IU) or units of biological activity, either per dosage-unit or volume, and with regard to the adjuvant and to the constituents of the excipients, the mass or the volume of each of them, with due allowance for the details provided in section B below.
Where an International Unit of biological activity has been defined, this shall be used.
The units of biological activity for which no published data exist shall be expressed in such a way as to provide unambiguous information on the activity of the ingredients, e.g. by stating the immunological effect on which the method of determining the dose is based.

4. Development pharmaceutics

An explanation shall be provided with regard to the composition, constituents and containers, supported by scientific data on development pharmaceutics. The overage, with justification thereof, shall be stated. The efficacy of any preservative system shall be demonstrated.

B. DESCRIPTION OF METHOD OF PREPARATION OF THE FINISHED PRODUCT

The description of the method of preparation accompanying the application for marketing authorization pursuant to point 4 of Article 5, second paragraph, of Directive 81/851/EEC, shall be drafted in such a way as to give an adequate description of the nature of the operations employed.
For this purpose the description shall include at least:

- the various stages of manufacture (including purification procedures) so that an assessment can be made of the reproducibility of the manufacturing procedure and of the risks of adverse effects on the finished products, such as microbiological contamination,

- in the case of continuous manufacture, full details concerning precautions taken to ensure the homogeneity and consistency of each batch of the finished product,
- mention of substances which cannot be recovered in the course of manufacture,
- the details of the blending, with the quantitative particulars of all the substances used,
- a statement of the stage of manufacture at which sampling is carried out for in-process control tests.

C. PRODUCTION AND CONTROL OF STARTING MATERIALS

For the purposes of this paragraph "starting materials" means all components used in the production of the immunological veterinary medicinal product. Culture media used for the production of the active ingredient are considered as one single starting material.
In the case of:

- an active ingredient not described in the European Pharmacopoeia or in the pharmacopoeia of a Member State,
or
- an active ingredient described in the European Pharmacopoeia or in the pharmacopoeia of a Member State when prepared by a method liable to leave impurities not mentioned in the pharmacopoeial monograph and for which the monograph is inappropriate adequately to control its quality,

which is manufactured by a person different from the applicant, the latter may arrange for the detailed description of the manufacturing method, quality control during manufacture and process validation to be supplied directly to the competent authorities by the manufacturer of the active ingredient. In this case, the manufacturer shall however provide the applicant with all the data which may be necessary for the latter to take responsibility for the medicinal product. The manufacturer shall confirm in writing to the applicant that he shall ensure batch-to-batch consistency and not modify the manufacturing process or specifications without informing the applicant. Documents and particulars supporting the application for such a change shall be supplied to the competent authorities.
The particulars and documents accompanying the application for marketing authorization pursuant to points 9 and 10 of the second paragraph of Article 5 of Directive 81/851/EEC shall include the results of the tests relating to quality control of all the components used and shall be submitted in accordance with the following provisions.

1. Starting materials listed in pharmacopoeias

The monographs of the European Pharmacopoeia shall be applicable to all substances appearing in it.
In respect of other substances, each Member State may require observance of its own national pharmacopoeia with regard to products manufactured in its territory.
Components fulfilling the requirements of the European Pharmacopoeia or the pharmacopoeia of one of the Member States shall be deemed to comply sufficiently with point 9 of the second paragraph of Article 5, second paragraph, of Directive 81/851/EEC. In this case the description of the analytical methods may be replaced by a detailed reference to the pharmacopoeia in question.
Reference to pharmacopoeias of third countries may be permitted in cases where the substance is described neither in the European Pharmacopoeia nor in the national pharmacopoeia concerned; in that case the monograph shall be submitted, accompanied where necessary by a translation for which the applicant will be responsible.
Colouring matter shall, in all cases, satisfy the requirements of Council Directive 78/25/EEC.
The routine tests carried out on each batch of starting materials must be as stated in the application for marketing authorization. If tests other than those mentioned in the pharmacopoeia are used, proof must be supplied that the starting materials meet the quality requirements of that pharmacopoeia.
In cases where a specification or other provisions contained in a monograph of the European Pharmacopoeia or in the national pharmacopoeia of a Member State might be insufficient to ensure the quality of the substance, the competent authorities may request more appropriate specifications from the person responsible for placing the product on the market.
The competent authorities shall inform the authorities responsible for the pharmacopoeia in question. The person responsible for placing the product on the market shall provide the authorities of that pharmacopoeia with the details of the alleged insufficiency and the additional specifications applied.
In cases where a starting material is described neither in the European Pharmacopoeia nor in the pharmacopoeia of a Member State, compliance with the monograph of a third country pharmacopoeia can be accepted; in such cases, the applicant shall submit a copy of the monograph accompanied where necessary by the validation of the test procedures contained in the monograph and by a translation where appropriate. For

active ingredients, demonstration of the ability of the monograph adequately to control their quality shall be presented.

2. Starting materials not in a pharmacopoeia

2.1. Starting materials of biological origin

The description shall be given in the form of a monograph.

Whenever possible, vaccine production shall be based on a seed lot system and on established cell banks. For the production of immunological veterinary medicinal products consisting of serums, the origin, general health and immunological status of the producing animals shall be indicated; defined pools of source materials shall be used.

The origin and history of starting materials shall be described and documented. For genetically engineered starting materials this information shall include details such as the description of the starting cells or strains, the construction of the expression vector (name, origin, function of the replicon, promoter enhancer and other regulator elements), control of the sequence of DNA or RNA effectively inserted, oligonucleotidic sequences of plasmid vector in cells, plasmid used for cotransfection, added or deleted genes, biological properties of the final construct and the genes expressed, copy number and genetic stability.

Seed materials, including cell banks and raw serum for anti-serum production shall be tested for identity and adventitious agents.

Information shall be provided on all substances of biological origin used at any stage in the manufacturing procedure. The information shall include:

- details of the source of the materials,
- details of any processing, purification and inactivation applied, with data on the validation of these process and in-process controls,
- details of any tests for contamination carried out on each batch of the substance.

If the presence of adventitious agents is detected or suspected, the corresponding material shall be discarded or used in very exceptional circumstances only when further processing of the product ensures their elimination and/or inactivation; elimination and/or inactivation of such adventitious agents shall be demonstrated.

When cell banks are used, the cell characteristics shall be shown to have remained unchanged up to the highest passage level used for the production.

For live attenuated vaccines, proof of the stability of the attenuation characteristics of the seed has to be given.

When required, samples of the biological starting material or reagents used in the testing procedures shall be provided to enable the competent authority to arrange for check tests to be carried out.

2.2. Starting materials of non-biological origin

The description shall be given in the form of a monograph under the following headings:

- the name of the starting material meeting the requirements of point 2 of paragraph A shall be supplemented by any trade or scientific synonyms,
- the description of the starting material, set down in a form similar to that used in a descriptive item in the European Pharmacopoeia,
- the function of the starting material,
- methods of identification,
- purity shall be described in relation to the sum total of predictable impurities, especially those which may have a harmful effect and, if necessary, those which, having regard to the combination of substances to which the application refers, may adversely affect the stability of the medicinal product or distort analytical results. A brief description shall be provided of the tests undertaken to establish the purity of each batch of the starting material,
- any special precautions which may be necessary during storage of the starting material and, if necessary, its storage life shall be given.

D. CONTROL TESTS DURING PRODUCTION

1. The particulars and documents accompanying an application for marketing authorization, pursuant to points 9 and 10 of Article 5, second paragraph, of Directive 81/851/EEC, shall include particulars relating to the control tests which are carried out on intermediate products with a view to verifying the consistency of the production process and the final product.

2. For inactivated or detoxified vaccines, inactivation or detoxification shall be tested during each production run immediately after the inactivation or detoxification process.

E. CONTROL TESTS ON THE FINISHED PRODUCT

The particulars and documents accompanying the application for marketing authorization pursuant to points 9 and 10 of Article 5, second paragraph, of Directive 81/851/EEC, shall include particulars relating to control tests on the finished product. Where appropriate monographs exist, if test procedures and limits other than those mentioned in the monographs of the European Pharmacopoeia, or failing this, in the national pharmacopoeia of a Member State, are used, proof must be supplied that the finished product would, if tested in accordance with those monographs, meet the quality requirements of that pharmacopoeia for the pharmaceutical form concerned. The application for marketing authorization shall list those tests which are carried out on representative samples of each batch of finished product. The frequency of the tests which are not carried out on each batch shall be stated. Release limits shall be indicated.

1. General characteristics of the finished product

Certain tests of the general characteristics of a product shall be included among the tests on the finished product, even if they have been carried out in the course of the manufacturing process.
These tests shall, wherever applicable, relate to the control of average masses and maximum deviations, to mechanical, physical, chemical or microbiological tests, physical characteristics such as density, pH, refractive index, etc. For each of these characteristics, specifications, with appropriate confidence limits, shall be established by the applicant in each particular case.

2. Identification and assay of active ingredient(s)

For all tests, the description of the techniques for analyzing the finished product shall be set out in sufficiently precise detail, so that they can be reproduced readily.
The assay of biological activity of the active ingredient(s) shall be carried out either in a representative sample from the production batch or in a number of dosage-units analysed individually.
Where necessary, a specific test for identification shall also be carried out.
In certain exceptional cases where assay of active ingredients which are very numerous or present in very low amounts would necessitate an intricate investigation difficult to carry out in respect of each production batch, the assay of one or more active ingredients in the finished product may be omitted, on the express condition that such assays are made at intermediate stages as late as possible in the production process. This relaxation may not be extended to the characterization of the substances concerned. This simplified technique shall be supplemented by a method of quantitative evaluation, enabling the competent authority to verify that the immunological veterinary medicinal product is in accordance with its formula after it has been placed on the market.

3. Identification and assay of adjuvants

In so far as testing procedures are available, the quantity and nature of the adjuvant and its constituents shall be verified on the finished product.

4. Identification and assay of excipient constituents

In so far as is necessary, the excipient(s) shall be subject at least to identification tests.
The test procedure proposed for identifying colouring matters must enable a verification to be made that such matters are permitted under Directive 78/25/EEC.
An upper and lower limit test shall be obligatory in respect of preserving agents; an upper limit test for any other excipient constituent liable to give rise to an adverse reaction shall be obligatory.

5. Safety tests

Apart from the results of tests submitted in accordance with Part 7 of this Annex, particulars of safety tests shall be submitted. These tests shall preferably be overdosage studies carried out in at least one of the most sensitive target species and by at least the recommended route of administration posing the greatest risk.

6. Sterility and purity test

Appropriate tests to demonstrate the absence of contamination by adventitious agents or other substances shall be carried out according to the nature of the immunological veterinary medicinal product, the method and the conditions of preparation.

7. Inactivation

Where applicable, a test to verify inactivation shall be carried out on the product in the final container.

8. Residual humidity

Each batch of lyophilized product shall be tested for residual humidity

9. Batch-to-batch consistency

In order to ensure that efficacy of the product is reproducible from batch to batch and to demonstrate conformity with specifications, potency tests based upon in vitro or in vivo methods, including appropriate reference materials whenever available, shall be carried out on each final bulk or each batch of finished product, with appropriate confidence limits; in exceptional circumstances, potency testing may be carried out at an intermediate stage, as late as possible in the production process.

F. STABILITY TESTS

The particulars and documents accompanying the application for marketing authorization pursuant to points 6 and 9 of Article 5, second paragraph, of Directive 81/851/EEC shall be submitted in accordance with the following requirements.

A description shall be given of the tests undertaken to support the shelf life proposed by the applicant. These tests shall always be real-time studies; they shall be carried out on a sufficient number of batches produced according to the described production process and on products stored in the final container(s); these tests include biological and physico-chemical stability tests.

The conclusions shall contain the results of analyses, justifying the proposed shelf-life under all proposed storage conditions.

In the case of products administered in the feed, information shall also be given as necessary on the shelf-life of the product, at the different stages of mixing, when mixed in accordance with the recommended instructions.

Where a finished product requires reconstitution prior to administration, details of the proposed shelf-life are required for the product reconstituted as recommended. Data in support of the proposed shelf-life for the reconstituted product shall be submitted.

PART 7

SAFETY TESTING

A. INTRODUCTION

1. The safety tests shall show the potential risks from the immunological veterinary medicinal product which may occur under the proposed conditions of use in animals: these shall be evaluated in relation to the potential benefits of the product.

Where immunological veterinary medicinal products consist of live organisms, especially those which could be shed by vaccinated animals, the potential risk to unvaccinated animals of the same or of any other potentially exposed species shall be evaluated.

2. The particulars and documents which shall accompany the application for marketing authorization pursuant to point 10 of the second paragraph of Article 5 of Directive 81/851/EEC shall be submitted in accordance with the requirements of section B below.

3. Member States shall ensure that the laboratory tests are carried out in conformity with the principles of good laboratory practice laid down in Council Directives 87/18/EEC and 88/320/EEC.

B. GENERAL REQUIREMENTS

1. The safety tests shall be carried out in the target species.

2. The dose to be used shall be that quantity of the product to be recommended for use and containing the maximum titre or potency for which the application is submitted.

3. The sample used for safety testing shall be taken from a batch or batches produced according to the manufacturing process described in the application for marketing authorization.

C. LABORATORY TESTS

1. Safety of the administration of one dose

The immunological veterinary medicinal product shall be administered at the recommended dose and by each recommended route of administration to animals of each species and category in which it is intended for use, including animals of the minimum age of administration. The animals shall be observed and examined for signs of systemic and local reactions. Where appropriate, these studies shall include detailed post-mortem macroscopic and microscopic examinations of the injection site. Other objective criteria shall be recorded, such as rectal temperature and performance measurements.
The animals shall be observed and examined until reactions may no longer be expected, but in all cases, the observation and examination period shall be at least 14 days after administration.

2. Safety of one administration of an overdose

An overdose of the immunological veterinary medicinal product shall be administered by each recommended route of administration to animals of the most sensitive categories of the target species. The animals shall be observed and examined for signs of systemic and local reactions. Other objective criteria shall be recorded, such as rectal temperature and performance measurements.
The animals shall be observed and examined for at least 14 days after administration.

3. Safety of the repeated administration of one dose

Repeated administration of one dose may be required to reveal any adverse effects induced by such administration. These tests shall be carried out on the most sensitive categories of the target species, using the recommended route of administration.
The animals shall be observed and examined for at least 14 days after the last administration for signs of systemic and local reactions. Other objective criteria shall be recorded, such as rectal temperature and performance measurements.

4. Examination of reproductive performance

Examination of reproductive performance shall be considered when data suggest that the starting material from which the product is derived may be a potential risk factor. Reproductive performance of males and non-pregnant and pregnant females shall be investigated with the recommended dose and by each of the recommended routes of administration. In addition, harmful effects on the progeny, as well as teratogenic and abortifacient effects, shall be investigated.
These studies may form part of the safety studies described in paragraph 1 above.

5. Examination of immunological functions

Where the immunological veterinary medicinal product might adversely affect the immune response of the vaccinated animal or of its progeny, suitable tests on the immunological functions shall be carried out.

6. Special requirements for live vaccines:

6.1. Spread of the vaccine strain

Spread of the vaccine strain from vaccinated to unvaccinated target animals shall be investigated, using the recommended route of administration most likely to result in spread. Moreover, it may be necessary to investigate spread to non target species which could be highly susceptible to a live vaccine strain.

6.2. Dissemination in the vaccinated animal

Faeces, urine, milk, eggs, oral, nasal and other secretions shall be tested for the presence of the organism. Moreover, studies may be required of the dissemination of the vaccine strain in the body, with particular attention being paid to the predilection sites for replication of the organism. In the case of live vaccines for well established zoonotic diseases for food producing animals, these studies must be undertaken.

6.3. Reversion to virulence of attenuated vaccines

Reversion to virulence shall be investigated with material from the passage level which is least attenuated between the master seed and the final product. The initial vaccination shall be carried out using the recommended route of administration most likely to lead to reversion to virulence. At least five serial passages through animals of the target species shall be undertaken. Where this is not technically possible due to failure of the organism to replicate adequately, as many passages as possible shall be carried out in the target species. If necessary, in vitro propagation of the organism may be carried out between passages in vivo. The passages shall be undertaken by the route of administration most likely to lead to reversion to virulence.

6.4. Biological properties of the vaccine strain

Other tests may be necessary to determine as precisely as possible the intrinsic biological properties of the vaccine strain (e.g. neurotropism).

6.5. Recombination or genomic reassortment of strains

The probability of recombination or genomic reassortment with field or other strains shall be discussed.

7. Study of residues

For immunological veterinary medicinal products, it will normally not be necessary to undertake a study of residues. However, where adjuvants and/or preservatives are used in the manufacture of immunological veterinary medicinal products, consideration shall be given to the possibility of any residue remaining in the foodstuffs. If necessary, the effects of such residues shall be investigated. Moreover, in the case of live vaccines for zoonotic diseases, the determination of residues at the injection site may be required in addition to the studies described in paragraph 6.2 above.

A proposal for a withdrawal period shall be made and its adequacy shall be discussed in relation to any residue studies which have been undertaken.

8. Interactions

Any known interactions with other products shall be indicated.

D. FIELD STUDIES

Unless justified, results from laboratory studies shall be supplemented with supportive data from field studies.

E. ECOTOXICITY

The purpose of the study of the ecotoxicity of an immunological veterinary medicinal product is to assess the potential harmful effects which the use of the product may cause to the environment and to identify any precautionary measures which may be necessary to reduce such risks.

An assessment of ecotoxicity shall be compulsory for any application for marketing authorization for an immunological veterinary medicinal product other than applications submitted in accordance with point 10 of Article 5, second paragraph, of Directive 81/851/EEC.

This assessment shall normally be conducted in two phases.

The first phase of the assessment shall always be carried out: the investigator shall assess the potential extent of exposure of the environment to the product, its active ingredients, or relevant metabolites, taking into account:

- the target species and the proposed pattern of use (for example, mass medication or individual animal medication),
- the method of administration, in particular the likely extent to which the product will enter directly into environmental system,

- the possible excretion of the product, its active ingredients or relevant metabolites into the environment by treated animals, persistence in such excretia,
- the disposal of unused or waste product.

Where the conclusions of the first phase indicate potential exposure of the environment to the product, the applicant shall proceed to the second phase and evaluate the potential ecotoxicity of the product. For this purpose, he shall consider the extent and duration of exposure of the environment to the product, and the information about the physical/chemical, pharmacological and/or toxicological properties of the compound obtained during the conduct of the other tests and trials required by this Directive. Where necessary further investigations on the impact of the product (soil, water, air, aquatic systems, non-target organisms) shall be carried out.

These further investigations shall be carried out in accordance with the test protocols laid down in Annex V to Council Directive 67/548/EEC of 27 June 1967 on the approximation of laws, regulations and administrative provisions relating to the classification, packaging and labelling of dangerous substances, as last amended by Commission Directive 91/632/EEC, or where an end point is not adequately covered by these protocols, in accordance with other internationally recognised protocols on the immunological veterinary medicinal product and/or the active substances and/or the excreted metabolites as appropriate. The number and types of tests and the criteria for their evaluation shall depend upon the state of scientific knowledge at the time the application is submitted.

PART 8

EFFICACY TRIALS

A. INTRODUCTION

1. The purpose of the trials described in this Part is to demonstrate or to confirm the efficacy of the immunological veterinary medicinal product. All claims made by the applicant with regard to the properties, effects and use of the product shall be fully supported by results of specific trials contained in the application for marketing authorization.

2. The particulars and documents which shall accompany applications for marketing authorizations pursuant to point 10 of Article 5, second paragraph, of Directive 81/851/EEC shall be submitted in accordance with the provisions below.

3. All veterinary clinical trials shall be conducted in accordance with a fully considered detailed trial protocol which shall be recorded in writing prior to commencement of the trial. The welfare of the trial animals shall be subject to veterinary supervision and shall be taken fully into consideration during the elaboration of any trial protocol and throughout the conduct of the trial.
Pre-established systematic written procedures for the organization, conduct, data collection, documentation and verification of clinical trials shall be required.

4. Before the commencement of any trial, the informed consent of the owner of the animals to be used in the trial shall be obtained and documented. In particular, the animal owner shall be informed in writing of the consequences of participation in the trial for the subsequent disposal of treated animals or for the taking of foodstuffs from treated animals. A copy of this notification, countersigned and dated by the animal owner, shall be included in the trial documentation.

5. Unless the trial is conducted with a blind design, the provisions of Articles 43 to 47 of Directive 81/851/EEC shall apply by analogy to the labelling of formulations intended for use in veterinary clinical trials. In all cases, the words " for veterinary clinical trial use only " shall appear prominently and indelibly upon the labelling.

B. GENERAL REQUIREMENTS

1. The choice of vaccine strains shall be justified on the basis of epizoological data.

2. Efficacy trials carried out in the laboratory shall be controlled trials, including untreated control animals.
In general, these trails shall be supported by trials carried out in field conditions, including untreated control animals.

All trials shall be described in sufficiently precise details so as to be reproducible in control trials, carried out at the request of the competent authorities. The investigator shall demonstrate the validity of all the techniques involved. All results shall be presented as precisely as possible.
All results obtained, whether favourable or unfavourable, shall be reported.

3. The efficacy of an immunological veterinary medicinal product shall be demonstrated for each category of each target species recommended for vaccination, by each recommended route of administration and using the proposed schedule of administration. The influence of passively acquired and maternally derived antibodies on the efficacy of a vaccine shall be adequately evaluated. Any claims regarding onset and duration of protection shall be supported by data from trials.

4. The efficacy of each of the components of multivalent and combined immunological veterinary medicinal products shall be demonstrated. If the product is recommended for administration in combination with or at the same time as another veterinary medicinal product, they shall be shown to be compatible.

5. Whenever a product forms part of a vaccination scheme recommended by the applicant the priming or booster effect or the contribution of the product to the efficacy of the scheme as a whole shall be demonstrated.

6. The dose to be used shall be that quantity of the product to be recommended for use and containing the minimum titre or potency for which the application is submitted.

7. The samples used for efficacy trials shall be taken from a batch or batches produced according to the manufacturing process described in the application for marketing authorization.

8. For diagnostic immunological veterinary medicinal products administered to animals, the applicant shall indicate how reactions to the product are to be interpreted.

C. LABORATORY TRIALS

1. In principle, demonstration of efficacy shall be undertaken under well controlled laboratory conditions by challenge after administration of the immunological veterinary medicinal product to the target animal under the recommended conditions of use. In so far as possible, the conditions under which the challenge is carried out shall mimic the natural conditions for infection, for example with regard to the amount of challenge organism and the route of administration of the challenge.

2. If possible, the immune mechanism (cell-mediated/humoral, local/general classes of immunoglobulin) which is initiated after the administration of the immunological veterinary medicinal product to target animals by the recommended route of administration shall be specified and documented.

D. FIELD TRIALS

1. Unless justified, results from laboratory trials shall be supplemented with data from field trials.

2. Where laboratory trials cannot be supportive of efficacy, the performance of field trials alone may be acceptable.

PART 9

PARTICULARS AND DOCUMENTS CONCERNING SAFETY TESTING AND EFFICACY TRIALS OF IMMUNOLOGICAL VETERINARY MEDICINAL PRODUCTS

A. INTRODUCTION

As in any scientific work, the dossier of safety and efficacy studies shall include an introduction defining the subject and indicating the tests which have been carried out in compliance with Parts 7 and 8, as well as a summary, with references to the published literature. Omission of any tests or trials listed in Parts 7 and 8 shall be indicated and discussed.

B. LABORATORY STUDIES

The following shall be provided for all studies:

1. a summary;

2. the name of the body having carried out the studies;

3. a detailed experimental protocol giving a description of the methods, apparatus and materials used, details such as species, breed or strain of animals, categories of animals, where they were obtained, their identification and number, the conditions under which they were housed and fed (stating inter alia whether they were free from any specified pathogens and/or specified antibodies, the nature and quantity of any additives contained in the feed), dose, route, schedule and dates of administration, a description of the statistical methods used;

4. in the case of control animals, whether they received a placebo or no treatment;

5. all general and individual observations and results obtained (with averages and standard deviations), whether favourable or unfavourable. The data shall be described in sufficient detail to allow the results to be critically evaluated independently of their interpretation by the author. The raw data shall be presented in tabular form. By way of explanation and illustration, the results may be accompanied by reproductions of recordings, photomicrographs, etc.;

6. the nature, frequency and duration of observed side-effects;

7. the number of animals withdrawn prematurely from the studies and reasons for such withdrawal;

8. a statistical analysis of the results, where such is called for by the test programme, and variance within the data;

9. occurrence and course of any intercurrent disease;

10. all details concerning medicinal products (other than the product under study), the administration of which was necessary during the course of the study;

11. an objective discussion of the results obtained, leading to conclusions on the safety and efficacy of the product.

C. FIELD STUDIES

Particulars concerning field studies shall be sufficiently detailed to enable an objective judgement to be made. They shall include the following:

1. a summary;

2. name, address, function and qualifications of the investigator in charge;

3. place and date of administration, name and address of the owner of the animal(s);

4. details of the trial protocol, giving a description of the methods, apparatus and materials used, details such as the route of administration, the schedule of administration, the dose, the categories of animals, the duration of observation, the serological response and other investigations carried out on the animals after administration;

5. in the case of control animals, whether they received a placebo or no treatment;

6. identification of the treated and control animals (collective or individual, as appropriate), such as species, breeds or strains, age, weight, sex, physiological status;

7. a brief description of the method of rearing and feeding, stating the nature and quantity of any additives contained in the feed;

8. all the particulars on observations, performances and results (with averages and standard deviation); individual data shall be indicated when tests and measurements on individuals have been carried out;

9. all observations and results of the studies, whether favourable or unfavourable, with a full statement of the observations and the results of the objective tests of activity required to evaluate the product; the techniques used must be specified and the significance of any variations in the results explained;

10. effect on the animals' performances (e.g. egg laying, milk production, reproductive performance);

11. the number of animals withdrawn prematurely from the studies and reasons for such withdrawal;

12. the nature, frequency and duration of observed side-effects;

13. occurrence and course of any intercurrent disease;

14. all details concerning medicinal products (other than the product under study) which have been administered either prior to or concurrently with the test product or during the observation period; details of any interactions observed;

15. an objective discussion of the results obtained, leading to conclusions on the safety and efficacy of the product.

D. GENERAL CONCLUSIONS

General conclusions on all results of tests and trials carried out in compliance with Parts 7 and 8 shall be given. They shall contain an objective discussion of all the results obtained and lead to a conclusion on the safety and efficacy of the immunological veterinary medicinal product.

E. BIBLIOGRAPHICAL REFERENCES

The bibliographical references cited in the summary mentioned under item A shall be listed in detail. " [2]

(1) OJ No L 317, 06/11/1981, p. 1.
(2) OJ No L 358, 18/12/1986, p. 1.
(3) OJ No L 11, 14/01/1978, p. 18.
(4) The competent authorities may also request the pK and pH values if they think this information is essential.
(5) OJ No L 15, 17/01/1987, p. 29.
(6) OJ No L 145, 11/06/1988, p. 35.
(7) OJ No L 196, 16/08/1967, p. 1.
(8) OJ No L 338, 10/12/1991, p. 23.

378L0025

78/25/EEC: COUNCIL DIRECTIVE OF 12 DECEMBER 1977 ON THE APPROXIMATION OF THE LAWS OF THE MEMBER STATES RELATING TO THE COLOURING MATTERS WHICH MAY BE ADDED TO MEDICINAL PRODUCTS

OFFICIAL JOURNAL No L 11, 14/01/1978, P. 18
DATE OF NOTIFICATION: 15/12/1977
DATE OF TRANSPOSITION: 15/06/1979; SEE ART. 7

AMENDED BY

179H
ACT CONCERNING THE CONDITIONS OF ACCESSION OF THE HELLENIC REPUBLIC AND THE ADJUSTMENTS TO THE TREATIES [1]
OFFICIAL JOURNAL No L 291, 19/11/1979, P. 111

381L0464
81/464/EEC: COUNCIL DIRECTIVE OF 24 JUNE 1981 [2]
OFFICIAL JOURNAL No L 183, 04/07/1981, P. 33
DATE OF NOTIFICATION: 02/07/1981
DATE OF TRANSPOSITION: 01/10/1981; SEE ART. 2

185I
ACT CONCERNING THE CONDITIONS OF ACCESSION OF THE KINGDOM OF SPAIN AND THE PORTUGUESE REPUBLIC AND THE ADJUSTMENTS TO THE TREATIES [3]
OFFICIAL JOURNAL No L 302, 15/11/1985, P. 217

(See above, page 135)

COMMISSION DIRECTIVE

of 23 July 1991

laying down the principles and guidelines of good manufacturing practice for veterinary medicinal products

(91/412/EEC)

THE COMMISSION OF THE EUROPEAN COMMUNITIES,

Having regard to the Treaty establishing the European Economic Community,

Having regard to Council Directive 81/851/EEC of 28 September 1981 concerning the approximation of the laws of the Member States relating to veterinary medicinal products (¹), as last amended by Directive 90/676/EEC (²), and in particular Article 27a,

Having regard to Council Directive 90/677/EEC of 13 December 1990 extending the scope of Directive 81/851/EEC on the approximation of the laws of the Member States relating to veterinary medicinal products and laying down additional provisions for immunological veterinary medicinal products (³),

Whereas all veterinary medicinal products manufactured or imported into the Community, including medicinal products intended for export should be manufactured in accordance with the principles and guidelines of good manufacturing practice ;

Whereas, in accordance with national legislation, Member States may require compliance with these principles of good manufacturing practice during the manufacture of products intended for use in clinical trials ;

Whereas the detailed guidelines mentioned in Article 27a of Directive 81/851/EEC have been published by the Commission after consultation with the pharmaceutical inspection services of the Member States in the form of a 'Guide to good manufacturing practice for medicinal products' ;

Whereas it is necessary that all manufacturers should operate an effective quality management of their manufacturing operations, and that this requires the implementation of a pharmaceutical quality assurance system ;

Whereas officials representing the competent authorities should report on whether the manufacturer complies with good manufacturing practice and that these reports should be communicated upon reasoned request to the competent authorities of another Member State ;

Whereas the principles and guidelines of good manufacturing practice should primarily concern personnel, premises and equipment, documentation, production, quality control, contracting out, complaints and product recall, and self inspection ;

Whereas the principles and guidelines envisaged by this Directive are in conformity with the opinion of the Committee for Adaptation of Technical Progress of the Directives on the Removal of Technical Barriers to Trade in the Veterinary Medicinal Products Sector created by Article 2b of Directive 81/852/EEC of 28 September 1981 concerning the approximation of the laws of Member States relating to analytical, pharmaco-toxicological and clinical standards and protocols in respect of the testing of veterinary medicinal products (⁴), as last amended by Directive 87/20/EEC (⁵),

HAS ADOPTED THIS DIRECTIVE :

CHAPTER I

GENERAL PROVISIONS

Article 1

This Directive lays down the principles and guidelines of good manufacturing practice for veterinary medicinal products whose manufacture requires the authorization referred to in Article 24 of Directive 81/851/EEC.

Article 2

For the purposes of this Directive, the definition of medicinal products set out in Article 1 (2) of Council Directive 65/65/EEC (⁶), and the definition of veterinary medicinal products set out in Article 1 (2) of Directive 81/851/EEC, shall apply.

In addition,

— 'manufacturer' shall mean any holder of the authorization referred to in Article 24 of Directive 81/851/EEC,

— 'qualified person' shall mean the person referred to in Article 29 of Directive 81/851/EEC,

---

(¹) OJ No L 317, 6. 11. 1981, p. 1.
(²) OJ No L 373, 31. 12. 1990, p. 15.
(³) OJ No L 373, 31. 12. 1990, p. 26.

(⁴) OJ No L 317, 6. 11. 1981, p. 16.
(⁵) OJ No L 15, 17. 1. 1987, p. 34.
(⁶) OJ No 22, 9. 2. 1965, p. 369/65.

— 'pharmaceutical quality assurance' shall mean the sum total of the organized arrangements made with the object of ensuring that veterinary medicinal products are of the quality required for their intended use,

— 'good manufacturing practice' shall mean the part of quality assurance with ensures that products are consistently produced and controlled to the quality standards appropriate to their intended use.

Article 3

By means of the repeated inspections referred to in Article 34 of Directive 81/851/EEC, the Member States shall ensure that manufacturers respect the principles and guidelines of good manufacturing practice laid down by this Directive.

For the interpretation of these principles and guidelines of good manufacturing practice, the manufacturers and the agents of the competent authorities refer to the detailed guidelines referred to in Article 27a of Directive 81/851/EEC. These detailed guidelines are published by the Commission in the 'Guide to good manufacturing practice for medicinal products' and in its annexes (Office for Official Publications of the European Communities, The Rules Governing Medicinal Products in the European Community, Volume IV).

Article 4

The manufacturers shall ensure that the manufacturing operations are carried out in accordance with good manufacturing practice and with the manufacturing authorization.

For veterinary medicinal products imported from third countries, the importer shall ensure that the veterinary medicinal products have been manufactured by manufacturers duly authorized and conforming to good manufacturing practice standards, at least equivalent to those laid down by the Community.

Article 5

The manufacturer shall ensure that all manufacturing operations subject to an authorization for marketing are carried out in accordance with the information given in the application for marketing authorization as accepted by the competent authorities.

The manufacturers shall regularly review their manufacturing methods in the light of scientific and technical progress. When a modification to the marketing authorization dossier is necessary, the application for modification must be submitted to the competent authorities.

CHAPTER II

PRINCIPLES AND GUIDELINES OF GOOD MANUFACTURING PRACTICE

Article 6

Quality management

The manufacturer shall establish and implement an effective pharmaceutical quality assurance system, involving the active participation of the management and personnel of the different services involved.

Article 7

Personnel

1. At each manufacturing site, the manufacturer shall have competent and appropriately qualified personnel at his disposal in sufficient number to achieve the pharmaceutical quality assurance objectives.

2. The duties of managerial and supervisory staff, including the qualified person(s), responsible for implementing and operating good manufacturing practice shall be defined in job descriptions. Their hierarchical relationships shall be defined in an organizational chart. Organizational charts and job descriptions shall be approved in accordance with the manufacturer's internal procedures.

3. Staff referred to in paragraph 2 shall be given sufficient authority to carry out their responsibilities correctly.

4. Personnel shall receive initial and continuing training including the theory and application of the concept of quality assurance and good manufacturing practice.

5. Hygiene programmes adapted to the activities to be carried out shall be established and observed. These programmes include procedures relating to health, hygiene and clothing of personnel.

Article 8

Premises and equipment

1. Premises and manufacturing equipment shall be located, designed, constructed, adapted and maintained to suit the intended operations.

2. Lay out, design and operation must aim to minimize the risk of errors and permit effective cleaning and maintenance in order to avoid contamination, cross contamination and, in general, any adverse effect on the quality of the product.

3. Premises and equipment intended to be used for manufacturing operations which are critical for the quality of the products shall be subjected to appropriate qualification.

Article 9

Documentation

1. The manufacturer shall have a system of documentation based upon specifications, manufacturing formulae and processing and packaging instructions, procedures and records covering the different manufacturing operations that they perform. Documents shall be clear, free from errors and kept up to-date. Pre-established procedures for general manufacturing operations and conditions shall be available, together with specific documents for the manufacture of each batch. This set of documents shall make it possible to trace the history of the manufacture of each batch. The batch documentation shall be retained for at least one year after the expiry date of the batches to which it relates, or at least five years after the certification referred to in Article 30 (2) of Directive 81/851/EEC, whichever is the longer.

2. When electronic, photographic or other data processing systems are used instead of written documents, the manufacturer shall have validated the system by proving that the data will be appropriately stored during the anticipated period of storage. Data stored by these systems shall be made readily available in legible form. The electronically stored data shall be protected against loss or damage of data (e.g. by duplication or back-up and transfer onto another storage system).

Article 10

Production

The different production operations shall be carried out according to pre-established instructions and procedures and in accordance with good manufacturing practice. Adequate and sufficient resources shall be made available for the in-process controls.

Appropriate technical and/or organizational measures shall be taken to avoid cross contamination and mix-ups.

Any new manufacture or important modification of a manufacturing process shall be validated. Critical phases of manufacturing process shall be regularly revalidated.

Article 11

Quality control

1. The manufacturer shall establish and maintain a quality control department. This department shall be placed under the authority of a person having the required qualifications and shall be independent of the other departments.

2. The quality control department shall have at its disposal one or more quality control laboratories appropriately staffed and equipped to carry out the necessary examination and testing of starting materials, packaging materials and intermediate and finished products testing. Resorting to outside laboratories is authorized in accordance with Article 12 of this Directive and after the authorization referred to in Article 10 (2) of Directive 81/851/EEC has been granted.

3. During the final control of finished products before their release for the sale or distribution, in addition to analytical results, the quality control department shall take into account essential information such as the production conditions, the results of in-process controls, the examination of the manufacturing documents and the conformity of the products to their specifications (including the final finished pack).

4. Samples of each batch of finished products shall be retained for at least one year after the expiry date. Unless in the Member State of manufacture a longer period is required, samples of starting materials (other than solvents, gases and water) used shall be retained for at least two years after the release of the product. This period may be shortened if their stability, as mentioned in the relevant specification, is shorter. All these samples shall be maintained at the disposal of the competent authorities.

For certain veterinary medicinal products manufactured individually or in small quantities, or when their storage could raise special problems, other sampling and retaining conditions may be defined in agreement with the competent authority.

Article 12

Work contracted out

1. Any manufacturing operation or operation linked with the manufacture which is carried out under contract, shall be the subject of a written contract between the contract giver and the contract acceptor.

2. The contract shall clearly define the responsibilities of each party and in particular the observance of good manufacturing practice by the contract acceptor and the manner in which the qualified person responsible for releasing each batch shall undertake his full responsibilities.

3. The contract acceptor shall not further sub-contract any of the work entrusted to him by the contract giver without the written authorization of the contract giver.

4. The contract acceptor shall respect the principles and guidelines of good manufacturing practice and shall submit to inspections carried out by the competent authorities as provided for by Article 34 of Directive 81/851/EEC.

Article 13

Complaints and product recall

The manufacturer shall implement a system for recording and reviewing complaints together with an effective system for recalling promptly and at any time the veterinary medicinal products in the distribution network. Any complaint concerning a quality defect shall be recorded and investigation by the manufacturer. The competent authority shall be informed by the manufacturer of any quality defect that could result in a recall or abnormal restriction on the supply. In so far as possible, the countries of destination shall also be indicated. Any recall shall be made in accordance with the requirements referred to in Article 42 of Directive 81/851/EEC.

Article 14

Self-inspection

The manufacturer shall conduct repeated self-inspections as part of the quality assurance system in order to monitor the implementation and respect of good manufacturing practice and to propose any necessary corrective measures. Records of such self-inspections and any further corrective action shall be maintained.

CHAPTER III

FINAL PROVISIONS

Article 15

Member States shall bring into force the laws, regulations and administrative provisions necessary to comply with this Directive before 23 July 1993. They shall forthwith inform the Commission thereof.

When Member States adopt these provisions, these shall contain a reference to this Directive or shall be accompanied by such reference at the time of their official publication. The procedure for such reference shall be adopted by Member States.

Article 16

This Directive is addressed to the Member States.

Done at Brussels, 23 July 1991.

For the Commission
Martin BANGEMANN
Vice-President

390R2377

2377/90/EEC: COUNCIL REGULATION OF 26 JUNE 1990 LAYING DOWN A COMMUNITY PROCEDURE FOR THE ESTABLISHMENT OF MAXIMUM RESIDUE LIMITS OF VETERINARY MEDICINAL PRODUCTS IN FOODSTUFFS OF ANIMAL ORIGIN

OFFICIAL JOURNAL No L 224, 18/08/1990, P. 1

AMENDED BY

392R0675
675/92/EEC: COMMISSION REGULATION OF 18 MARCH 1992 [1]
OFFICIAL JOURNAL No L 73, 19/03/1992, P. 8

392R0762
762/92/EEC: COMMISSION REGULATION OF 27 MARCH 1992 [2]
OFFICIAL JOURNAL No L 83, 28/03/1992, P. 14

392R3093
3093/92/EEC: COMMISSION REGULATION OF 27 OCTOBER 1992 [3]
OFFICIAL JOURNAL No L 311, 27/10/1992, P. 18

392R3093
895/93/EEC: COMMISSION REGULATION OF 16 APRIL 1993 [4]
OFFICIAL JOURNAL No L 93, 17/04/1993, P. 10

393R2901
2901/93/EEC: COMMISSION REGULATION OF 18 OCTOBER 1993 [5]
OFFICIAL JOURNAL No L 264, 23/10/1993, P. 1

393R3425
3425/93/EC: COMMISSION REGULATION OF 14 DECEMBER 1993 [6]
OFFICIAL JOURNAL No L 312, 15/12/1993, P. 12

393R3426
3426/93/EC: COMMISSION REGULATION OF 14 DECEMBER 1993 [7]
OFFICIAL JOURNAL No L 312, 15/12/1993, P. 15

394R0955
955/94/EC: COMMISSION REGULATION OF 28 APRIL 1994 [8]
OFFICIAL JOURNAL No L 108, 29/04/1994, P. 8

394R1430
1430/94/EC: COMMISSION REGULATION OF 22 JUNE 1994 [9]
OFFICIAL JOURNAL No L 156, 23/06/1994, P. 6

394R2701
2701/94/EC: COMMISSION REGULATION OF 7 NOVEMBER 1994   **[10]**
OFFICIAL JOURNAL No L 287, 8/11/1994, P. 7

394R2703
2703/94/EC: COMMISSION REGULATION OF 7 NOVEMBER 1994   **[11]**
OFFICIAL JOURNAL No L 287, 8/11/1994, P. 19

394R3059
3059/94/EC: COMMISSION REGULATION OF 15 DECEMBER 1994   **[12]**
OFFICIAL JOURNAL No L 323, 16/12/1994, P. 15

Article 1

1. For the purposes of this Regulation, the following definitions shall apply:

(a) "residues of veterinary medicinal products": means all pharmacologically active substances, whether active principles, excipients or degradation products, and their metabolites which remain in foodstuffs obtained from animals to which the veterinary medicinal product in question has been administered;

(b) "maximum residue limit": means the maximum concentration of residue resulting from the use of a veterinary medicinal product (expressed in mg/kg or µg/kg on a fresh weight basis) which may be accepted by the Community to be legally permitted or recognized as acceptable in or on a food.
It is based on the type and amount of residue considered to be without any toxicological hazard for human health as expressed by the acceptable daily intake (ADI), or on the basis of a temporary ADI that utilizes an additional safety factor. It also takes into account other relevant public health risks as well as food technology aspects.
When establishing a maximum residue limit (MRL), consideration is also given to residues that occur in food of plant origin and/or come from the environment. Furthermore, the MRL may be reduced to be consistent with good practices in the use of veterinary drugs and to the extent that practical analytical methods are available.

2. This Regulation shall not apply to active principles of biological origin intended to produce active or passive immunity or to diagnose a state of immunity used in immunological veterinary medicinal products.

Article 2

The list of pharmacologically active substances used in veterinary medicinal products in respect of which maximum residue limits have been established shall be contained in Annex I, which shall be adopted in accordance with the procedure laid down in Article 8. Except as provided for in Article 9, any amendments to Annex I shall be adopted in accordance with the same procedure.

Article 3

Where, following an evaluation of a pharmacologically active substance used in veterinary medicinal products, it appears that it is not necessary for the protection of public health to establish a maximum residue limit, that substance shall be included in a list in Annex II, which shall be adopted in accordance with the procedure laid down in Article 8. Except as provided for in Article 9, any amendments to Annex II shall be adopted in accordance with the same procedure.

Article 4

A provisional maximum residue limit may be established for a pharmacologically active substance used in veterinary medicinal products on the date of entry into force of this Regulation, provided that there are no grounds for supposing that residues of the substance concerned at the level proposed present a hazard for the health of the consumer. A provisional maximum residue limit shall apply for a defined period of time, which shall not exceed five years. That period may be extended once only in exceptional cases for a period not in excess of two years if that proves expedient for the completion of scientific studies in progress.

In exceptional circumstances, a provisional maximum residue limit may also be established for a pharmacologically active substance not previously used in veterinary medicinal products on the date of entry into force of this Regulation provided that there are no grounds for supposing that residues of the substance concerned at the limit proposed present a hazard for the health of the consumer.

The list of pharmacologically active substances used in veterinary medicinal products in respect of which provisional maximum residue limits have been established shall be contained in Annex III, which shall be adopted in accordance with the procedure laid down in Article 8. Except as provided for in Article 9, any amendments to Annex III shall be adopted in accordance with the same procedure.

Article 5

Where it appears that a maximum residue limit cannot be established in respect of a pharmacologically active substance used in veterinary medicinal products because residues of the substances concerned, at whatever limit, in foodstuffs of animal origin constitute a hazard to the health of the consumer, that substance shall be included in a list in Annex IV, which shall be adopted in accordance with the procedure laid down in Article 8. Except as provided for in Article 9, any amendments to Annex IV shall be adopted in accordance with the same procedure.

The administration of the substances listed in Annex IV to food-producing animals shall be prohibited throughout the Community.

Article 6

1. In order to obtain the inclusion in Annex I, II, or III of a new pharmacologically active substance which is:

- intended for use in veterinary medicinal products for administration to food-producing animals, and
- intended to be placed on the market of one or more Member States which have not previously authorized the use of the substance concerned in food-producing animals,

the person responsible for marketing shall submit an application to the Commission. The application shall contain the information and particulars referred to in Annex V and shall comply with the principles laid down in Directive 81/852/EEC (1).

2. After verifying within a period of 30 days that the application is submitted in correct form, the Commission shall forthwith submit the application for examination by the Committee for Veterinary Medicinal Products set up under Article 16 of Directive 81/851/EEC (2). The Committee shall appoint one of its members to act as rapporteur and to undertake an initial evaluation of the application.

3. Within 120 days of referral of the application to the Committee for Veterinary Medicinal Products, and having regard to the observations formulated by the members of the Committee, the Commission shall prepare a draft of the measures to be taken. If the information submitted by the person responsible for marketing is insufficient to enable such a draft to be prepared, that person will be requested to provide the Committee with additional information for examination. The rapporteur shall update the evaluation report to take account of the additional information received.

4. Within 90 days of receipt of the additional information referred to in paragraph 3, the Commission shall prepare a draft of the measures to be taken, which shall forthwith be communicated to the Member States and the person responsible for marketing. Within a further 60 days, the person responsible for marketing may, at his

request, provide oral or written explanations for consideration by the Committee for Veterinary Medicinal Products. The Commission may, at the request of the applicant, extend this time limit.

5. Within a further 60 days the Commission shall submit the draft measures to the Committee for the Adaptation to Technical Progress of the Directives on the Removal of Technical Barriers to Trade in the Veterinary Medicinal Products Sector, set up under Article 2b of Directive 81/852/EEC, for the application of the procedure laid down in Article 8.

Article 7

1. Paragraphs 2 to 6 shall apply in respect of pharmacologically active substances which are authorized for use in veterinary medicinal products on the date of entry into force of this Regulation.

2. After consulting the Committee on Veterinary Medicinal Products, the Commission shall publish a timetable for the consideration of these substances, including time limits for submission of the information referred to in Annex V.
The persons responsible for marketing the veterinary medicinal products concerned shall ensure that all relevant information is submitted to the Commission in accordance with the requirements of Annex V and in conformity with the principles laid down in Directive 81/852/EEC before expiry of the relevant time limits. The competent authorities of the Member States shall bring any other relevant information to the attention of the Commission.

3. After verifying within 30 days that the information is submitted in correct form, the Commission shall forthwith submit the information for examination to the Committee for Veterinary Medicinal Products, which shall deliver its opinion within a renewable period of 120 days. That Committee shall appoint one of its members to act as rapporteur and to undertake an evaluation of the information.

4. Having regard to the observations formulated by the members of the Committee for Veterinary Medicinal Products, the Commission shall prepare, within a maximum period of 30 days, a draft of the measures to be taken. If the information submitted by the person responsible for marketing is insufficient to enable such a draft to be prepared, that person will be requested to provide additional information, within a specified period, for examination by the Committee. The rapporteur shall update the evaluation report to take account of the additional information received.

5. The draft of the measures to be taken shall be communicated forthwith by the Commission to the Member States and those persons responsible for marketing who have submitted information to the Commission before expiry of the time limit established in accordance with paragraph 2. These persons may, at their request, provide oral or written explanations to the Committee for Veterinary Medicinal Products.

6. The Commission shall forthwith submit the draft measures to the Committee for Adaptation to Technical Progress of the Directives on Veterinary Medicinal Products for the application of the procedure laid down in Article 8.

Article 8

1. Where the procedure laid down in this Article is to be followed, the chairman shall, without delay, refer the matter to the Committee for Adaptation to Technical Progress of the Directives on Veterinary Medicinal Products either on his own initiative or at the request of a representative of a Member State.

2. The representative of the Commission shall submit a draft of the measures to be adopted to the Committee for Adaptation to Technical Progress. The Committee shall deliver its opinion on the draft within a time limit set by the chairman, having regard to the urgency of the matter. It shall act by a qualified majority, the votes of the Member States being weighted as provided for in Article 148 (2) of the Treaty. The chairman shall not vote.

3. (a) The Commission shall adopt the measures envisaged where they are in accordance with the opinion of the Committee.

(b) Where the measures envisaged are not in accordance with the opinion of the Committee, or if no opinion is adopted, the Commission shall without delay propose to the Council the measures to be adopted. The Council shall act by a qualified majority.

(c) If, after a period of three months of the proposal being referred to it, the Council has not acted, the proposed measures shall be adopted by the Commission, unless the Council has voted against them by a simple majority.

Article 9

1. Where a Member State, as a result of new information or a reassessment of existing information, considers that the urgent amendment of a provision contained in Annexes I to IV is necessary in order to protect human or animal health, and therefore requires swift action to be taken, that Member State may temporarily suspend the operation of the provision concerned in its own territory. In that case, it shall immediately notify the other Member States and the Commission of the measures, attaching a statement of the reasons therefor.

2. The Commission shall as soon as possible examine the grounds given by the Member State concerned and, after consulting the Member States within the Committee for Veterinary Medicinal Products, it shall then deliver its opinion forthwith and take appropriate measures; the person responsible for marketing may be requested to provide the Committee with oral or written explanations. The Commission shall immediately notify the Council and the Member States of any measures taken. Any Member State may refer the Commission's measures to the Council within 15 days of such notification. The Council, acting by a qualified majority, may take a different decision within 30 days of the date on which the matter was referred to it.

3. If the Commission considers that it is necessary to amend the provision of Annex I to IV concerned in order to resolve the difficulties referred to in paragraph 1 and to ensure the protection of human health, it shall initiate the procedure laid down in Article 10 with a view to adopting those amendments; the Member State which has taken measures under paragraph 1 may maintain them until the Council or the Commission has taken a decision in accordance with the abovementioned procedure.

Article 10

1. Where the procedure laid down in this Article is to be followed, the chairman shall, without delay, refer the matter to the Committee for Adaptation to Technical Progress of the Directives on Veterinary Medicinal Products either on his own initiative or at the request of a representative of a Member State.

2. The representative of the Commission shall submit to the Committee a draft of the measures to be adopted. The Committee shall deliver its opinion on the draft within a time limit set by the chairman, having regard to the urgency of the matter. It shall act by a qualified majority, the votes of the Member States being weighted as provided for in Article 148 (2) of the Treaty. The chairman shall not vote.

3. (a) The Commission shall adopt the measures envisaged, where they are in accordance with the opinion of the Committee.

(b) Where the measures envisaged are not in accordance with the opinion of the Committee, or if no opinion is adopted, the Commission shall without delay propose to the Council the measures to be adopted. The Council shall act by a qualified majority.

(c) If within 15 days of the proposals being submitted to it, the Council has not acted, the proposed measures shall be adopted by the Commission.

Article 11

Any changes which are necessary to adapt Annex V to take account of scientific and technical progress shall be adopted in accordance with the procedure laid down in Article 2c of Directive 81/852/EEC.

Article 12

As soon as possible after the amendment of Annexes I, II, III or IV, the Commission shall publish a summary of the assessment of the safety of the substances concerned by the Committee for Veterinary Medicinal Products. The confidential nature of any proprietary data shall be respected.

Article 13

Member States may not prohibit or impede the putting into circulation within their territories of foodstuffs of animal origin originating in other Member States on the grounds that they contain residues of veterinary medicinal products if the quantity of residue does not exceed the maximum residue limit provided for in Annex I or III, or if the substance concerned is listed in Annex II.

Article 14

With effect from 1 January 1997, the administration to food-producing animals of veterinary medicinal products containing pharmacologically active substances which are not mentioned in Annexes I, II or III shall be prohibited within the Community, except in the case of clinical trials accepted by the competent authorities following notification or authorization in accordance with the legislation in force and which do not cause foodstuffs obtained from livestock participating in such trials to contain residues which constitute a hazard to human health.

Article 15

This Regulation shall in no way prejudice the application of Community legislation prohibiting the use in livestock farming of certain substances having a hormonal action.
Nothing in this Regulation shall prejudice the measures taken by Member States to prevent the unauthorized use of veterinary medicinal products.

Article 16

This Regulation shall enter into force on 1 January 1992.

This Regulation shall be binding in its entirety and directly applicable in all Member States.

" ANNEX I

List of pharmacologically active substances for which maximum residue limits have been fixed

1. *Anti-infectious agents*

1.1. Chemotherapeutics

1.1.1. Sulfonamides

Pharmacologically active substance(s)	Marker residue	Animal species	MRLs	Target tissues	Other provisions
All substances belonging to the sulfonamide group	Parent drug	All food producing species	100 µg/kg	Muscle, liver, kidney, fat	The combined total residues of all substances within the sulfonamide group should not exceed 100 µg/kg

1.2. Antibiotics

1.2.1. Penicillins

Pharmacologically active substance(s)	Marker residue	Animal species	MRLs	Target tissues	Other provisions
1.2.1.1. Benzylpenicillin	Benzylpenicillin	All food producing species	50 µg/kg 4 µg/kg	Muscle, liver, kidney, fat Milk	
1.2.1.2. Ampicillin	Ampicillin	All food producing species	50 µg/kg 4 µg/kg	Muscle, liver, kidney, fat Milk	
1.2.1.3. Amoxicillin	Amoxicillin	All food producing species	50 µg/kg 4 µg/kg	Muscle, liver, kidney, fat Milk	
1.2.1.4. Oxacillin	Oxacillin	All food producing species	300 µg/kg 30 µg/kg	Muscle, liver, kidney, fat Milk	
1.2.1.5. Cloxacillin	Cloxacillin	All food producing species	300 µg/kg 30 µg/kg	Muscle, liver, kidney, fat Milk	
1.2.1.6. Dicloxacillin	Dicloxacillin	All food producing species	300 µg/kg 30 µg/kg	Muscle, liver, kidney, fat Milk	

1.2.2 Cephalosporins

Pharmacologically active substance(s)	Marker residue	Animal species	MRLs	Target tissues	Other provisions
1.2.2.1. Cefquinome	Cefquinome	Bovine	200 µg/kg 100 µg/kg 50 µg/kg 50 µg/kg	Kidney Liver Muscle Fat	

1.2.3. Quinolones

Pharmacologically active substance(s)	Marker residue	Animal species	MRLs	Target tissues	Other provisions
1.2.3.1. Enrofloxacin	Sum of enrofloxacin and ciprofloxacin	Bovine Porcine Poultry	30 µg/kg	Muscle, liver, kidney	

1.2.4. Macrolides

Pharmacologically active substance(s)	Marker residue	Animal species	MRLs	Target tissues	Other provisions
1.2.4.1. Tilmicosin	Tilmicosin	Bovine	1000 µg/kg 50 µg/kg	Liver, kidney Muscle, fat	

' 1.2.5. Florfenicol and related compounds

Pharmacologically active substance(s)	Marker residue	Animal species	MRLs	Target tissues	Other provisions
1.2.5.1. Florfenicol	Sum of florfenicol and its metabolites measured as florfenicol-amine	Bovine	200 µg/kg 300 µg/kg 3000 µg/kg	Muscle Kidney Liver	' [11]

2. Antiparasitic agents

2.1. Agents acting against endoparasites

2.1.1. Avermectins

Pharmacologically active substance(s)	Marker residue	Animal species	MRLs	Target tissues	Other provisions
2.1.1.1. Ivermectin	22,23-Dihydro-avermectin B1a	Bovine	100 µg/kg 40 µg/kg	Liver Fat	
		Porcine Ovine Equidae	15 µg/kg 20 µg/kg	Liver Fat	
2.1.1.2. Abamectin	Avermectin B1a	Bovine	20 µg/kg 10 µg/kg	Liver Fat	
2.1.1.3. Doramectin	Doramectin	Bovine	15 µg/kg 25 µg/kg	Liver Fat	

2.1.2. Salicylanilides

Pharmacologically active substance(s)	Marker residue	Animal species	MRLs	Target tissues	Other provisions
2.1.2.1. Closantel	Closantel	Bovine	1000 µg/kg 3000 µg/kg	Muscle, liver Kidney, fat	
		Ovine	1500 µg/kg 5000 µg/kg 2000 µg/kg	Muscle, liver Kidney Fat	" [10]

" 2.1.3. Tetra-hydro-imidazoles (imidazolthiazoles)

Pharmacologically active substance(s)	Marker residue	Animal species	MRLs	Target tissues	Other provisions
2.1.3.1. Levamisole	Levamisole	Bovine, ovine, porcine, poultry	10 µg/kg	Muscle, kidney, fat	
			100 µg/kg	Liver	" [12]

" ANNEX II

List of substances not subject to maximum residue limits

1. Inorganic chemicals

Pharmacologically active substance(s)	Animal species	Other provisions
1.1. Hydrogen peroxide	Fish	
1.2. Sulphur	Bovine Porcine Ovine Caprine Equidae	
1.3. Iodine and iodine inorganic compounds including : – Sodium and potassium iodide – Sodium and potassium iodate – Iodophors including polyvinylpyrrolidone iodine	All food producing species	
1.4. Sodium chlorite	Bovine	For topical use only

2. Organic compounds

Pharmacologically active substance(s)	Animal species	Other provisions
2.1. Etiproston tromethamine	Bovine Porcine	
2.2. Ketanserin tartrate	Equidae	
2.3. Fertirelin acetate	Bovine	
2.4. Human menopausal urinary gonadotrophin	Bovine	
2.5. Lactic acid	All food producing species	
2.6. Melatonin	Ovine Caprine	
2.7. Iodine organic compounds - Iodoform	All food producing species	
2.8. Acetyl cysteine	All food producing species	" [10]
"2.9. Gonadotrophin releasing hormone	All food producing species	" [11]
"2.10. Pregnant mare serum gonadotrophin	All food producing species	
2.11. 17β-Oestradiol	All food producing mammals	For therapeutic and zootechnical uses only " [12]

" ANNEX III

List of pharmacologically active substances used in veterinary medicinal products for which provisional maximum residue limits have been fixed

I. *Anti-infectious agents*

1.1.   Chemotherapeutics

1.1.1.   Sulfonamides

Pharmacologically active substance(s)	Marker residue	Animal species	MRLs	Target tissues	Other provisions
All substances belonging to the sulfonamide group	Parent drug	Bovine, ovine, caprine	100 µg/kg	Milk	Provisional MRL expires on 1. 1. 1996. The combined total residues of all substances within the sulfonamide group should not exceed 100 µg/kg

1.1.2.   Diamino pyrimidine derivates

Pharmacologically active substance(s)	Marker residue	Animal species	MRLs	Target tissues	Other provisions
1.1.2.1. Trimethoprim	Trimethoprim	All food producing species	50 µg/kg	Muscle, liver, kidney, fat, milk	Provisional MRL expires on 1. 1. 1996

1.1.3.   Nitrofurans

Pharmacologically active substance(s)	Marker residue	Animal species	MRLs	Target tissues	Other provisions
1.1.3.1. Furazolidone	All residues with intact 5-nitro structure	All food producing species	5 µg/kg	Muscle, liver, kidney, fat	Provisional MRL expires on 1. 7. 1995

1.1.4.   Nitroimidazoles

Pharmacologically active substance(s)	Marker residue	Animal species	MRLs	Target tissues	Other provisions
1.1.4.1. Dimetridazole	All residues with intact nitroimidazole structure	All food producing species	10 µg/kg	Muscle, liver, kidney, fat	Provisional MRL expires on 1. 1. 1995

1.2.   Antibiotics

1.2.1.   Tetracyclines

Pharmacologically active substance(s)	Marker residue	Animal species	MRLs	Target tissues	Other provisions
All substances belonging to the tetracycline group	Parent drug	All food producing species	600 µg/kg 300 µg/kg 200 µg/kg 100 µg/kg 100 µg/kg	Kidney Liver Eggs Muscle Milk	Provisional MRLs expire on 1. 1. 1996. The combined total residues of all substances within the tetracycline group should not exceed the limits indicated

1.2.2. Macrolides

Pharmacologically active substance(s)	Marker residue	Animal species	MRLs	Target tissues	Other provisions
1.2.2.1. Spiramycin	Spiramycin	Bovine, porcine	300 µg/kg 200 µg/kg 50 µg/kg	Liver Kidney Muscle	Provisional MRLs expire on 1. 7. 1995 The MRLs for liver, kidney and muscle apply to both the bovine and porcine species
		Bovine	150 µg/kg	Milk	
1.2.2.2. Tylosin	Tylosin	Bovine, porcine, poultry	100 µg/kg	Muscle, liver, kidney	Provisional MRLs expire on 1. 7. 1995
		Bovine	50 µg/kg	Milk	

1.2.3. Thiamphenicol and related compounds

Pharmacologically active substance(s)	Marker residue	Animal species	MRLs	Target tissues	Other provisions
1.2.3.1. Thiamphenicol	Thiamphenicol	Bovine, poultry	40 µg/kg	Muscle, liver, kidney, fat	Provisional MRL expires on 1. 1. 1996

' 1.2.4.   Cephalosporins

Pharmacologically active substance(s)	Marker residue	Animal species	MRLs	Target tissues	Other provisions
1.2.4.1. Ceftiofur	Sum of all residues retaining the betalactam structure expressed as desfuroylceftiofur	Bovine	2000 µg/kg 200 µg/kg 600 µg/kg 100 µg/kg	Kidney, liver Muscle Fat Milk	Provisional MRLs expire on 1 July 1997
		Porcine	4000 µg/kg 3000 µg/kg 500 µg/kg 600 µg/kg	Kidney Liver Muscle Fat	' [11]

' 1.2.5.   Aminoglycosides

Pharmacologically active substance(s)	Marker residue	Animal species	MRLs	Target tissues	Other provisions
1.2.5.1. Spectinomycin	Spectinomycin	Bovine, porcine, poultry	5000 µg/kg 2000 µg/kg 300 µg/kg 500 µg/kg	Kidney Liver Muscle Fat	Provisional MRLs expire on 1 July 1998
		Bovine	200 µg/kg	Milk	' [12]

2. Antiparasitic agents

2.1. Agents acting against endo-parasites

2.1.1. Benzimidazoles and pro-benzimidazoles

Pharmacologically active substance(s)	Marker residue	Animal species	MRLs	Target tissues	Other provisions
2.1.1.1. Febantel	Combined residues of oxfendazole, oxfendazole sulfone and fenbendazole	All food producing species	1000 µg/kg 10 µg/kg 10 µg/kg	Liver Muscle, kidney, fat Milk	Provisional MRLs expire on 1. 7. 1995. The MRLs cover all residues of febantel, fenbendazole and oxfendazole
2.1.1.2. Fenbendazole	Combined residues of oxfendazole, oxfendazole sulfone and fenbendazole	All food producing species	1000 µg/kg 10 µg/kg 10 µg/kg	Liver Muscle, kidney, fat Milk	Provisional MRLs expire on 1. 7. 1995. The MRLs cover all residues of febantel, fenbendazole and oxfendazole
2.1.1.3. Oxfendazole	Combined residues of oxfendazole, oxfendazole sulfone and fenbendazole	All food producing species	1000 µg/kg 10 µg/kg 10 µg/kg	Liver Muscle, kidney, fat Milk	Provisional MRLs expire on 1. 7. 1995. The MRLs cover all residues of febantel, fenbendazole and oxfendazole
2.1.1.4. Albendazole	Sum of albendazole and metabolites which are measured as 2-amino-benzimidazole sulphone	Bovine Ovine	100 µg/kg 500 µg/kg 1000 µg/kg	Muscle, fat, milk Kidney Liver	Provisional MRLs expire on 1. 1. 1996

Pharmacologically active substance(s)	Marker residue	Animal species	MRLs	Target tissues	Other provisions
2.1.1.5. Thiabendazole	Sum of thiabendazole and 5-hydroxythiabendazole	Bovine Ovine Caprine	100 µg/kg	Muscle, liver, kidney, fat, milk	Provisional MRLs expire on 1. 1. 1996
2.1.1.6. Triclabendazole	Sum of extractable residues that may be oxidized to keto-triclabendazole	Bovine Ovine	150 µg/kg 50 µg/kg	Muscle, liver, kidney Fat	Provisional MRLs expire on 1. 7. 1995
2.1.1.7. Flubendazole	Flubendazole	Poultry Game birds Porcine	500 µg/kg 200 µg/kg 400 µg/kg 10 µg/kg	Liver Muscle Eggs Muscle, liver, kidney, fat	Provisional MRLs expire on 1. 1. 1996
2.1.1.8. Oxibendazole	Oxibendazole	Bovine Ovine Porcine Equidae	100 µg/kg 50 µg/kg 100 µg/kg	Muscle, liver, kidney, fat Milk Muscle, liver, kidney, fat	Provisional MRLs expire on 1. 1. 1996

2.1.2. Tetra-hydro-imidazoles (imidazolthiazoles)

Pharmacologically active substance(s)	Marker residue	Animal species	MRLs	Target tissues	Other provisions
2.1.2.1. Levamisole	Levamisole	All food producing species	10 µg/kg	Muscle, liver, kidney, fat, milk	Provisional MRL expires on 1. 1. 1995

2.2. Agents acting against ectoparasites

Pharmacologically active substance(s)	Marker residue	Animal species	MRLs	Target tissues	Other provisions
2.2.1. Amitraz	Sum of amitraz and metabolites which are measured as 2.4-dimethylaniline	Porcine	50 µg/kg 200 µg/kg	Muscle Kidney, liver	Provisional MRLs expire on 1. 7. 1996

' 2.3. Agents acting against endo- and ectoparasites

2.3.1. Avermectins

Pharmacologically active substance(s)	Marker residue	Animal species	MRLs	Target tissues	Other provisions
2.3.1.1. Moxidectin	Moxidectin	Bovine, Ovine	200 µg/kg 20 µg/kg	Fat Kidney, liver	Provisional MRLs expire on 1 July 1997 ' [11]

3. Agents acting on the nervous system

3.1. Agents acting on the central nervous system

3.1.1. Butyrophenone tranquillizers

Pharmacologically active substance(s)	Marker residue	Animal species	MRLs	Target tissues	Other provisions
3.1.1.1. Azaperone	Azaperol	All food producing species	100 µg/kg 50 µg/kg	Kidney Liver, muscle, fat	Provisional MRLs expire on 1. 1. 1996

3.2. Agents acting on the autonomic nervous system

3.2.1. Anti-adrenergics

Pharmacologically active substance(s)	Marker residue	Animal species	MRLs	Target tissues	Other provisions
3.2.1.1. Carazolol	Carazolol	All food producing species	30 µg/kg 5 µg/kg	Liver, kidney Muscle, fat	Provisional MRLs expire on 1. 7. 1995 " [10]

" ANNEX IV

List of pharmacologically active substances for which no maximum levels can be fixed

1.   Nitrofurans, except furazolidone (see Annex III)

2.   Ronidazole

3.   Dapsone

4.   Chloramphenicol " [10]

ANNEX V

" Information and particulars to be included in an application for the establishment of a maximum residue limit for a pharmacologically active substance used in veterinary medicinal products

Administrative particulars

1. Name or corporate name and permanent address of the applicant.

2. Name of the veterinary medicinal product.

3. Qualitative and quantitative composition in terms of active principles, with mention of the international non-proprietary name recommended by the World Health Organization, where such name exists.

4. Manufacturing authorization, if any.

5. Marketing authorization, if any.

6. Summary of the characteristics of the veterinary medicinal product(s) prepared in accordance with Article 5a of Directive 81/851/EEC.

A. Safety documentation

A.0. Expert report

A.1. Precise identification of the substance concerned by the application

1.1. International non-proprietary name (INN).

1.2. International Union of Pure and Applied Chemistry (IUPAC) name.

1.3. Chemical Abstract Service (CAS) name.

1.4. Classification:

- therapeutic;
- pharmacological.

1.5. Synonyms and abbreviations.

1.6. Structural formula.

1.7. Molecular formula.

1.8. Molecular weight.

1.9. Degree of impurity.

1.10. Qualitative and quantitative composition of impurities.

1.11. Description of physical properties:

- melting point;
- boiling point;
- vapour pressure;
- solubility in water and organic solvents, expressed in grams per litre, with indication of temperature;
- density;

- refractive index, rotation, etc.

A.2. Relevant pharmacological studies

2.1. Pharmacodynamics.

2.2. Pharmacokinetics.

A.3. Toxicological studies

3.1. Single dose toxicity.

3.2. Repeated dose toxicity.

3.3. Tolerance in the target species of animal.

3.4. Reproductive toxicity, including teratogenicity.

3.4.1. Study of the effects on reproduction.
3.4.2. Embryotoxicity/fetotoxicity, including teratogenicity.

3.5. Mutagenicity.

3.6. Carcinogenicity.

A.4. Studies of other effects

4.1. Immunotoxicity.

4.2. Microbiological properties of residues.

4.2.1. On the human gut flora;
4.2.2. On the organisms and microorganisms used for industrial food-processing.

4.3. Observations in humans.

B. Residue documentation

B.0. Expert report

B.1. Precise identification of the substance concerned by the application

The substance concerned should be identified in accordance with point A.1. However, where the application relates to one or more veterinary medicinal products, the product itself should be identified in detail, including:

- qualitative and quantitative composition;
- purity;
- identification of the manufacturer's batch used in the studies; relationship to the final product;
- specific activity and radio-purity of labelled substances;
- position of labelled atoms on the molecule.

B.2. Residue studies

2.1. Pharmacokinetics (absorption, distribution, biotransformation, excretion).

2.2. Depletion of residues.

2.3. Elaboration of maximum residue limits (MRLS).

B.3. Routine analytical method for the detection of residues

3.1. Description of the method.

3.2. Validation of the method.

3.2.1. specificity;
3.2.2. accuracy, including sensitivity;
3.2.3. precision;
3.2.4. limit of detection;
3.2.5. limit of quantitation;
3.2.6. practicability and applicability under normal laboratory conditions;
3.2.7. susceptibility to interference. " [2]

(1) OJ No L 317, 06/11/1981, p. 16.
(2) OJ No L 317, 06/11/1981, p. 1.

II

(Acts whose publication is not obligatory)

COUNCIL

COUNCIL DIRECTIVE
of 26 March 1990
laying down the conditions governing the preparation, placing on the market and use of medicated feedingstuffs in the Community

(90/167/EEC)

THE COUNCIL OF THE EUROPEAN COMMUNITIES,

Having regard to the Treaty establishing the European Economic Community, and in particular Article 43 thereof,

Having regard to the proposal from the Commission ([1]),

Having regard to the opinion of the European Parliament ([2]),

Having regard to the opinion of the Economic and Social Committee ([3]),

Whereas the conditions with which medicated feedingstuffs should comply, in particular as concerns their preparation, supply, use and administration to animals, have no small influence on the rational development of the keeping and on the rearing of animals and the production of products of animal origin ;

Whereas the keeping and rearing of animals constitutes a major portion of the common agricultural policy ;

Whereas, to safeguard public health from any dangers arising from the use of medicated feedingstuffs for animals intended for food production, and to prevent distortions in competition in the keeping and rearing of farm animals, conditions should be laid down regarding the preparation, placing on the market and use of medicated feedingstuffs and regarding intra-Community trade in those products ;

Whereas Community rules regarding veterinary medicinal products, and in particular Council Directive 81/851/EEC of 28 September 1981 on the approximation of the laws of Member States relating to veterinary medicinal

products ([4]), and Council Directive 81/852/EEC of 28 September 1981 on the approximation of the laws of Member States relating to analytical, pharmaco-toxicological and clinical standards and protocols in respect of the testing of veterinary medicinal products ([5]), as amended by Directive 87/20/EEC ([6]), should be taken into account ;

Whereas medicated feedingstuffs must, with regard to the medicinal components, comply with the rules applicable to veterinary medicinal products ; whereas, however, in the manufacture of medicated feedingstuffs simple mixing is the main process ; whereas only authorized medicated pre-mixes may be used and precise instructions must be given for the use of these medicated feedingstuffs ; whereas, in addition, the person responsible for manufacture must have at his disposal sufficient staff and premises so that can meet the requirements of this Directive ;

Whereas it is the manufacturer's responsibility to carry out a quality control on the products placed on the market ; whereas, however, the manufacturing unit should be placed under satisfactory official control ;

Whereas, for the purposes of this Directive, the rules concerning checks and the safeguard measures laid down by Council Directive 89/662/EEC of 11 December 1989 concerning veterinary checks in intra-Community trade with a view to the completion of the internal market ([7]) should be used ;

([1]) OJ No C 41, 16. 2. 1982, p. 3 ; and
    OJ No C 182, 8. 7. 1983, p. 7.
([2]) OJ No C 128, 16. 5. 1983, p. 76.
([3]) OJ No C 114, 6. 5. 1982, p. 17.

([4]) OJ No L 317, 6. 11. 1981, p. 1.
([5]) OJ No L 317, 6. 11. 1981, p. 16.
([6]) OJ No L 15, 17. 1. 1987, p. 34.
([7]) OJ No L 395, 30. 12. 1989, p. 13.

Whereas the supply of medicated feedingstuffs to stock-farmers may only be on prescription of a veterinarian, who must himself comply with particular conditions when issuing the prescription;

Whereas, in order for there be to effective control, the persons concerned must be required to keep a register or, where appropriate, to retain the documents for a specified period of time;

Whereas, pending the complete harmonization of the rules authorizing the placing of veterinary medicinal products on the market, the possibility of making national derogations, in particular with respect to the manufacture of intermediate products or certain medicated pre-mixes, should be kept,

HAS ADOPTED THIS DIRECTIVE:

Article 1

This Directive lays down, without prejudice to the adoption of the list laid down in Article 2 (3) of Directive 81/851/EEC, the conditions other than those of animal health, governing the preparation, placing on the market and use of medicated feedingstuffs within the Community.

This Directive shall not affect Community rules applicable to additives used in feedingstuffs, or national rules adopted pursuant to the said rules, and in particular those applicable to the additives entered in Annex II of Directive 70/524/EEC ('), as last amended by Commission Directive 89/583/EEC (²).

Article 2

For the purposes of this Directive the definitions appearing in Article 1 (2) of Directive 81/851/EEC and Article 2 of Council Directive 79/373/EEC of 2 April 1979 on the marketing of compound feedingstuffs (³), as last amended by Directive 90/44/EEC (⁴), shall apply as necessary.

The following definitions shall also apply:

(a) 'authorized medicated pre-mix': any pre-mix for the manufacture of medicated feedingstuffs as defined in Article 1 (2) of Directive 81/851/EEC which has been granted an authorization in accordance with Article 4 of that Directive;

(b) 'placing on the market': the holding in the territory of the Community for sale or disposal in any other form whatever to third parties, whether or not for consideration, and actual sale or disposal.

(') OJ No L 270, 14. 12. 1970, p. 1.
(²) OJ No L 325, 10. 11. 1989, p. 33.
(³) OJ No L 86, 6. 4. 1979, p. 30.
(⁴) OJ No L 27, 31. 1. 1990, p. 35.

Article 3

1.   Member States shall prescribe that, as regards the medicinal component, medicated feedingstuffs may be manufactured from authorized medicated pre-mixes only.

By way of derogation from the first subparagraph, Member States may, provided they comply with the requirements of Article 4 (4) of Directive 81/851/EEC:

— subject to any specific conditions laid down in authorizations to place authorized medicated pre-mixes on the market, authorize intermediate products which are prepared from such medicated pre-mixes authorized in accordance with Article 4 of Directive 81/851/EEC and from one or more feedingstuffs and which are intended for the subsequent manufacture of medicated feedingstuffs ready for use.

Member States shall take all necessary steps to ensure that intermediate products are manufactured only by establishments authorized in accordance with Article 4 and that they are the subject of a declaration to the competent authority,

— authorize the veterinarian to have manufactured under the conditions laid down in Article 4 (3) of Directive 81/851/EEC, and under his responsibility and on prescription, medicated feedingstuffs from several authorized medicated pre-mixes, provided that there is no specific authorized therapeutic agent in pre-mix form for the disease to be treated or for the species concerned.

Until the date on which the Member States have to comply with the new rules laid down in Article 4 (3) of Directive 81/851/EEC, national rules governing the above conditions shall remain applicable, with due regard for the general provisions of the Treaty.

2.   Products authorized pursuant to paragraph 1 shall be subject to the rules laid down in Articles 24 to 50 of Directive 81/851/EEC.

Article 4

1.   Member States shall take all necessary measures to ensure that medicated feedingstuffs are manufactured only under the conditions set out below:

(a) the manufacturer shall have premises which have been previously approved by the competent national authority, technical equipment and suitable and adequate storage and inspection facilities;

(b) the medicated feedingstuffs manufacturing plant shall be manned by staff whose knowledge of and qualifications in mixing technology are adequate;

(c) the producer shall be responsible for ensuring that:

— only feedingstuffs or combinations thereof which comply with Community provisions on feedingstuffs are used,

— the feedingstuff used produces a homogeneous and stable mix with the authorized medicated pre-mix,

— the authorized medicated pre-mix is used during the manufacturing process in accordance with the conditions laid down when authorization for placing on the market was given and, in particular, that :

(i) there is no possibility of any undesirable interaction between veterinary medicinal products, additives and feedingstuffs ;

(ii) the medicated feedingstuff will keep for the stipulated period ;

(iii) the feedingstuff to be used for producing the medicated feedingstuff does not contain the same antibiotic or the same coccidiostat as those used as an active substance in the medicated pre-mix ;

— the daily dose of medicinal product is contained in a quantity of feedingstuff corresponding to at least half the daily feed ration of the animals treated or, in the case of ruminants, corresponding to at least half the daily requirement of nonmineral supplementary feedingstuffs ;

(d) premises, staff and equipment used and participating in the entire manufacturing process must comply with the manufacturing hygiene rules and principles of the Member State in question ; the manufacturing process must conform to the rules of good manufacturing practice ;

(e) the medicated feedingstuffs manufactured shall undergo regular checks — including appropriate laboratory tests of homogeneity — by the manufacturing establishments, under the supervision and periodic control of the official department, to ensure that the medicated feedingstuff complies with the requirements of this Directive, especially in respect of its homogeneity, stability and storability ;

(f) manufacturers shall be obliged to keep daily records of the types and quantities of the authorized medicated pre-mixes and feedingstuffs used and of the medicated feedingstuffs manufactured, held or dispatched, together with the names and addresses of the breeders or holders of the animals, and in the case provided for in Article 10 (2), the name and address of the authorized distributor and, where appropriate, the name and address of the prescribing veterinarian. The records, which must meet the requirements of Article 5 of Directive 81/851/EEC, must be kept for at least three years after the date of the last entry and must be made available at any time to the competent authorities in case of checking ;

(g) pre-mixes and medicated feedingstuffs shall be stored in suitable separate and secured rooms or hermetic containers which are specially designed for the storage of such products.

2. Member States may, by way of derogation from paragraph 1, subject to any additional guarantees appropriate, authorize the manufacture of medicated feedingstuffs on farms provided that the said paragraph is complied with.

Article 5

1. Member States shall prescribe that medicated feedingstuffs may be placed on the market only in packages or containers sealed in such a way that, when the package is opened, the closure or seal is damaged and they cannot be re-used.

2. Where road tankers or similar containers are used to place medicated feedingstuffs on the market, these must be cleaned before any re-use in order to prevent any subsequent undesirable interaction or contamination.

Article 6

1. Member States shall take all necessary measures to ensure that medicated feedingstuffs are not put into circulation unless the labelling complies with the Community provisions in force.

Furthermore, the packages or containers referred to in Article 5 (1) shall be clearly marked 'Medicated Feedingstuffs'.

2. Where road tankers or similar containers are used to place medicated feedingstuffs on the market, it shall be sufficient for the information referred to in paragraph 1 to be contained in the accompanying documents.

Article 7

1. Member States shall take all necessary measures to ensure that a medicated feedingstuff cannot be held, placed on the market or used unless it has been manufactured in accordance with this Directive.

2. Subject to the requirements of Article 4 (2) of Directive 81/851/EEC with regard to the tests to be carried out on veterinary medicinal products, Member States may, however, for scientific purposes, provide for derogations from this Directive, provided there is adequate official control.

Article 8

1. Member States shall ensure that medicated feedingstuffs are not supplied to stockfarmers or holders of animals except on presentation of a prescription from a registered veterinarian on the following terms :

(a) the veterinarian's prescription shall be made out on a form which contains the headings shown on the specimen in Annex A ; the original form shall be for the manufacturer or, where appropriate, a distributor approved by the competent authority of the Member State of destination of the medicated feedingstuffs ;

(b) the competent national authorities shall determine the number of copies of the prescription form, the persons who are to receive a copy and the period for which the original and the copies must be kept;

(c) medicated feedingstuffs may not be used for more than one treatment under the same prescription.

The veterinary prescription shall be valid only for a period determined by the competent national authority which may not exceed three months;

(d) the veterinarian's prescription may be used only for animals treated by him. He must first satisfy himself that:

(i) the use of this medication is justified for the species concerned on veterinary grounds;

(ii) administration of the medicinal product is not incompatible with a previous treatment or use and that there is no contra-indication or interaction where several pre-mixes are used;

(e) the veterinarian must:

(i) prescribe the medicated feedingstuffs only in such quantities as, within the maximum limits laid down by the national authorization for placing medicated pre-mixes on the market, are necessary for the purpose of the treatment;

(ii) satisfy himself that the medicated feedingstuff and the feedingstuff currently used to feed treated animals do not contain the same antibiotic or the same coccidiostat as active substances.

2. However, in the case of anthelmintic medicinal products (vermifuges), Member States may, pending the review to be carried out under Directive 81/851/EEC of the risks associated with the use of these groups of substances, derogate for five years after the adoption of this Directive from the obligation laid down in paragraph 1 not to supply medicated feedingstuffs obtained from authorized medicated pre-mixes except on presentation of a veterinary prescription, provided that:

— the medicated pre-mixes used do not contain active substances which belong to the chemical groups used, in their territory, on medical prescription for human medicine,

— the medicated feedingstuffs accorded such authorization are used in their territory only prophylactically and in the dosages necessary for the purpose in question.

Member States applying such a derogation shall inform the Commission and the other Member States thereof within the Standing Veterinary Committee, before the date provided for in the first indent of the first subparagraph of Article 15, specifying in particular the nature of the medicinal products and animal species that it covers.

Not more than six months before the expiry of the five-year period laid down in the first subparagraph the Commission shall report to the Council on the risks associated with the use of these groups of substances and may include proposals on which the Council will decide by a qualified majority.

3. Where medicated feedingstuffs are administered to animals whose meat, flesh, offal or products are intended for human consumption, the stockfarmer or holder of the animals concerned must ensure that treated animals are not slaughtered in order to be offered for consumption before the end of the withdrawal period and that products obtained from a treated animal before the end of such a withdrawal period are not disposed of with a view to their being offered for human consumption.

Article 9

1. Member States shall take all necessary measures to ensure that medicated feedingstuffs are issued directly to the stockfarmer or holder of the animals only by the manufacturer or distributor specially approved by the competent authority of the Member State of destination.

Furthermore, medicated feedingstuffs for the treatment of animals whose meat, flesh, offal or products are intended for human consumption may not be issued unless:

— they do not exceed the quantities prescribed for the treatment, in accordance with the veterinary prescription where this is provided for,

— they are not issued in quantities greater than one month's requirements as established in accordance with the stipulations of the first indent.

2. However, notwithstanding paragraph 1, Member States may in special cases authorize distributors specifically approved for that purpose to issue, on the basis of a veterinary prescription, medicated feedingstuffs in small quantities, prepacked and ready for use, and prepared, without prejudice to Article 8 (2) in accordance with the requirements of this Directive, provided that these distributors:

— comply with the same conditions as the manufacturer regarding the keeping of registers and the storage, transport and issue of the products concerned,

— are subject to special checking for the purpose, under the supervision of the competent veterinary authority,

— may supply only prepacked or prepackaged medicated feedingstuffs ready for use by the holder or stockfarmer that have on the packaging or containers instructions for the use of the said medicated feedingstuffs and, in particular, an indication of the withdrawal period.

3. The provisions of paragraph 2 shall not affect national rules on the legal ownership of the medicated feedingstuffs.

Article 10

1. Member States shall ensure that, without prejudice to animal-health rules, there are no prohibitions, limitations or obstacles in respect of intra-Community trade

— in medicated feedingstuffs which have been manufactured in accordance with the requirements of this Directive, and in particular Article 4 thereof, with authorized pre-mixes which have the same active substances as pre-mixes authorized by the Member State of destination, in accordance with the criteria of Directive 81/852/EEC, and a quantitative and qualitative composition similar thereto,

— subject to the specific provisions of Council Directive 86/469/EEC of 16 September 1986 concerning the examination of animals and fresh meat for the presence of residues [1] and Council Directive 88/299/EEC of 17 May 1988 on trade in animals treated with certain substances having a hormonal action and their meat, as referred to in Article 7 of Directive 88/146/EEC [2], in animals to which those medicated feedingstuffs except those produced pursuant to the second subparagraph of Article 3 (1), have been administered, or in meat, flesh, offal or their products from such animals.

2. Where the application of paragraph 1 gives rise to dispute, in particular as concerns recognition of the similar nature of the pre-mix, the Member States concerned or the Commission may submit the dispute to assessment by an expert appearing on a list of Community experts to be drawn up by the Commission on a proposal from the Member States.

If the two Member States so agree beforehand, the parties shall abide by the opinion of the expert, in compliance with Community legislation.

3. The Member State of destination may require that each consignment of a medicated feedingstuff be accompanied by a certificate issued by the competent authority, corresponding to the specimen form in Annex B.

Article 11

1. The safeguard measures laid down by Directive 89/662/EEC shall apply to trade in authorized medicated pre-mixes or medicated feedingstuffs.

2. The rules laid down concerning veterinary control and, in particular, the requirements laid down in Article 5 (2) and Article 20 of Directive 89/662/EEC shall apply to trade in authorized pre-mixes or medicated feedingstuffs to the extent that they are subject to veterinary control.

Article 12

The Council, acting by a qualified majority on proposals from the Commission, shall adopt any amendments and additions to be made to this Directive.

Article 13

Member States shall take all necessary measures to ensure that their competent authorities satisfy themselves :

(i) by making sampling checks at all stages of the production and marketing of the products referred to by this Directive, that the provisions of this Directive are complied with ;

(ii) in particular, by making sampling checks on farms and slaughterhouses, that medicated feedingstuffs are used in compliance with the conditions of use, and that withdrawal periods have been complied with.

Article 14

Pending the implementation of Community measures relating to imports of medicated feedingstuffs from third countries, Member States shall apply to those imports measures which are at least equivalent to those of this Directive.

Article 15

Member States shall bring into force the laws, regulations and administrative provisions necessary to comply :

— with the requirements of Article 11 (2) on the date on which they must conform with the Community rules on the protection of feedingstuffs against pathogenic agents, but at the latest by 31 December 1992,

— before 1 October 1991, with the other provisions of this Directive.

They shall forthwith inform the Commission thereof.

Article 16

This Directive is addressed to the Member States.

Done at Luxembourg, 26 March 1990.

For the Council
The President
M. O'KENNEDY

---

[1] OJ No L 275, 26. 9. 1986, p. 36.
[2] OJ No L 128, 21. 5. 1988, p. 36.

ANNEX A

....

....

Surname, forename and address of the prescribing veterinarian :

(Copy for the manufacturer or authorized distributor) (¹)

(to be kept for ....) (²)

PRESCRIPTION FOR A MEDICATED FEEDINGSTUFF

| This prescription may not be re-used |

Name or business name and address of the manufacturer or supplier of the medicated feedingstuff :

....

....

Name and address of the stockfarmer or holder of the animals : ....

....

Identification and number of animals : ....

Disease to be treated (³) : ....

Designation of the authorized medicated pre-mixes :

....

....

....

....

Quantity of medicated feedingstuff : .... kg

Special instructions for the stockfarmer :

Percentage of medicated feedingstuff in the daily ration, frequency and duration of treatment : ....

....

Withdrawal time before slaughtering, or waiting time before placing on the market products from treated

animals : ....

....

....
Personal signature of veterinarian

To be completed by the manufacturer or authorized distributor :

Date of delivery : ....

To be used before : ....

....
Signature of manufacturer or supplier

_____

(¹) To be filled in in accordance with Article 8 (1) (b).
(²) To be specified by the competent national authorities.
(³) To be entered only on the copy for the veterinarian.

ANNEX B

ACCOMPANYING CERTIFICATE IN RESPECT OF MEDICATED FEEDINGSTUFFS FOR ANIMALS INTENDED FOR TRADE

Name and address of the manufacturer or approved distributor :

....

....

....

Name of the medicated feedingstuff : ....

— Type of animal for which the medicated feedingstuff is intended : ....

— Name and composition of the authorized medicated pre-mix : ....

....

— Dosage of the medicated pre-mix authorized in the medicated feeding stuff :

....

Quantity of medicated feedingstuff : ....

Name and address of the recipient : ....

....

....

It is hereby certified that the medicated feedingstuff as described above has been manufactured by an authorized person in accordance with Directive 90/167/EEC.

....
Place and date

Stamp of the veterinary authority
or other competent authority

....
(signature)
Name and position

Economic environment
of veterinary medicinal products

I

(Acts whose publication is obligatory)

COUNCIL REGULATION (EEC) No 1768/92

of 18 June 1992

concerning the creation of a supplementary protection certificate for medicinal products

THE COUNCIL OF THE EUROPEAN COMMUNITIES,

Having regard to the Treaty establishing the European Economic Community, and in particular Article 100a thereof,

Having regard to the proposal from the Commission (¹),

In cooperation with the European Parliament (²),

Having regard to the opinion of the Economic and Social Committee (³),

Whereas pharmaceutical research plays a decisive role in the continuing improvement in public health;

Whereas medicinal products, especially those that are the result of long, costly research will not continue to be developed in the Community and in Europe unless they are covered by favourable rules that provide for sufficient protection top encourage such research;

Whereas at the moment the period that elapses between the filing of an application for a patent for a new medicinal product and authorization to place the medicinal product on the market makes the period of effective protection under the patent insufficient to cover the investment put into the research;

Whereas this situation leads to a lack of protection which penalizes pharmaceutical research;

Whereas the current situation is creating the risk of research centres situated in the Member States relocating to countries that already offer greater protection;

Whereas a uniform solution at Community level should be provided for, thereby preventing the heterogeneous development of national laws leading to further disparities which would be likely to create obstacles to the free movement of medicinal products within the Community and thus directly affect the establishment and the functioning of the internal market;

Whereas, therefore, the creation of a supplementary protection certificate granted, under the same conditions, by each of the Member States at the request of the holder of a national or European patent relating to a medicinal product for which marketing authorization has been granted is necessary; whereas a Regulation is therefore the most appropriate legal instrument;

Whereas the duration of the protection granted by the certificate should be such as to provide adequate effective protection; whereas, for this purpose, the holder of both a patent and a certificate should be able to enjoy an overall maximum of fifteen years of exclusively from the time the medicinal product in question first obtains authorization to be placed on the market in the Community;

Whereas all the interests at stake, including those of public health, in a sector as complex and sensitive as the pharmaceutical sector must nevertheless be taken into account; whereas, for this purpose, the certificate cannot be granted for a period exceeding five years; whereas the protection granted should furthermore be strictly confined to the product which obtained authorization to be placed on the market as a medicinal product;

Whereas a fair balance should also be struck with regard to the determination of the transitional arrangements; whereas such arrangements should enable the Community pharmaceutical industry to catch up to some extent with its main competitors who, for a number of years, have been covered by laws guaranteeing them more adequate protection, while making sure that the arrangements do not compromise the achievement of other legitimate objectives concerning the health policies pursued both at national and Community level;

Whereas the transitional arrangements applicable to applications for certificates filed and to certificates granted under national legislation prior to the entry into force of this Regulation should be defined;

(¹) OJ No C 114, 8. 5. 1990, p. 10.
(²) OJ No C 19, 28. 1. 1991, p. 94 and
    OJ No C 150, 15. 6. 1992.
(³) OJ No C 69, 18. 3. 1991, p. 22.

Whereas special arrangements should be allowed in Member States whose laws introduced the patentability of pharmaceutical products only very recently;

Whereas provision should be made for appropriate limitation of the duration of the certificate in the special case where a patent term has already been extended under a specific national law,

HAS ADOPTED THIS REGULATION:

Article 1

Definitions

For the purposes of this Regulation:

(a) 'medicinal product' means any substance or combination of substances presented for treating or preventing disease in human beings or animals and any substance or combination of substances which may be administered to human beings or animals with a view to making a medical diagnosis or to restoring, correcting or modifying physiological functions in humans or in animals;

(b) 'product' means the active ingredient or combination of active ingredients of a medicinal product;

(c) 'basic patent' means a patent which protects a product as defined in (b) as such, a process to obtain a product or an application of a product, and which is designated by its holder for the purpose of the procedure for grant of a certificate;

(d) 'certificate' means the supplementary protection certificate.

Article 2

Scope

Any product protected by a patent in the territory of a Member State and subject, prior to being placed on the market as a medicinal product, to an administrative authorization procedure as laid down in Council Directive 65/65/EEC (¹) or Directive 81/851/EEC (²) may, under the terms and conditions provided for in this Regulation, be the subject of a certificate.

Article 3

Conditions for obtaining a certificate

A certificate shall be granted if, in the Member State in which the application referred to in Article 7 is submitted and at the date of that application:

(¹) OJ No L 22, 9. 12. 1965, p. 369. Last amended by Directive 89/341/EEC (OJ No L 142, 25. 5. 1989, p. 11).
(²) OJ No L 317, 6. 11. 1981, p. 1. Amended by Directive 90/676/EEC (OJ No L 373, 31. 12. 1990, p. 15).

(a) the product is protected by a basic patent in force;

(b) a valid authorization to place the product on the market as a medicinal product has been granted in accordance with Directive 65/65/EEC or Directive 81/851/EEC, as appropriate;

(c) the product has not already been the subject of a certificate;

(d) the authorization referred to in (b) is the first authorization to place the product on the market as a medicinal product.

Article 4

Subject-matter of protection

Within the limits of the protection conferred by the basic patent, the protection conferred by a certificate shall extend only to the product covered by the authorization to place the corresponding medicinal product on the market and for any use of the product as a medicinal product that has been authorized before the expiry of the certificate.

Article 5

Effects of the certificate

Subject to the provisions of Article 4, the certificate shall confer the same rights as conferred by the basic patent and shall be subject to the same limitations and the same obligations.

Article 6

Entitlement to the certificate

The certificate shall be granted to the holder of the basic patent or his successor in title.

Article 7

Application for a certificate

1. The application for a certificate shall be lodged within six months of the date on which the authorization referred to in Article 3 (b) to place the product on the market as a medicinal product was granted.

2. Notwithstanding paragraph 1, where the authorization to place the product on the market is granted before the basic patent is granted, the application for a certificate shall be lodged within six months of the date on which the patent is granted.

Article 8

Content of the application for a certificate

1.   The application for a certificate shall contain :

(a) a request for the grant of a certificate, stating in particular :

  (i) the name and address of the applicant ;

  (ii) if he has appointed a representative, the name and address of the representative ;

  (iii) the number of the basic patent and the title of the invention ;

  (iv) the number and date of the first authorization to place the product on the market, as referred to in Article 3 (b) and, if this authorization is not the first authorization for placing the product on the market in the Community, the number and date of that authorization ;

(b) a copy of the authorization to place the product on the market, as referred to in Article 3 (b), in which the product is identified, containing in particular the number and date of the authorization and the summary of the product characteristics listed in Article 4a of Directive 65/65/EEC or Article 5a of Directive 81/851/EEC ;

(c) if the authorization referred to in (b) is not the first authorization for placing the product on the market as a medicinal product in the Community, information regarding the identity of the product thus authorized and the legal provision under which the authorization procedure took place, together with a copy of the notice publishing the authorization in the appropriate official publication.

2.   Member States may provide that a fee is to be payable upon application for a certificate.

Article 9

Lodging of an application for a certificate

1.   The application for a certificate shall be lodged with the competent industrial property office of the Member State which granted the basic patent or on whose behalf it was granted and in which the authorization referred to in Article 3 (b) to place the product on the market was obtained, unless the Member State designates another authority for the purpose.

2.   Notification of the application for a certificate shall be published by the authority referred to in paragraph 1. The notification shall contain at least the following information :

(a) the name and address of the applicant ;

(b) the number of the basic patent ;

(c) the title of the invention ;

(d) the number and date of the authorization to place the product on the market, referred to in Article 3 (b), and the product identified in that authorization ;

(e) where relevant, the number and date of the first authorization to place the product on the market in the Community.

Article 10

Grant of the certificate or rejection of the application

1.   Where the application for a certificate and the product to which it relates meet the conditions laid down in this Regulation, the authority referred to in Article 9 (1) shall grant the certificate.

2.   The authority referred to in Article 9 (1) shall, subject to paragraph 3, reject the application for a certificate if the application or the product to which it relates does not meet the conditions laid down in this Regulation.

3.   Where the application for a certificate does not meet the conditions laid down in Article 8, the authority referred to in Article 9 (1) shall ask the applicant to rectify the irregularity, or to settle the fee, within a stated time.

4.   If the irregularity is not rectified or the fee is not settled under paragraph 3 within the stated time, the authority shall reject the application.

5.   Member States may provide that the authority referred to in Article 9 (1) is to grant certificates without verifying that the conditions laid down in Article 3 (c) and (d) are met.

Article 11

Publication

1.   Notification of the fact that a certificate has been granted shall be published by the authority referred to in Article 9 (1). The notification shall contain at least the following information :

(a) the name and address of the holder of the certificate ;

(b) the number of the basic patent ;

(c) the title of the invention ;

(d) the number and date of the authorization to place the product on the market referred to in Article 3 (b) and the product identified in that authorization ;

(e) where relevant, the number and date of the first authorization to place the product on the market in the Community ;

(f) the duration of the certificate.

2. Notification of the fact that the application for a certificate has been rejected shall be published by the authority referred to in Article 9 (1). The notification shall contain at least the information listed in Article 9 (2).

Article 12

Annual fees

Member States may require that the certificate be subject to the payment of annual fees.

Article 13

Duration of the certificate

1. The certificate shall take effect at the end of the lawful term of the basic patent for a perid equal to the period which elapsed between the date on which the application for a basic patent was lodged and the date of the first authorization to place the product on the market in the Community reduced by a period of five years.

2. Notwithstanding paragraph 1, the duration of the certificate may not exceed five years from the date on which it takes effect.

Article 14

Expiry of the certificate

The certificate shall lapse :

(a) at the end of the period provided for in Article 13 ;

(b) if the certificate-holder surrenders it ;

(c) if the annual fee laid down in accordance with Article 12 is not paid in time ;

(d) if and as long as the product covered by the certificate may no longer be placed on the market following the withdrawal of the appropriate authorization or authorizations to place on the market in accordance with Directive 65/65/EEC or Directive 81/851/EEC. The authority referred to in Article 9 (1) may decide on the lapse of the certificate either of its own motion or at the request of a third party.

Article 15

Invalidity of the certificate

1. The certificate shall be invalid if :

(a) it was granted contrary to the provisions of Article 3 ;

(b) the basic patent has lapsed before its lawful term expires ;

(c) the basic patent is revoked or limited to the extent that the product for which the certificate was granted would no longer be protected by the claims of the basic patent or, after the basic patent has expired, grounds for revocation exist which would have justified such revocation or limitation.

2. Any person may submit an application or bring an action for a declaration of invalidity of the certificate before the body responsible under national law for the renovation of the corresponding basic patent.

Article 16

Notification of lapse or invalidity

If the certificate lapses in accordance with Article 14 (b), (c) or (d) or is invalid in accordance with Article 15, notification thereof shall be published by the authority referred to in Article 9 (1).

Article 17

Appeals

The decisions of the authority referred to in Article 9 (1) or of the body referred to in Article 15 (2) taken under this Regulation shall be open to the same appeals as those provided for in national law against similar decisions taken in respect of national patents.

Article 18

Procedure

1. In the absence of procedural provisions in this Regulation, the procedural provisions applicable under national law to the corresponding basic patent shall apply to the certificate, unless that law lays down special procedural provisions for certificates.

2. Notwithstanding paragraph 1, the procedure for opposition to the granting of a certificate shall be excluded.

Article 19

Transitional provisions

1. Any product which, on the date on which this Regulation enters into force, is protected by a valid basic patent and for which the first authorization to place it on the market as a medicinal product in the Community was obtained after 1 January 1985 may be granted a certificate.

In the case of certificates to be granted in Denmark and in Germany, the date of 1 January 1985 shall be replaced by that of 1 January 1988.

In the case of certificates to be granted in Belgium and in Italy, the date of 1 January 1985 shall be replaced by that of 1 January 1982.

2. An application for a certificate as referred to in paragraph 1 shall be submitted within six months of the date on which this Regulation enters into force.

Article 20

This Regulation shall not apply to certificates granted in accordance with the national legislation of a Member State before the date on which this Regulation enters into force or to applications for a certificate filed in accordance with that legislation before the date of publication of this Regulation in the *Official Journal of the European Communities*.

Article 21

In those Member States whose national law did not on 1 January 1990 provide for the patentability of pharmaceutical products, this Regulation shall apply five years after the entry into force of this Regulation.

Article 19 shall not apply in those Member States.

Article 22

Where a certificate is granted for a product protected by a patent which, before the date on which this Regulation enters into force, has had its term extended or for which such extension was applied for, under national patent law, the term of protection to be afforded under this certificate shall be reduced by the number of years by which the term of the patent exceeds 20 years.

FINAL PROVISION

Article 23

Entry into force

This Regulation shall enter into force six months after its publication in the *Official Journal of the European Communities*.

This Regulation shall be binding in its entirety and directly applicable in all Member States.

Done at Luxembourg, 18 June 1992.

For the Council
The President
Vitor MARTINS

Other relevant texts applicable to medicinal products for human and/or veterinary use

COUNCIL DIRECTIVE

of 25 July 1985

on the approximation of the laws, regulations and administrative provisions of the Member States concerning liability for defective products

(85/374/EEC)

THE COUNCIL OF THE EUROPEAN COMMUNITIES,

Having regard to the Treaty establishing the European Economic Community, and in particular Article 100 thereof,

Having regard to the proposal from the Commission (¹),

Having regard to the opinion of the European Parliament (²),

Having regard to the opinion of the Economic and Social Committee (³),

Whereas approximation of the laws of the Member States concerning the liability of the producer for damage caused by the defectiveness of his products is necessary because the existing divergences may distort competition and affect the movement of goods within the common market and entail a differing degree of protection of the consumer against damage caused by a defective product to his health or property;

Whereas liability without fault on the part of the producer is the sole means of adequately solving the problem, peculiar to our age of increasing technicality, of a fair apportionment of the risks inherent in modern technological production;

Whereas libility without fault should apply only to movables which have been industrially produced; whereas, as a result, it is appropriate to exclude liability for agricultural products and game, except where they have undergone a processing of an industrial nature which could cause a defect in these products; whereas the liability provided for in this Directive should also apply to movables which are used in the construction of immovables or are installed in immovables;

Whereas protection of the consumer requires that all producers involved in the production process should be made liable, in so far as their finished product, component part or any raw material supplied by them

was defective; whereas, for the same reason, liability should extend to importers of products into the Community and to persons who present themselves as producers by affixing their name, trade mark or other distinguishing feature or who supply a product the producer of which cannot be identified;

Whereas, in situations where several persons are liable for the same damage, the protection of the consumer requires that the injured person should be able to claim full compensation for the damage from any one of them;

whereas, to protect the physical well-being and property of the consumer, the defectiveness of the product should be determined by reference not to its fitness for use but to the lack of the safety which the public at large is entitled to expect; whereas the safety is assessed by excluding any misuse of the product not reasonable under the circumstances;

Whereas a fair apportionment of risk between the injured person and the producer implies that the producer should be able to free himself from liability if he furnishes proof as to the existence of certain exonerating circumstances;

Whereas the protection of the consumer requires that the liability of the producer remains unaffected by acts or omissions of other persons having contributed to cause the damage; whereas, however, the contributory negligence of the injured person may be taken into account to reduce or disallow such liability;

Whereas the protection of the consumer requires compensation for death and personal injury as well as compensation for damage to property; whereas the latter should nevertheless be limited to goods for private use or consumption and be subject to a deduction of a lower threshold of a fixed amount in order to avoid litigation in an excessive number of cases; whereas this Directive should not prejudice compensation for pain and suffering and other non-material damages payable, where appropriate, under the law applicable to the case;

Whereas a uniform period of limitation for the bringing of action for compensation is in the interests both of the injured person and of the producer;

(¹) OJ No C 241, 14. 10. 1976, p. 9 and OJ No C 271, 26. 10. 1979, p. 3.
(²) OJ No C 127, 21. 5. 1979, p. 61.
(³) OJ No C 114, 7. 5. 1979, p. 15.

Whereas products age in the course of time, higher safety standards are developed and the state of science and technology progresses; whereas, therefore, it would not be reasonable to make the producer liable for an unlimited period for the defectiveness of his product; whereas, therefore, liability should expire after a reasonable length of time, without prejudice to claims pending at law;

Whereas, to achieve effective protection of consumers, no contractual derogation should be permitted as regards the liability of the producer in relation to the injured person;

Whereas under the legal systems of the Member States an injured party may have a claim for damages based on grounds of contractual liability or on grounds of non-contractual liability other than that provided for in this Directive; in so far as these provisions also serve to attain the objective of effective protection of consumers, they should remain unaffected by this Directive; whereas, in so far as effective protection of consumers in the sector of pharmaceutical products is already also attained in a Member State under a special liability system, claims based on this system should similarly remain possible;

Whereas, to the extent that liability for nuclear injury or damage is already covered in all Member States by adequate special rules, it has been possible to exclude damage of this type from the scope of this Directive;

Whereas, since the exclusion of primary agricultural products and game from the scope of this Directive may be felt, in certain Member States, in view of what is expected for the protection of consumers, to restrict unduly such protection, it should be possible for a Member State to extend liability to such products;

Whereas, for similar reasons, the possibility offered to a producer to free himself from liability if he proves that the state of scientific and technical knowledge at the time when he put the product into circulation was not such as to enable the existence of a defect to be discovered may be felt in certain Member States to restrict unduly the protection of the consumer; whereas it should therefore be possible for a Member State to maintain in its legislation or to provide by new legislation that this exonerating circumstance is not admitted; whereas, in the case of new legislation, making use of this derogation should, however, be subject to a Community stand-still procedure, in order to raise, if possible, the level of protection in a uniform manner throughout the Community;

Whereas, taking into account the legal traditions in most of the Member States, it is inappropriate to set any financial ceiling on the producer's liability without

fault; whereas, in so far as there are, however, differing traditions, it seems possible to admit that a Member State may derogate from the principle of unlimited liability by providing a limit for the total liability of the producer for damage resulting from a death or personal injury and caused by identical items with the same defect, provided that this limit is established at a level sufficiently high to guarantee adequate protection of the consumer and the correct functioning of the common market;

Whereas the harmonization resulting from this cannot be total at the present stage, but opens the way towards greater harmonization; whereas it is therefore necessary that the Council receive at regular intervals, reports from the Commission on the application of this Directive, accompanied, as the case may be, by appropriate proposals;

Whereas it is particularly important in this respect that a re-examination be carried out of those parts of the Directive relating to the derogations open to the Member States, at the expiry of a period of sufficient length to gather practical experience on the effects of these derogations on the protection of consumers and on the functioning of the common market,

HAS ADOPTED THIS DIRECTIVE:

Article 1

The producer shall be liable for damage caused by a defect in his product.

Article 2

For the purpose of this Directive 'product' means all movables, with the exception of primary agricultural products and game, even though incorporated into another movable or into an immovable. 'Primary agricultural products' means the products of the soil, of stock-farming and of fisheries, excluding products which have undergone initial processing. 'Product' includes electricity.

Article 3

1. 'Producer' means the manufacturer of a finished product, the producer of any raw material or the manufacturer of a component part and any person who, by putting his name, trade mark or other distinguishing feature on the product presents himself as its producer.

2. Without prejudice to the liability of the producer, any person who imports into the Community a product for sale, hire, leasing or any form of distribution in the course of his business shall be deemed to be a producer within the meaning of this Directive and shall be responsible as a producer.

3. Where the producer of the product cannot be identified, each supplier of the product shall be treated as its producer unless he informs the injured person, within a reasonable time, of the identity of the producer or of the person who supplied him with the product. The same shall apply, in the case of an imported product, if this product does not indicate the identity of the importer referred to in paragraph 2, even if the name of the producer is indicated.

Article 4

The injured person shall be required to prove the damage, the defect and the causal relationship between defect and damage.

Article 5

Where, as a result of the provisions of this Directive, two or more persons are liable for the same damage, they shall be liable jointly and severally, without prejudice to the provisions of national law concerning the rights of contribution or recourse.

Article 6

1. A product is defective when it does not provide the safety which a person is entitled to expect, taking all circumstances into account, including:

(a) the presentation of the product;

(b) the use to which it could reasonably be expected that the product would be put;

(c) the time when the product was put into circulation.

2. A product shall not be considered defective for the sole reason that a better product is subsequently put into circulation.

Article 7

The producer shall not be liable as a result of this Directive if he proves:

(a) that he did not put the product into circulation; or

(b) that, having regard to the circumstances, it is probable that the defect which caused the damage did not exist at the time when the product was put into circulation by him or that this defect came into being afterwards; or

(c) that the product was neither manufactured by him for sale or any form of distribution for economic purpose nor manufactured or distributed by him in the course of his business; or

(d) that the defect is due to compliance of the product with mandatory regulations issued by the public authorities; or

(e) that the state of scientific and technical knowledge at the time when he put the product into circulation was not such as to enable the existence of the defect to be discovered; or

(f) in the case of a manufacturer of a component, that the defect is attributable to the design of the product in which the component has been fitted or to the instructions given by the manufacturer of the product.

Article 8

1. Without prejudice to the provisions of national law concerning the right of contribution or recourse, the liability of the producer shall not be reduced when the damage is caused both by a defect in product and by the act or omission of a third party.

2. The liability of the producer may be reduced or disallowed when, having regard to all the circumstances, the damage is caused both by a defect in the product and by the fault of the injured person or any person for whom the injured person is responsible.

Article 9

For the purpose of Article 1, 'damage' means:

(a) damage caused by death or by personal injuries;

(b) damage to, or destruction of, any item of property other than the defective product itself, with a lower threshold of 500 ECU, provided that the item of property:

  (i) is of a type ordinarily intended for private use or consumption, and

  (ii) was used by the injured person mainly for his own private use or consumption.

This Article shall be without prejudice to national provisions relating to non-material damage.

Article 10

1. Member States shall provide in their legislation that a limitation period of three years shall apply to proceedings for the recovery of damages as provided for in this Directive. The limitation period shall begin to run from the day on which the plaintiff became aware, or should reasonably have become aware, of the damage, the defect and the identity of the producer.

2. The laws of Member States regulating suspension or interruption of the limitation period shall not be affected by this Directive.

Article 11

Member States shall provide in their legislation that the rights conferred upon the injured person pursuant to this Directive shall be extinguished upon the expiry of a period of 10 years from the date on which the producer put into circulation the actual product which caused the damage, unless the injured person has in the meantime instituted proceedings against the producer.

Article 12

The liability of the producer arising from this Directive may not, in relation to the injured person, be limited or excluded by a provision limiting his liability or exempting him from liability.

Article 13

This Directive shall not affect any rights which an injured person may have according to the rules of the law of contractual or non-contractual liability or a special liability system existing at the moment when this Directive is notified.

Article 14

This Directive shall not apply to injury or damage arising from nuclear accidents and covered by international conventions ratified by the Member States.

Article 15

1. Each Member State may:

(a) by way of derogation from Article 2, provide in its legislation that within the meaning of Article 1 of this Directive 'product' also means primary agricultural products and game;

(b) by way of derogation from Article 7 (e), maintain or, subject to the procedure set out in paragraph 2 of this Article, provide in this legislation that the producer shall be liable even if he proves that the state of scientific and technical knowledge at the time when he put the product into circulation was not such as to enable the existence of a defect to be discovered.

2. A Member State wishing to introduce the measure specified in paragraph 1 (b) shall communicate the text of the proposed measure to the Commission. The Commission shall inform the other Member States thereof.

The Member State concerned shall hold the proposed measure in abeyance for nine months after the Commission is informed and provided that in the meantime the Commission has not submitted to the Council a proposal amending this Directive on the relevant matter. However, if within three months of receiving the said information, the Commission does not advise the Member State concerned that it intends submitting such a proposal to the Council, the Member State may take the proposed measure immediately.

If the Commission does submit to the Council such a proposal amending this Directive within the aforementioned nine months, the Member State concerned shall hold the proposed measure in abeyance for a further period of 18 months from the date on which the proposal is submitted.

3. Ten years after the date of notification of this Directive, the Commission shall submit to the Council a report on the effect that rulings by the courts as to the application of Article 7 (e) and of paragraph 1 (b) of this Article have on consumer protection and the functioning of the common market. In the light of this report the Council, acting on a proposal from the Commission and pursuant to the terms of Article 100 of the Treaty, shall decide whether to repeal Article 7 (e).

Article 16

1. Any Member State may provide that a producer's total liability for damage resulting from a death or personal injury and caused by identical items with the same defect shall be limited to an amount which may not be less than 70 million ECU.

2. Ten years after the date of notification of this Directive, the Commission shall submit to the Council a report on the effect on consumer protection and the functioning of the common market of the implementation of the financial limit on liability by those Member States which have used the option provided for in paragraph 1. In the light of this report the Council, acting on a proposal from the Commission and pursuant to the terms of Article 100 of the Treaty, shall decide whether to repeal paragraph 1.

Article 17

This Directive shall not apply to products put into circulation before the date on which the provisions referred to in Article 19 enter into force.

Article 18

1. For the purposes of this Directive, the ECU shall be that defined by Regulation (EEC) No 3180/78 (¹), as amended by Regulation (EEC) No 2626/84 (²). The equivalent in national currency shall initially be calculated at the rate obtaining on the date of adoption of this Directive.

2. Every five years the Council, acting on a proposal from the Commission, shall examine and, if need be, revise the amounts in this Directive, in the light of economic and monetary trends in the Community.

(¹) OJ No L 379, 30. 12. 1978, p. 1.
(²) OJ No L 247, 16. 9. 1984, p. 1.

Article 19

1.   Member States shall bring into force, not later than three years from the date of notification of this Directive, the laws, regulations and administrative provisions necessary to comply with this Directive. They shall forthwith inform the Commission thereof (¹).

2.   The procedure set out in Article 15 (2) shall apply from the date of notification of this Directive.

Article 20

Member States shall communicate to the Commission the texts of the main provisions of national law which they subsequently adopt in the field governed by this Directive.

Article 21

Every five years the Commission shall present a report to the Council on the application of this Directive and, if necessary, shall submit appropriate proposals to it.

Article 22

This Directive is addressed to the Member States.

Done at Brussels, 25 July 1985.

For the Council
The President
J. POOS

(¹) This Directive was notified to the Member States on 30 July 1985.

390L0219

90/219/EEC: COUNCIL DIRECTIVE OF 23 APRIL 1990 ON THE CONTAINED USE OF GENETICALLY MODIFIED MICRO-ORGANISMS

OFFICIAL JOURNAL No L 117, 05/05/1990, P. 1
DATE OF NOTIFICATION: 02/05/1990
DATE OF TRANSPOSITION: 23/10/1991; SEE ART. 22

AMENDED BY

394L0051
94/51/EC: COMMISSION DIRECTIVE OF 7 NOVEMBER 1994 [1]
OFFICIAL JOURNAL No L 297, 18/11/1994, P. 29
DATE OF TRANSPOSITION: 30/04/1995; SEE ART. 2

Article 1

This Directive lays down common measures for the contained use of genetically modified micro-organisms with a view to protecting human health and the environment.

Article 2

For the purposes of this Directive:

(a) 'micro-organism' shall mean any microbiological entity, cellular or non-cellular, capable of replication or of transferring genetic material;

(b) 'genetically modified micro-organism' shall mean a micro-organism in which the genetic material has been altered in a way that does not occur naturally by mating and/or natural recombination.

Within the terms of this definition:

(i) genetic modification occurs at least through the use of the techniques listed in Annex I A, Part 1;

(ii) the techniques listed in Annex I A, Part 2, are not considered to result in genetic modification;

(c) 'contained use' shall mean any operation in which micro-organisms are genetically modified or in which such genetically modified micro-organisms are cultured, stored, used, transported, destroyed or disposed of and for which physical barriers, or a combination of physical barriers together with chemical and/or biological barriers, are used to limit their contact with the general population and the environment;

(d) Type A operation shall mean any operation used for teaching, research, development, or non-industrial or non-commercial purposes and which is of a small scale (e.g. 10 litres culture volume or less);

(e) Type B operation shall mean any operation other than a Type A operation;

(f) 'accident' shall mean any incident involving a significant and unintended release of genetically modified micro-organisms in the course of their contained use which could present an immediate or delayed hazard to human health or the environment;

(g) 'user' shall mean any natural or legal person responsible for the contained use of genetically modified micro-organisms;

(h) 'notification' shall mean the presentation of documents containing the requisite information to the competent authorities of a Member State.

Article 3

This Directive shall not apply where genetic modification is obtained through the use of the techniques listed in Annex I B.

Article 4

1. For the purposes of this Directive, genetically modified micro-organisms shall be classified as follows:

Group I: those satisfying the criteria of Annex II;

Group II: those other than in Group I.

2. For Type A operations, some of the criteria in Annex II may not be applicable in determining the classification of a particular genetically modified micro-organism. In such a case, the classification shall be provisional and the competent authority shall ensure that relevant criteria are used with the aim of obtaining equivalence as far as possible.

3. Before this Directive is implemented, the Commission shall draw up guidelines for classification under the procedures of Article 21.

Article 5

Articles 7 to 12 shall not apply to the transport of genetically modified micro-organisms by road, rail, inland waterway, sea or air. This Directive shall not apply to the storage, transport, destruction or disposal of genetically modified micro-organisms which have been placed on the market under Community legislation, which includes a specific risk assessment similar to that provided in this Directive.

Article 6

1. Member States shall ensure that all appropriate measures are taken to avoid adverse effects on human health and the environment which might arise from the contained use of genetically modified micro-organisms.

2. To this end, the user shall carry out a prior assessment of the contained uses as regards the risks to human health and the environment that they may incur.

3. In making such an assessment the user shall, in particular, take due account of the parameters set out in Annex III, as far as they are relevant, for any genetically modified micro-organisms he is proposing to use.

4. A record of this assessment shall be kept by the user and made available in summary form to the competent authority as part of the notification under Articles 8, 9 and 10 or upon request.

Article 7

1. For genetically modified micro-organisms in Group I, principles of good microbiological practice, and the following principles of good occupational safety and hygiene, shall apply:

(i) to keep workplace and environmental exposure to any physical, chemical or biological agent to the lowest practicable level;

(ii) to exercise engineering control measures at source and to supplement these with appropriate personal protective clothing and equipment when necessary;

(iii) to test adequately and maintain control measures and equipment;

(iv) to test, when necessary, for the presence of viable process organisms outside the primary physical containment;

(v) to provide training of personnel;

(vi) to establish biological safety committees or subcommittees as required;

(vii) to formulate and implement local codes of practice for the safety of personnel.

2. In addition to these principles, the containment measures set out in Annex IV shall be applied, as appropriate, to contained uses of genetically modified micro-organisms in Group II so as to ensure a high level of safety.

3. The containment measures applied shall be periodically reviewed by the user to take into account new scientific or technical knowledge relative to risk management and treatment and disposal of wastes.

Article 8

When a particular installation is to be used for the first time for operations involving the contained use of genetically modified micro-organisms, the user shall be required to submit to the competent authorities, before commencing such use, a notification containing at least the information listed in Annex V A.

A separate notification shall be made for first use of genetically modified micro-organisms in Group I and Group II respectively.

Article 9

1. Users of genetically modified micro-organisms classified in Group I in Type A operations shall be required to keep records of the work carried out which shall be made available to the competent authority on request.

2. Users of genetically modified micro-organisms classified in Group I in Type B operations shall, before commencing the contained use, be required to submit to the competent authorities a notification containing the information listed in Annex V B.

Article 10

1.   Users of genetically modified micro-organisms classified in Group II in Type A operations shall, before commencing the contained use, be required to submit to the competent authorities a notification containing the information listed in Annex V C.

2.   Users of genetically modified micro-organisms classified in Group II in Type B operations shall, before commencing the contained use, be required to submit to the competent authorities a notification containing:

— information on the genetically modified micro-organism(s),

— information on personnel and training,

— information on the installation,

— information on waste management,

— information on accident prevention and emergency response plans,

— the assessment of the risks to human health and the environment referred to in Article 6,

the details of which are listed in Annex V D.

Article 11

1.   Member States shall designate the authority or authorities competent to implement the measures which they adopt in application of this Directive and to receive and acknowledge the notifications referred to in Article 8, Article 9 (2) and Article 10.

2.   The competent authorities shall examine the conformity of the notifications with the requirements of this Directive, the accuracy and completeness of the information given, the correctness of the classification and, where appropriate, the adequacy of the waste management, safety, and emergency response measures.

3.   If necessary, the competent authority may:

(a) ask the user to provide further information or to modify the conditions of the proposed contained use. In this case the proposed contained use cannot proceed until the competent authority has given its approval on the basis of the further information obtained or of the modified conditions of the contained use;

(b) limit the time for which the contained use should be permitted or subject it to certain specific conditions.

4.   In the case of first-time use in an installation as referred to in Article 8:

— where such use involves genetically modified micro-organisms in Group I, the contained use may, in the absence of any indication to the contrary from the competent authority, proceed 90 days after submission of the notification, or earlier with the agreement of the competent authority;

— where such use involves genetically modified micro-organisms in Group II, the contained use may not proceed without the consent of the competent authority. The competent authority shall communicate its decision in writing at the latest 90 days after submission of the notification.

5. (a) Operations notified under Article 9 (2) and Article 10 (1), may, in the absence of any indication to the contrary from the competent authority, proceed 60 days after submission of the notification, or earlier with the agreement of the competent authority.

(b) Operations notified under Article 10 (2) may not proceed without the consent of the competent authority. The competent authority shall communicate its decision in writing at the latest 90 days after submission of the notification.

6.   For the purpose of calculating the periods referred to in paragraphs 4 and 5, any periods of time during which the competent authority:

— is awaiting any further information which it may have requested from the notifier in accordance with paragraph 3 (a) or

— is carrying out a public inquiry or consultation in accordance with Article 13

shall not be taken into account.

Article 12

1.   If the user becomes aware of relevant new information or modifies the contained use in a way which could have significant consequences for the risks posed by the contained use, or if the category of genetically modified micro-organisms used is changed, the competent authority shall be informed as soon as possible and the notification under Articles 8, 9 and 10 modified.

2.   If information becomes available subsequently to the competent authority which could have significant consequences for the risks posed by the contained use, the competent authority may require the user to modify the conditions of, suspend or terminate the contained use.

Article 13

Where a Member State considers it appropriate, it may provide that groups or the public shall be consulted on any aspect of the proposed contained use.

Article 14

The competent authorities shall ensure that, where necessary, before an operation commences:

(a) an emergency plan is drawn up for the protection of human health and the environment outside the installation in the event of an accident and the emergency services are aware of the hazards and informed thereof in writing;

(b) information on safety measures and on the correct behaviour to adopt in the case of an accident is supplied in an appropriate manner, and without their having to request it, to persons liable to be affected by the accident. The information shall be repeated and updated at appropriate intervals. It shall also be made publicly available.

The Member States concerned shall at the same time make available to other Member States concerned, as a basis for all necessary consultation within the framework of their bilateral relations, the same information as that which is disseminated to their nationals.

Article 15

1. Member States shall take the necessary measures to ensure that, in the event of an accident, the user shall be required immediately to inform the competent authority specified in Article 11 and provide the following information:

— the circumstances of the accident,

— the identity and quantities of the genetically modified micro-organisms released,

— any information necessary to assess the effects of the accident on the health of the general population and the environment,

— the emergency measures taken.

2. Where information is given under paragraph 1, the Member States shall be required to:

— ensure that any emergency, medium and long-term measures necessary are taken, and immediately alert any Member State which could be affected by the accident;

— collect, where possible, the information necessary for a full analysis of the accident and, where appropriate, make recommendations to avoid similar accidents in the future and to limit the effects thereof.

Article 16

1. Member States shall be required to:

(a) consult with other Member States liable to be affected in the event of an accident in the drawing up and implementation of emergency plans;

(b) inform the Commission as soon as possible of any accident within the scope of this Directive, giving details

of the circumstances of the accident, the identity and quantities of the genetically modified micro-organisms released, the emergency response measures employed and their effectiveness, and an analysis of the accident including recommendations to limit its effects and avoid similar accidents in the future.

2. The Commission, in consultation with the Member States, shall establish a procedure for the exchange of information under paragraph 1. It shall also set up and keep at the disposal of the Member States a register of accidents within the scope of this Directive which have occurred, including an analysis of the causes of the accidents, experience gained and measures taken to avoid similar accidents in the future.

Article 17

Member States shall ensure that the competent authority organizes inspections and other control measures to ensure user compliance with this Directive.

Article 18

1. Member States shall send to the Commission, at the end of each year, a summary report on the contained uses notified under Article 10 (2) including the description, proposed uses and risks of the genetically modified micro-organisms.

2. Every three years, Member States shall send the Commission a summary report on their experience with this Directive, the first time being on 1 September 1992.

3. Every three years, the Commission shall publish a summary based on the reports referred to in paragraph 2, the first time being in 1993.

4. The Commission may publish general statistical information on the implementation of this Directive and related matters, as long as it contains no information likely to cause harm to the competitive position of a user.

Article 19

1. The Commission and the competent authorities shall not divulge to third parties any confidential information notified or otherwise provided under this Directive and shall protect intellectual property rights relating to the data received.

2. The notifier may indicate the information in the notifications submitted under this Directive, the disclosure of which might harm his competitive position, that should be treated as confidential. Verifiable justification must be given in such cases.

3. The competent authority shall decide, after consultation with the notifier, which information will be kept confidential and shall inform the notifier of its decision.

4. In no case may the following information, when submitted according to Articles 8, 9 or 10, be kept confidential:

— description of the genetically modified micro-organisms, name and address of the notifier, purpose of the contained use, and location of use;

— methods and plans for monitoring of the genetically modified micro-organisms and for emergency response;

— the evaluation of foreseeable effects, in particular any pathogenic and/or ecologically disruptive effects.

5. If, for whatever reasons, the notifier withdraws the notification, the competent authority must respect the confidentiality of the information supplied.

Article 20

Amendments necessary to adapt Annexes II to V to technical progress shall be decided in accordance with the procedure defined in Article 21.

Article 21

1. The Commission shall be assisted by a committee composed of the representatives of the Member States and chaired by the representative of the Commission.

2. The representative of the Commission shall submit to the committee a draft of the measures to be taken. The committee shall deliver its opinion on the draft within a time limit which the chairman may lay down according to the urgency of the matter. The opinion shall be delivered by the majority laid down in Article 148 (2) of the Treaty in the case of decisions which the Council is required to adopt on a proposal from the Commission. The votes of the representatives of the Member States within the committee shall be weighted in the manner set out in that Article. The chairman shall not vote.

3. (a) The Commission shall adopt the measures envisaged if they are in accordance with the opinion of the committee.

(b) If the measures envisaged are not in accordance with the opinion of the committee, or if no opinion is delivered, the Commission shall, without delay, submit to the Council a proposal relating to the measures to be taken. The Council shall act by a qualified majority.

If, on the expiry of a period of three months from the date of referral to the Council, the Council has not acted, the proposed measures shall be adopted by the Commission, save where the Council has decided against the said measures by a simple majority.

Article 22

Member States shall bring into force the laws, regulations and administrative provisions necessary to comply with this Directive not later than 23 October 1991. They shall forthwith inform the Commission thereof.

Article 23

This Directive is addressed to the Member States.

Done at Luxembourg, 23 April 1990.

For the Council
The President
A. REYNOLDS

ANNEX I A

PART 1

Techniques of genetic modification referred to in Article 2 (b) (i) are, *inter alia:*

  (i) recombinant DNA techniques using vector systems as previously covered by Recommendation 82/472/EEC (¹);

 (ii) techniques involving the direct introduction into a micro-organism of heritable material prepared outside the micro-organism including micro-injection, macro-injection and micro-encapsulation;

(iii) cell fusion or hybridization techniques where live cells with new combinations of heritable genetic material are formed through the fusion of two or more cells by means of methods that do not occur naturally.

PART 2

Techniques referred to in Article 2 (b) (ii) which are not considered to result in genetic modification, on condition that they do not involve the use of recombinant-DNA molecules or genetically modified organisms:

(1) *in vitro* fertilization;

(2) conjugation, transduction, transformation or any other natural process;

(3) polyploidy induction.

———

ANNEX I B

Techniques of genetic modification to be excluded from the Directive, on condition that they do not involve the use of genetically modified micro-organisms as recipient or parental organisms:

(1) mutagenesis;

(2) the construction and use of somatic animal hybridoma cells (e.g. for the production of monoclonal antibodies);

(3) cell fusion (including protoplast fusion) of cells from plants which can be produced by traditional breeding methods;

(4) self-cloning of non-pathogenic naturally occurring micro-organisms which fulfil the criteria of Group I for recipient micro-organisms.

———

(¹) OJ No 213, 21. 7. 1982, p. 15.

ANNEX II

" CRITERIA FOR CLASSIFYING GENETICALLY MODIFIED MICRO-ORGANISMS INTO GROUP I

A genetically modified micro-organism is classified as falling within Group I when all the following criteria are fulfilled :

  (i) the recipient or parental micro-organism is unlikely to cause disease to humans, animals or plants ;

 (ii) the nature of the vector and the insert is such that they do not endow the genetically modified micro-organism with a phenotype likely to cause disease to humans, animals or plants, or likely to cause adverse effects in the environment ;

(iii) the genetically modified micro-organism is unlikely to cause disease to humans, animals or plants and is unlikely to have adverse effects on the environment. " [1]

ANNEX III

SAFETY ASSESSMENT PARAMETERS TO BE TAKEN INTO ACCOUNT, AS FAR AS THEY ARE RELEVANT, IN ACCORDANCE WITH ARTICLE 6 (3)

A. Characteristics of the donor, recipient or (where appropriate) parental organism(s)

B. Characteristics of the modified micro-organism

C. Health considerations

D. Environmental considerations

A. Characteristics of the donor, recipient or (where appropriate) parental organism(s)

— names and designation;

— degree of relatedness;

— sources of the organism(s);

— information on reproductive cycles (sexual/asexual) of the parental organism(s) or, where applicable, of the recipient micro-organism;

— history of prior genetic manipulations;

— stability of parental or of recipient organism in terms of relevant genetic traits;

— nature of pathogenicity and virulence, infectivity, toxicity and vectors of disease transmission;

— nature of indigenous vectors:

  sequence,

  frequency of mobilization,

  specificity,

  presence of genes which confer resistance;

— host range;

— other potentially significant physiological traits;

— stability of these traits;

— natural habitat and geographic distribution. Climatic characteristics of original habitats;

— significant involvement in environmental processes (such as nitrogen fixation or pH regulation);

— interaction with, and effects on, other organisms in the environment (including likely competitive or symbiotic properties);

— ability to form survival structures (such as spores or sclerotia).

B. Characteristics of the modified micro-organism

— the description of the modification including the method for introducing the vector-insert into the recipient organism or the method used for achieving the genetic modification involved;

— the function of the genetic manipulation and/or of the new nucleic acid;

— nature and source of the vector;

— structure and amount of any vector and/or donor nucleic acid remaining in the final construction of the modified micro-organism;

— stability of the micro-organism in terms of genetic traits;

— frequency of mobilization of inserted vector and/or genetic transfer capability;

— rate and level of expression of the new genetic material. Method and sensitivity of measurement;

— activity of the expressed protein.

C. Health considerations

— toxic or allergenic effects of non-viable organisms and/or their metabolic products;

— product hazards;

— comparison of the modified micro-organism to the donor, recipient or (where appropriate) parental organism regarding pathogenicity;

— capacity for colonization;

— if the micro-organism is pathogenic to humans who are immunocompetent:

  (a) diseases caused and mechanism of pathogenicity including invasiveness and virulence;

  (b) communicability;

  (c) infective dose;

  (d) host range, possibility of alteration;

  (e) possibility of survival outside of human host;

  (f) presence of vectors or means of dissemination;

  (g) biological stability;

  (h) antibiotic-resistance patterns;

  (i) allergenicity;

  (j) availability of appropriate therapies.

D. Environmental considerations

— factors affecting survival, multiplication and dissemination of the modified micro-organism in the environment;

— available techniques for detection, identification and monitoring of the modified micro-organism;

— available techniques for detecting transfer of the new genetic material to other organisms;

— known and predicted habitats of the modified micro-organism;

— description of ecosystems to which the micro-organism could be accidentally disseminated;

— anticipated mechanism and result of interaction between the modified micro-organism and the organisms or micro-organisms which might be exposed in case of release into the environment;

— known or predicted effects on plants and animals such as pathogenicity, infectivity, toxicity, virulence, vector of pathogen, allergenicity, colonization;

— known or predicted involvement in biogeochemical processes;

— availability of methods for decontamination of the area in case of release to the environment.

———

ANNEX IV

CONTAINMENT MEASURES FOR MICRO-ORGANISMS IN GROUP II

The containment measures for micro-organisms from Group II shall be chosen by the user from the categories below as appropriate to the micro-organism and the operation in question in order to ensure the protection of the public health of the general population and the environment.

Type B operations shall be considered in terms of their unit operations. The characteristics of each operation will dictate the physical containment to be used at that stage. This will allow selection and design of process, plant and operating procedures best fitted to assure adequate and safe containment. Two important factors to be considered when selecting the equipment needed to implement the containment are the risk of, and the effects consequent on, equipment failure. Engineering practice may require increasingly stringent standards to reduce the risk of failure as the consequence of that failure becomes less tolerable.

Specific containment measures for Type A operations shall be established taking into account the containment categories below and bearing in mind the specific circumstances of such operations.

Specifications	Containment Categories		
	1	2	3
1. Viable micro-organisms should be contained in a system which physically separates the process from the environment (closed system)	Yes	Yes	Yes
2. Exhaust gases from the closed system should be treated so as to:	Minimize release	Prevent release	Prevent release
3. Sample collection, addition of materials to a closed system and transfer of viable micro-organisms to another closed system, should be performed so as to:	Minimize release	Prevent release	Prevent release
4. Bulk culture fluids should not be removed from the closed system unless the viable micro-organisms have been:	Inactivated by validated means	Inactivated by validated chemical or physical means	Inactivated by validated chemical or physical means
5. Seals should be designed so as to:	Minimize release	Prevent release	Prevent release
6. Closed systems should be located within a controlled area	Optional	Optional	Yes, and purpose-built
(a) Biohazard signs should be posted	Optional	Yes	Yes
(b) Access should be restricted to nominated personnel only	Optional	Yes	Yes, via airlock
(c) Personnel should wear protective clothing	Yes, work clothing	Yes	A complete change
(d) Decontamination and washing facilities should be provided for personnel	Yes	Yes	Yes
(e) Personnel should shower before leaving the controlled area	No	Optional	Yes
(f) Effluent from sinks and showers should be collected and inactivated before release	No	Optional	Yes

Specifications	Containment Categories		
	1	2	3
(g) The controlled area should be adequately ventilated to minimize air contamination	Optional	Optional	Yes
(h) The controlled areas should be maintained at an air pressure negative to atmosphere	No	Optional	Yes
(i) Input air and extract air to the controlled area should be HEPA filtered	No	Optional	Yes
(j) The controlled area should be designed to contain spillage of the entire contents of the closed system	Optional	Yes	Yes
(k) The controlled area should be sealable to permit fumigation	No	Optional	Yes
7. Effluent treatment before final discharge	Inactivated by validated means	Inactivated by validated chemical or physical means	Inactivated by validated chemical means

ANNEX V

PART A

Information required for the notification referred to in Article 8:

— name of person(s) responsible for carrying out the contained use including those responsible for supervision, monitoring and safety and information on their training and qualifications;

— address of installation and grid reference; description of the sections of the installation;

— a description of the nature of the work which will be undertaken and in particular the classification of the micro-organism(s) to be used (Group I or Group II) and the likely scale of the operation;

— a summary of the risk assessment referred to in Article 6 (2).

PART B

Information required for the notification referred to in Article 9 (2):

— the date of submission of the notification referred to in Article 8;

— the parental micro-organism(s) used or, where applicable the host-vector system(s) used;

— the source(s) and the intended function(s) of the genetic material(s) involved in the manipulation(s);

— identity and characteristics of the genetically modified micro-organism;

— the purpose of the contained use including the expected results;

— the culture volumes to be used;

— a summary of the risk assessment referred to in Article 6 (2).

PART C

Information required for the notification referred to in Article 10 (1):

— the information required in Part B;

— description of the sections of the installation and the methods for handling the micro-organisms;

— description of the predominant meteorological conditions and of the potential sources of danger arising from the location of the installation;

— description of the protective and supervisory measures to be applied throughout the duration of the contained use;

— the containment category allocated specifying waste treatment provisions and the safety precautions to be adopted.

PART D

Information required for the notification referred to in Article 10 (2):

If it is not technically possible, or if it does not appear necessary to give the information specified below, the reasons shall be stated. The level of detail required in response to each subset of considerations is likely to vary according to the nature and the scale of the proposed contained use. In the case of information already submitted to the competent authority under the requirements of this Directive, reference can be made to this information by the user:

(a) the date of submission of the notification referred to in Article 8 and the name of the responsible person(s);

(b) information about the genetically modified micro-organism(s):

— the identity and characteristics of the genetically modified micro-organism(s),

— the purpose of the contained use or the nature of the product,

— the host-vector system to be used (where applicable),

— the culture volumes to be used,

— behaviour and characteristics of the micro-organism(s) in the case of changes in the conditions of containment or of release to the environment,

— overview of the potential hazards associated with the release of the micro-organism(s) to the environment,

— substances which are or may be produced in the course of the use of the micro-organism(s) other than the intended product;

(c) information about personnel:

— the maximum number of persons working in the installation and the number of persons who work directly with the micro-organism(s);

(d) information about the installation:

— the activity in which the micro-organism(s) is to be used,

— the technological processes used,

— a description of the sections of the installation,

— the predominant meteorological conditions, and specific hazards arising from the location of the installation;

(e) information about waste management:

— types, quantities, and potential hazards of wastes arising from the use of the micro-organism(s),

— waste management techniques used, including recovery of liquid or solid wastes and inactivation methods,

— ultimate form and destination of inactivated wastes;

(f) information about accident prevention and emergency response plans:

— the sources of hazards and conditions under which accidents might occur,

— the preventive measures applied such as safety equipment, alarm systems, containment methods and procedures and available resources,

— a description of information provided to workers,

— the information necessary for the competent authority to enable them to draw up or establish the necessary emergency response plans for use outside the installation in accordance with Article 14;

(g) a comprehensive assessment (referred to in Article 6 (2)) of the risks to human health and the environment which might arise from the proposed contained use;

(h) all other information required under Parts B and C if it is not already specified above.

COMMISSION DECISION

of 29 July 1991

concerning the guidelines for classification referred to in Article 4 of Directive 90/219/EEC

(91/448/EEC)

THE COMMISSION OF THE EUROPEAN COMMUNITIES,

Having regard to the Treaty establishing the European Economic Community,

Having regard to Council Directive 90/219/EEC of 23 April 1990 on the contained use of genetically modified micro-organisms ([1]), and in particular Article 4 thereof,

Whereas, for the purposes of this Directive, genetically modified micro-organisms need to be classified into Groups I and II using the criteria of Annex II and the Guidelines for classification referred to in Article 4 (3);

Whereas the Commission is required to establish before the entry into force of Directive 90/219/EEC, these guidelines for classification;

Whereas the provisions of this Decision have received the favourable opinion of the Committee of Member States representatives in accordance with the procedure laid down in Article 21 of Directive 90/219/EEC,

HAS ADOPTED THIS DECISION:

Article 1

When a classification of genetically modified micro-organisms is made under Article 4 of Directive 90/219/EEC, the annexed Guidelines for classification should be used to interpret Annex II of Directive 90/219/EEC.

Article 2

This Decision is addressed to the Member States.

Done at Brussels, 29 July 1991.

For the Commission

Carlo RIPA DI MEANA

Member of the Commission

([1]) OJ No L 117, 8. 5. 1990, p. 1.

ANNEX

GUIDELINES FOR THE CLASSIFICATION OF GENETICALLY MODIFIED MICRO-ORGANISMS INTO GROUP I ACCORDING TO ARTICLE 4 (3) OF DIRECTIVE 90/129/EEC

For classification into Group I, the following guidelines should be used for further interpret Annex II of Directive 90/219/EEC:

A.   **Characteristics of the recipient or parental organism(s)**

1.   *Non-pathogenic*

     The recipient or parental organisms can be classified as non-pathogenic if they satisfy the conditions of one of the following paragraphs:

     (i) the recipient or parental strain should have an established record of safety in the laboratory and/or industry, with no adverse effects on human health and the environment;

     (ii) the recipient or parental strain does not meet the conditions of paragraph (i) but it belongs to a species for which there is a long record of biological work including safety in the lab and/or industry, showing no adverse effects on human health and the environment;

     (iii) if the recipient or parental organism is a strain which does not satisfy the conditions of paragraph (i) and belongs to a species for which there is no record of biological work including safe use in the laboratory and/or industry, appropriate testing (including, if necessary, animals) must be carried out, in order to establish non-pathogenicity and safety in the environment;

     (iv) if a non-virulent strain of an acknowledged pathogenic species is used, the strain should be as deficient as possible in genetic material that determines virulence so as to ensure no reversion to pathogenicity. In the case of bacteria, special attention should be given to plasmid or phage-borne virulence determinants.

2.   *No adventitious agents*

     The recipient or parental strain/cell line should be free of known biological contaminating agents (symbionts, mycoplasma, viruses, viroids, etc.), which are potentially harmful.

3.   The recipient or parental strain/cell line should have proven and extended history of safe use or built-in biological barriers, which, without interfering with optimal growth in the reactor or fermentor, confer limited survivability and replicability, without adverse consequences in the environment (applicable only for type B operations).

B.1.   **Characteristics of the vector**

1.1.   *The vector should be well characterized*

     For this purpose the following characteristics should be taken into account.

1.1.1.   Information on composition and construction

     (a) The type of the vector should be defined (virus, plasmid, cosmid, phasmid, transposable element, minichromosome, etc.);

     (b) The following information on the constituent fragments of the vector should be available:

         (i) the origin of each fragment (progenitor genetic element, strain of organism in which the progenitor genetic element naturally occurred);

         (ii) if some fragments are synthetic, their function should be known.

     (c) The methods used for construction should be known.

1.1.2.   Information on vector structure

     (a) The size of the vector should be known and expressed in basepairs or D.

     (b) The function and relative position of the following should be known:

         (i) structural genes;

         (ii) marker genes for selection (antibiotic resistance, heavy metal resistance, phage immunity, genes coding for degradation of xenobiotics, etc.);

(iii) regulatory elements ;

(iv) target sites (nic-sites, restriction endonuclease sites, linkers, etc.) ;

(v) transposable elements (including provirus sequences) ;

(vi) genes related to transfer and mobilization function (e.g. with respect to conjugation, transduction or chromosomal integration) ;

(vii) replicon(s)

1.2.   *The vector should be free from harmful sequences*

The vector should not contain genes coding for potentially harmful or pathogenic traits (e.g. virulence determinants, toxins, etc.), (unless, for type A operations, such genes constitute an essential feature of the vector without, under any conditions or circumstances, resulting in a harmful or pathogenic phenotype of the genetically modified micro-organism).

1.3.   The vector should be limited in size as much as possible to the genetic sequences required to perform the intended function.

1.4.   The vector should not increase the stability of the genetically modified micro-organism in the environment (unless that is a requirement of the intended function).

1.5.   *The vector should be poorly mobilizable*

1.5.1.   If the vector is a plasmid :

(i) it should have a restricted host-range ;

(ii) it should be defective in transfer-mobilization factors e.g. Tra $^-$, Mob$^+$, for type A operations or Tra $^-$, Mob $^-$, for type B operations.

1.5.2.   If the vector is a virus, cosmid, or phasmid :

(i) it should have a restricted host range ;

(ii) it should be rendered non-lysogenic when used as a cloning vector (e.g. defective in the CI-lamda repressor).

1.6.   It should not transfer any resistance markers to micro-organisms not known to acquire them naturally (if such acquisition could compromise use of drug to control disease agents)

B.2.   **Required characteristics of the insert**

2.1.   *The insert should be well characterized*

For this purpose, the following characteristics should be taken into account :

2.1.1.   The origin of the insert should be known (genus, species, strain).

2.1.2.   The following information on the library from which the insert originated, should be known :

(i) the source and method for obtaining the nucleic acid of interest (cDNA, chromosomal mitochondrial, etc.) ;

(ii) the vector in which the library was constructed (e.g. lamda GT 11, pBR 322, etc.) and the site in which the DNA was inserted ;

(iii) the method used for identification (colony, hybridization, immuno-blot, etc.) ;

(iv) the strain used for library construction.

2.1.3.   If the insert is synthetic, its intended function should be identified.

2.1.4.   The following information on the structure of the insert is required :

(i) information on structural genes, regulatory elements ;

(ii) size of the insert ;

(iii) restriction endonuclease sites flanking the insert ;

(iv) information on transposable elements and provirus sequences.

2.2.   *The insert should be free from harmful sequences*

(i) The function of each genetic unit in the insert should be defined (not applicable for type A operations) ;

(ii) the insert should not contain genes coding for potential pathogenic traits (e.g. virulence determinants, toxins, etc.), (unless for type A operations, such genes constitute an essential part of the insert without, under any circumstances resulting in a harmful or pathogenic phenotype of the genetically modified micro-organism).

2.3.   The insert should be limited in size as much as possible to the genetic sequences required to perform the intended function.

2.4.   The insert should not increase the stability of the construct in the environment (unless that is a requirement of intended function).

2.5.   *The insert should be poorly mobilizable*

For instance, it should not contain transposing or transferrable provirus sequences and other functional transposing sequences.

C.   **Required characteristics of the genetically modified micro-organism**

1.   *The genetically modified micro-organism should be non-pathogenic*

This requirement is reasonably assured by compliance with all the requirements above.

2.   (a) The genetically modified micro-organism should be as safe (to man and the environment) as the recipient or parental strains) (applicable only for type A operations).

      (b) The genetically modified micro-organisms should be as safe in the reactor or fermentor as the recipient or parental strains, but with limited survivability and/or replicability outside the reactor or fermentor without adverse consequences in the environment (applicable only for type B operations).

D.   **Other genetically modified micro-organisms that could be included in Group 1 if they meet the conditions in C above :**

1.   Those constructed entirely from a single prokaryotic recipient (including its indigenous plasmids and viruses) or from a single eukaryotic recipient (including its chloroplats, mitochondria, plasmids, but excluding viruses).

2.   Those that consist entirely of genetic sequences from different species that exchange these sequences by known physiological processes.

90/220/EEC: COUNCIL DIRECTIVE OF 23 APRIL 1990 ON THE DELIBERATE RELEASE INTO THE ENVIRONMENT OF GENETICALLY MODIFIED ORGANISMS

OFFICIAL JOURNAL No L 117, 08/05/1990, P. 15
DATE OF NOTIFICATION: 02/05/1990
DATE OF TRANSPOSITION: 23/10/1991; SEE ART. 23

AMENDED BY

394L0015
94/15/EC: COMMISSION DIRECTIVE OF 15 APRIL 1994 [1]
OFFICIAL JOURNAL No L 103, 22/04/1994, P. 20
DATE OF TRANSPOSITION: 30/06/1994; SEE ART. 2

PART A

General provisions

Article 1

1. The objective of this Directive is to approximate the laws, regulations and administrative provisions of the Member States and to protect human health and the environment:

— when carrying out the deliberate release of genetically modified organisms into the environment,

— when placing on the market products containing, or consisting of, genetically modified organisms intended for subsequent deliberate release into the environment.

2. This Directive shall not apply to the carriage of genetically modified organisms by rail, road, inland waterway, sea or air.

Article 2

For the purposes of this Directive:

(1) 'organism' is any biological entity capable of replication or of transferring genetic material;

(2) 'genetically modified organism (GMO)' means an organism in which the genetic material has been altered in a way that does not occur naturally by mating and/or natural recombination.

Within the terms of this definition:

(i) genetic modification occurs at least through the use of the techniques listed in Annex I A Part 1;

(ii) the techniques listed in Annex I A Part 2 are not considered to result in genetic modification;

(3) 'deliberate release' means any intentional introduction into the environment of a GMO or a combination of GMOs without provisions for containment such as physical barriers or a combination of physical barriers together with chemical and/or biological barriers used to limit their contact with the general population and the environment;

(4) 'product' means a preparation consisting of, or containing, a GMO or a combination of GMOs, which is placed on the market;

(5) 'placing on the market' means supplying or making available to third parties;

(6) 'notification' means the presentation of documents containing the requisite information to the competent authority of a Member State. The person making the presentation shall be referred to as 'the notifier';

(7) 'use' means the deliberate release of a product which has been placed on the market. The persons carrying out this use will be referred to as 'users';

(8) 'environmental risk assessment' means the evaluation of the risk to human health and the environment (which includes plants and animals) connected with the release of GMOs or products containing GMOs.

Article 3

This Directive shall not apply to organisms obtained through the techniques of genetic modification listed in Annex I B.

Article 4

1. Member States shall ensure that all appropriate measures are taken to avoid adverse effects on human health and the environment which might arise from the deliberate release or placing on the market of GMOs.

2. Member States shall designate the competent authority or authorities responsible for carrying out the requirements of this Directive and its Annexes.

3. Member States shall ensure that the competent authority organizes inspections and other control measures as appropriate, to ensure compliance with this Directive.

PART B

Deliberate release of GMOs into the environment for research and development purposes or for any other purpose than for placing on the market

Article 5

Member States shall adopt the provisions necessary to ensure that:

(1) any person, before undertaking a deliberate release of a GMO or a combination of GMOs for the purpose of research and development, or for any other purpose than for placing on the market, must submit a notification to the competent authority referred to in Article 4 (2) of the Member State within whose territory the release is to take place;

(2) the notification shall include:

(a) a technical dossier supplying the information specified in Annex II necessary for evaluating the foreseeable risks, whether immediate or delayed, which the GMO or combination of GMOs may pose to human health or the environment, together with the methods used and the bibliographic reference to them and covering, in particular:

(i) general information including information on personnel and training,

(ii) information relating to the GMO(s),

(iii) information relating to the conditions of release and the receiving environment,

(iv) information on the interactions between the GMO(s) and the environment,

(v) information on monitoring, control, waste treatment and emergency response plans;

(b) a statement evaluating the impacts and risks posed by the GMO(s) to human health or the environment from the uses envisaged;

(3) the competent authority may accept that releases of a combination of GMOs on the same site or of the same GMO on different sites for the same purpose and within a limited period may be notified in a single notification;

(4) the notifier shall include in the notification information on data or results from releases of the same GMOs or the same combination of GMOs previously or currently notified and/or carried out by him either inside or outside the Community.

The notifier may also refer to data or results from notifications previously submitted by other notifiers, provided that the latter have given their agreement in writing;

(5) in the case of a subsequent release of the same GMO or combination of GMOs previously notified as part of the same research programme, the notifier shall be required to submit a new notification. In this case, the notifier may refer to data from previous notifications or results from previous releases;

(6) in the event of any modification of the deliberate release of GMOs or a combination of GMOs which could have consequences with regard to the risks for human health or the environment or if new information has become available on such risks, either while the notification is being examined by the competent authority or after that authority has given its written consent, the notifier shall immediately:

(a) revise the measures specified in the notification,

(b) inform the competent authority in advance of any modification or as soon as the new information is available,

(c) take the measures necessary to protect human health and the environment.

Article 6

1. On receipt and after acknowledgment of the notification the competent authority shall:

— examine it for compliance with this Directive,

— evaluate the risks posed by the release,

— record its conclusions in writing,

and, if necessary,

— carry out tests or inspections as may be necessary for control purposes.

2. The competent authority, having considered, where appropriate, any comments by other Member States made in accordance with Article 9, shall respond in writing to the notifier within 90 days of receipt of the notification by either:

(a) indicating that it is satisfied that the notification is in compliance with this Directive and that the release may proceed, or

(b) indicating that the release does not fulfil the conditions of this Directive and the notification is therefore rejected.

3. For the purpose of calculating the 90-day period referred to in paragraph 2, any periods of time during which the competent authority:

— is awaiting further information which it may have requested from the notifier,

or

— is carrying out a public inquiry or consultation in accordance with Article 7

shall not be taken into account.

4. The notifier may proceed with the release only when he has received the written consent of the competent authority, and in conformity with any conditions required in this consent.

5. If the competent authority considers that sufficient experience has been obtained of releases of certain GMOs, it may submit to the Commission a request for the application of simplified procedures for releases of such types of GMOs. The Commission shall, in accordance with the procedures laid down in Article 21, establish appropriate criteria and take a decision accordingly on each application. The criteria shall be based on safety to human health and the environment and on the evidence available on such safety.

6. If information becomes available subsequently to the competent authority which could have significant consequences for the risks posed by the release, the competent authority may require the notifier to modify the conditions of, suspend or terminate the deliberate release.

Article 7

Where a Member State considers it appropriate, it may provide that groups or the public shall be consulted on any aspect of the proposed deliberate release.

Article 8

After completion of a release, the notifier shall send to the competent authority the result of the release in respect of any risk to human health or the environment, with particular reference to any kind of product that the notifier intends to notify at a later stage.

Article 9

1. The Commission shall set up a system of exchange of the information contained in the notifications. The competent authorities shall send to the Commission, within 30 days of its receipt, a summary of each notification received. The format of this summary will be established by the Commission in accordance with the procedure laid down in Article 21.

2. The Commission shall immediately forward these summaries to the other Member States, which may, within 30 days, ask for further information or present observations through the Commission or directly.

3. The competent authorities shall inform the other Member States and the Commission of the final decisions taken in compliance with Article 6 (2).

PART C

Placing on the market of products containing GMOs

Article 10

1. Consent may only be given for the placing on the market of products containing, or consisting of, GMOs, provided that:

— written consent has been given to a notification under Part B or if a risk analysis has been carried out based on the elements outlined in that Part;

— the products comply with the relevant Community product legislation;

— the products comply with the requirements of this Part of this Directive, concerning the environmental risk assessment.

2. Articles 11 to 18 shall not apply to any products covered by Community legislation which provides for a specific environmental risk assessment similar to that laid down in this Directive.

3. Not later than 12 months after notification of this Directive, the Commission, in accordance with the procedure laid down in Article 21, shall establish a list of Community legislation covering the products referred to in paragraph 2. This list will be re-examined periodically and, as necessary, revised in accordance with the said procedure.

Article 11

1. Before a GMO or a combination of GMOs are placed on the market as or in a product, the manufacturer or the importer to the Community shall submit a notification to the competent authority of the Member State where such a product is to be placed on the market for the first time. This notification shall contain:

— the information required in Annex II, extended as necessary to take into account the diversity of sites of use of the product, including information on data and results obtained from research and developmental releases concerning the ecosystems which could be affected by the use of the product and an assessent of any risks for human health and the environment related to the GMOs or a combination of GMOs contained in the product, including information obtained from the research and development stage on the impact of the release on human health and the environment;

— the conditions for the placing on the market of the product, including specific conditions of use and handling and a proposal for labelling and packaging which should comprise at least the requirements laid down in Annex III.

If on the basis of the results of any release notified under Part B of this Directive, or on substantive, reasoned scientific grounds, a notifier considers that the placing on the market and use of a product do not pose a risk to human health and the environment, he may propose not to comply with one or more of the requirements of Annex III B.

2. The notifier shall include in this notification information on data or results from releases of the same GMOs or the same combination of GMOs previously or currently notified and/or carried out by the notifier either inside or outside the Community.

3. The notifier may also refer to data or results from notifications previously submitted by other notifiers, provided that the latter have given their agreement in writing.

4. Each new product which, containing or consisting of the same GMO or combination of GMOs, is intended for a different use, shall be notified separately.

5. The notifier may proceed with the release only when he has received the written consent of the competent authority in accordance with Article 13, and in conformity with any conditions, including reference to particular ecosystems/environments, required in that consent.

6. If new information has become available with regard to the risks of the product to human health or the environment, either before or after the written consent, the notifier shall immediately:

— revise the information and conditions specified in paragraph 1,

— inform the competent authority, and

— take the measures necessary to protect human health and the environment.

Article 12

1. On receipt and after acknowledgement of the notification referred to in Article 11, the competent authority shall examine it for compliance with this Directive, giving particular attention to the environmental risk assessment and the recommended precautions related to the safe use of the product.

2. At the latest 90 days after receipt of the notification, the competent authority shall either:

(a) forward the dossier to the Commission with a favourable opinion, or

(b) inform the notifier that the proposed release does not fulfil the conditions of this Directive and that it is therefore rejected.

3. In the case referred to in paragraph 2 (a), the dossier forwarded to the Commission shall include a summary of the notification together with a statement of the conditions under which the competent authority proposes to consent to the placing on the market of the product.

The format of this summary shall be established by the Commission in accordance with the procedure laid down in Article 21.

In particular where the competent authority has acceded to the request of the notifier, under the terms of the last subparagraph of Article 11 (1), not to comply with some of the requirements of Annex III B, it shall at the same time inform the Commission thereof.

4. If the competent authority receives additional information pursuant to Article 11 (6), it shall immediately inform the Commission and the other Member States.

5. For the purpose of calculating the 90-day period referred to in paragraph 2, any periods of time during which the competent authority is awaiting further information which it may have requested from the notifier shall not be taken into account.

Article 13

1. On receipt of the dossier referred to in Article 12 (3), the Commission shall immediately forward it to the competent authorities of all Member States together with any other information it has collected pursuant to this Directive and advise the competent authority responsible for forwarding the document of the distribution date.

2. The competent authority, in the absence of any indication to the contrary from another Member State within 60 days following the distribution date referred to in paragraph 1, shall give its consent in writing to the notification so that the product can be placed on the market and shall inform the other Member States and the Commission thereof.

3. In cases where the competent authority of another Member State raises an objection — for which the reasons must be stated — and should it not be possible for the competent authorities concerned to reach an agreement within the period specified in paragraph 2, the Commission shall take a decision in accordance with the procedure laid down in Article 21.

4. Where the Commission has taken a favourable decision, the competent authority that received the original notification shall give consent in writing to the notification so that the product may be placed on the market and shall inform the other Member States and the Commission thereof.

5. Once a product has received a written consent, it may be used without further notification throughout the Community in so far as the specific conditions of use and the environments and/or geographical areas stipulated in these conditions are strictly adhered to.

6. Member States shall take all necessary measures to ensure that users comply with the conditions of use specified in the written consent.

Article 14

Member States shall take all necessary measures to ensure that products containing, or consisting of, GMOs will be placed on the market only if their labelling and packaging is that specified in the written consent referred to in Articles 12 and 13.

Article 15

Member States may not, on grounds relating to the notification and written consent of a deliberate release under this Directive, prohibit, restrict or impede the placing on the market of products containing, or consisting of, GMOs which comply with the requirements of this Directive.

Article 16

1. Where a Member State has justifiable reasons to consider that a product which has been properly notified and has received written consent under this Directive constitutes a risk to human health or the environment, it may provisionally restrict or prohibit the use and/or sale of that product on its territory. It shall immediately inform the Commission and the other Member States of such action and give reasons for its decision.

2. A decision shall be taken on the matter within three months in accordance with the procedure laid down in Article 21.

Article 17

The Commission shall publish in the *Official Journal of the European Communities* a list of all the products receiving final written consent under this Directive. For each product, the GMO or GMOs contained therein and the use or uses shall be clearly specified.

Article 18

1. Member States shall send to the Commission, at the end of each year, a brief factual report on the control of the use of all products placed on the market under this Directive.

2. The Commission shall send to the European Parliament and the Council, every three years, a report on the control by the Member States of the products placed on the market under this Directive.

3. When submitting this report for the first time, the Commission shall at the same time submit a specific report on the operation of this Part of this Directive including an assessment of all its implications.

PART D

Final provisions

Article 19

1. The Commission and the competent authorities shall not divulge to third parties any confidential information notified or exchanged under this Directive and shall protect intellectual property rights relating to the data received.

2. The notifier may indicate the information in the notification submitted under this Directive, the disclosure of which might harm his competitive position, that should therefore be treated as confidential. Verifiable justification must be given in such cases.

3. The competent authority shall decide, after consultation with the notifier, which information will be kept confidential and shall inform the notifier of its decisions.

4. In no case may the following information when submitted according to Articles 5 or 11 be kept confidential:

— description of the GMO or GMOs, name and address of the notifier, purpose of the release and location of release;

— methods and plans for monitoring of the GMO or GMOs and for emergency response;

— the evaluation of foreseeable effects, in particular any pathogenic and/or ecologically disruptive effects.

5. If, for whatever reasons, the notifier withdraws the notification, the competent authorities and the Commission must respect the confidentiality of the information supplied.

Article 20

According to the procedure laid down in Article 21, the Commission shall adapt Annexes II and III to technical progress in particular by amending the notification requirements to take into account the potential hazard of the GMOs.

Article 21

The Commission shall be assisted by a committee composed of the representatives of the Member States and chaired by the representative of the Commission.

The representative of the Commission shall submit to the committee a draft of the measures to be taken. The committee shall deliver its opinion on the draft within a time limit which the chairman may lay down according to the urgency of the matter. The opinion shall be delivered by the majority laid down in Article 148 (2) of the Treaty in the case of decisions which the Council is required to adopt on a proposal from the Commission. The votes of the representatives of the Member States within the committee shall be weighted in the manner set out in that Article. The chairman shall not vote.

The Commission shall adopt the measures envisaged if they are in accordance with the opinion of the committee.

If the measures envisaged are not in accordance with the opinion of the committee, or if no opinion is delivered, the Commission shall, without delay, submit to the Council a proposal relating to the measures to be taken. The Council shall act by a qualified majority.

If, on the expiry of a period of three months from the date of referral to the Council, the Council has not acted, the proposed measures shall be adopted by the Commission.

Article 22

1. Member States and the Commission shall meet regularly and exchange information on the experience acquired with regard to the prevention of risks related to the release of GMOs into the environment.

2. Every three years, Member States shall send the Commission a report on the measures taken to implement the provisions of this Directive, the first time being on 1 September 1992.

3. Every three years, the Commission shall publish a summary based on the reports referred to in paragraph 2, the first time being in 1993.

Article 23

1. Member States shall bring into force the laws, regulations and administrative provisions necessary to comply with this Directive before 23 October 1991.

2. Member States shall immediately inform the Commission of all laws, regulations and administrative provisions adopted in implementation of this Directive.

Article 24

This Directive is addressed to the Member States.

Done at Luxembourg, 23 April 1990.

For the Council
The President
A. REYNOLDS

ANNEX I A

TECHNIQUES REFERRED TO IN ARTICLE 2 (2)

PART 1

Techniques of genetic modification referred to in Article 2 (2) (i) are *inter alia:*

(1) recombinant DNA techniques using vector systems as previously covered by Council Recommendation 82/472/EEC ([1]);

(2) techniques involving the direct introduction into an organism of heritable material prepared outside the organism including micro-injection, macro-injection and micro-encapsulation;

(3) cell fusion (including protoplast fusion) or hybridization techniques where live cells with new combinations of heritable genetic material are formed through the fusion of two or more cells by means of methods that do not occur naturally.

PART 2

Techniques referred to in Article 2 (2) (ii) which are not considered to result in genetic modification, on condition that they do not involve the use of recombinant DNA molecules or GMOs, are:

(1) *in vitro* fertilization,

(2) conjugation, transduction, transformation or any other natural process,

(3) polyploidy induction.

—

ANNEX I B

TECHNIQUES REFERRED TO IN ARTICLE 3

Techniques of genetic modification to be excluded from this Directive, on condition that they do not involve the use of GMOs as recipient or parental organisms, are:

(1) mutagenesis,

(2) cell fusion (including protoplast fusion) of plant cells where the resulting organisms can also be produced by traditional breeding methods.

—

([1]) OJ NO L 213, 21. 7. 1982, p. 15.

" ANNEX II

INFORMATION REQUIRED IN THE NOTIFICATION

The notification for a deliberate release referred to in Article 5 and of the placing on the market referred to in Article 11 is to include, as appropriate, the information set out below in the sub-Annexes.

Not all points included will apply to every case. It is to be expected that individual notifications will address only the particular subset of considerations which is appropriate to individual situations.

The level of detail required in response to each subset of considerations is also likely to vary according to the nature and scale of the proposed release.

Annex II A applies to releases of all types of genetically modified organisms other than higher plants. Annex II B applies to releases of genetically modified higher plants.

The term "higher plants" means plants which belong to the taxonomic groups *Gymnospermae* and *Angiospermae*.

ANNEX II A

INFORMATION REQUIRED IN NOTIFICATIONS CONCERNING RELEASES OF GENETICALLY MODIFIED ORGANISMS OTHER THAN HIGHER PLANTS

I. GENERAL INFORMATION

A. Name and address of the notifier (company or institute)

B. Name, qualifications and experience of the responsible scientist(s)

C. Title of the project

II. INFORMATION RELATING TO THE GMO

A. Characteristics of (a) the donor, (b) the recipient or (c) (where appropriate) parental organism(s):

1. scientific name;

2. taxonomy;

3. other names (usual name, strain name, etc.);

4. phenotypic and genetic markers;

5. degree of relatedness between donor and recipient or between parental organisms;

6. description of identification and detection techniques;

7. sensitivity, reliability (in quantitative terms) and specificity of detection and identification techniques;

8. description of the geographic distribution and of the natural habitat of the organism including information on natural predators, preys, parasites and competitors, symbionts and hosts;

9. potential for genetic transfer and exchange with other organisms;

10. verification of the genetic stability of the organisms and factors affecting it;

11. pathological, ecological and physiological traits:

   (a) classification of hazard according to existing Community rules concerning the protection of human health and/or the environment;

   (b) generation time in natural ecosystems, sexual and asexual reproductive cycle;

   (c) information on survival, including seasonability and the ability to form survival structures e.g.: seeds, spores or sclerotia;

   (d) pathogenicity: infectivity, toxigenicity, virulence, allergenicity, carrier (vector) of pathogen, possible vectors, host range including non-target organism. Possible activation of latent viruses (proviruses). Ability to colonize other organisms;

   (e) antibiotic resistance, and potential use of these antibiotics in humans and domestic organisms for prophylaxis and therapy;

   (f) involvement in environmental processes: primary production, nutrient turnover, decomposition of organic matter, respiration, etc.

12. Nature of indigenous vectors:

   (a) sequence;

   (b) frequency of mobilization;

   (c) specificity;

   (d) presence of genes which confer resistance.

13. History of previous genetic modifications.

B. Characteristics of the vector:

1. nature and source of the vector;

2. sequence of transposons, vectors and other non-coding genetic segments used to construct the GMO and to make the introduced vector and insert function in the GMO;

3. frequency of mobilization of inserted vector and/or genetic transfer capabilities and methods of determination ;

4. information on the degree to which the vector is limited to the DNA required to perform the intended function.

C. Characteristics of the modified organism :

1. Information relating to the genetic modification :

   (a) methods used for the modification ;

   (b) methods used to construct and introduce the insert(s) into the recipient or to delete a sequence ;

   (c) description of the insert and/or vector construction ;

   (d) purity of the insert from any unknown sequence and information on the degree to which the inserted sequence is limited to the DNA required to perform the intended function ;

   (e) sequence, functional identity and location of the altered/inserted/deleted nucleic acid segment(s) in question with particular reference to any known harmful sequence.

2. Information on the final GMO :

   (a) description of genetic trait(s) or phenotypic characteristics and in particular any new traits and characteristics which may be expressed or no longer expressed ;

   (b) structure and amount of any vector and/or donor nucleic acid remaining in the final construction of the modified organism ;

   (c) stability of the organism in terms of genetic traits ;

   (d) rate and level of expression of the new genetic material. Method and sensitivity of measurement ;

   (e) activity of the expressed protein(s) ;

   (f) description of identification and detection techniques including techniques for the identification and detection of the inserted sequence and vector ;

   (g) sensitivity, reliability (in quantitative terms) and specificity of detection and identification techniques ;

   (h) history of previous releases or uses of the GMO ;

   (i) health considerations :

   (i) toxic or allergenic effects of the non-viable GMOs and/or their metabolic products ;

   (ii) product hazards ;

   (iii) comparison of the modified organism to the donor, recipient or (where appropriate) parental organism regarding pathogenicity ;

   (iv) capacity for colonization ;

   (v) if the organism is pathogenic to humans who are immunocompetent :

   — diseases caused and mechanism of pathogenicity including invasiveness and virulence,

   — communicability,

   — infective dose,

   — host range, possibility of alteration,

   — possibility of survival outside of human host,

   — presence of vectors or means of dissemination,

   — biological stability,

   — antibiotic-resistance patterns,

   — allergenicity,

   — availability of appropriate therapies.

III. INFORMATION RELATING TO THE CONDITIONS OF RELEASE AND THE RECEIVING ENVIRONMENT

A. Information on the release :

1. description of the proposed deliberate release, including the purpose(s) and foreseen products ;

2. foreseen dates of the release and time planning of the experiment including frequency and duration of releases ;

3. preparation of the site previous to the release ;

4. size of the site ;

5. method(s) to be used for the release;

6. quantities of GMOs to be released;

7. disturbance on the site (type and method of cultivation, mining, irrigation, or other activities);

8. worker protection measures taken during the release;

9. post-release treatment of the site;

10. techniques foreseen for elimination or inactivition of the GMOs at the end of the experiment;

11. information on, and results of, previous releases of the GMOs, especially at different scales and in different ecosystems.

B. Information on the environment (both on the site and in the wider environment):

1. geographical location and grid reference of the site(s) (in case of notifications under Part C the site(s) of release will be the foreseen areas of use of the product);

2. physical or biological proximity to humans and other significant biota;

3. proximity to significant biotopes or protected areas;

4. size of local population;

5. economic activities of local populations which are based on the natural resources of the area;

6. distance to closest areas protected for drinking water and/or environmental purpose;

7. climatic characteristics of the region(s) likely to be affected;

8. geographical, geological and pedological characteristics;

9. flora and fauna, including crops, livestock and migratory species;

10. description of target and non-target ecosystems likely to be affected;

11. a comparison of the natural habitat of the recipient organism with the proposed site(s) of release;

12. any known planned developments or changes in land use in the region which could influence the environmental impact of the release.

IV. INFORMATION RELATING TO THE INTERACTIONS BETWEEN THE GMOs AND THE ENVIRONMENT

A. Characteristics affecting survival, multiplication and dissemination:

1. biological features which affect survival, multiplication and dispersal;

2. known or predicted environmental conditions which may affect survival, multiplication and dissemination (wind, water, soil, temperature, pH, etc.);

3. sensitivity to specific agents.

B. Interactions with the environment:

1. predicted habitat of the GMOs;

2. studies of the behaviour and characteristics of the GMOs and their ecological impact carried out in simulated natural environments, such as microcosms, growth rooms, greenhouses;

3. genetic transfer capability:

(a) post-release transfer of genetic material from GMOs into organisms in affected ecosystems;

(b) post-release transfer of genetic material from indigenous organisms to the GMOs;

4. likelihood of post-release selection leading to the expression of unexpected and/or undesirable traits in the modified organism;

5. measures employed to ensure and to verify genetic stability. Description of genetic traits which may prevent or minimize dispersal of genetic material. Methods to verify genetic stability;

6. routes of biological dispersal, known or potential modes of interaction with the disseminating agent, including inhalation, ingestion, surface contact, burrowing, etc.;

7. description of ecosystems to which the GMOs could be disseminated.

390L0220 EN - 11

C. Potential environmental impact :

1. potential for excessive population increase in the environment ;

2. competitive advantage of the GMOs in relation to the unmodified recipient or parental organism(s) ;

3. identification and description of the target organisms ;

4. anticipated mechanism and result of interaction between the released GMOs and the target organism ;

5. identification and description of non-target organisms which may be affected unwittingly ;

6. likelihood of post-release shifts in biological interactions or in host range ;

7. known or predicted effects on non-target organisms in the environment, impact on population levels of competitors : preys, hosts, symbionts, predators, parasites and pathogens ;

8. known or predicted involvement in biogeochemical processes ;

9. other potentially significant interactions with the environment.

V. INFORMATION ON MONITORING, CONTROL, WASTE TREATMENT AND EMERGENCY RESPONSE PLANS

A. Monitoring techniques :

1. methods for tracing the GMOs, and for monitoring their effects ;

2. specificity (to identify the GMOs, and to distinguish them from the donor, recipient or, where appropriate, the parental organisms), sensitivity and reliability of the monitoring techniques ;

3. techniques for detecting transfer of the donated genetic material to other organisms ;

4. duration and frequency of the monitoring.

B. Control of the release :

1. methods and procedures to avoid and/or minimize the spread of the GMOs beyond the site of release or the designated area for use ;

2. methods and procedures to protect the site from intrusion by unauthorized individuals ;

3. methods and procedures to prevent other organisms from entering the site.

C. Waste treatment :

1. type of waste generated ;

2. expected amount of waste ;

3. possible risks ;

4. description of treatment envisaged.

D. Emergency response plans :

1. methods and procedures for controlling the GMOs in case of unexpected spread ;

2. methods for decontamination of the areas affected, e.g. eradication of the GMOs ;

3. methods for disposal or sanitation of plants, animals, etc., that were exposed during or after the spread ;

4. methods for the isolation of the area affected by the spread ;

5. plans for protecting human health and the environment in case of the occurrence of an undesirable effect.

———

ANNEX II B

INFORMATION REQUIRED IN NOTIFICATIONS CONCERNING RELEASES OF GENETICALLY MODIFIED HIGHER PLANTS (GMHPs) *(GYMNOSPERMAE* AND *ANGIOSPERMAE)*

A. GENERAL INFORMATION

1. Name and address of the notifier (company or institute)

2. Name, qualifications and experience of the responsible scientist(s)

3. Title of the project

B. INFORMATION RELATING TO (A) THE RECIPIENT OR (B) (WHERE APPROPRIATE) PARENTAL PLANTS

1. Complete name :

   (a) family name ;

   (b) genus ;

   (c) species ;

   (d) subspecies ;

   (e) cultivar/breeding line ;

   (f) common name.

2. (a) Information concerning reproduction :

   (i) mode(s) of reproduction ;

   (ii) specific factors affecting reproduction, if any ;

   (iii) generation time.

   (b) Sexual compatibility with other cultivated or wild plant species.

3. Survivability :

   (a) ability to form structures for survival or dormancy ;

   (b) specific factors affecting survivability, if any.

4. Dissemination :

   (a) ways and extent of dissemination ;

   (b) specific factors affecting dissemination, if any.

5. Geographical distribution of the plant.

6. In the case of plant species not normally grown in the Member State(s), description of the natural habitat of the plant, including information on natural predators, parasites, competitors and symbionts.

7. Potentially significant interactions of the plant with organisms other than plants in the ecosystem where it is usually grown, including information on toxic effects on humans, animals and other organisms.

C. INFORMATION RELATING TO THE GENETIC MODIFICATION

1. Description of the methods used for the genetic modification.

2. Nature and source of the vector used.

3. Size, source (name of donor organism(s) and intended function of each constituent fragment of the region intended for insertion.

D. INFORMATION RELATING TO THE GENETICALLY MODIFIED PLANT

1. Description of the trait(s) and characteristics which have been introduced or modified.

2. Information on the sequences actually inserted/deleted :

   (a) size and structure of the insert and methods used for its characterization, including information on any parts of the vector introduced in the GMHP or any carrier or foreign DNA remaining in the GMHP ;

   (b) in case of deletion, size and function of the deleted region(s) ;

   (c) location of the insert in the plant cells (integrated in the chromosome, chloroplasts, mitochondria, or maintained in a non-integrated form), and methods for its determination ;

   (d) copy number of the insert.

3. Information on the expression of the insert :

   (a) information on the expression of the insert and methods used for its characterization ;

   (b) parts of the plant where the insert is expressed (e.g. roots, stem, pollen etc.).

4. Information on how the genetically modified plant differs from the recipient plant in :

(a) mode(s) and/or rate of reproduction ;

(b) dissemination ;

(c) survivability.

5. Genetic stability of the insert.

6. Potential for transfer of genetic material from the genetically modified plants to other organisms.

7. Information on any toxic or harmful effects on human health and the environment, arising from the genetic modification.

8. Mechanism of interaction between the genetically modified plant and target organisms (if applicable).

9. Potentially significant interactions with non-target organisms.

10. Description of detection and identification techniques for the genetically modified plant.

11. Information about previous releases of the genetically modified plant, if applicable.

E. INFORMATION RELATING TO THE SITE OF RELEASE (ONLY FOR NOTIFICATIONS SUBMITTED PURSUANT TO ARTICLE 5)

1. Location and size of the release site(s).

2. Description of the release site ecosystem, including climate, flora and fauna.

3. Presence of sexually compatible wild relatives or cultivated plant species.

4. Proximity to officially recognized biotopes or protected areas which may be affected.

F. INFORMATION RELATING TO THE RELEASE (ONLY FOR NOTIFICATIONS SUBMITTED PURSUANT TO ARTICLE 5)

1. Purpose of the release.

2. Foreseen date(s) and duration of the release.

3. Method by which the genetically modified plants will be released.

4. Method for preparing and managing the release site, prior to, during and post-release, including cultivation practices and harvesting methods.

5. Approximate number of plants (or plants per m²).

G. INFORMATION ON CONTROL, MONITORING, POST-RELEASE AND WASTE TREATMENT PLANS (ONLY FOR NOTIFICATIONS SUBMITTED PURSUANT TO ARTICLE 5)

1. Any precautions taken :

(a) distance(s) from sexually compatible plant species ;

(b) any measures to minimize/prevent pollen or seed dispersal.

2. Description of methods for post-release treatment of the site.

3. Description of post-release treatment methods for the genetically modified plant material including wastes.

4. Description of monitoring plans and techniques.

5. Description of any emergency plans.

H. INFORMATION ON THE POTENTIAL ENVIRONMENTAL IMPACT FROM THE RELEASE OF THE GENETICALLY MODIFIED PLANTS

1. Likelihood of the GMHP becoming more persistent than the recipient or parental plants in agricultural habitats or more invasive in natural habitats.

2. Any selective advantage or disadvantage conferred to other sexually compatible plants species, which may result from genetic transfer from the genetically modified plant.

3. Potential environmental impact of the interaction between the genetically modified plant and target organisms (if applicable).

4. Possible environmental impact resulting from potential interactions with non-target organisms. " [1]

ANNEX III

ADDITIONAL INFORMATION REQUIRED IN THE CASE OF NOTIFICATION FOR PLACING ON THE MARKET

A. The following information shall be provided in the notification for placing on the market of products, in addition to that of Annex II:

1. name of the product and names of GMOs contained therein;

2. name of the manufacturer or distributor and his address in the Community;

3. specificity of the product, exact conditions of use including, when appropriate, the type of environment and/or the geographical area(s) of the Community for which the product is suited;

4. type of expected use: industry, agriculture and skilled trades, consumer use by public at large.

B. The following information shall be provided, when relevant, in addition to that of point A, in accordance with Article 11 of this Directive:

1. measures to take in case of unintended release or misuse;

2. specific instructions or recommendations for storage and handling;

3. estimated production in and/or imports to the Community;

4. proposed packaging. This must be appropriate so as to avoid unintended release of the GMOs during storage, or at a later stage;

5. proposed labelling. This must include, at least in summarized form, the information referred to in points A. 1, A. 2, A. 3, B. 1 and B. 2.

_____

II

(Acts whose publication is not obligatory)

COUNCIL

COUNCIL DIRECTIVE
of 18 December 1986

on the harmonization of laws, regulations and administrative provisions relating to the application of the principles of good laboratory practice and the verification of their applications for tests on chemical substances

(87/18/EEC)

THE COUNCIL OF THE EUROPEAN COMMUNITIES,

Having regard to the Treaty establishing the European Economic Community, and in particular Article 100 thereof,

Having regard to the proposal from the Commission,

Having regard to the opinion of the European Parliament ([1]),

Having regard to the opinion of the Economic and Social Committee ([2]),

Whereas Council Directive 67/548/EEC of 27 June 1967 on the approximation of laws, regulations and administrative provisions relating to the classification, packaging and labelling of dangerous substances ([3]), as last amended by Directive 84/449/EEC ([4]), requires tests to be carried out on chemical substances in order to enable their potential risk to man and the environment to be determined;

Whereas Directive 75/318/EEC ([5]) as amended by Directive 87/19/EEC ([6]), and Directive 81/852/EEC ([7]) as amended by Directive 87/20/EEC ([8]) lay down that non-clinical tests on pharmaceutical products shall be carried out in accordance with the principles of good laboratory practice in force in the Community for chemical substances;

Whereas when the active substances in pesticides undergo tests they shall do so in accordance with the protocols provided for by Directive 67/548/EEC, and hence in accordance with good laboratory practice for chemical substances;

Whereas the methods to be used for these tests are laid down in Annex V to Directive 67/548/EEC;

Whereas it is necessary to comply with the principles of good laboratory practice in carrying out the tests laid down by Directive 67/548/EEC so as to ensure that the results are comparable and of high quality;

Whereas the Commission intends shortly to submit a proposal to the Council for a Directive aiming at verifying compliance with the principles of good laboratory practice;

Whereas the resources devoted to the tests must not be wasted by having to repeat tests owing to differences in laboratory practice from one Member State to another;

Whereas the Council of the Organization for Economic Cooperation and Development (OECD) took a Decision on 12 May 1981 on the mutual acceptance of data for the evaluation of chemical products; whereas it issued a recommendation on 26 July 1983 concerning the mutual recognition of compliance with good laboratory practice;

Whereas animal protection requires that the number of experiments conducted on animals be restricted; whereas mutual recognition of the results of tests obtained using standard and recognized methods is an essential condition for reducing the number of experiments in this area;

([1]) OJ No C 120, 20. 5. 1986, p. 177.
([2]) OJ No C 354, 31. 12. 1985, p. 5.
([3]) OJ No 196, 16. 8. 1967, p. 1.
([4]) OJ No L 251, 19. 9. 1984, p. 1.
([5]) OJ No L 147, 9. 6. 1975, p. 1.
([6]) See page 31 of this Official Journal.
([7]) OJ No L 317, 6. 11. 1981, p. 16.
([8]) See page 34 of this Official Journal.

Whereas it is necessary to set up a procedure allowing rapid adaptation of the principles of good laboratory practice,

HAS ADOPTED THIS DIRECTIVE:

Article 1

1. Member States shall take all measures necessary to ensure that laboratories carrying out tests on chemical products, in accordance with Directive 67/548/EEC, comply with the principles of good laboratory practice specified in Annex 2 to the Decision of 12 May 1981 of the Council of the OECD on the mutual acceptance of data for the evaluation of chemical products.

2. Paragraph 1 shall apply also where other Community provisions provide for the application of the principles of good laboratory practice in respect of tests on chemical products to evaluate their safety for man and/or the environment.

Article 2

When submitting results, the laboratories referred to in Article 1 must certify that the tests have been carried out in conformity with the principles of good laboratory practice referred to in that Article.

Article 3

1. Member States shall adopt the measures necessary for verification of compliance with the principles of good laboratory practice. These measures shall include, in particular, inspections and study checks in accordance with the recommendations of the OECD in this area.

2. Member States shall notify to the Commission the name or names of the authority or authorities responsible for verifying compliance with the principles of good laboratory practice, as referred to in paragraph 1. The Commission shall inform the other Member States thereof.

Article 4

Adaptations to the principles of good laboratory practice mentioned in Article 1 may be adopted in accordance with the procedure laid down in Article 21 of Directive 67/548/EEC.

Article 5

1. Where Community provisions require application of the principles of good laboratory practice following the entry into force of this Directive for tests on chemical products, Member States may not, on grounds relating to the principles of good laboratory practice, prohibit, restrict or impede the placing on the market of chemical products if the principles applied by the laboratories concerned are in conformity with those mentioned in Article 1.

2. Should a Member State establish on the basis of detailed evidence that the application of the principles of good laboratory practice and the verification of their application for tests on chemical substances show that, although a chemical substance has been examined in accordance with the requirements of this Directive, it presents a danger to man and the environment, the Member State may provisionally prohibit or make subject to special conditions the marketing of that substance on its territory. It shall immediately inform the Commission and the other Member States thereof and give the grounds for its decision.

The Commission shall, within six weeks, consult the Member States concerned and then give its opinion and take suitable measures without delay.

Should the Commission consider that technical adaptations to this Directive are necessary, those adaptations shall be adopted either by the Commission or by the Council in accordance with the procedure laid down in Article 4. In that case, the Member State which adopted the safeguard measures may maintain them until entry into force of those adaptations.

Article 6

Member States shall bring into force the laws, regulations and administrative provisions necessary to comply with this Directive not later than 30 June 1988. They shall forthwith inform the Commission thereof.

Article 7

This Directive is addressed to the Member States.

Done at Brussels, 18 December 1986.

For the Council
The President
M. JOPLING

II

(Acts whose publication is not obligatory)

COUNCIL

COUNCIL DIRECTIVE

of 24 November 1986

on the approximation of laws, regulations and administrative provisions of the Member States regarding the protection of animals used for experimental and other scientific purposes

(86/609/EEC)

THE COUNCIL OF THE EUROPEAN COMMUNITIES,

Having regard to the Treaty establishing the European Economic Community, and in particular Article 100 thereof,

Having regard to the proposal from the Commission (¹),

Having regard to the opinion of the European Parliament (²),

Having regard to the opinion of the Economic and Social Committee (³),

Whereas there exist between the national laws at present in force for the protection of animals used for certain experimental purposes disparities which may affect the functioning of the common market;

Whereas, in order to eliminate these disparities, the laws of the Member States should be harmonized; whereas such harmonization should ensure that the number of animals used for experimental or other scientific purposes is reduced to a minimum, that such animals are adequately cared for, that no pain, suffering, distress or lasting harm are inflicted unnecessarily and ensure that, where unavoidable, these shall be kept to the minimum;

Whereas, in particular, unnecessary duplication of experiments should be avoided,

(¹) OJ No C 351, 31. 12. 1985, p. 16.
(²) OJ No C 255, 13. 10. 1986, p. 250.
(³) OJ No C 207, 18. 8. 1986, p. 3.

HAS ADOPTED THIS DIRECTIVE:

Article 1

The aim of this Directive is to ensure that where animals are used for experimental or other scientific purposes the provisions laid down by law, regulation or administrative provisions in the Member States for their protection are approximated so as to avoid affecting the establishment and functioning of the common market, in particular by distorsions of competition or barriers to trade.

Article 2

For the purposes of this Directive the following definitions shall apply:

(a) *'animal'* unless otherwise qualified, means any live non-human vertebrate, including free-living larval and/or reproducing larval forms, but excluding foetal or embryonic forms;

(b) *'experimental animals'* means animals used or to be used in experiments;

(c) *'bred animals'* means animals specially bred for use in experiments in facilities approved by, or registered with, the authority;

(d) *'experiment'* means any use of an animal for experimental or other scientific purposes which may cause it pain, suffering, distress or lasting harm, including any course of action intended, or liable, to result in the birth of an animal in any such condition, but excluding the least painful methods accepted in modern practice (i.e. 'humane' methods) of killing or marking an animal; an experiment starts when an animal is first prepared for use and ends when no further observations are to be made for that experiment; the elimination of pain, suffering, distress or lasting harm by the successful use of anaesthesia or analgesia or other methods does not place the use of an animal outside the scope of this definition. Non experimental, agricultural or clinical veterinary practices are excluded;

(e) *'authority'* means the authority or authorities designated by each Member State as being responsible for supervising the experiments within the meaning of this Directive;

(f) *'competent person'* means any person who is considered by a Member State to be competent to perform the relevant function described in this Directive;

(g) *'establishment'* means any installation, building, group of buildings or other premises and may include a place which is not wholly enclosed or covered and mobile facilities;

(h) *'breeding establishment'* means any establishment where animals are bred with a view to their use in experiments;

(i) *'supplying establishment'* means any establishment, other than a breeding establishment, from which animals are supplied with a view to their use in experiments;

(j) *'user establishment'* means any establishment where animals are used for experiments;

(k) *'properly anaesthetized'* means deprived of sensation by methods of anaesthesia (whether local or general) as effective as those used in good veterinary practice;

(l) *'humane method of killing'* means the killing of an animal with a minimum of physical and mental suffering, depending on the species.

Article 3

This Directive applies to the use of animals in experiments which are undertaken for one of the following purposes:

(a) the development, manufacture, quality, effectiveness and safety testing of drugs, foodstuffs and other substances or products:

    i) for the avoidance, prevention, diagnosis or treatment of disease, ill-health or other abnormality or their effects in man, animals or plants;

    (ii) for the assessment, detection, regulation or modification of physiological conditions in man, animals or plants;

(b) the protection of the natural environment in the interests of the health or welfare of man or animal.

Article 4

Each Member State shall ensure that experiments using animals considered as endangered under Appendix I of the Convention on International Trade in Endangered Species of Fauna and Flora and Annex C.I. of Regulation (EEC) No 3626/82 ([1]) are prohibited unless they are in conformity with the above Regulation and the objects of the experiment are:

— research aimed at preservation of the species in question, or

— essential biomedical purposes where the species in question exceptionally proves to be the only one suitable for those purposes.

Article 5

Member States shall ensure that, as far as the general care and accommodation of animals is concerned:

(a) all experimental animals shall be provided with housing, an environment, at least some freedom of movement, food, water and care which are appropriate to their health and well-being;

(b) any restriction on the extent to which an experimental animal can satisfy its physiological and ethological needs shall be limited to the absolute minimum;

(c) the environmental conditions in which experimental animals are bred, kept or used must be checked daily;

(d) the well-being and state of health of experimental animals shall be observed by a competent person to prevent pain or avoidable suffering, distress or lasting harm;

(e) arrangements are made to ensure that any defect or suffering discovered is eliminated as quickly as possible.

For the implementation of the provisions of paragraphs (a) and (b), Member States shall pay regard to the guidelines set out in Annex II.

Article 6

1. Each Member State shall designate the authority or authorities responsible for verifying that the provisions of this Directive are properly carried out.

2. In the framework of the implementation of this Directive, Member States shall adopt the necessary measures in order that the designated authority mentioned in paragraph 1 above may have the advice of experts competent for the matters in question.

_____
([1]) OJ No L 384, 31. 12. 1982, p. 1.

Article 7

1.   Experiments shall be performed solely by competent authorized persons, or under the direct responsibility of such a person, or if the experimental or other scientific project concerned is authorized in accordance with the provisions of national legislation.

2.   An experiment shall not be performed if another scientifically satisfactory method of obtaining the result sought, not entailing the use of an animal, is reasonably and practicably available.

3.   When an experiment has to be performed, the choice of species shall be carefully considered and, where necessary, explained to the authority. In a choice between experiments, those which use the minimum number of animals, involve animals with the lowest degree of neurophysiological sensitivity, cause the least pain, suffering, distress or lasting harm and which are most likely to provide satisfactory results shall be selected.

Experiments on animals taken from the wild may not be carried out unless experiments on other animals would not suffice for the aims of the experiment.

4.   All experiments shall be designed to avoid distress and unnecessary pain and suffering to the experimental animals. They shall be subject to the provisions laid down in Article 8. The measures set out in Article 9 shall be taken in all cases.

Article 8

1.   All experiments shall be carried out under general or local anaesthesia.

2.   Paragraph 1 above does not apply when:

(a) anaesthesia is judged to be more traumatic to the animal than the experiment itself;

(b) anaesthesia is incompatible with the object of the experiment. In such cases appropriate legislative and/or administrative measures shall be taken to ensure that no such experiment is carried out unnecessarily.

Anaesthesia should be used in the case of serious injuries which may cause severe pain.

3.   If anaesthesia is not possible, analgesics or other appropriate methods should be used in order to ensure as far as possible that pain, suffering, distress or harm are limited and that in any event the animal is not subject to severe pain, distress or suffering.

4.   Provided such action is compatible with the object of the experiment, an anaesthetized animal, which suffers considerable pain once anaesthesia has worn off, shall be treated in good time with pain-relieving means or, if this is not possible, shall be immediately killed by a humane method.

Article 9

1.   At the end of any experiment, it shall be decided whether the animal shall be kept alive or killed by a humane method, subject to the condition that it shall not be kept alive if, even though it has been restored to normal health in all other respects, it is likely to remain in lasting pain or distress.

2.   The decisions referred to in paragraph 1 shall be taken by a competent person, preferably a veterinarian.

3.   Where, at the end of an experiment:

(a) an animal is to be kept alive, it shall receive the care appropriate to its state of health, be placed under the supervision of a veterinarian or other competent person and shall be kept under conditions conforming to the requirements of Article 5. The conditions laid down in this subparagraph may, however, be waived where, in the opinion of a veterinarian, the animal would not suffer as a consequence of such exemption;

(b) an animal is not to be kept alive or cannot benefit from the provisions of Article 5 concerning its well-being, it shall be killed by a humane method as soon as possible.

Article 10

Member States shall ensure that any re-use of animals in experiments shall be compatible with the provisions of this Directive.

In particular, an animal shall not be used more than once in experiments entailing severe pain, distress or equivalent suffering.

Article 11

Notwithstanding the other provisions of this Directive, where it is necessary for the legitimate purposes of the experiment, the authority may allow the animal concerned to be set free, provided that it is satisfied that the maximum possible care has been taken to safeguard the animal's well-being, as long as its state of health allows this to be done and there is no danger for public health and the environment.

Article 12

1.   Member States shall establish procedures whereby experiments themselves or the details of persons conducting such experiments shall be notified in advance to the authority.

2. Where it is planned to subject an animal to an experiment in which it will, or may, experience severe pain which is likely to be prolonged, that experiment must be specifically declared and justified to, or specifically authorized by, the authority. The authority shall take appropriate judicial or administrative action if it is not satisfied that the experiment is of sufficient importance for meeting the essential needs of man or animal.

Article 13

1. On the basis of requests for authorization and notifications received, and on the basis of the reports made, the authority in each Member State shall collect, and as far as possible periodically make publicly available, the statistical information on the use of animals in experiments in respect of:

(a) the number and kinds of animals used in experiments;

(b) the number of animals, in selected categories, used in the experiments referred to in Article 3;

(c) the number of animals, in selected categories, used in experiments required by legislation.

2. Member States shall take all necessary steps to ensure that the confidentiality of commercially sensitive information communicated pursuant to this Directive is protected.

Article 14

Persons who carry out experiments or take part in them and persons who take care of animals used for experiments, including duties of a supervisory nature, shall have appropriate education and training.

In particular, persons carrying out or supervising the conduct of experiments shall have received instruction in a scientific discipline relevant to the experimental work being undertaken and be capable of handling and taking care of laboratory animals; they shall also have satisfied the authority that they have attained a level of training sufficient for carrying out their tasks.

Article 15

Breeding and supplying establishments shall be approved by or registered with, the authority and comply with the requirements of Articles 5 and 14 unless an exemption is granted under Article 19 (4) or Article 21. A supplying establishment shall obtain animals only from a breeding or other supplying establishment unless the animal has been lawfully imported and is not a feral or stray animal. General or special exemption from this last provision may be granted to a supplying establishment under arrangements determined by the authority.

Article 16

The approval or the registration provided for in Article 15 shall specify the competent person responsible for the establishment entrusted with the task of administering, or arranging for the administration of, appropriate care to the animals bred or kept in the establishment and of ensuring compliance with the requirements of Articles 5 and 14.

ticle 17

1. Breeding and supplying establishments shall record the number and the species of animals sold or supplied, the dates on which they are sold or supplied, the name and address of the recipient and the number and species of animals dying while in the breeding or supplying establishment in question.

2. Each authority shall prescribe the records which are to be kept and made available to it by the person responsible for the establishments mentioned in paragraph 1; such records shall be kept for a minimum of three years from the date of the last entry and shall undergo periodic inspection by officers of the authority.

Article 18

1. Each dog, cat or non-human primate in any breeding, supplying or user establishment shall, before it is weaned, be provided with an individual identification mark in the least painful manner possible except in the cases referred to in paragraph 3.

2. Where an unmarked dog, cat or non-human primate is taken into an establishment for the first time after it has been weaned it shall be marked as soon as possible.

3. Where a dog, cat or non-human primate is transferred from one establishment as referred to in paragraph 1 to another before it is weaned, and it is not practicable to mark it beforehand, a full documentary record, specifying in particular its mother, must be maintained by the receiving establishment until it can be so marked.

4. Particulars of the identity and origin of each dog, cat or non-human primate shall be entered in the records of each establishment.

Article 19

1. User establishments shall be registered with, or approved by, the authority. Arrangements shall be made for user establishments to have installations and equipment suited to the species of animals used and the performance of the experiments conducted there; their design, construction and method of functioning shall be such as to ensure that the experiments are performed as effectively as possible, with the

object of obtaining consistent results with the minimum number of animals and the minimum degree of pain, suffering, distress or lasting harm.

2. In each user establishment:

(a) the person or persons who are administratively responsible for the care of the animals and the functioning of the equipment shall be identified;

(b) sufficient trained staff shall be provided;

(c) adequate arrangements shall be made for the provision of veterinary advice and treatment;

(d) a veterinarian or other competent person should be charged with advisory duties in relation to the well-being of the animals.

3. Experiments may, where authorized by the authority, be conducted outside user establishments.

4. In user establishments, only animals from breeding or supplying establishments shall be used unless a general or special exemption has been obtained under arrangements determined by the authority. Bred animals shall be used whenever possible. Stray animals of domestic species shall not be used in experiments. A general exemption made under the conditions of this paragraph may not extend to stray dogs and cats.

5. User establishments shall keep records of all animals used and produce them whenever required to do so by the authority. In particular, these records shall show the number and species of all animals acquired, from whom they were acquired and the date of their arrival. Such records shall be kept for a minimum of three years and shall be submitted to the authority which asks for them. User establishments shall be subject to periodic inspection by representatives of the authority.

Article 20

When user establishments breed animals for use in experiments on their own premises, only one registration or approval is needed for the purposes of Article 15 and 19. However, the establishments shall comply with the relevant provisions of this Directive concerning breeding and user establishments.

Article 21

Animals belonging to the species listed in Annex I which are to be used in experiments shall be bred animals unless a general or special exemption has been obtained under arrangements determined by the authority.

Article 22

1. In order to avoid unnecessary duplication of experiments for the purposes of satisfying national or Community health and safety legislation, Member States shall as far as possible recognize the validity of data generated by experiments carried out in the territory of another Member State unless further testing is necessary in order to protect public health and safety.

2. To that end, Member States shall, where practicable and without prejudice to the requirements of existing Community Directives, furnish information to the Commission on their legislation and administrative practice relating to animal experiments, including requirements to be satisfied prior to the marketing of products; they shall also supply factual information on experiments carried out in their territory and on authorizations or any other administrative particulars pertaining to these experiments.

3. The Commission shall establish a permanent consultative committee within which the Member States would be represented, which will assist the Commission in organizing the exchange of appropriate information, while respecting the requirements of confidentiality, and which will also assist the Commission in the other questions raised by the application of this Directive.

Article 23

1. The Commission and Member States should encourage research into the development and validation of alternative techniques which could provide the same level of information as that obtained in experiments using animals but which involve fewer animals or which entail less painful procedures, and shall take such other steps as they consider appropriate to encourage research in this field. The Commission and Member States shall monitor trends in experimental methods.

2. The Commission shall report before the end of 1987 on the possibility of modifying tests and guidelines laid down in existing Community legislation taking into account the objectives referred to in paragraph 1.

Article 24

This Directive shall not restrict the right of the Member States to apply or adopt stricter measures for the protection of animals used in experiments or for the control and restriction of the use of animals for experiments. In particular, Member States may require a prior authorization for experiments or programmes of work notified in accordance with the provisions of Article 12 (1).

Article 25

1. Member States shall take the measures necessary to comply with this Directive by 24 November 1989. They shall forthwith inform the Commission thereof.

2.   Member States shall communicate to the Commission the provisions of national law which they adopt in the field covered by this Directive.

Article 26

At regular intervals not exceeding three years, and for the first time five years following notification of this Directive, Member States shall inform the Commission of the measures taken in this area and provide a suitable summary of the information collected under the provisions of Article 13. The Commission shall prepare a report for the Council and the European Parliament.

Article 27

This Directive is addressed to the Member States.

Done at Brussels, 24 November 1986.

For the Council
The President
W. WALDEGRAVE

ANNEX I

LIST OF EXPERIMENTAL ANIMALS COVERED BY THE PROVISIONS OF ARTICLE 21

— Mouse	— *Mus musculus*
— Rat	— *Rattus norvegicus*
— Guinea Pig	— *Cavia porcellus*
— Golden Hamster	— *Mesocricetus auratus*
— Rabbit	— *Oryctolagus cuniculus*
— Non-human Primates	
— Dog	— *Canis familiaris*
— Cat	— *Felis catus*
— Quail	— *Coturnix coturnix*

ANNEX II

GUIDELINES FOR ACCOMMODATION AND CARE OF ANIMALS

(Article 5 of the Directive)

INTRODUCTION

1. The Council of the European Economic Community has decided that the aim of the Directive is to harmonize the laws of the Member States for the protection of animals used for experimental and other scientific purposes in order to eliminate disparities which at present may affect the functioning of the common market. Harmonization should ensure that such animals are adequately cared for, that no pain, suffering, distress or lasting harm are inflicted unnecessarily and that where unavoidable the latter shall be kept to the minimum.

2. It is true that some experiments are conducted under field conditions on free-living, self-supporting, wild animals, but such experiments are relatively few in number. The great majority of animals used in experiments must for practical reasons be kept under some sort of physical control in facilities ranging from outdoor corrals to cages for small animals in a laboratory animal house. This is a situation where there are highly conflicting interests. On the one hand, the animal whose needs in respect of movement, social relations and other manifestations of life must be restricted, on the other hand, the experimenter and his assistants who demand full control of the animal and its environment. In this confrontation of interests the animal may sometimes be given secondary consideration.

3. Therefore, the Directive provides in Article 5 that: 'as far as the general care and accommodation of animals is concerned:

   (a) all experimental animals shall be provided with housing, an environment, at least some freedom of movement, food, water and care which are appropriate to their health and well-being;

   (b) any restriction on the extent to which an experimental animal can satisfy its physiological and ethological needs shall be limited to the absolute minimum'.

4. This Annex draws up certain guidelines based on present knowledge and practice for the accommodation and care of animals. It explains and supplements the basic principles adopted in Article 5. The object is thus to help authorities, institutions and individuals in their pursuit of the aims of the Directive in this matter.

5. Care is a word which, when used in connection with animals intended for or in actual use in experiments covers all aspects of the relationship between animals and man. Its substance is the sum of material and non-material resources mobilized by man to obtain and maintain an animal in a physical and mental state where it suffers least and performs best in experiments. It starts from the moment the animal is destined to be used in experiments and continues until it is killed by a humane method or otherwise disposed of by the establishment in accordance with Article 9 of the Directive after the close of the experiment.

6. This Annex aims to give advice about the design of appropriate animal quarters. There are, however, several methods of breeding and keeping laboratory animals that differ chiefly in the degree of control of the microbiological environment. It has to be borne in mind that the staff concerned will sometimes have to judge from the character and condition of the animals where the recommended standards of space may not be sufficient, as with especially aggressive animals. In applying the guidelines described in this Annex the requirements of each of these situations should be taken into account. Furthermore, it is necessary to make clear the status of these guidelines. Unlike the provisions of the Directive itself, they are not mandatory; they are recommendations to be used with discretion, designed as guidance to the practices and standards which all concerned should conscientiously strive to achieve. It is for this reason that the term 'should' has had to be used throughout the text even where 'must' might seem to be the more appropriate word. For example, it is self-evident that food and water *must* be provided (see 3.7.2 and 3.8).

7. Finally, for practical and financial reasons, existing animal quarters equipment should not need to be replaced before it is worn out, or has otherwise become useless. Pending replacement with equipment conforming with the present guidelines, these should as far as practicable be complied with by adjusting the numbers and sizes of animals placed in existing cages and pens.

DEFINITIONS

In this Annex, in addition to the definitions contained in Article 2 of the Directive:

(a) *'holding rooms'* mean rooms where animals are normally housed, either for breeding and stocking or during the conduct of an experiment;

(b) *'cage'* means a permanently fixed or movable container that is closed by solid walls and, at least on one side, by bars or meshed wire or, where appropriate, nets and in which one or more animals are kept or transported; depending on the stocking density and the size of the container, the freedom of movement of the animals is relatively restricted;

(c) *'pen'* means an area enclosed, for example, by walls, bars or meshed wire in which one or more animals are kept; depending on the size of the enclosure and the stocking density the freedom of movement of the animals is usually less restricted than in a cage;

(d) *'run'* means an area closed, for example, by fences, walls, bars or meshed wire and frequently situated outside permanently fixed buildings in which animals kept in cages or pens can move freely during certain periods of time in accordance with their ethological and physiological needs, such as exercise;

(e) *'stall'* means a small enclosure with three sides, usually a feed-rack and lateral separations, where one or two animals may be kept tethered.

1.　　THE PHYSICAL FACILITIES

1.1.　Functions and general design

1.1.1.　Any facility should be so constructed as to provide a suitable environment for the species housed. It should also be designed to prevent access by unauthorized persons.

Facilities that are part of a larger building complex should also be protected by proper building measures and arrangements that limit the number of entrances and prevent unauthorized traffic.

1.1.2.　It is recommended that there should be a maintenance programme for the facilities in order to prevent any defect of equipment.

1.2.　Holding rooms

1.2.1.　All necessary measures should be taken to ensure regular and efficient cleaning of the rooms and the maintenance of a satisfactory hygienic standard. Ceilings and walls should be damage-resistant with a smooth, impervious and easily washable surface. Special attention should be paid to junctions with doors, ducts, pipes and cables. Doors and windows, if any, should be constructed or protected so as to keep out unwanted animals. Where appropriate, an inspection window may be fitted in the door. Floors should be smooth, impervious and have a non-slippery, easily washable surface which can carry the weight of racks and other heavy equipment without being damaged. Drains, if any, should be adequately covered and fitted with a barrier which will prevent animals from gaining access.

1.2.2.　Rooms where the animals are allowed to run freely should have walls and floors with a particularly resistant surface material to stand up to the heavy wear and tear caused by the animals and the cleaning process. The material should not be detrimental to the health of the animals and be such that the animals cannot hurt themselves. Drains are desirable in such rooms. Additional protection must be given to any equipment or fixtures so that they may not be damaged by the animals or hurt the animals themselves. Where outdoor exercise areas are provided measures should be taken when appropriate to prevent access by the public and animals.

1.2.3.　Rooms intended for the holding of farm animals (cattle, sheep, goats, pigs, horses, poultry, etc.) should at least conform with the standards laid down in the European Convention for the Protection of Animals kept for Farming Purposes and by national veterinary and other authorities.

1.2.4.　The majority of holding rooms are usually designed to house rodents. Frequently such rooms may also be used to house larger species. Care should be taken not to house together species which are incompatible.

1.2.5.　Holding rooms should be provided with facilities for carrying out minor experiments and manipulations, where appropriate.

1.3.   **Laboratories and general and special purpose experiment rooms**

1.3.1.   At breeding or supplying establishments suitable facilities for making consignments of animals ready for dispatch should be made available.

1.3.2.   All establishments should also have available as a minimum laboratory facilities for the carrying out of simple diagnostic tests, post-mortem examinations, and/or the collection of samples which are to be subjected to more extensive laboratory investigations elsewhere.

1.3.3.   Provision should be made for the receipt of animals in such a way that incoming animals do not put at risk animals already present in the facility, for example by quarantining. General and special purpose experiment rooms should be available for situations where it is undesirable to carry out the experiments or observations in the holding room.

1.3.4.   There should be appropriate accommodation for enabling animals which are ill or injured to be housed separately.

1.3.5.   Where appropriate, there should be provision for one or more separate operating rooms suitably equipped for the performance of surgical experiments under aseptic conditions. There should be facilities for post-operative recovery where this is warranted.

1.4.   **Service rooms**

1.4.1.   Store rooms for food should be cool, dry, vermin and insect proof and those for bedding, dry, vermin and insect proof. Other materials, which may be contaminated or present a hazard, should be stored separately.

1.4.2.   Store rooms for clean cages, instruments and other equipment should be available.

1.4.3.   The cleaning and washing room should be large enough to accommodate the installations necessary to decontaminate and clean used equipment. The cleaning process should be arranged so as to separate the flow of clean and dirty equipment to prevent the contamination of newly cleaned equipment. Walls and floors should be covered with a suitably resistant surface material and the ventilation system should have ample capacity to carry away the excess heat and humidity.

1.4.4.   Provision should be made for the hygienic storage and disposal of carcasses and animal waste. If incineration on the site is not possible or desirable, suitable arrangements should be made for the safe disposal of such material having regard to local regulations and by-laws. Special precautions should be taken with highly toxic or radioactive waste.

1.4.5.   The design and construction of circulation areas should correspond to the standards of the holding rooms. The corridors should be wide enough to allow easy circulation of movable equipment.

2.   **THE ENVIRONMENT IN THE HOLDING ROOMS AND ITS CONTROL**

2.1.   **Ventilation**

2.1.1.   Holding rooms should have an adequate ventilation system which should satisfy the requirements of the species housed. The purpose of the ventilation system is to provide fresh air and to keep down the level of odours, noxious gases, dust and infectious agents of any kind. It also provides for the removal of excess heat and humidity.

2.1.2.   The air in the room should be renewed at frequent intervals. A ventilation rate of 15—20 air changes per hour is normally adequate. However, in some circumstances, where stocking density is low, 8—10 air changes per hour may suffice or mechanical ventilation may not even be needed at all. Other circumstances may necessitate a much higher rate of air change. Recirculation of untreated air should be avoided. However, it should be emphasized that even the most efficient system cannot compensate for poor cleaning routines or negligence.

2.1.3.   The ventilation system should be so designed as to avoid harmful draughts.

2.1.4.   Smoking in rooms where there are animals should be forbidden.

2.2.   **Temperature**

2.2.1.   Table 1 gives the range within which it is recommended that the temperature should be maintained. It should also be emphasized that the figures apply only to adult, normal animals. Newborn and young animals will often require a much higher temperature level. The temperature of the premises should be regulated according to possible changes in the animals' thermal regulation which may be due to special physiological conditions or to the effects of the experiment.

2.2.2.   Under the climatic conditions prevailing in Europe it may be necessary to provide a ventilation system having the capacity both to heat and to cool the air supplied.

2.2.3.   In user establishments a precise temperature control in the holding rooms may be required, because the environmental temperature is a physical factor which has a profound effect on the metabolism of all animals.

2.3.   Humidity

Extreme variations in relative humidity (RH) have an adverse effect on the health and well-being of animals. It is therefore recommended that the RH level in holding rooms should be appropriate to the species concerned and should ordinarily be maintained at 55 % ± 10 %. Values below 40 % and above 70 % RH for prolonged periods should be avoided.

2.4.   Lighting

In windowless rooms, it is necessary to provide controlled lighting both to satisfy the biological requirements of the animals and to provide a satisfactory working environment. It is also necessary to have a control of the intensity and of the light-dark cycle. When keeping albino animals, one should take into account their sensitivity to light (see also 2.6).

2.5.   Noise

Noise can be an important disturbing factor in the animal quarters. Holding rooms and experiment rooms should be insulated against loud noise sources in the audible and in the higher frequencies in order to avoid disturbances in the behaviour and the physiology of the animals. Sudden noises may lead to considerable change in organ functions but, as they are often unavoidable, it is sometimes advisable to provide holding and experiment rooms with a continous sound of moderate intensity such as soft music.

2.6.   Alarm systems

A facility housing a large number of animals is vulnerable. It is therefore recommended that the facility is duly protected by the installation of devices to detect fires and the intrusion of unauthorized persons. Technical defects or a breakdown of the ventilation system is another hazard which could cause distress and even the death of animals, due to suffocation and overheating or, in less serious cases, have such negative effects on an experiment that it will be a failure and have to be repeated. Adequate monitoring devices should therefore be installed in connection with the heating and ventilation plant to enable the staff to supervise its operation in general. If warranted, a stand-by generator should be provided for the maintenance of life support systems for the animals and lighting in the event of a breakdown or the withdrawal of supply. Clear instructions on emergency procedures should be prominently displayed. Alarms for fish tanks are recommended in case of failure of the water supply. Care should be taken to ensure that the operation of an alarm system causes as little disturbance as possible to the animals.

3.   CARE

3.1.   Health

3.1.1.   The person in charge of the establishment should ensure regular inspection of the animals and supervision of the accommodation and care by a veterinarian or other competent person.

3.1.2.   According to the assessment of the potential hazard to the animals, appropriate attention should be paid to the health and hygiene of the staff.

3.2.   Capture

Wild and feral animals should be captured only by humane methods and by experienced persons who have a thorough knowledge of the habits and habitats of the animals to be caught. If an anaesthetic or any other drug has to be used in the capturing operation, it should be administered by a veterinarian or other competent person. Any animal which is seriously injured should be presented as soon as possible to a veterinarian for treatment. If the animal, in the opinion of the veterinarian, can only go on living with suffering or pain it should be killed at once by a humane method. In the absence of a veterinarian, any animal which may be seriously injured should be killed at once by a humane method.

3.3.   **Packing and transport conditions**

All transportation is undoubtedly, for the animals, a stressful experience, which should be mitigated as far as possible. Animals should be in good health for transportation and it is the duty of the sender to ensure that they are so. Animals which are sick or otherwise out of condition should never be subjected to any transport which is not necessary for therapeutic or diagnostic reasons. Special care should be exercised with female animals in an advanced state of pregnancy. Female animals which are likely to give birth during the transport or which have done so within the preceding forty-eight hours, and their offspring, should be excluded from transportation. Every precaution should be taken by sender and carrier in packing, stowing and transit to avoid unnecessary suffering through inadequate ventilation, exposure to extreme temperatures, lack of feed and water, long delays, etc. The receiver should be properly informed about the transport details and documentary particulars to ensure quick handling and reception in the place of arrival. It is recalled that, as far as international transport of animals is concerned, Directives 77/489/EEC and 81/389/EEC apply; strict observance of national laws and regulations as well as of the regulations for live animals of the International Air Transport Association and the Animal Air Transport Association is also recommended.

3.4.   **Reception and unpacking**

The consignments of animals should be received and unpacked without avoidable delay. After inspection, the animals should be transferred to clean cages or pens and be supplied with feed and water as appropriate. Animals which are sick or otherwise out of condition should be kept under close observation and separately from other animals. They should be examined by a veterinarian or other competent person as soon as possible and, where necessary, treated. Animals which do not have any chance to recover should be killed at once by a humane method. Finally, all animals received must be registered and marked in accordance with the provisions of Articles 17, 18, 19 (5) of the Directive. Transport boxes should be destroyed immediately if proper decontamination is impossible.

3.5.   **Quarantine, isolation and acclimatization**

3.5.1.   The objects of quarantine are:

(a) to protect other animals in the establishment;

(b) to protect man against zoonotic infection;

(c) to foster good scientific practice.

Unless the state of health of animals introduced into an establishment is satisfactory, it is recommended that they should undergo a period of quarantine. In some cases, that of rabies, for example, this period may be laid down in the national regulations of the Member State. In others, it will vary and should be determined by a competent person, according to the circumstances, normally the veterinarian appointed by the establishment (see also Table 2).

Animals may be used for experiments during the quarantine period as long as they have become acclimatized to their new environment and they present no significant risk to other animals or man.

3.5.2.   It is recommended that facilities should be set aside in which to isolate animals showing signs of or suspected of ill-health and which might present a hazard to man or to other animals.

3.5.3.   Even when the animals are seen to be in sound health it is good husbandry for them to undergo a period of acclimatization before being used in an experiment. The time required depends on several factors, such as the stress to which the animals have been subjected which in turn depends on several factors such as the duration of the transportation and the age of the animal. This time shall be decided by a competent person.

3.6.   **Caging**

3.6.1.   It is possible to make a distinction between two broad systems of housing animals.

Firstly, there is the system found in breeding, supplying and user establishments in the bio-medical field designed to accommodate animals such as rodents, rabbits, carnivores, birds and non-human primates, sometimes also ruminants, swine and horses. Suggested guidelines for cages, pens, runs and stalls suitable for such facilities are presented in Tables 3 to 13. Supplementary guidance on minimum cage areas is found in Figures 1 to 7. Furthermore, a corresponding guidance for the appraisal of the stocking density in cages is presented in Figures 8 to 12.

Secondly, there is the system frequently found in establishments conducting experiments only on farm or similar large animals. The facilities in such establishments should not be less than those required by current veterinary standards.

3.6.2. Cages and pens should not be made out of material that is detrimental to the health of the animals, and their design should be such that the animals cannot injure themselves and, unless they are disposable, they should be made from a resistant material adapted to cleaning and decontamination techniques. In particular, attention should be given to the design of cage and pen floors which should vary according to the species and age of the animals and be designed to facilitate the removal of excreta.

3.6.3. Pens should be designed for the well-being of the species. They should permit the satisfaction of certain ethological needs (for example the need to climb, hide or shelter temporarily) and be designed for efficient cleaning and freedom from contact with other animals.

3.7. **Feeding**

3.7.1. In the selection, production and preparation of feed, precautions should be taken to avoid chemical, physical and microbiological contamination. The feed should be packed in tight, closed bags, stamped with the production date when appropriate. Packing, transport and storing should also be such as to avoid contamination, deterioration or destruction. Store rooms should be cool, dark, dry, and vermin and insect proof. Quickly perishable feed like greens, vegetables, fruit, meat, fish, etc. should be stored in cold rooms, refrigerators or freezers.

All feed hoppers, troughs or other utensils used for feeding should be regularly cleaned and if necessary sterilized. If moist feed is used or if the feed is easily contaminated with water, urine, etc., daily cleaning is necessary.

3.7.2. The feed distribution process may vary according to the species but it should be such as to satisfy the physiological needs of the animal. Provision should be made for each animal to have access to the feed.

3.8. **Water**

3.8.1. Uncontaminated drinking water should always be available to all animals. During transport, it is acceptable to provide water as part of a moist diet. Water is however a vehicle of micro-organisms and the supply should therefore be so arranged that the hazard involved is minimized. Two methods are in common use, bottles and automatic systems.

3.8.2. Bottles are often used with small animals like rodents and rabbits. When bottles are used, they should be made from translucent material in order to enable their contents to be monitored. The design should be wide-mouthed for easy and efficient cleaning and, if plastic material is used, it should not be leachable. Caps, stoppers and pipes should also be sterilizable and easy to clean. All bottles and accessories should be taken to pieces, cleaned and sterilized at appropriate and regular periods. It is preferable that the bottles should be replaced by clean, sterilized ones rather than be refilled in the holding rooms.

3.8.3. Automatic drinking systems should be regularly checked, serviced and flushed to avoid accidents and the spread of infections. If solid-bottom cages are used, care should be taken to minimize the risk of flooding. Regular bacteriological testing of the system is also necessary to monitor the quality of the water.

3.8.4. Water received from public waterworks contains some micro-organisms which are usually considered to be harmless unless one is dealing with microbiologically defined animals. In such cases, the water should be treated. Water supplied by public waterworks is usually chlorinated to reduce the growth of micro-organisms. Such chlorination is not always enough to keep down the growth of certain potential pathogens, as for example Pseudomonas. As an additional measure, the level of chlorine in the water could be increased or the water could be acidified to achieve the desired effect.

3.8.5. In fishes, amphibians and reptiles, tolerance for acidity, chlorine and many other chemicals differs widely from species to species. Therefore provision should be made to adapt the water supply for aquariums and tanks to the needs and tolerance limits of the individual species.

3.9.   **Bedding**

Bedding should be dry, absorbent, non-dusty, non-toxic and free from infectious agents or vermin, or any other form of contamination. Special care should be taken to avoid using sawdust or bedding material derived from wood which has been treated chemically. Certain industrial by-products or waste, such as shredded paper, may be used.

3.10.   **Exercising and handling**

3.10.1. It is advisable to take every possible opportunity to let animals take exercise.

3.10.2. The performance of an animal during an experiment depends very much on its confidence in man, something which has to be developed. The wild or feral animal will probably never become an ideal experimental animal. It is different with the domesticated animal born and raised in contact with man. The confidence once established should however be preserved. It is therefore recommended that frequent contact should be maintained so that the animals become familiar with human presence and activity. Where appropriate, time should be set aside for talking, handling and grooming. The staff should be sympathetic, gentle and firm when associating with the animals.

3.11.   **Cleaning**

3.11.1. The standard of a facility depends very much on good hygiene. Clear instructions should be given for the changing of bedding in cages and pens.

3.11.2. Adequate routines for the cleaning, washing, decontamination and, when necessary, sterilization of cages and accessories, bottles and other equipment should be established. A very high standard of cleanliness and order should also be maintained in holding, washing and storage rooms.

3.11.3. There should be regular cleaning and, where appropriate, renewal of the material forming the ground surface in outdoor pens, cages and runs to avoid them becoming a source of infection and parasite infestation.

3.12.   **Humane killing of animals**

3.12.1. All humane methods of killing animals require expertise which can only be attained by appropriate training.

3.12.2. A deeply unconscious animal can be exsanguinated but drugs which paralyse muscles before unconsciousness occurs, those with curariform effects and electrocution without passage of current through the brain, should not be used without prior anaesthesia.

Carcass disposal should not be allowed until *rigor mortis* occurs.

TABLE 1

Guidelines for room temperature

(animals kept in cages, pens or indoor runs)

Species or groups of species	Optimal range in °C
Non-human New World primates	20 – 28
Mouse	20 – 24
Rat	20 – 24
Syrian hamster	20 – 24
Gerbil	20 – 24
Guinea pig	20 – 24
Non-human Old World primates	20 – 24
Quail	20 – 24
Rabbit	15 – 21
Cat	15 – 21
Dog	15 – 21
Ferret	15 – 21
Poultry	15 – 21
Pigeon	15 – 21
Swine	10 – 24
Goat	10 – 24
Sheep	10 – 24
Cattle	10 – 24
Horse	10 – 24

Note: In special cases, for example when housing very young or hairless animals, higher room temperatures than those indicated may be required.

———

TABLE 2

Guidelines for local quarantine periods

Introductory note: For imported animals, all quarantine periods should be subject to the Member States' national regulations. In regard to local quarantine periods, the period should be determined by a competent person according to circumstances, normally a veterinarian appointed by the establishment.

Species	Days
Mouse	5 – 15
Rat	5 – 15
Gerbil	5 – 15
Guinea pig	5 – 15
Syrian hamster	5 – 15
Rabbit	20 – 30
Cat	20 – 30
Dog	20 – 30
Non-human primates	40 – 60

TABLE 3

Guidelines for caging small rodents and rabbits

(in stock and during experiments)

Species	Minimum cage floor area cm²	Minimum cage height cm
Mouse	180	12
Rat	350	14
Syrian hamster	180	12
Guinea pig	600	18
Rabbit 1 kg	1 400	30
2 kg	2 000	30
3 kg	2 500	35
4 kg	3 000	40
5 kg	3 600	40

Note: 'Cage height' means the vertical distance between the cage floor and the upper horizontal part of the lid or cage.

When designing experiments, consideration should be given to the potential growth of the animals to ensure adequate room according to this table in all phases of the experiments.

See also Figures 1 to 5 and 8 to 12.

TABLE 4

Guidelines for caging small rodents in breeding

Species	Minimum cage floor area for mother and litter cm²	Minimum cage height cm
Mouse	200	12
Rat	800	14
Syrian hamster	650	12
Guinea pig	1 200	18
Guinea pig in harems	1 000 per adult	18

Note: For definition of 'cage height' see note to Table 3.

TABLE 5

Guidelines for caging breeding rabbits

Weight of doe kg	Minimum cage floor area per doe and litter m²	Minimum cage height cm	Minimum nest box floor m²
1	0,30	30	0,10
2	0,35	30	0,10
3	0,40	35	0,12
4	0,45	40	0,12
5	0,50	40	0,14

Note: For definition of 'cage height' see note to Table 3.

The minimum cage floor area per doe and litter includes the area of the nest box floor.

See also Figure 6.

———

TABLE 6

Guidelines for housing cats

(during experiments and breeding)

Weight of cat kg	Minimum cage floor area per cat m²	Minimum cage height cm	Minimum cage floor area per queen and litter m²	Minimum pen floor area per queen and litter m²
0,5 – 1	0,2	50	—	—
1 – 3	0,3	50	0,58	2
3 – 4	0,4	50	0,58	2
4 – 5	0,6	50	0,58	2

Note: The housing of cats in cages should be strictly limited. Cats confined in this way should be let out for exercising at least once a day, where it does not interfere with the experiment. Cat pens should be equipped with dirt trays, ample shelf room for resting and objects suitable for climbing and claw-trimming.

'Cage height' means the vertical distance between the highest point on the floor and the lowest point in the top of the cage.

For the purpose of calculating the minimum floor area, the shelf area may be included. The minimum cage floor area per queen and litter includes the 0,18 m² area of the kittening box.

See also Figure 7.

———

TABLE 7

Guidelines for housing dogs in cages

(during experiments)

Height of dog to point of shoulder cm	Minimum cage floor area per dog m²	Mininum height of cage cm
30	0,75	60
40	1,00	80
70	1,75	140

Note: Dogs should not be kept in cages any longer than is absolutely necessary for the purpose of the experiment. Caged dogs should be let out for exercise at least once a day unless it is incomptabile with the purpose of the experiment. A time-limit should be set beyond which a dog should not be confined without daily exercise. Exercise areas should be large enough to allow the dog freedom of movement. Grid floors should not be used in dog cages unless the experiment requires it.

In the light of the great differences in height and the limited interdependence of height and weight of various breeds of dogs, the cage height should be based on the body height to the shoulder of the individual animal. As a general rule the minimum cage height should be twice the height to the shoulder.

For definition of 'cage height', see note to Table 6.

TABLE 8

Guidelines for housing dogs in pens

(in stock and during experiments and breeding)

Weight of dog kg	Minimum pen floor area per dog m²	Minimum adjacent exercise area per dog	
		up to 3 dogs m²	more than 3 dogs m²
< 6	0,5	0,5 (1,0)	0,5 (1,0)
6 – 10	0,7	1,4 (2,1)	1,2 (1,9)
10 – 20	1,2	1,6 (2,8)	1,4 (2,6)
20 – 30	1,7	1,9 (3,6)	1,6 (3,3)
>30	2,0	2,0 (4,0)	1,8 (3,8)

Note: Figures in brackets give the total area per dog, that is, the pen floor area plus the adjacent exercise area. Dogs kept permanently outdoors should have access to a sheltered place to find protection against unfavourable weather conditions. Where dogs are housed on grid floors, a solid area should be provided for sleeping. Grid floors should not be used unless the experiment requires it. Partitions between pens should be such as to prevent dogs from injuring each other.

All pens should have adequate drainage.

TABLE 9

Guidelines for caging non-human primates

(in stock and during experiments and breeding)

Introductory note: Because of the wide variations in sizes and characteristics of primates, it is especially important to match the shape and internal fittings as well as the dimensions of their cages to their particular needs. The total volume of the cage is just as important to primates as the floor area. As a general principle, the height of a cage, at least for apes and other simians, should be its greatest dimension. Cages should be high enough at least to allow the animals to stand up erect. The minimum cage height for brachiators should be such as to allow them to swing in full extension from the ceiling without their feet touching the cage floor. Where appropriate, perches should be fitted to allow the primates to use the upper part of the cage.

Compatible primates may be kept two to a cage. Where they cannot be kept in pairs, their cages should be so placed that they can see one another, but it should also be possible to prevent this when required.

Subject to these observations, the following table constitutes a general guideline for caging the groups of species most commonly used (superfamilies *Ceboidea* and *Cercopithecoidea).*

Weight of primate kg	Minimum cage floor area for one or two animals m²	Minimum cage height cm
< 1	0,25	60
1 – 3	0,35	75
3 – 5	0,50	80
5 – 7	0,70	85
7 – 9	0,90	90
9 – 15	1,10	125
15 – 25	1,50	125

Note: For definition of 'cage height' see note to Table 6.

TABLE 10

Guidelines for caging pigs

(in stock and during experiments)

Weight of pig kg	Minimum cage floor area per pig m²	Minimum cage height cm
5 – 15	0,35	50
15 – 25	0,55	60
25 – 40	0,80	80

Note: The table would also apply to piglets. Pigs should not be kept in cages unless absolutely necessary for the purpose of the experiment and then only for a minimum period of time.

For definition of 'cage height' see note to Table 6.

TABLE 11

Guidelines for accommodating farm animals in pens

(in stock and during experiments in user establishments)

Species and weights	Minimum pen floor area	Minimum pen length	Minimum pen partition height	Minimum pen floor area for groups	Minimum length of feed rack per head
kg	m²	m	m	m²/animal	m
Pigs 10 – 30	2	1,6	0,8	0,2	0,20
30 – 50	2	1,8	1,0	0,3	0,25
50 – 100	3	2,1	1,2	0,8	0,30
100 – 150	5	2,5	1,4	1,2	0,35
>150	5	2,5	1,4	2,5	0,40
Sheep <70	1,4	1,8	1,2	0,7	0,35
Goats <70	1,6	1,8	2,0	0,8	0,35
Cattle <60	2,0	1,1	1,0	0,8	0,30
60 – 100	2,2	1,8	1,0	1,0	0,30
100 – 150	2,4	1,8	1,0	1,2	0,35
150 – 200	2,5	2,0	1,2	1,4	0,40
200 – 400	2,6	2,2	1,4	1,6	0,55
>400	2,8	2,2	1,4	1,8	0,65
Adult horses	13,5	4,5	1,8	—	—

TABLE 12

Guidelines for accommodating farm animals in stalls

(in stock and during experiments in user establishments)

Species and weights	Minimum stall area	Minimum stall length	Minimum stall partition height
kg	m²	m	m
Pigs 100 – 150	1,2	2,0	0,9
>150	2,5	2,5	1,4
Sheep <70	0,7	1,0	0,9
Goats <70	0,8	1,0	0,9
Cattle 60 – 100	0,6	1,0	0,9
100 – 150	0,9	1,4	0,9
150 – 200	1,2	1,6	1,4
200 – 350	1,8	1,8	1,4
350 – 500	2,1	1,9	1,4
>500	2,6	2,2	1,4
Adult horses	4,0	2,5	1,6

Note: Stalls should be sufficiently wide to allow an animal to lie comfortably.

TABLE 13

Guidelines for caging birds

(in stock and during experiments in user establishments)

Species and weights	Minimum area for one bird	Minimum area for 2 birds	Minimum area for 3 birds or more	Minimum cage height	Minimum length of feed trough per bird
g	cm²	cm²/bird	cm²/bird	cm	cm
Chickens 100 – 300	250	200	150	25	3
300 – 600	500	400	300	35	7
600 – 1 200	1 000	600	450	45	10
1 200 – 1 800	1 200	700	550	45	12
1 800 – 2 400	1 400	850	650	45	12
(Adult males)					
> 2 400	1 800	1 200	1 000	60	15
Quails 120 – 140	350	250	200	15	4

Note: 'Area' means the product of cage length and cage width measured internally and horizontally. *Not* the product of the floor length and floor width.

For definition of 'cage height' see note to Table 6.

Mesh size in grid floors should not be greater than 10×10 mm for young chicks, and 25×25 mm for pullets and adults. The wire thickness should be at the least 2 mm. The sloping gradient should not exceed 14 % (8°). Water troughs should be of the same length as the feed troughs. If nipples or cups are provided, each bird should have access to two. Cages should be fitted with perches and allow birds in single cages to see each other.

FIGURE 1

Mice
(in stock and during experiments)

Minimum cage floor area

Given the weight of a mouse, the full-drawn line, EU—EU, gives the minimum area that it should be allocated.

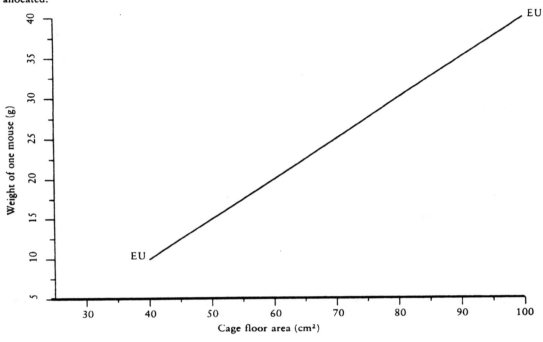

FIGURE 2

Rats
(in stock and during experiments)

Minimum cage floor area

Given the weight of a rat, the full-drawn line, EU—EU, gives the minimum area that it should be allocated.

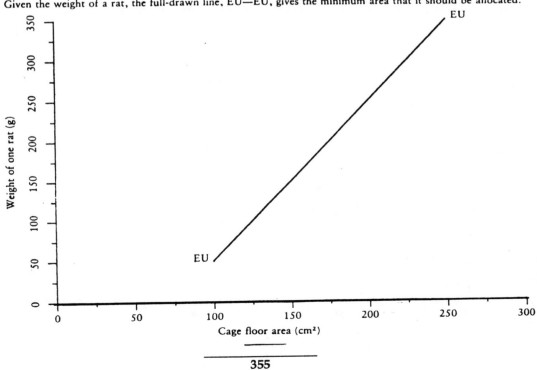

FIGURE 3

Syrian hamsters

(in stock and during experiments)

Minimum cage floor area

Given the weight of a Syrian hamster, the full-drawn line, EU—EU, gives the minimum area that it should be allocated.

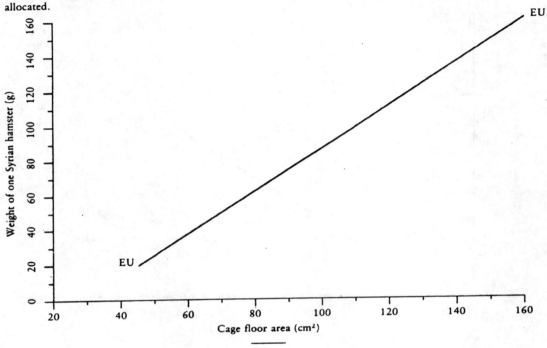

FIGURE 4

Guinea pigs

(in stock and during experiments)

Minimum cage floor area

Given the weight of a guinea pig, the full-drawn line, EU—EU, gives the minimum area that it should be allocated.

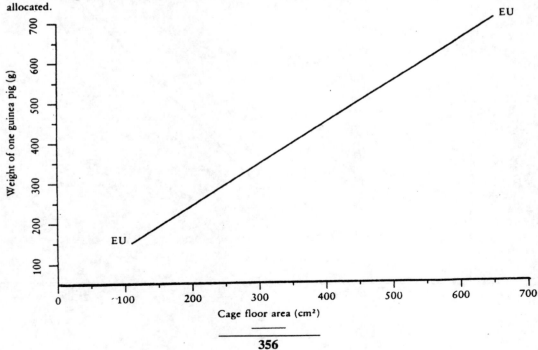

FIGURE 5

Rabbits

(in stock and during experiments)

Minimum cage floor area

Given the weight of a rabbit, the full-drawn line, EU—EU, gives the minimum area that it should be allocated.

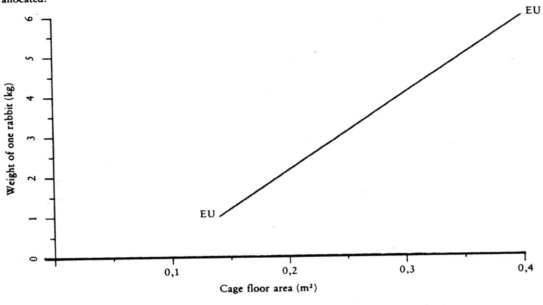

FIGURE 6

Rabbits

(in breeding)

Minimum cage floor area for doe with unweaned litter

Given the weight of a doe, the full-drawn line, EU—EU, gives the minimum area that it should be allocated.

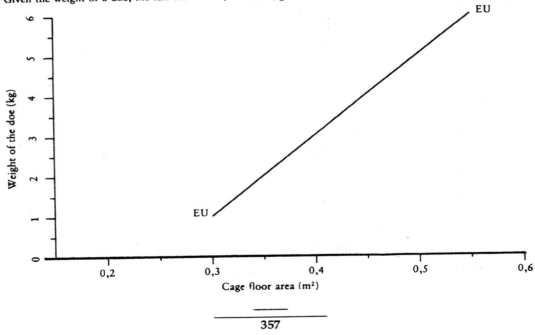

FIGURE 7

Cats

(in stock and during experiments)

Minimum cage floor area

Given the weight of a cat, the full-drawn line, EU—EU, gives the minimum area that it should be allocated.

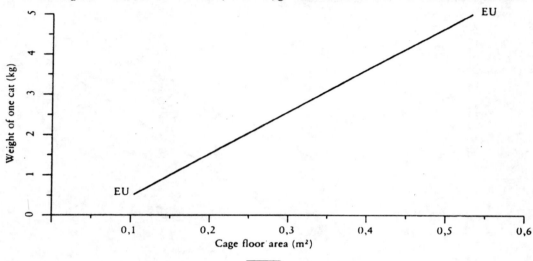

FIGURE 8

Guide to the relationship between number of mice per cage and cage floor area

(in stock and during experiments)

The lines represent the average weights and correspond to the line EU—EU in Figure 1.

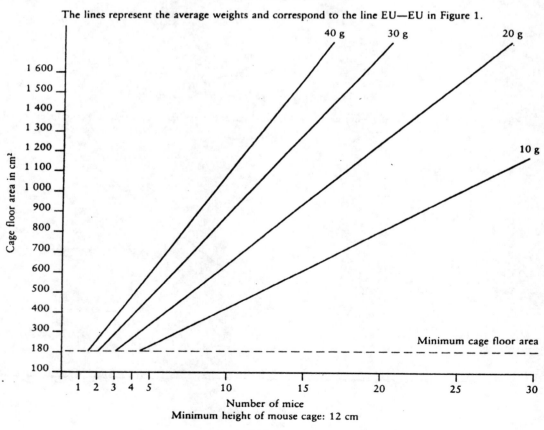

Minimum height of mouse cage: 12 cm

FIGURE 9

Guide to the relationship between number of rats per cage and cage floor area

(in stock and during experiments)

The lines represent the average weights and correspond to the line EU—EU in Figure 2.

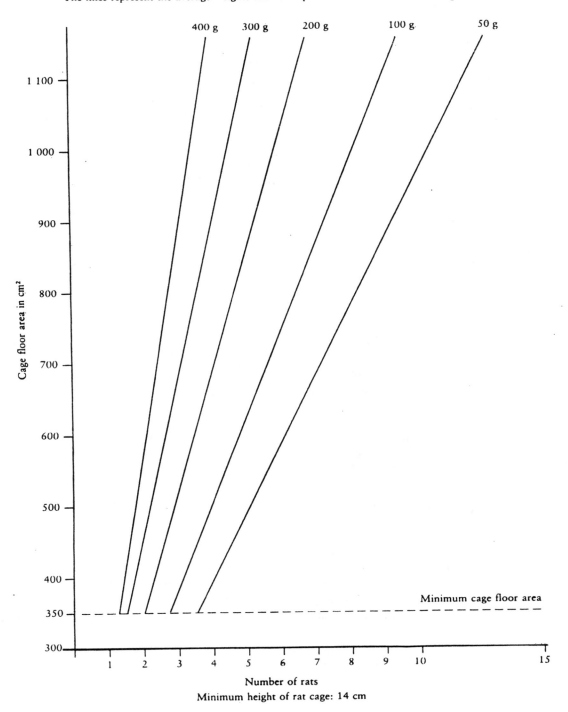

Number of rats

Minimum height of rat cage: 14 cm

FIGURE 10

Guide to the relationship between number of hamsters per cage and cage floor area

(in stock and during experiments)

The lines represent the average weights and correspond to the EU—EU in Figure 3.

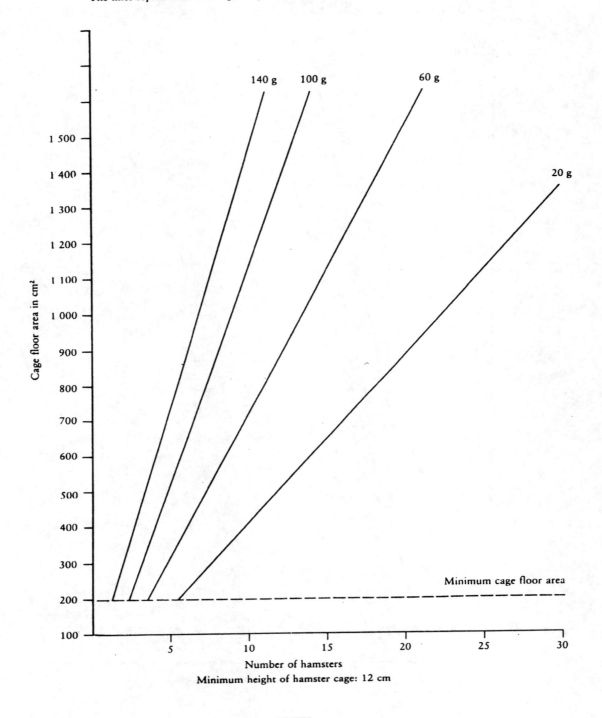

FIGURE 11

Guide to the relationship between number of guinea pigs per cage and cage floor area

(in stock and during experiments)

The lines represent the average weights and correspond to the line EU—EU in Figure 4.

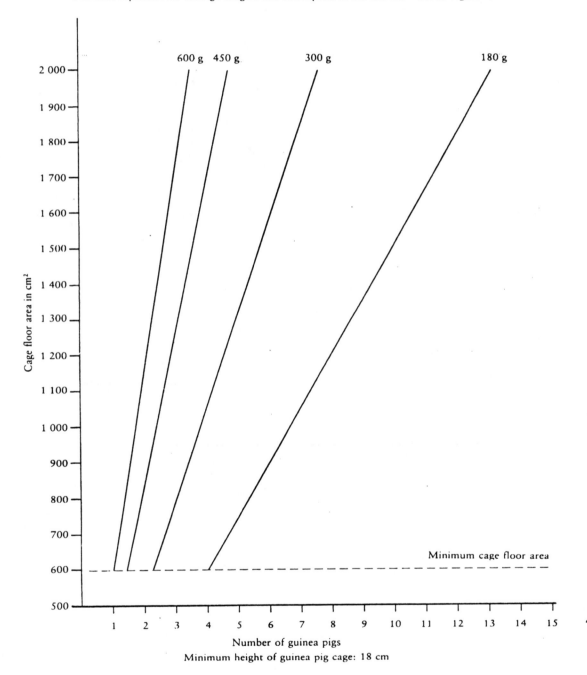

Number of guinea pigs

Minimum height of guinea pig cage: 18 cm

FIGURE 12

Guide to the relationship between number of rabbits per cage and cage floor area
(in stock and during experiments)

The lines represent the average weights and correspond to the ine EU—EU in Figure 5.

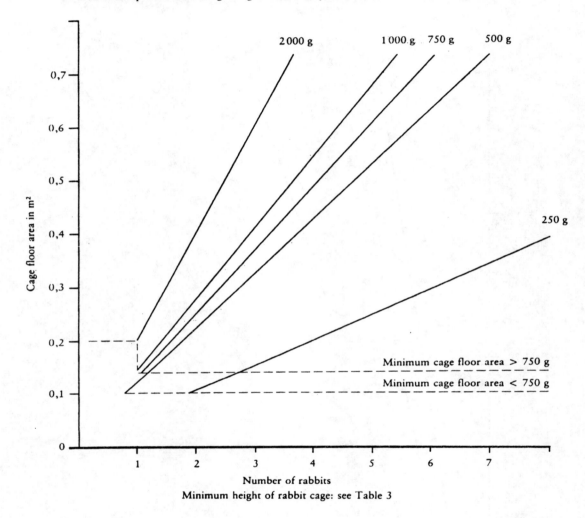

Minimum height of rabbit cage: see Table 3

COUNCIL DECISION

of 20 May 1975

setting up a pharmaceutical committee

(75/320/EEC)

THE COUNCIL OF THE EUROPEAN COMMUNITIES,

Having regard to the Treaty establishing the European Economic Community;

Having regard to the proposal from the Commission;

Whereas the implementation of the measures adopted by the Council as regards the approximation of the laws relating to proprietary medicinal products for human use may raise problems which should be jointly examined;

Whereas, to this end, a Committee should be set up, chaired by a representative of the Commission and composed of representatives of the Member States from those States' administrations,

HAS DECIDED AS FOLLOWS:

Article 1

A Committee called the 'Pharmaceutical Committee' shall be set up and attached to the Commission.

Article 2

Without prejudice to the tasks of the Committee for Proprietary Medicinal Products referred to in Article 8 of the Second Council Directive 75/319/EEC (¹) of 20 May 1975 on the approximation of provisions laid down by law, regulation or administrative action relating to proprietary medicinal products, the task of this Committee shall be to examine:

— any question relating to the application of Directives on proprietary medicinal products which are brought up by its Chairman — either on his initiative or at the request of the representative of a Member State;

— any other question in the field of proprietary medicinal products brought up by its Chairman — either on his initiative or at the request of the representative of a Member State.

The Commission shall consult the Committee when preparing proposals for Directives in the field of proprietary medicinal products, and in particular when it considers any amendments to Council Directive 65/65/EEC (²) of 26 January 1965 on the approximation of provisions laid down by law, regulation or administrative action relating to proprietary medicinal products which it might have occasion to propose.

Article 3

1. The Committee shall consist of senior experts in public health matters from the Member States' administrations and each Member State shall have one representative.

2. There shall be one deputy for each representative. This deputy shall be entitled to participate in meetings of the Committee.

3. A representative of the Commission shall chair the Committee.

Article 4

The Committee shall adopt its rules of procedure.

Done at Brussels, 20 May 1975.

For the Council
The President
R. RYAN

(¹) See page 13 of this Official Journal.

(²) OJ No 22, 9. 2. 1965, p. 369/65.

European Commission

Pharmaceutical Sector — Coordinated instruments

Luxembourg: Office for Official Publications of the European Communities

1995 —363 pp. — 21 x 29.7 cm

ISBN 92-827-0020-8

Price (excluding VAT) in Luxembourg: ECU 52